History Of Russia: From The Foundation Of The Monarchy By Rurik, To The Accession Of Catharine The Second, Volume 2

William Tooke

Nabu Public Domain Reprints:

You are holding a reproduction of an original work published before 1923 that is in the public domain in the United States of America, and possibly other countries. You may freely copy and distribute this work as no entity (individual or corporate) has a copyright on the body of the work. This book may contain prior copyright references, and library stamps (as most of these works were scanned from library copies). These have been scanned and retained as part of the historical artifact.

This book may have occasional imperfections such as missing or blurred pages, poor pictures, errant marks, etc. that were either part of the original artifact, or were introduced by the scanning process. We believe this work is culturally important, and despite the imperfections, have elected to bring it back into print as part of our continuing commitment to the preservation of printed works worldwide. We appreciate your understanding of the imperfections in the preservation process, and hope you enjoy this valuable book.

HISTORY

OF

RUSSIA.

VOL. II.

HISTORY
OF
RUSSIA,

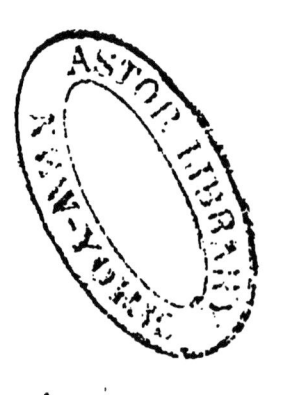

FROM THE

FOUNDATION OF THE MONARCHY BY RURIK,

TO THE

ACCESSION OF CATHARINE THE SECOND.

By W. TOOKE, F.R.S.
MEMBER OF THE IMPERIAL ACADEMY OF SCIENCES AND OF THE
FREE ECONOMICAL SOCIETY AT ST. PETERSBURG.

IN TWO VOLUMES.

VOL. II.

LONDON:
Printed by *A. Strahan, Printers-Street,*
FOR T. N. LONGMAN AND O. REES, PATERNOSTER-ROW.
1800.

ASTOR, LENOX AND
TILDEN FOUNDATION

Drawn & Engraved by J. Chapman from a Series of Medals in the possession of the Rev.d W.m Tooke

SOVEREIGNS OF RUSSIA.

Explanatory of the Plates.

PLATE III.

FAMILY OF RURIK.

The names of the Princes who afterwards succeed to the throne, are distinguished by small capitals.

31. VEL. KN. ANDREI ALEKSANDROVITCH, reigned in 1281, was expelled, afterwards restored, and died in 1304.

No mention is found of his marriage or of his progeny.

32. Vīkīĭ knž DANIIL ALEXANDROVITCH, began to reign in 1296 at Mosco, and lived to the age of 42.

33. VEL. KN. MIXAÏLA YAROSLAVITCH, born in 1271, began to reign in 1304, was slain at the horde in 1317, after reigning 13 years.

He had to wife Anne, daughter of a prince Dmitri Borissovitch.

His sons were: DMITRI, ALEXANDER, Constantine, and Vassilly.

34. VEL. KN. YURIE DANILOVITCH Moscov, reigned from 1317 to 1323, was killed in 1324.

He married Koptshana, named at her baptism Agaphia, daughter of Usbek, khan of the Golden Horde.

35. VEL.

35. Vel. kn. Aleksandr Mixailovitch Yaroslavitcha Tverskie, assumed the sovereign power in 1326, and reigned two years, being punished with death at the Horde.

Who was his wife is not known. His sons were: Feodor, executed at the same time with his father, Vsevolode, and Mikhaïla.

He had likewise two daughters: 1. Mary wife of Simeon Ivanovitch, grand prince of Mosco. 2. Yuliana, wife of Olgard, grand prince of Lithuania.

Posterity of Yuliana.

From this princess sprung the kings of Poland: Yagellon, named at his baptism Vladislas V; John I; Alexander, who married Helena, daughter of Ivan Vassillievitch, grand prince of Mosco; Sigismond I; Sigismond II; and Sigismond III; Vladislas, styled tzar of Russia by the rebels in the time of the troubles; and John II. Likewise from this princess descended Catharine, wife of John, king of Sweden; and Anne, wife of Stephen Battori king of Poland.

Yagellon, king of Poland, the son of Olgard and Yuliana, was father of Casimir IV. Anne, daughter of Casimir became wife of Boguslaf, duke of Pomerania. Their daughter Sophia was married to Frederic I. king of Denmark, and of this marriage was born Adolphus, who was the parent stock of the dukes of Holstein. From him issued: John Adolphus, Frederic III. Christian Albert, Frederic IV. Peter III. emperor of Russia, and Paul Petrovitch who now fills that throne.

36. Velikii knẑ Ioan Danilovitch, reigned from 1328 to his death, which happened in 1341.

His wife, whose former name is unknown, on taking the veil adopted that of Helena.

His

His sons were: SIMEON, IVAN, and Andrew.

His daughter was united in marriage to Constantine Vassilievitch, prince of Rostof.

37. VEL. KN. SEMEN IVANOVITCH GORDIE, born in 1317, reigned in 1341, died of the plague in 1353, at the age of thirty-six.

During his short life he had three wives: 1. Avgusta, named at her baptism Anastasia, princess of Lithuania. 2. Paraskovia, daughter of Feodor Sviatoslavitch, prince of Smolensk. 3. Mary daughter of Alexander, prince of Tver.

His sons were Ivan and Semen, or Simeon.

His daughter was joined in wedlock to Mikhaïla Vassilievitch, prince of Tver.

38. VELIKII KNIAZ IOAN IOANOVITCH, born in 1325, began to reign in 1353, and died in 1358.

He had two wives: 1. Pheodosia, daughter of Dmitri, prince of Briansk. 2. Alexandra, afterwards a religious under the name of Maria.

By the second he had DMITRI and Ivan.

39. V. K. DMITRI KONSTANTINOVITCH SUZDAL, was invested with the sovereignty by the Tartars in 1360, and divested of it in 1362.

He had sons: Vassilly, Simeon, and Ivan.

His daughter, Evdokhia, married the grand-prince Dmitri Donski.

40. VELIKII KNIAZ DIMITRII IOANNOVITCH, born in 1349, received from the Tartars the sovereignty in 1362; built the Kreml at Mosco, of stone; died in 1389, at the age of forty.

His wife was Evdokhia, daughter of Dmitri, prince of Suzdal, and some time grand-prince of Mosco.

His sons: Danila, VASSILLY, Yury, Andrew, Peter, Ivan, and Constantine.

His daughter, named Sophia, was married to Feodor, prince of Riazan.

41. VELIKII KNIAZ VASILII DIMITRIEVITCH, born in 1370, succeeded his father in 1389; died in 1425, aged fifty-five years.

He married Sophia, daughter of Vitolde, grand-prince of Lithuania.

His sons: Ivan and VASSILLY.

His daughters were: 1. Anne, married to John Paleologus, emperor of Constantinople. 2. The second espoused George son of Patrick, prince of Lithuania. 3. Vassilissa, was first married to Alexander Ivanovitch, prince of Suzdal, and in second nuptials to Alexander Danilovitch, likewise prince of Suzdal.

42. VELIKII KNIAZ VASILII VASILIEVITCH, surnamed the Blind, born in 1415, succeeded his father in 1425; died in 1462 at the age of forty-seven.

He married Mary, daughter of a prince Yaroslaf, descended in the fourth generation from the grand-prince Ivan Danilovitch.

His sons were: Yury, IVAN, Yury, Andrey, Boris, Andrey.

His daughter Marpha was married to the prince Ivan Vassillievitch Belski.

43. VELIKII KNIAZ IOANN VASILIEVITCH, born in 1438, succeeded his father in 1462, and died in 1505, in his sixtieth year, after a reign of forty-three years.

He had two wives: 1. Mary, daughter of Boris, prince of Tver. 2. Sophia, daughter of Thomas Paleologus, and niece of John and Constantine, emperors of Constantinople.

He

He had, by his first consort, Ivan; and by the second: VASSILLY, Yury, Dmitri, Simeon, and Andrew.

His daughters were: 1. Helena, consort of Alexander, king of Poland. 2. Evdokhia, married to Kudailuk, son of Ibrahim, khan of Kazan, who was converted to christianity, and received at the font the name of Peter. 3. The Third, whose name is unknown, gave her hand to Daniel, prince of Tver. 4. Sophia, the spouse of Vassilly Danilovitch, prince of Kholm.

44. VELIKII KNIAZ VASILII IOANNOVITCH, born in 1458, succeeded his father in 1505; died in 1533, aged 55.

He had two wives: 1. Solomona, daughter of Yury Zaburof. 2. Helena, daughter of prince Vassilly Glinsky.

By the second were born to him: IVAN and Yury.

45. TZAR I VEL. KN. IOANN VASILIEVITCH, B. P. born in 1530, succeeded his father in 1533; died in 1584, aged 54.

Foreigners give him seven wives; the russian historians consent to no more than five, who were: 1. Anastasia, daughter of Romane Yurievitch Zakhariin. 2. Maria, daughter of Temruke, prince of the highland Circassians. 3. Marpha, daughter of Vassilly Sobakin, forced by her husband to enter a convent. 4. Daria, daughter of Ivan Koltofsky, forced likewise to take the veil. 5. Maria, daughter of Feodor, of the race of the Nogays.

He had by the first: Dmitri, Ivan, and FEODOR; and by the second, Dmitri, who is thought to have been assassinated at Uglitch.

He had likewise two daughters: Anne and Mary, who died in their infancy.

THE END OF THE THIRD PLATE.

PLATE IV.

46. Tzar i vel. kn. Pheodore Ivannovitch, b. p. [*Vfé Roffijkiye*], born in 1557, succeeded his father in 1584; died in 1598, aged forty-one.

His wife was Irene, daughter of Feodor Godunof. She retired to a convent under the name of Alexandra.

His only child was a daughter, named Phedosia, who died in early infancy.

This dynasty occupied the throne during a period of 643 years, and produced a series of 46 sovereigns; which gives for each reign only a mean duration of thirteen years eleven months and some days. As it was long the custom for brothers to succeed in prejudice to their nephews, the sovereigns were not young when they came to the crown; and some of them only just appear on the throne, from which they are presently after expelled.

It is likewise observable that extremely few of these princes attain to an advanced age.

Sovereigns of different Families.

47. Tzar i vel. kn. Boris Pheodorovitch, b. p. succeeded his father in 1598, and reigned seven years and a half.

48. Tzar Pheodor Borissovitch Godunof, on the death of his father, succeeded as tzar in 1604, and reigned six weeks.

49. Tzar i vel. kn. Vasilii Ivanovitch, b. p. became tzar in 1606, and reigned five years.

Drawn & Engraved by J. Chapman from a Series of Medals in the possession of the Rev.

THE HOUSE OF ROMANOF,
Still reigning.

Andrew, son of John, said to have been brother to a prince of Prussia, came into Russia towards the middle of the fourteenth century, during the reign of the grand-prince Ivan Ivanovitch.

Feodor, the last of his five sons, was father of Zachariah, who arrived at the highest honours at the court of the grand-prince Vassilly Vassillievitch, the Blind.

He had three sons, of whom the second, named

Yury Zakharievitch, was boyar and voivode in the reign of the grand-prince Ivan Vassillievitch. Mention is made of him, for the last time, in 1501. His third son was

Romane Yurievitch Zakharin, who served in several campaigns in quality of voivode. He died the 12th of February 1543.

His daughter Nastasia, or Anastasia, was the first wife of tzar Ivan Vassillievitch.

The youngest of his sons was

Nikité [Nicetas] Romanovitch Yurief, who attained to the dignity of boyar. He died in 1586.

His eldest son was

Feodor Nikititch Yurief, one of the principal boyars at the court of tzar Feodor. Became a monk in the reign of Boris, and on adopting the monastic state took the name of Philarete.

All his sons died in their infancy, except

50. Tzar i vel. kn. Mikhaïl Feodorovitch, B. P. Romanof, elected tzar in 1613; died in 1645, at the age of forty-nine.

He

xii EXPLANATION OF THE PLATES.

He had two wives: 1. Maria, daughter of prince Mikhaïla Dolgoruky. 2. Evdokhia, daughter of Lukiane Strechnefi.

By his second nuptials he had: ALEXEY, Vaffilly, and Ivan.

And the princeffes Irene, Pelagia, Marpha, Sophia, Evdokhia, Anna, and Tatiana.

51. TZAR I VEL. KN. ALEKSEI MIKHAILOVITCH, B. P. acceded to the tzarian dignity in 1646, reigned 31 years, and died at the age of forty-seven.

He had two wives: 1. Maria, daughter of Ilia Miloflaffky. 2. Natalia, daughter of Kyril Narifhkin.

By the former he had: Dmitri, Alexei, FEODOR, Simeon, and IVAN.

And the princeffes Evdokhia, Marpha, Sophia, Catharine, Maria, Anna, Feodofia, Feodora.

By the second, PETER and the princefs Natalia.

52. TZAR I VEL. KN. PHEODOR ALEKSIEVITCH, B. P. acceded to the fovereignty in 1676; died in 1682, at the age of twenty-five years.

He married twice: 1. Agaphia, daughter of Simeon Gruchetfki. 2. Marpha, daughter of Matfey Apraxin.

By the former he had the tzarevitch Ilia, who died in his infancy.

53. TZAR I VEL. KN. IOANN ALEKSIEVITCH, B. P. began to reign in 1682, at firft alone, afterwards conjointly with Peter I. died in 1695, aged twenty-five.

By his wife Prafkovia, daughter of Feodor Soltikof: Catharine, ANNA, Prafkovia, who died unmarried, Maria and Feodofia, who died infants.

Catharine was married to Leopold, duke of Meklenburg. The princefs their daughter efpoufed Anthony Ulric of
Brunfwick

Brunſwick Bevern. She was named Cathaŕine after her mother; but took the name of Anna on embracing the greek religion. She was mother of the unhappy

Ivan, emperor in his cradle, 1740; ſhut up in a fortreſs in 1741; baſely murdered in priſon in 1764.

Anne married Frederic William, duke of Courland; ſhe was choſen to be empreſs of Ruſſia in 1730.

54. b. m. Petr I. imperat. i samoder. vseross. i. e. Bojiye Miloſtvo, *by the grace of God*, Peter I. emperor and autocrator of all the Ruſſias, began to reign in 1682, reigned 43 years, died at the age of 52 and eight months.

Peter I. had two empreſſes: Evdokhia, daughter of Feodor Lapukhine, and

Catharine Skavronſky, who reigned after the demiſe of her huſband.

He had by the former: Alexius and Alexander, and by the ſecond two princes named Paul, and two named Peter. Of all theſe princes only Alexius ſurvived his infancy.

By the ſecond he had alſo, the princeſſes Anne, Elizabeth, Natalia, Margaret, and another Natalia: the three laſt died infants.

The tzarevitch Alexius, too famous for his misfortunes and his unhappy end, married the princeſs Charlotta Sophia of Brunſwick Wolfenbuttle, and had by her a ſon named Peter.

55. Ekatarina I. imperat. i samoder. vseross. i. e. Catharine I. imperatritza and ſamoderjitza of all the Ruſſias, crowned in 1724, acceded to the ſovereignty in 1725, and died in 1727.

56. b. m. Petr II. imperat. i samoder. vseross. aſcended the throne in 1727, and died in 1730, aged fifteen.

57. Anna

57. ANNA B. M. IMPERATRITZA I SAMODERJITSA VSEROSS. mounted the throne in 1730, reigned ten years, died in 1740, at the age of forty-seven.

58. B. M. ELIZAVET I. IMPERAT. I SAMODER. VSEROSS. took the crown by birthright in 1741, reigned 20 years, and died at the age of fifty-two.

59. PETR III. B. M. IMP. I. SAMODERJ. VSEROSS. succeeded to the throne in 1762, and was cruelly murdered after a reign of six months.

He married Sophia, princess of Anhalt Zerbst, who, at her baptism into the orthodox greek communion, assumed the name of CATHARINE.

By her he had the tzarevitch PAUL, grand-duke of Russia, born in 1754.

60. B. M. EKATERINA II. IMP. I SAMOD. VSEROSS. born April 21, 1729, began to reign in 1762, reigned 34 years, and died in 1796, at the age of sixty-five.

She was succeeded by her son the emperor PAUL, now reigning.

His first marriage, with Natalia Alexievna, born princess of Hesse Darmstadt, was without issue.

By his second marriage, with Maria Feodorevna, born princess of Virtemburg Stutgard, he has the grand-dukes:

Alexander Pavlovitch, born December 12, 1777. Married Elizaveta Alexievna, born January 13, 1779.

Constantine Pavlovitch, born April 27, 1779. Married Anna Feodorovna, born September 12, 1781.

Nikolai Pavlovitch, born June 25, 1796.

Mikhaila Pavlovitch, born January 28, 1798.

EXPLANATION OF THE PLATES.

Grand-duchesses.

Alexandra Pavlovna, born July 29, 1783.
Elena Pavlovna, born December 13, 1784.
Maria Pavlovna, born February 4, 1786.
Ekatarina Pavlovna, born May 10, 1788.
Anna Pavlovna, born January 7, 1795.

THE END OF THE EXPLANATION OF THE PLATES.

The Binder is requested to beat the Book before he inserts the Plates.—Plates I. *and* II. *to be placed in Vol.* I. *and Plates* III. *and* IV. *in Vol.* II. *to face the first page of the Explanation of each.*

HIS-

HISTORY
OF
RUSSIA.

Troubles and confusions, engendered by the discontents and ambition of the great, and fomented by rancorous competitors for the throne, had torn the vitals of the russian monarchy, at the conclusion of the sixteenth and the beginning of the seventeenth centuries, and at the same time raised up against it two powerful adversaries, the kings of Sweden and Poland, who disguised their real views under a contest for the throne. How little reliance could be made upon the Poles, or their fidelity as friends and allies, had been sufficiently evinced by repeated experience; and there was the greatest probability that the same disasters would ensue from engaging in an intimate alliance with Sweden. It seemed to admit of no doubt that the election of

a polish or a swedish prince would neither be for the happiness of the Russians nor the quiet of their empire; and therefore no alternative was left but for the whole to concur in placing a native Russian on the throne, to disown all attachment to foreign candidates, to unite cordially together, and in one general union, with a true-born patriot at their head, to secure themselves from a dismemberment or violent possession with which the empire was threatened by the Swedes and Poles. The longing for a tranquil and stable government, after so many storms, was so great, that deputies from all parts of the empire appeared at Mosco for giving their votes at the election of a tzar. It was the general wish that the throne might be filled by a Russian; but the gratification of it was involved in many difficulties, and might again open a wide field for discontents, and jealousies, and cabals. The very election which was designed to provide against a renewal of the late disturbances and confusions, might have a contrary effect, by strewing the seeds of fresh turbulence and confusion. The dangers into which the nation had lately been plunged, of being ruined by intestine broils and subjugated by foreign enemies, had called up the patriotism of a numerous party of Russians, and afforded them an opportunity of performing
important

important service to their country both in the council and in the field. These persons therefore now might prefer their claims on the national gratitude, and aspire to the crown, or even strive for it, and, by various methods, as Schuiskoy had formerly done, extort it from their countrymen in proof of their sense of obligation. Yet it was to be feared that the election of any one of these patriots might be felt as an affront to the rest, who had been equally serviceable to the state, and, by inciting their jealousy, create divisions, and so reduce the country again to the brink of destruction. Accordingly the electors wavered long in irresolution and doubt.

In the meantime a party was imperceptibly forming among them, whose wish it was to put a youth upon the throne who had hitherto lived remote from the grand theatre of administration and war, and consequently was without adherents, and had neither friends nor foes. MIKHAILA ROMANOF was the name of this youth, a descendant of the ancient family of the tzars. This relationship indeed was very distant; but, as there was no nearer progeny, it yielded him some pretension to the throne of his relations. Besides, his father Philaretes, from his eminent station as metropolitan of Rostof, and still

still more on account of the patriotism he had displayed during the troubles of the empire, and on account of the many salutary counsels which he had given, was held in very high respect, and had therefore been appointed one of the embassy that carried to the king of Poland the account of the election of his son Vladislaf to be tzar of Russia. All the time that Philaretes, with the other ambassadors, was detained in the king's camp, his wife and their son Mikhaila lived in perfect retirement and almost unknown, in a convent at Kostroma. Now, that it was proposed to call this Mikhaila to the government, one part of the electors refused him their votes because he had no knowledge of state affairs. However, the testimony that was given to his good conduct and excellent intellectual endowments by persons who knew him, prevailed with a majority sufficient for carrying his election, as the most effectual means of preventing the interference of faction. The clergy was most interested in this choice. They were particularly desirous that a Russian, born and brought up in the orthodox greek communion, should be raised to the throne, as an effectual means of preventing the poison of protestant or catholic heresy from being propagated in the ancient, pure, and orthodox church of Russia by a swedish or

polish

polish prince. — Accordingly the voice of an ecclesiastic at last gave the decision in favour of Mikhaila Romanof. " It had been announced " to him," — for so a metropolitan declared in the hall of election, — " by a divine revelation, " that the young Romanof would prove the " most fortunate and prosperous of all the tzars " that had sat on the throne." — To believe that even the Deity interposed in the election, and by so manifest an indication had pointed out the fittest ruler for them, was much too flattering to the generality of the voters for them not to feel it their duty to obey the suggestion of heaven; and their reverence for the superior clergy, the patriarch, the metropolitans, and bishops was so great, that no man would presume to doubt the veracity of a person of that rank, though every unbiassed individual might easily perceive that this pretended revelation was either a stratagem of policy or fanaticism, or at the very utmost was perhaps founded on a dream. In the meantime, this revelation being once known, the people at large expressed so plainly their desire to have the young Romanof for their sovereign, that all were presently united in their choice. The young man himself, however, refused to accept the offered crown. — Indeed what was there in the state of the empire,

pire, what in the fates of a Boris or a Schuiſkoy to make him deſirous of becoming the ſucceſſor of theſe men? and it could by no means be taken amiſs in Mikhaila's mother, that ſhe implored with tears the deputies who were ſent to her and her ſon, to ſpare him the intended honour. But this very refuſal confirmed numbers ſtill more in the belief that Mikhaila was the worthieſt candidate for the throne, and would prove the happieſt tzar. At length the deputies returned to Moſco, bringing with them the conſent of the monarch elect; and all men promiſed themſelves more calm and peaceable times, when Mikhaila Romanof was crowned and had ſworn to obſerve the articles that were ſubmitted to his aſſent*.

The two royal neighbours of Poland and Sweden were now therefore fruſtrated in the expectations they had formed on the ruſſian throne; but the new ſovereign found it no eaſy taſk to free himſelf from thoſe foreign candidates, eſpecially as they had put themſelves at the head of an armed force, and were not only on the borders of the country, but had already made advances into the empire itſelf. Moreover, the embers of the ancient feuds were ſtill ſmoaking,

* Theſe events took place the 11th of June 1613.

and several parts of the empire were haunted by the partizans of Dmitri. But after Mikhaila's accession the government was conducted on a wise and prudent plan. His first efforts were directed to quell entirely the internal ferments; and, by uniting the nation under their new head, to employ the general force against the foreign enemy.

Though the second Dmitri had been slain, yet Marina did not abandon her purpose, by the means of her adherents, if not to ascend the throne of Russia, yet to fix her sovereignty in some part of the empire. A boy whom she declared to have had by Dmitri, but who probably was suppositious, was by her partizans announced to be the future successor of the father; and an adventurer, named Zaruski, an accomplice of Marina, appointed guardian to the pretended son. But this new artifice of Marina was of short duration. The boy, the guardian, and the mother were presently clapped into prison and punished for their contrivance. Thus was dispersed the whole party of Dmitri, which, with various degrees of strength at various times, had brought the empire into many troubles. However the success that had attended the first Dmitri had called up yet another successor to

him

him in Pscove; but he finished his part very soon at the gallows.

Mikhaila now made it his next concern to rid himself of the Poles and Swedes, who were already masters of those parts of the empire that lay contiguous to their several frontiers. Schuiskoy had called in the Swedes to his assistance; and in 1609 they marched a body of five thousand men to the frontiers, defeated the Poles that were in connection with the second Dmitri, delivered Mosco, and might probably have contributed much towards quelling the disturbances in the empire, if Schuiskoy had punctually paid them the stipulated subsidies. But, distrusting one of his relations, the prince of Novgorod, who was successfully carrying on an underhand negotiation with Sweden, and whom Schuiskoy therefore suspected of aspiring to the throne by the assistance of that court, it followed that the swedish troops were neglected; and, in order to enforce payment, remained in the empire, took possession of the country bordering on Sweden, took Kexholm by famine, and Novgorod by stratagem, and therefore could not be immediately expelled.

The empire was in too weak a condition to cope at once with two such enemies as Sweden and

and Poland. Accordingly Mikhaila first attempted the gentler mode of negotiation, and made a beginning with Sweden. The Poles were held in the greatest aversion, as having afforded support to Dmitri, laid Mosco in ashes, and done exceeding great harm to the empire. Besides, they would never abandon the hope of seeing Vladislaf on the russian throne. For however resolutely the king of Poland had formerly refused [*] to send out this prince, he seemed now to be as forward to do so, on hearing that his scruples had rendered the whole election fruitless, and given occasion to another. The Swedes indeed, after Mikhaila's election, made some attempts to repulse the latter: though too late. Mikhaila maintained his ground, and the Swedes thought it most advisable, in 1617, to conclude a treaty of peace, which however was purchased on the side of Russia by the cession of Ingria and Karelia, and was once more obliged to evacuate Esthonia and Livonia. However, one enemy was pacified, and the empire on one side quieted: within two years a pacification with Poland was also brought to effect. For, when the king of Poland saw that his delays had utterly and irrecoverably ruined the cause of his

[*] See before, vol. i. p. 285.

son, and that the nation unanimously adhered to the young tzar, of which he had a sufficient proof, when an army with Vladiflaf at its head penetrated into Russia, in order, if possible, to assert the priority of his election against that of Romanof. It being drawn into ambuscades, first on one side, and then on another, by the russian commander, pushed into districts already desolated, where they suffered much by cold and hunger, a treaty of peace for fourteen years and a half, was concluded in 1619, by which the Russians evacuated Smolensk, and several other towns with their territories to the Poles. A sacrifice to which, however, they agreed only in compliance with the then posture of affairs, and in the hopes of more fortunate conjunctures, when they might redemand the ceded territories as an expired loan.

The russian embassy that had formerly been deputed to Vladiflaf on his election, now returned from Poland, and with them the tzar's father. The place of patriarch just now falling vacant, the tzar his son conferred upon him this supreme spiritual dignity, whom, as the patriarchs always resided at Mosco, he had therefore continually near him, and profited so well by the experience and advice of his father, that the latter was generally regarded as co-regent, and
sat,

fat, whenever audiences were given, at the right hand of his son. Foreign ministers brought credentials not only to the tzar, but also to his father, the patriarch; and it is affirmed by all the writers of those times, that the father's influence was extremely great; and, as Philaretes, in quality of patriarch, often spoke in behalf of peace, it was owing in a great measure to him, that the reign of his son was so distinguished for clemency, gentleness, and acts of benevolence.

As Mikhaila had shewn himself desirous of living in amity with Sweden and Poland, he was not less eager to form connections with other european states; and accordingly sent ambassadors to England, Denmark, Holland, and the german emperor. Thus Russia, which had hitherto been considered rather in the light of an asiatic than an european power, became more and more known to the rest of Europe, and rivalships now rose for obtaining treaties and alliances with that empire.

The peace with Poland being only for a stated term of years, could be considered no otherwise than as a temporary accommodation, (though even what are denominated treaties of everlasting amity scarcely last so long as this stipulated period,) it was to be supposed that, on the expiration of that term, hostilities were to be re-commenced.

menced. Mikhaila, therefore, juftly thought it advifable to put his frontiers in the beft ftate of defence, and to have his troops placed in fuch a condition by foreign officers, that in cafe the Poles fhould have recourfe to arms at the termination of the truce, he might be able to defend himfelf, or perhaps even to act on the offenfive, and reconquer the countries that had been ceded to the Poles. Nay, ere the time agreed on for the armiftice was expired, on the death of Sigifmond, he made fome attempts to recover thefe territories, under the idle pretext that he had concluded a peace with Sigifmond, and not with his fucceffor. But the very ruffian commander, who had valiantly defended Smolenfk with a fmall number of troops againft the Poles, now lay two whole years indolently with an army of 50,000 men, and provided with good artillery, before that town, and at length retreated on capitulation. A retreat for which he and his friends were brought to anfwer with their heads. In the meantime the ruffian nation were fo diffatisfied with this campaign, and the king of Sweden, whom Mikhaila wanted to perfuade into an alliance with him againft the Poles, fhewing fo little inclination to comply, the tzar thought it the wifeft courfe he could purfue, to return to the former amicable relation with Poland. Peace
was

was therefore again agreed on, and matters remained, as so frequently happens, after shedding the blood of thousands of human beings, as they were before. Mikhaila plainly perceived that russian troops were able to effect but little against the polish *.

Mikhaila had, moreover, during his reign, which continued till 1645, employment enough in endeavouring to heal the wounds which the many-headed spirit of party had inflicted on his country; to compose the disorders that had arisen; to restore the administration which had been so often disjointed and relaxed; to give new vigour and activity to the laws, disobeyed and inefficient during the general confusions; and to communicate fresh life to expiring commerce. It

* Into what different circumstances and relations, quite opposite to the former, may states and empires fall! At that time the Russians could not make head against the Poles: how totally is the case altered in our times! At that time it was earnestly insisted on the russian side at the negotiation for peace, that the Poles should deliver up the diploma of election which had been sent to Vladislaf, for fear that they might at some future time make use of it to the disadvantage of Russia; which the Poles even refused to do, pretending that this diploma was lost. Russia has nothing now to apprehend on that score, especially since all the archives of Poland have been brought from Warsaw to St. Petersburg.

redounds

cumulation of wealth seemed to be the general characteristic of all men in office. From the same corrupt fountain flowed a multitude of monopolies, and excessive taxes on the prime necessaries of life. The consequence of all this was the oppression of the people by privileged extortioners, and murmurs against injustice and the exorbitance of imposts. In addition to this, those grandees who had now the reins of government in their hands, assumed a haughty, austere behaviour towards the subjects, whereas Mikhaila and his father had been friendly and indulgent, and their gentleness communicated itself to all who at that time took part in the administration. From these several causes arose discontents in the nation; such great men as were neglected and disappointed, contributed what they could to fan these discontents, and to bring them to overt act. Mosco, the seat of the principal magistrate, who, himself in the highest degree unjust, connived at the iniquities of his subordinate judges, was the place where the people first applied for redress. They began by presenting petitions for the tzar at court, implored the removal of these disorders, and exposed to him in plain terms the abuses committed by the favourite and his adherents. But these petitions were of no avail, as none of the courtiers liers would venture to put them into the hand of the tzar, for fear of Morofof's long arm. The populace, therefore, once ftopped the tzar, as he was returning from church to his palace, calling aloud for righteous judges. Alexey promifed them to make ftrict inquiry into their grievances, and to inflict impartial punifhment on the guilty; the people, however, had not patience to wait this tardy procefs, but proceeded to plunder the houfes of fuch of the great as were moft obnoxious to them. At length they were pacified only on condition that the author of their oppreffions fhould be brought to condign punifhment; not however till they had killed the principal magiftrate, and forced from the tzar the death of another nefarious judge, could they be induced to fpare the life of Morofof, though the tzar himfelf intreated for him with tears, and vowed an effectual amendment of conduct in his name. Thus was tranquillity reftored in Mofco, and fhortly afterwards in Novgorod and Pfcove, where likewife difcontents had broke out on account of the exorbitances of the great. At Novgorod on this occafion, the metropolitan Nikon acquired great merit; a man, who, fprung from an inferior ftation, raifed himfelf by a reputation for extraordinary piety and holinefs to the patriarchal dignity, and was in high favour with tzar Alexey;

but likewife, beguiled by his good fortune, he interfered too much in ftate affairs, and, in one word, would willingly have played the fame part with Alexey, as the patriarch Philaretes performed with his fon the tzar Mikhaila: a project which at length ejected him from the patriarchate [*].

Thefe difturbances in Mofco, Novgorod, and Pfcove, which, however, had no farther confequences, than that fome flagitious peculators were reftrained from farther mifchief, and others put out of the way, having entirely fubfided, the empire was threatened with new dangers from a different quarter, by the appearance of another man, who one while gave himfelf out for Dmitri's, and at another for Schuifkoy's fon, and under both thefe names laid claim to the throne. Happy it was for Alexey and Ruffia, that neither the Poles nor the Swedes, whom the impoftor, in reality the fon of a linen-draper, endeavoured to induce to efpoufe his caufe, fhewed any great zeal in his fupport; otherwife it is probable that the turbulent times of the former impoftors under the name of Dmitri would have been renewed. On the contrary, however, the

[*] Concerning this remarkable perfonage more will be feen in the fequel.

pretender very soon fell into the hands of the Russians; and, instead of being promoted to the throne, was raised to the gallows.

The empire therefore remained quiet within. It was, however, presently disturbed on the frontiers towards Poland, with which kingdom a war broke out, originally occasioned by the Kozaks. This people, whose name is probably of tartarian origin, and signifies a light armed warrior, took its rise in the fourteenth century, when Kief the primitive russian realm, was conjoined with Lithuania *. A great part of the subjects of the kievian principality being dissatisfied with the lithuanian government, deserted their country, and settled in districts lying more to the southward, almost destitute of people, about the mouth of the Dniepr. For this emigration undoubtedly the catholic clergy were most to blame, who left no means untried to unite the inhabitants of the kievian, now belonging to the lithuanian empire, and who were not catholics, but firmly attached to the greek ritual, to the communion of the church of Rome. Their abhorrence to this union induced them to emigrate; and, as the new colonies formed on the Dniepr by these emigrations were always

* See before, vol. i. p. 277.

c 2   greatly

greatly annoyed by the neighbouring Poles, Lithuanians, and Tartars, a particular form of government gradually created itself among these colonists, who afterwards obtained the name of Kozaks. It was a military democracy. Every man was a soldier, and the chief (the ataman or hetman) was elected by the voice of the people assembled, which was also decisive on every matter of public concern. The Kozaks being at first under tartarian protection, on the dissolution of the tartarian empire, and their numbers being increased by a multitude of tartarian families that took refuge among them, they acknowledged the king of Poland as their paramount guardian. An attack upon their constitution, however, which the Poles thought proper to make, and the attempts which the polish clergy never gave up, to incorporate these greek christians into the latin church, alienated the minds of the Kozaks from the polish supremacy, and induced them to apply for admission under the patronage of Russia, especially as the greek mode of christian faith, so highly revered by them, was predominant in the russian empire. Alexey was much disposed to comply with their wishes to own him for their guardian sovereign, on their declaration to that effect about the year 1654. Even Nikon, now elevated to the patriarchate,

triarchate, encouraged him not a little to adopt these persecuted sheep of the orthodox church, and reduce them to the patriarchal fold. His spiritual motives were convincing enough to Alexey, who was desirous of the same thing for political reasons, especially as the tzar might foresee that Poland would not regard this with complacency, but would strive to prevent it by force of arms. On this occasion he was in hopes not only to become the paramount lord of the kozaks, but even perhaps to recover from the Poles what his father had been obliged by a series of disasters to evacuate to them. It was curious, however, that Alexey, while he earnestly wished to form a connection with the Poles, should begin by making complaints, that, in a number of writings published in Poland, the honour of his father and of the empire was insulted. Nay, in compensation for the injuries thereby cast upon him, he directly demanded the restoration of the countries ceded by his father to Poland. The king of Poland rejected the demand, as might easily be expected. Thus then, on the side of Russia, there was already a pretence for war, which indeed as to its validity seemed slight enough, yet, however, might pass for a pretence. Besides, the tzar offered to act as mediator between the discontented kozaks
and

and the polish government. But Poland would not accept the mediation, and thus it came to an open rupture between them. In this war the Russians, assisted by the kozaks, were so successful against Poland, that even the king of Sweden, jealous at Alexey's good fortune, was apprehensive lest the latter might hereafter employ the force he was thus increasing to the detriment of Sweden, and by the vanquishing of one neighbour, might be the more dangerous to him as the other. He, therefore, took precautionary means of defence in case of an attack. The Tartars, who came to the assistance of Poland, in the meantime put a check to Alexey's conquests; and Lithuania, that she might not fall into the hands of the tzar, implored the protection of the king of Sweden. By this step Alexey, who thought by conquering Poland to get possession of Lithuania as an appanage to it, felt himself affronted, and now also, in 1656, broke measures with Sweden. If pillaging, ravaging, desolating, and seizing on towns and villages, and even massacring unarmed enemies, may be called a successful war, then it must be said, that Alexey's arms were likewise successful in Sweden; but only in those respects. The Russians would not dare to contend with the swedish warriors face to face in the open field,

even

even with a far greater superiority of numbers; and therefore Alexey found it highly advisable in 1658 to conclude a three years' truce with Sweden, which three years afterwards, in 1661, was confirmed into a peace, at which it was agreed that, disregarding all that had passed between the two powers, everything should be fixed on the former footing, as had been settled at the treaty of peace made at Stolbova in 1617. But Alexey's war with Poland terminated more honourably for Russia. An armistice for thirteen years, agreed upon at Andrussof in Lithuania in 1667, and afterwards prolonged from time to time, was the forerunner of a complete pacification, which was brought to effect in 1686, and restored to the empire Smolensk, Severia, Tchernigof, and Kief, that primeval principality of the russian tzars. The king of Poland likewise relinquished the supremacy he had hitherto asserted over the kozaks to the tzar; and that people became now a protected relative of the russian empire.

Successful as Alexey had been against the Poles, his empire, nevertheless, had nearly fallen into new intestine troubles. Dolgoruki, the russian commander, caused an officer of the Don-kozaks to be hanged, and thereby, in the opinion of the kozaks, grievously infringed their liberty.

A brother

A brother of the deceased, therefore, Stenka (Stephen) Radzin, found no difficulty in enticing numbers of his countrymen, under pretence that attempts were making to contract their privileges, to stand forth and revenge the insult committed on them all by putting to death this member of their community. Prompted by a love of licentiousness, plunder, and excesses of all kinds, which Radzin allowed, his followers rallied round his banner, soon increased to great numbers, particularly attracted by the piratical expeditions on the Caspian, and even to Persia, in which considerable booty was to be made. In the meantime the proceedings of this fellow, and the crew that had flocked to him, were not confined to the kozaks: he sent out several of his people, who sounded forth the praises of their great leader in various parts of the country, and took advantage of every slight murmur against the government, every expression of discontent at one ordinance or another of the tzar, for ostentatiously promising help and redress to every kind of oppression, by the arm of their mighty Radzin. These envoys took particular care to raise hopes in the populace that Radzin would deliver them from the gripe of power. Radzin himself proceeded to greater excesses from day to day. As many of the Russians still adhered to the pa-

triarch

triarch Nikon, who had been depofed and fent into a monaftery, he fpread it abroad that Nikon was with him, that even the eldeft of the tzarian princes had put himfelf under his protection, and that he had been requefted by the tzar himfelf to come to Mofco, in order by his affiftance to rid himfelf of thofe unpatriotic grandees by whom, to the misfortune of the empire, he was unhappily furrounded. Thefe artifices, together with the permiffion to rob and plunder all without fcruple, which Radzin granted to every one that came to his ftandard, were a lure which operated fo ftrongly, that the rebel found himfelf at length at the head of 200,000 men. Indeed his power was not formidable, though his numbers were fo great. Without difcipline, without knowledge in the art of war, moft of his adherents even without inclination to fight, what was to be dreaded from fuch a banditti when oppofed by a military force? for it was not a manly ardour and courage that had collected this band about Radzin, but rapine and the thirft of plunder. Accordingly, how little fervice this great mafs was of to the man himfelf, and how little qualified he was to bring them into a well regulated activity, and how deftitute he was of the neceffary prudence for acting fuch a part as he had adopted, was feen at length in his fuffering
himfelf

himself to be persuaded that the tzar had forgiven him, and was desirous of nothing more than to see him at Mosco. Radzin put implicit faith in this report, on the declaration of an ataman of the Don-kozaks, and travelled thither with his brother. Though the latter repeatedly represented to him on the journey that punishment and death would more probably be their lot at Mosco than a pardon, yet Radzin was still simple enough to trust in the assurance he had received, and only perceived his mistake — certainly too late — when at a little distance from the capital, he was accosted by a gallows in a cart which had been sent to meet him: a terrible harbinger of the fate that awaited him there. — His execution had the proper effect on his accomplices, who gradually dispersed: and though another miscreant took upon him to play Radzin's part, yet the party did not long hold together. Astrakhan, the chief seat of these Russians, where Radzin had for some time ruled with unlimited sway, and where he had resolved to take up his residence as *king of Astrakhan*, was surrounded by the russian troops; and *twelve thousand* of Radzin's followers — as a dreadful example to all future rebels — were gibbeted on the high roads of Astrakhan. Such was the catastrophe of an enterprise which might

have

have been attended with lamentable consequences to the russian empire if Radzin had only been as prudent as he was daring. Disturbances of a very extensive nature might in that case perhaps have been easily excited, especially as a great part of the warlike nation of kozaks were implicated in the rebellion.

The turkish emperor, in the meantime, had not looked on with complacency from the very beginning, while Alexey was taking measures for making himself protector of the kozaks, as Russia by this nation obtained a strong rampart against the incursions of the Tartars dependent on the turkish empire, who were perpetually infesting the russian territory. He accordingly strove to prevent it; first by farther humbling Poland, already weakened by Alexey's forces, and then by attacking Russia. In 1671 the Turks made themselves masters of Kaminietz, a fortress on the frontiers belonging to Poland, and extended themselves throughout the Ukraine. At the treaty of Andrussof the Russians and Poles having promised mutual assistance to each other against their mohammedan neighbour, Alexey was obliged now, in pursuance of that agreement, again to take arms. In order to give employment to the Turks on all sides, and totally to reduce the inveterate foe to his empire,

empire, Alexey sent ambassadors to several of the christian potentates, exhorting them to take part in the war against the implacable enemy of the christian name. But the christian potentates had similar business enough of their own, and were obliged to be perpetually on their guard against the depredations of each other. Accordingly, the general league of the christians against the Turks was never brought to effect, and only remained a pious wish of the tzar. — The turkish army being for some years successively victorious, and making many conquests in Poland, was consequently becoming every day more dangerous to the tzar. At length, however, a stop was put to their conquests by the great commander Sobiesky, who smoothed his way to the throne by his victorious arms against these enemies of his country. Indeed Alexey had formed the project for making one of his sons king of Poland, and so to unite that kingdom with his own; but the plan proved abortive. He did not live to see the termination of the war with the Turks, in which Alexey had taken a very active part. His death happened in 1676; and it is highly probable that he fell a victim to the empyrical remedies of an old polish woman, in whom he had more confidence than in his physicians.

That

That Alexey was fuccefsful in his wars with Poland; that he procured a reftitution of the countries torn from his empire, and laid the foundation of a fovereignty over the kozaks, were not his only merits in behalf of Ruffia. He was as provident for the improvement of the empire within, as for its aggrandizement without. He in a particular manner attached to himfelf the gratitude of his fubjects, by a reformation of the laws, in which he confulted the nobility, the clergy, and the clafs of burghers. He encouraged the trade of the country, and was attentive to advance the cultivation of the empire: whereas formerly the prifoners of war always belonged as flaves to thofe who had taken them, he acted far more wifely, by fending the captives from the enemy into uncultivated regions, that they might be peopled by their means. The mildnefs of his government allured Germans, Dutch, Italians, and about three thoufand Scotfmen into Ruffia. He had already formed the defign, which his fon Peter afterwards put into execution, of making the Ruffians acquainted with the art of conftructing fhips and with maritime commerce, and refolved to keep merchant-fhips in the Cafpian; but Radzin's rebellion had fruftrated the attempts to that end which he had already made. Ruffia had therefore yet much to expect from Alexey,

if

if death had not prematurely carried him off in the forty-seventh year of his age.

It may with the strictest justice be affirmed, that under Alexey the russian empire made some progress in civilization, and that this prince, in many respects, already trod the path which his son Peter afterwards pursued with more firm and certain steps.

For the better understanding of the transactions that next ensued in the reigning family, which, as it could not be otherwise, had great influence on the empire itself, I shall here mention the manner in which the tzars of Russia were wont to select their consorts — a manner that indeed had a nearer resemblance with asiatic than with european customs. When a tzar was resolved to marry, the most beautiful of the unmarried daughters of the country, particularly of the principal families, were summoned to court. They appeared in their holiday cloaths, met with sumptuous entertainment; and the young lady who had the good fortune to be chosen by the tzar for his bride remained at court, while the rest were dismissed with favours *. Indeed it is possible that in most

cases

* The account generally received among foreigners is as follows: Solent autem moschovitæ quum de uxore ducenda deliberant,

cases it was determined prior to this exhibition on which of the fair the election would fall. — By this practice, therefore, all that influence which foreign princesses as consorts so often exercise over the sovereign, and through them upon the interests of the country, was prevented: this mode observed by the tzars in contracting marriage had a tendency likewise to what all of them prior to Peter the Great seemed most to desire, that this empire should have as little connection with other countries as possible *. But even this election of a tzaritza

from

---

deliberant, omnium toto regno puellarum virginum delectum habere, ac forma virtuteque animi præstantiores ad se perduci jubere, quas demum per idoneos homines, fidelesque matronas inspiciunt, ita diligenter, ut secretiora quoque ab iis contrectari explorarique fas sit. Ex iis vero magna atque solicita parentum exspectatione, quæ ad principis animum responderit regiis nuptiis digna pronunciatur. Cæteræ vero, quæ deformæ pudicitiæque, & morum dignitate contenderant, sæpe eadem die in gratiam principum, proceribus atque militibus nubunt, sic ut mediocri loco natæ plerumque dum principes regiæ stirpis clara stemmata contemnunt, ad summum regalis thori fastigium, uti & Turcas ottomannas solitos esse videmus, pulchritudinis auspiciis evehantur. *Paulus Jovius in Moschovia*, p. 32.

* The following is delivered as the true state of the business by that profound russian antiquarian M. Boltin:

Inquiries

from the daughters of the natives proved at times the fruitful source of the disasters to the empire, as the relations of the new tzaritza, by the assistance of their aunts, now raised to be great ladies, strove to make themselves of consequence, and did not always pursue this aim by the directest means; as, for example, in the case of Boris. Should it happen that a tzar married more than once, then a door was imme-

---

Inquiries were privately made after the most beautiful and sensible young women of the country; but no ukases were ever issued to that effect, as has been pretended by some foreign authors. Some of the principal lords and ladies received the commission to bring such as they deemed the worthiest to the house of the monarch, where each of them found a decent chamber ready for her reception. They ate all at one table, and various kinds of pastime were provided for their amusement. The monarch observed them privately and listened to their conversations. It is affirmed by some that he even visited them by night, in order to see which of them slept quietly or unquietly. After reiterated visitation and inspection of the understandings, tempers, and dispositions, and having made up his mind in consequence, he came and sat down at table with them, where he presented her on whom he had fixed his choice for a bride with a handkerchief and a ring. On the same day he dismissed the rest from his house with presents consisting of the several articles of dress. The name of the bride elect was then publicly declared, and the title of grand-princess conferred upon her.

diately

diately opened to the spirit of faction: several families became related to the sovereign; one exerting itself to circumvent the other; the new relations endeavouring by all means to subvert the elder. The case here supposed, by no means advantageous to the empire, actually happened with Alexey. He married twice; and herein lay principally the foundation of the troubles which threatened to break out immediately on his death; and though at that time suppressed, burst forth with greater violence and fury, six years afterwards, when Feodor died.

Two princes, named Feodor and Ivan, and six princesses, of whom Sophia afterwards made herself particularly famous, were the children of the first, Peter and Natalia the offspring of the second marriage, whom Alexey left behind him at his death. By his first consort, born a Miloslafskoy, the family of Miloslafskoy acquired great influence at court; which, however, declined on Alexey's marrying a second time a Narishkin, and this consort favoured *her* relations. As now, moreover, the two princes of the former marriage, Feodor and Ivan, were not only of a very feeble temperament, but also appeared to have no great intellectual abilities, (which was particularly the case with Ivan,) it was natural for the Narishkin family to conceive the design of nominating, after Alexey's death, the young Peter, fourteen years of age, the only prince of the second marriage, as successor to his father, and to exclude the two elder princes, on account of their incapacity, from the succession. But this project failed: Feodor was appointed tzar; and, though he was sickly and infirm of body, and this infirmity was even increased by an illness shortly after his accession to the throne, yet he proved, that the conclusion from the weakness of his body to an imbecility of mind was too hasty. On the contrary, during his reign of six years he displayed many excellent talents for government; and it was much to be lamented, that the tenement of his spirit was so frail. The war against the Turks which he inherited from his father he prosecuted four years longer, and terminated it in 1680 by a truce for twenty years, by which the Turks not only reaped no advantage, but were compelled to acknowledge the sovereignty of the tzars over the Kozaks, whom the sultan was greatly desirous to incorporate with his empire.

The pains bestowed by Feodor in his administration related chiefly to the interior of the empire; evincing in the whole of his conduct that the benefit of his people was his ruling object,

object. In a country like Russia, where even after all the trouble that Alexey had taken to form a code of laws, there were not statutes adapted to all cases, too many opportunities offered where chicane or money could influence the decision of the judge. The offices of the magistrature were almost exclusively filled by the nobility; and it was extremely difficult for any of the burghers or peasantry, and for the poor almost impossible, to gain a verdict, even though the law was on their side, whenever the adversary was a noble or a wealthy man, as the former was commonly favoured by the court on account of his rank, and the latter for the weighty arguments which he brought. Indeed under Alexey's government some great men, as before related, received sad wages for their iniquities; but these examples presently lost their warning virtue, and Feodor saw himself obliged to make it a primary object of his care that law and equity were impartially administered, and that even the poor and needy of his subjects should at least have justice. — With equal diligence he provided that the necessaries of life should not be kept at too high a price, nor the dealers in them oppress the poor. For the encouragement of persons in slender circumstances, desirous to engage in useful undertakings that

exceeded

exceeded their means, he affisted them with pecuniary advances for several years. Mosco was already indebted to his father for having a well constituted police: he added to it many wise regulations, and at length crowned his reign by an ordinance, eminently important and beneficial to the empire, by which he gave a violent blow to the hurtful and ridiculous conceit of privileges of birth.

Nothing could equal the care with which the noble families kept the books of their pedigrees, in which were set down, not only every one of their ancestors, but also the posts and offices which these their forefathers held at court, in the army, or in the civil department. Had these genealogies and registers of descent been confined to the purpose of determining the ancestry and the relationship of families, no objection could be alleged against them. But these books of record were carried to the most absurd abuse, attended with a host of pernicious consequences. If a nobleman were appointed to a post in the army or at court, or to some civil station, and it appeared that the person to whom he was now subordinate numbered fewer ancestors than he, it was with the utmost difficulty that he could be brought to accept of the office to which he was called. Nay, this folly

was

was carried still greater lengths: a man would even refuse to take upon him an employ, if thereby he would be subordinate to one whose ancestors formerly stood under the ancestors of him who was now offered the place. It is easy to imagine that a prejudice of this kind must have been productive of the most disagreeable effects, and that discontents, murmurs at slights and trifling neglects, disputes, quarrels, and disorders in the service, must have been its natural attendants. It was therefore become indispensably necessary that a particular office should be instituted at court, in which exact copies of the genealogical tables and service-registers of the noble families were deposited; and this office was incessantly employed in settling the numberless disputes that arose from this inveterate prejudice. Feodor, observing the pernicious effects of this fond conceit that the father's capacity must necessarily devolve on the son, and that consequently he ought to inherit his posts, wished to put a stop to it; and, with the advice of his sagacious minister prince Vassilly Galitzin, of whom we shall frequently have occasion to speak, fell upon the following method for putting an end to this ridiculous practice. He caused it to be proclaimed, that all the families should deliver into court faithful copies of their service-rolls, in order that they might be corrected of a number of errors that had crept into them. This delivery being made, he convoked the great men and the superior clergy before him. In eloquent speeches it was represented to them by him in arguments drawn from reason, and by the patriarch in arguments drawn from religion, that the prejudice which had hitherto prevailed of forming pretensions from the posts that had been filled by their ancestors, was as irrational as it was contrary to the dictates of christianity, which required humility and brotherly love. These discourses being ended, the assembly were asked their opinion, when they unanimously assented; the generality however not from full conviction to the judgment of the tzar and the patriarch. No sooner was this assent declared, than the whole heap of these records of service was brought into the square before the palace, and, in presence of the clergy and a multitude of noblemen, — burnt to ashes. By way of conclusion to this singular ceremony, the patriarch denounced an anathema against every one who should presume to contravene this ordinance of the tzar; and the justice of the sentence was ratified by the assembly in a general shout of Amen. It was by no means Feodor's intention to efface nobility; and

and accordingly he ordered new books to be made in which the noble families were inscribed; but thus was abolished that extremely pernicious custom which made it a disgrace to be under the orders of another if his ancestry did not reach so high, or even — in case of equal pedigree — if a forefather of the commander had once been subordinate in the service to the progenitor of him who was now to acknowledge him for his superior.

Feodor, therefore, did much good in his generation, combated many prejudices, and contributed what he could to rouse his people from that sluggishness which generally prevailed among them; by many of his actions strove to cure them of the idle notion, that every thing is best as it is, and therefore that nothing should be altered. He destroyed, as we have just seen, the extravagant pretensions of the nobility, so highly detrimental to the state; in like manner he did away the prejudice that the tzaritza must always be a native Russian, by marrying a lady of Poland, for whom he had conceived an affection, and roundly told the patriarch, on his declaring the marriage invalid, that he either never would marry at all, or only according to his private inclination: upon which the former retracted. He attempted to bring about an

alteration

alteration in the national drefs of the Ruffians, which had more of the afiatic than the european; not by a decree, as Peter afterwards did, but by appointing, occafionally, feftivities at court, and making it a condition on all who would partake in them, that they fhould appear in a particular drefs fomewhat altered by him, and bearing a refemblance to the polifh. — Thus Feodor in many refpects fet a pattern to his great fucceffor Peter. It was much to be wifhed that the period of his life had been protracted *; but the empire would more deeply ftill have felt his lofs, if he had not been fucceeded by Peter, who ftrove to complete the good which Alexey and Feodor had begun, who brought to maturity what they had fown, who combined with the talents for government, which feemed hereditary in the houfe of Romanof, a more reftlefs zeal, a more indefatigable activity than his predeceffors poffeffed; and by his deeds as fovereign acquired that renown which has claffed him with the greateft monarchs.

Feodor's death in 1682 was in a manner the fignal for fanguinary fcenes, being the occafion

---

* " Feodor lived," fays the ruffian hiftorian Sumarokof, " the joy and delight of his people, and died amidft " their fighs and tears. On the day he died Mofco was " in the fame ftate of diftrefs as Rome was on the death " of Titus."

of a struggle for the sovereignty of the empire, between brother and sister, which lasted sixteen years, and in 1698 * terminated in favour of Peter, the brother.

Feodor had already been aware that Ivan, half-blind, and in general very infirm, was not adequate to the business of a tzar of Russia, and for that reason had shortly before his death ordained, that his step-brother Peter, then ten years old, who already discovered uncommon abilities, should be his successor. Ivan himself avowed his incapacity for governing, and would willingly now have relinquished the throne to Peter, as he afterwards actually did; but to this SOPHIA, the own sister of Feodor and Ivan, and half-sister of Peter, would not assent. This princess was just then in the full bloom of youth, of exquisite beauty, and of rare accomplishments. She had ambition enough to aspire to the throne, courage enough to make her way to it by any kind of means, and prudence enough to have maintained herself upon it †.

* When Sophia's last effort, the rebellion of the Strelitzes, raised by her and her party in Peter's absence, was defeated.

† Peter himself afterwards frequently said, that if his sister had bridled her ambition, he would have left to her the helm of government, and contentedly have served his country under her authority.

That

That Ivan, a prince of the former marriage, was intended to be passed by in the succession to the throne, furnished her with the fittest pretence for making herself of consequence. She took upon her the tone of a patroness of the claims of her full brother, demanding justice apparently for him alone, regardless of herself. Accordingly, in the same proportion as the Narishkin party were endeavouring to promote Peter's succession, Sophia was industrious in contriving to oppose it. In order to facilitate the accomplishment of her design, she secured to herself, by promises and money, the concurrence of the strelitzes, that band of soldiers who at Mosco were what the janisaries are at Constantinople, a corps which, by its strength, consisting of upwards of 14,000 men, were enabled to give powerful support to any plot. To get rid of the Narishkins, as the friends and dependants of prince Peter, was the first and grand aim of Sophia, as by that means she hoped to have a freer scope for her stratagems. To effect this the more readily, a rumour was spread that the Narishkins were guilty of Feodor's death; that foreign physicians, bribed by this family, had dispatched the tzar by poison, and their relations only wanted to raise Peter to the throne, and to that end to exclude, nay even to murder

Sophia's

Sophia's own brother Ivan, who had a prior right. The efforts of the Narishkins to procure the succession for Peter, which were not to be dissembled, gave to this report an air of probability, which every method was used to reduce to certainty. The beautiful Sophia, by her arts of persuasion, ingeniously gave impression to these allegations, particularly among the chiefs of the strelitzes, while her creatures were incessantly assiduous in gaining over the common people of that body by various artifices. Galitzin, Feodor's wife and active minister *, was also Sophia's favourite and counsellor; and even the vulgar owned it to be reasonable that the crown should be given to prince Ivan, as the eldest son. Sophia was therefore preparing to ascend the throne; for that was her real intention, though she concealed it under her sisterly love for Ivan, who in that case would never have had any thing more than the title of tzar, as was afterwards plainly seen. Hitherto, indeed, it seemed as if Sophia had no design of making any attempts against the life of Peter; but some years

* To this a foreigner, who at that time lived in Russia, bears the following testimony: He was polite, fertile in invention, and of greater sagacity than any of his countrymen; of an active mind, diligent; was, in understanding, far beyond his times, and capable of working a great alteration in Russia, if his time and authority had been commensurate with his inclination.

after

after she shewed, by her actions, that she would have made no scruple of sacrificing this half-brother to her ambition. Sophia would perhaps too have found arguments sufficient for justifying her conduct, and for proving to her country and to the world that she was necessitated so to act for the benefit of the empire. Had she then, supported by Galitzin, a shrewd and enterprising man, and whom, as has since been believed, she would have owned for her husband, wisely and happily conducted her reign, it would scarcely ever have been mentioned, perhaps it would even gradually have been forgotten, that she made her way to the throne over the corpse of her brother. But fate would have it otherwise. Peter, the persecuted prince, was to conquer all plots and machinations against him, and at length to become sole monarch; while Sophia, for her often unsuccessful, but always repeated attempts to place herself on the throne, was doomed at length to do penance by the loss of her liberty.

In perfect consistence with her plan, by which the strelitzes had been dextrously enticed, the whole crew of them consorted together soon after Feodor's death, committed all manner of excesses for three days in succession, in which they met with no check whatever, sacrificed to

their

their fury several of the chief officers of state, that were against Sophia, forced their way even into the palace of the tzars, and demanded the death of the Narishkins *, who, as they pretended, were bent on depriving Ivan of the throne, and then of his life. At length they declared by acclamation prince Ivan to be tzar. He, however, having a sincere affection for his half-brother Peter, wished him to be co-sovereign with him; which was granted: but Sophia was at the same time declared co-sovereign with the two tzars. This was on the 6th of May 1681, and in June the coronation of Ivan and Peter was solemnized in due form. Sophia immediately married tzar Ivan, in order that if any children were born of this marriage, Peter might lose for ever all hope of obtaining the crown. Thus, one step of Sophia's succeeded; she had now the government in her hands; for Ivan,

* Two brothers of the widowed tzaritza Natalia, Alexey's second consort, of the family of Narishkin, were murdered. This was the fatal lot in all of about sixty persons, mostly of the first distinction. The Miloslafskys, Sophia's kinsmen, were particularly busy in this sedition. The property of such as were executed was confiscated and divided among the strelitzes. A public monument was likewise erected, on which the names of the deceased were inscribed, as traitors to their country.

from

from his imbecility; and Peter from his youth, being only ten years of age, had nothing more than the title of tzars. Their names stood at bottom of the decrees and ordinances that were issued; but Sophia and her favourite Galitzin were alone their authors. Afterwards, in the year 1687, Sophia began to add her name to those of the tzars, and to cause her image to be stamped on the coin.

In the meantime, the strelitzes whom Sophia had chosen as her instruments in the downfal which she had prepared for Peter, had nearly, after that first insurrection in her favour, been dangerous to herself. Prince Kovanskoi, their commander, who was privy to the plans of Sophia, had probably too much ambition for submitting to be the passive instrument by which she was to obtain the sovereign power, also might be desirous of having himself a share in the government, and was accordingly jealous of Galitzin. The proposal which he made to Sophia, that she would marry one of her sisters to his son, perhaps caused some alarm on account of the consequences by which it might possibly be attended; and her refusal, which made Kovanskoi the adversary of Sophia, wrought also so powerfully on his strelitzes, that Sophia, the two tzars, and the whole court were reduced to

the

the neceffity of making the ftrong monaftery of the Trinity, twelve leagues from Mofco, their fanctuary. Ere, however, the enraged ftrelitzes could follow them thither, the court collected together a great body of armed foldiers, among whom were many foreigners. Kovanfkoi being taken prifoner, was beheaded; and as the ftrelitzes, ftill more exafperated by this act, were advancing againft the monaftery, they learnt that they were likely to meet with a ftout refiftance there. This intelligence immediately converted their apparent courage into defpondency, and their fury into confternation. The court demanded that the principal ringleaders fhould be delivered up, which was done; and, moreover, the tenth man of every regiment was felected as a victim for the reft. Thefe wretches, thus decimated, being condemned to die at Mofco, where moft of the ftrelitzes were ftationary, took an affectionate leave of their wives and children, prepared themfelves for death by receiving the facrament, and went back to the monaftery in fuch order, that every two of them carried a block, and the third was the bearer of an axe. In this tremendous proceffion, attended by a great concourfe of people, particularly of their relations, they came to the place before the monaftery, laid their heads on the blocks they had brought

brought with them, and in that situation waited their doom, which at length amounted to this, that some of the most guilty were made an atonement for all. Sophia henceforward placed no more confidence in the strelitzes. The majority of them were draughted off into the other regiments on the frontiers, in order to remove them from the capital *.

This insurrection being quelled, all now wore a tranquil appearance; and the government, which Sophia had in her hands, proceeded in the ordinary course. Certain persons, however, of both parties, that is, the friends of Sophia and of Peter, were in the meantime very busy in private. The former to preserve the government in the hands of that princess, and the latter to ravish it from her in time, and to confer it upon Peter. A good opportunity soon offered for the party of this tzar to raise clamours against Vaffilly Galitzin the favourite of Sophia, and the measures they pursued; and thus to take one step in behalf of Peter. In 1686 the peace abovementioned † was concluded with Poland,

* The beforementioned monument, a testimony of rewarded insurrection, dishonourable to the government, was removed, and another with a warning against rebellion set up in its place.
† See before, p. 28.

But

But new hostilities with Turkey soon broke out. The Turks were at the same time involved in a war with Poland and with the german emperor. Both powers sollicited the court of Russia to take part in the contest, in order to employ the common foe on the side of the krimean Tartars. Sophia at first would not hearken to this request. But among the few great men whose counsel was of any moment, were several secret friends to Peter. These shewed by a multitude of arguments, that it behoved them, as tending to the good of the country, to cut out more work for the sultan, already harassed on two sides, and thus by dividing, to weaken his forces. Doubtless these advisers cared less about weakening the Turks than of lessening the credit of the present administration. They foresaw that little glory would redound from this war, and were in hopes that the displeasure, if it turned out badly, would fall upon Sophia. Besides, a war offered the best means for getting rid of Galitzin, and in his absence of being more active in favour of Peter, who now already [1686] shewed himself worthy of sitting on the throne of his ancestors. They were therefore so incessant, and so earnest in their sollicitations with Sophia and Galitzin, and asserted so vehemently that Galitzin was the only man qualified for conducting this war with success, that the latter, though so strenuously against it at the first, at length complied, and put himself at the head of the army. He was thoroughly sensible of what his enemies knew, and what the sequel proved, that he had no talents for a military commander. He consumed the whole campaign in marches and countermarches, without gaining, though with an army of 300,000 men, a single advantage over the enemy, and yet 40,000 of his people fell sacrifices to this fruitless campaign. Indeed the friends of Sophia and Galitzin were continually causing false accounts of victories gained by the Russians to be circulated in Mosco; and, casting the blame of the failure of the campaign on the hetman of the kozaks, whom they actually sent to Siberia, on disbanding the soldiers at the end of the campaign they even distributed rewards among them — for nothing. But all this did not impose upon the people; and a general aversion ensued against Sophia and Galitzin, which was greatly increased by an equal want of success in the following campaign of 1687. Undoubtedly one circumstance contributed in no small degree to diminish the lustre of both these campaigns, that one part of the army wished well to Peter, and therefore was not desirous that Galitzin should be successful, and the influence of him and

Sophia

Sophia be thereby augmented, but rather devoutly hoped to see the downfall of the present government and the elevation of Peter *.

Peter's friends, during the absence of Galitzin, were extremely industrious in supporting the claims of that prince to the absolute monarchy. The following was one of the methods adopted for forming a party in his behalf. He repaired to a village not far from Mosco, where he admitted a number of young people to his company and into his service, many of whom were sons of the principal families of the empire. They were generally called the tzar's playmates †, and it even seemed at first, that the object of this connection was nothing more than diversion, entertainment, and pleasure. The real aim of it, however, was far greater and more extensive; for the youths who here daily associated with Peter acquired such an attachment to his person as was never to be effaced, and became his most faithful adherents. The probability that he would one day be sole tzar brought constantly new accessions of young men into this society; and it grew up into a small

* Such were the sentiments, for example, of Lefort and Gordon, both firm friends of Peter, who made the campaign with him; and certainly many of the officers and privates in the army held the same opinion.

† Potefchniye.

company,

company, at the head of which was Lefort*. The tzar himself began as a drummer, and served

* It cannot be doubted that Lefort had great influence in the forming of Peter's character, and on his undertakings afterwards, though all that Peter did cannot properly be ascribed to him; for, without the thirst of knowledge, the perseverance and the unabated emulation by which the latter was actuated, all his intercourse with Lefort would have operated nothing. On a different soil the same seed would never have come to maturity, much less have borne the fruit it did with Peter. Lefort was born at Geneva in 1652, and designed by his parents for commerce. But his active mind and lively imagination led him into a dissolute way of life, in consequence of which he got deeply in debt, and in consequence of his debts left Geneva, went to Marseilles, and became a cadet. After remaining there some time, he travelled to Holland, enlisted under an officer who was raising soldiers for tzar Alexey, and so came to Archangel. Alexey in the meantime dying, no farther concern was taken at Archangel about the new raised foreign troops. Upon this Lefort proceeded to Mosco, where he as speedily made himself master of the russian language, as he had before acquired the dutch and german, and became secretary to the danish ambassador. His striking figure and engaging manners procured him access to the most distinguished families, and he soon married a young lady with a large fortune. In these circumstances he found an opportunity of making himself known to the tzar, who presently felt an attachment for the foreigner who had entirely educated himself, and who, without any literary acquirements, possessed extensive knowledge, and became his avowed patron and friend. Peter learnt dutch and german

of

served progressively upwards through the several ranks, as every one was obliged to do who was admitted into this corps. The novelty of the affair, the affability of Peter, and Lefort's exertions, co-operated in continually adding to its numbers; so that in a short time the village was too small to contain it, and a part was obliged to remove into another. Sophia at first foresaw none of the effects which might, and indeed must

---

of him, and Lefort was his daily companion. The tzar, finding between him and Lefort such a conformity of inclinations and ideas, made him the confident of all his projects, and constantly applied to him for advice. He even authorized him to check him in his extravagances, and to soothe him in those bursts of passion to which he was unfortunately subject, and sometimes, mixing with the intoxication arising from strong liquors, rendered him furious. At such times only Lefort could dare to speak to him; and, in reproving him for his intemperance and madness, he has even been known to use violence for checking his impetuous career. It was not, however, without danger that Lefort could venture on these bold offices of zeal. Peter was once on the point of stabbing him; but on regaining the equipoise of his mind, he embraced Lefort and asked his pardon. Peter having given him a company, next made him general, then admiral, lived with him on the footing of a friend, and on his death interred him like a prince. Pity that Lefort, by his excesses in the early part of life, brought on himself a premature death, being only in his forty-sixth year when he died.

naturally

naturally flow from such an inftitution; or, perhaps, fhe thought herfelf too fecure to allow any fuggeftion of alarm to enter her mind, and took no farther notice of it than as an infignificant youthful paftime. Befides, as feveral of this company, with whom the tzar was extremely familiar, Lefort, a certain Galitzin*, and others, lived rather diforderly, had frequent entertainments, carouzings, and the like jovial parties, and were therefore more likely to lead Peter into extravagancies, than to ufeful knowledge and to habits of activity, Sophia gave herfelf no concern about them, in the hopes that this licentious mode of life would prevent the tzar from turning his mind to the affairs of government, might even at length draw upon him the odium of the nation, and thereby confirm her authority the more. But fhe was miftaken. Amidft the libertinifm and diffipation in which Peter was apparently paffing his days, his great mind was ever watchful, his underftanding was unfolding itfelf from day to day, and his activity was conftantly increafing. Lefort imparted to him much knowledge in their converfations, at their repafts, and even over their wine, called his attention to a variety of objects, rouzed his curio-

* A coufin of the minifter.

ſty, explained to him ſuch difficulties as he ſtarted, and Peter now ſoon began to reflect on himſelf, on his ſtation, and on the nature of the country which he was called to govern. He then made it his buſineſs to gain ſome knowledge in the arts of policy and war. Lefort, who had been an attentive obſerver of whatever had paſſed within his view, had acquired a conſiderable ſtore of various kinds of information, and was naturally of a thoughtful and penetrating diſpoſition, at the ſame time ingenious in uſing the ſkill and experience he had acquired, took every occaſion of inſtilling into Peter's mind the improvements and advantages of other kingdoms and ſtates, in regard to military diſcipline, government, laws, commerce, arts, manufactures, and trade. Peter preſently felt an ardent deſire to procure theſe advantages to his empire. To this end it was abſolutely neceſſary that he ſhould have the government ſolely in his own hands. As throughout the whole ruſſian hiſtory to that time there had not been one example of a female reign; as Peter, who had now attained his ſeventeenth year, had a right to claim the government, the incapacity of Ivan being generally allowed; in ſhort, encouraged by the unanimous intreaty of his friends and adherents to ſecure to himſelf the ſole ſovereignty, the ſpirit of Peter was rouzed. The very prince whom Sophia had all along regarded as a frivolous youth, fit for no continued and regular courſe of action, and incompetent to the arduous affairs of government, diſplayed all at once ſuch a ſpirit of enterpriſe, with ſuch energy and perſeverance in whatever he undertook, that Sophia and her party were alarmed, the friends and adherents of Peter were delighted and concurred zealouſly with him, while the nation at large admired and feared the courageous tzar.

In July 1689 the diſagreements between Peter and Sophia came to a formal rupture [*], on occaſion of the meeting at a ſolemn office of religion. Peter was preſent as tzar, and Sophia inſiſted on attending the ſolemnity as regent; it is even affirmed that ſhe demanded the principal place. This Peter refuſed to allow; Sophia was peremptory in her claim; on which the tzar entirely withdrew in diſpleaſure. The theatre on which the ſovereignty was to be contended for was now opened, the two parties had in a manner declared war, a war which muſt end in the victory of the one and the downfall of the other.

[*] Sophia and Peter had had frequent altercations, when the latter frequented the ſittings of the national council where ſhe preſided, and would not accommodate himſelf to her inclination in everything.

Peter,

Peter, with his court and his friends, repaired in the month of August once more to the fortified monastery of the holy trinity, whither he was followed by most of the foreigners among the troops, officers and privates, as his bodyguard to secure his person from an attack. Sophia now again threw herself into the arms of the strelitzes. Their leader, named Scheglovitoï, engaged to remove Peter out of the way, but — the project miscarried. In the mean time, as a great number of defenders had resorted to Peter, as even the public voice of the nation was on the side of the enterprising tzar, and as particularly the black design of Sophia to have him made away with had degraded her still lower in the eyes of the people; and the strelitzes, as they had already shewn, not being soldiers on whose bravery any reliance could be made, the co-sovereign held it best to abandon the way of violence and to adopt the arts of gentleness. She offered her hand to an accommodation, and sent mediators to that purpose; but Peter convinced them of Sophia's base designs, and they remained with him. Sophia at length set out herself. On the road she was met by persons sent from Peter, who informed her that he would not speak to her, and ordered, as tzar, the immediate surrender of the commander

mander of the ſtrelitzes. He was beheaded, and the other conſpirators puniſhed. Galitzin paid forfeit by an exile to the borders of Archangel *, and the co-ſovereign Sophia had her head ſhaved and was obliged to retire to a nunnery under the name of ſiſter Sufanna. — Thus Peter now ſat without a partner upon the throne, to which his right had been conteſted; for Ivan, though he lived till 1696, was a mere nonentity. He was paſſive in all theſe tranſactions, and both from reverence and affection for Peter had never approved of the machinations of his ſiſter againſt his brother. — On the eleventh of September a proclamation was made, that for the future in all public papers and records the name of the late regent Sophia would no longer be mentioned.

No ſooner had Peter the ſole ſovereignty in his hands than he gave the moſt unequivocal proofs of his active mind, and ſhewed that he was thoroughly acquainted with the defects and infirmities of his empire. He plainly perceived that a diſciplined, well-trained valiant army, according to the preſent eſtabliſhment in other countries, was much wanted in his own; and

* He received for himſelf and each perſon of his family the daily allowance of — three kopeeks (about three halfpence) for their maintainance.

accordingly

accordingly he made it one of his first businesses, as monarch, to put the army on a better footing. Except a few regiments stationed on the frontiers, the strelitzes at Mosco were the only standing troops; and that these possessed less courage and discipline than brutal ferocity, they had furnished several glaring proofs. On the breaking out of a war, besides the strelitzes, the nobility were summoned to the field with their retainers; but they appeared undisciplined, armed in various methods, some well-cloathed but others in ragged array. Such a constitution was attended by many disadvantages: Peter therefore resolved to form a great standing army, to be at once better disciplined and better exercised; and to this end he appointed Gordon, a Scotsman, and Lefort, the Genevan, to raise regiments *, which in their whole constitution, dress, and military exercises should be formed entirely after the model of the european troops.

* Lefort had a regiment of 12,000 men. The greater part, as in Gordon's regiments, consisted of foreigners. In Lefort's regiments there were about 300 huguenots alone who had fled from France on account of the revocation of the edict of Nantes in 1685. Among Gordon's soldiers were great numbers of Scotsmen who had left their native country on account of the troubles with which it was then afflicted.

While

While Peter was thus industriously employed in reforming his army, he conceived the still more ardent desire of having a navy, and soon set himself to work at its accomplishment. What first prompted his zeal to this undertaking was the following circumstance, though it would certainly have arisen sooner or later in Peter's mind without that occasion. Being at a pleasure-house of his father's he saw an english boat lying neglected. This attracted his ever-active curiosity; and, in the course of his inquiries about it, he learnt that the builder of this vessel was Brandt, a Dutchman, who was still living in Mosco. The boat-builder was immediately sent for and received orders from Peter to construct several vessels in which the monarch and his attendants might sail about the rivers and lakes in the vicinity of Mosco. By this practice he got in a short time such a taste for the art of ship-building and the whole system of marine, that he took a journey to Archangel in order to inspect the several ships in that harbour, and to acquaint himself still farther with naval affairs. At Archangel he caused a large vessel to be built, was an attentive observer of the whole work as it proceeded, employed himself in making drawings and models of ships, occasionally put his hand to the labour, and very often acted the

part

part of the steersman. It soon occurred to such a reflecting mind as Peter's, that a marine must be of signal advantage to a country. He saw in the port of Archangel the influence of a haven on the trade, the commerce, and the whole business of a nation; and all this accelerated the completion of the wish he had already formed to have a navy. To incite his people to commerce, and thereby to diligence and activity by navigation, and by a fleet to increase the respect and the power of his empire, were the two plans, in the execution whereof he was now as sedulously employed as in the better formation of his army. To the accomplishment of his design, however, it was a great impediment that Russia had so little water. The port of Archangel was adapted to the purposes of commerce; but it was not entirely fit for the uses of a navy, as the White-sea is scarcely navigable six months in the year, and Archangel is situate at a great distance from the rest of Europe. Peter was rather desirous to acquire water on the side of the Euxine and the Caspian, or in the parts of the Baltic, as more convenient for the fitting out of a fleet and offering greater opportunities for commerce. Both of these views in the sequel succeeded.

The

The war between the Turks and the Poles was not yet brought to a termination. Peter refolved, notwithftanding the unfuccefsful campaign of Galitzin, to take once more a fhare in it, placing no fmall confidence at this time in the new regulations he had introduced into the army. Indeed he would have been able to accomplifh more, if in the firft campaign he could have acted by fea; but the veffels which he caufed to be built for that purpofe were not yet [1695] ready, and therefore all depended on this occafion on the land forces. To get poffeffion of Azof, then belonging to the Turks, and, as that fortrefs ftands at the exit of the Don into the Euxine, to gain an intercourfe with that fea, was Peter's plan.

In this campaign he gave a good leffon to the nobility of the empire. The monarch declined to take upon him the chief command, chufing rather to ferve as a volunteer; though it would have been very eafy for him, even fuppofing him to have underftood but very little of military orders, to have acted as commander in chief by the advice of a council: intending by this to teach his nobles that talents and fkill are not innate, but muft be acquired; and therefore he appointed Gordon, Lefort, Scheremetof, and Schein commanders of his army, while he himfelf attended

this

this campaign as a pupil in the military art. However, the fuccefs of the campaign was by no means brilliant; only the capture of a couple of forts before Azof: the affailants found it impoffible to take the citadel itfelf even by ftorm, and they were obliged to abandon the fiege. Peter, however, was not difheartened by this failure, but applied himfelf to repair the miftakes and neglects to which the ill-fuccefs of the campaign was owing, that he might proceed with fresh vigour to the accomplifhment of his defign. That the whole army was divided into three corps independent on each other; that there was a great deficiency in artillery, and efpecially in tranfport veffels, for preventing the Turks from fupplying the fortrefs with provifions from the water-fide, were the caufes which rendered ineffectual the firft attack on Azof. Peter removed them all. He gave the chief command to Schein, obtained artillerifts and engineers from the emperor, from the elector of Brandenburg, and from the Dutch; and had likewife the fatisfaction of being now fupported in the fecond campaign [1696] by feveral tranfports, with the affiftance whereof he beat the Turks at fea, and thereby at length became mafter of Azof. This firft victory of his partly new-conftituted army, and of his newly-acquired

quired little fleet, he resolved to display before his people, whose affections he had captivated in the interim between the two campaigns, by his care in procuring a supply of corn in a season of great scarcity, in order thereby to rouze them from their inactivity, and to inspire them with confidence in the tzar's innovations, which in either respect could not be better done than by shewing them their fruits. He accordingly appointed a triumphal procession into Mosco, similar to the triumphal entries of the ancient Romans; thus by publicly rewarding the soldiers for their bravery, he strove to quicken their sense of honour, and by this solemnity to raise in the breasts of the spectators a veneration for courage and intrepidity. Lefort, as admiral, and Schein as commander in chief of the land forces, were the principal personages in this triumphal procession, while Peter was lost without distinction in the crowd of officers, thus publicly shewing his own greatness of mind and testifying to the whole nation, for their encouragement to excel, that he would only recompense merit.

Immediately on his happy return from this second campaign, Peter employed his thoughts in forming plans for benefiting his empire by the vicinity of the Euxine thus forcibly obtained.

tained. He resolved to construct a fleet in that sea; but, as his revenues alone were not sufficient for its equipment at once, he put out a proclamation commanding the patriarch and the other dignitaries of the church, the nobility, and merchants, to shew their patriotism by a pecuniary contribution for fitting out a certain number of ships, while he himself engaged to get ready several others. Within three years the fleet was to be fit for sea, and therefore the work was immediately begun and continued with the utmost expedition, as any omission of compliance with the orders in the decree was rigorously attended with heavy penalties.

As none other than foreign workmen, particularly Dutchmen and Italians, could be employed in the building and fitting out of these ships, Peter sent several young Russians, to qualify themselves for being their assistants afterwards, to Venice, Leghorn and Holland, to study the art of ship-building there, and others to Germany to learn the science of war, as the german artillerists and engineers had been of very great service to him at Azof. But, not content with merely prescribing to others the way for acquiring several branches of knowledge beneficial to the nation, he came to the resolution to travel himself into foreign countries, to examine with his own eyes their several advantages, to propagate them in his empire, to transfuse more activity, industry, and diligence into the great mass of his subjects, and by that means to render his country more prosperous and powerful.

Shortly before this journey, however, Peter very narrowly escaped being sent into another world, as a great number of his subjects were highly dissatisfied with the various alterations that were going forward. Whatever he did was unlike to anything they had been accustomed to in the former tzars; nay, his behaviour in general was the very reverse of theirs. The former tzars, for instance, shewed themselves very rarely to the people, appearing only on particular solemnities in asiatic pomp and a cumbersome parade, to excite the awful admiration of a wondering populace, who gazed at them with the same religious veneration with which they beheld the relics of their saints; and, having thus gratified their slavish curiosity, returned in majestic state to the Kremlin, the tzarian palace at Mosco. — But Peter was every day to be seen, one while exercising his troops, at another conversing in the public places, and then visiting the workshops and private persons. His whole behaviour therefore was extremely different from that

that of the ancient tzars, and consequently numbers of Russians shook their heads at it. But likewise the regulations he introduced naturally excited discontent, since they were innovations; and even in enlightened countries as they are called, every innovation, however rational and profitable, is loudly enough decried to prevent us from being surprised at the Russians of Peter's times for their not approving of his alterations. That Peter kept up a greater standing army — that he was constantly limiting the power of the strelitzes — that he made no greater account of a nobleman than of a burgher — that he had many foreigners about him, whom he promoted and rewarded — that he himself served upwards in the army from the lowest ranks — that he caused a navy to be built, and compelled the clergy and others to open their coffers for the equipment of it — that he sent a number of young Russians into heretical countries, even to Italy, the seat of the pope, the abomination of the Russians, though it had always been prohibited to travel out of the country — that, in short, he, the tzar himself, was determined to travel abroad, and probably at his return would pester them with still more innovations: — all these circumstances seemed to a great part of the Russians so entirely

tirely out of rule, and so utterly hostile to all their hereditary usages, that murmurs began to be pretty plainly heard in several parts of the empire. Indeed they arose merely from the ignorant and vulgar; for the more sensible part of the nation very clearly perceived that the plans and regulations of the tzar were calculated for the lasting advantage of the country. Some malignants, however, conceived the horrible design of first murdering Peter, then massacring the foreigners who had gained his esteem, and lastly, of fetching Sophia out of the convent and proclaiming her sovereign. But this plot was likewise happily defeated *, and Peter rescued.

The

---

* The circumstances of this plot to murder Peter are related in a very credible narrative in the following manner. A number of strelitzes, particularly exasperated at the reform of the troops and the employment of foreigners, had agreed to make away with the tzar. They met therefore one day at noon at the house of a strelitz, named Sukanin, the chief of the conspiracy, intending to remain there till about midnight, then to set fire to a house adjacent to the tzar's palace, and when the tzar, according to his custom, should appear to give directions about the means of stopping its progress, to assassinate him in the crowd. But, two of these conspirators, being stung with remorse previous to the execution of their plot, opened themselves to each other, and obtained leave of the rest to go home and pass in sleep the hours till midnight that they might be the

more

HISTORY OF RUSSIA. 69

The tzar now undertook his first journey, committing the government for a time to some of his trusty counsellors, for the sake of acquiring, by travel and converse, more skill in the art of government, and thus to qualify himself more worthily to discharge the duties of a ruler.

---

more alert for their purpose at that time. Instead, however, of doing as they proposed, they repaired to Peter, and disclosed to him the whole of the horrid design. Peter immediately wrote to the captain of one of the regiments of guards, commanding him to invest Sukanin's house in perfect silence at ten o'clock. In his hurry he wrote *eleven* instead of ten. He himself proceeded, just after ten, to the neighbourhood of the house, in the expectation of finding all in readiness; but was much surprised at not seeing the guard. Hearing a great noise in the house, he even ventured in, and suddenly found himself in the midst of his sworn enemies. Instead of being struck with awe at his presence, they thought this the luckiest opportunity for making sure of their purpose. He desired that he might not interrupt them at their mirth, sat down and drank with them, and shewed himself in high spirits. The conspirators drank boldly to him, and were giving one another the wink to fall upon him, when the captain of the guard, who had surrounded the house in perfect silence, entered the room with some of his people, rescued Peter, and arrested the conspirators, who were afterwards cruelly put to death. Peter, in a passion, gave the captain a box on the ear for coming too late. But he produced the tzar's order in which eleven o'clock was plainly written. Peter immediately kissed him on the forehead, and declared him blameless.

It would lead me too far from my purpose were I to accompany Peter on his journey, and to describe everything remarkable in this extraordinary man. That belongs rather to his biographer. My province extends only to those transactions which had an influence on his empire. Lefort and a few other persons travelling under the name of a russian embassy to several european courts, he went incognito in their train, through Riga and Kœnigsberg, to Holland, England, thence back to Holland, and by Dresden to Vienna. His absence awakened in the breast of Sophia — who had perhaps been implicated in the plot just related against Peter's life — the desire of prosecuting afresh her old plan, to which indeed the journey of the tzar seemed to afford a convenient opportunity.

The strelitzes were now again to assist Sophia in the accomplishment of her project. In the double election that had been made [1697] of a king of Poland, one party having chosen the french prince de Conti, and the other the elector of Saxony, Frederic Augustus, Peter declared himself on the side of Augustus, and in Holland signed an edict, by which a body of his troops, chiefly strelitzes, were ordered to march to the polish frontiers, to be ready in case of necessity

to

to support Augustus against the opposite party. But this very body suffered itself to be inveigled into Sophia's present attempt to seize upon the throne, though the horrid punishments which had been inflicted on the late rebels were so recent. Under pretence that Peter had died abroad, and that they must go back to Mosco to deliver the throne to the young Alexey Petrovitch, these strelitzes quitted their camp, degraded several of their officers, who would not turn about with them, made choice of others from their own body, and took the road to the capital. Those troops, however, which were stationed in and about Mosco, and were mostly foreigners, marched by command of the regency against the rebellious strelitzes. Gordon, who was at the head of these troops, first had recourse to gentle methods. But these failing, and the strelitzes finding great concurrence, numbers even of the clergy uniting with them, from their hatred to Peter as the friend of foreign heretics, Gordon attacked the rebels in form, beat them, and kept them in custody till Peter's return. On the arrival of the tzar he inflicted dreadful punishments on the ringleaders, drafted the other strelitzes into different regiments, abolished that appellation, gave all his troops the name of soldiers, and took two particular

In the meantime Peter had no sooner concluded an armistice for thirty years with the Turks, 1699, than he also took part in the war against Charles; and, in 1700, penetrating into Ingria, laid siege to the citadel of Narva. The russian army was very numerous, and though it might not, as has been affirmed, consist of 80,000, yet it certainly amounted to at least 40,000 men. But among them were only a few well-disciplined regiments, in the whole perhaps 12,000 men, the rest of the troops being nobility summoned to attend with their retinue. Add to this the unfortunate jealousy and dissentions among the commanders. Peter's presence indeed kept them under some restraint; but, on his departure for the purpose of raising more troops in the territories of Pscove and Novgorod, all union was dissolved, and Charles, who appeared with 8000 men, mostly cavalry, on the 30th of November 1700, entirely routed the great russian army, which in numbers four or five times exceeded his own. Ere Peter could come with his reinforcements to Narva, he already received an account of the unsuccessful event of the siege by the total defeat of his army. Charles, moreover, had such a thorough contempt for the russian soldiers, that he would not even detain the privates he had taken prisoners,

but

but sent them home. If the fortunate hero had now followed up his conquests; had he pursued the flying Russians to the heart of the country, Peter would certainly have had enough to do to make an adequate resistance to such an enemy; and what Charles afterwards in vain proposed, namely to dictate terms of peace to Peter in Mosco, he might now probably have effected, as the dread of him and his soldiers, who were held in Russia for supernatural men or necromancers, would have prepared the way for him.

But the youthful conqueror at Narva resolved first to humble Augustus, to deprive him of his crown, and then to attack Peter, and as he confidently expected compel him to submit. " If I remain fifty years in Poland, I will not " quit it till I have driven the king from the " throne." Such was his arrogant declaration, to which he inflexibly adhered; for he was undoubtedly the most conceited man that ever sat upon a throne, and never would listen to the advice of his counsellors: a conceitedness which turned greatly to the advantage of Peter and of Russia.

Charles, in the meantime, utterly regardless of Peter, and despising the Russians, marched against Poland, in order to execute his favourite plan; the dethroning of Augustus; and thus gave

Peter

Peter time to recruit his armies, to recover from the disaster he had sustained, and with new forces to distress Charles, who was penetrating into foreign countries, in the interior of his own. As all the artillery at Narva, about 150 pieces of cannon, had fallen into the hands of the Swedes, Peter had now recourse to the same means for casting more, which in our time have been employed by the French. He caused the superfluous bells of the churches and monasteries to be melted: and to refute the superstitious notion that this was a profanation of the sacred metal by an argument of a like nature, he declared that it was only this holy metal that could be of any service against the swedish magicians. In order to augment his army he proclaimed all vassals to be free who should enlist. In a short time he had again cannon enough, and withal a very numerous army which he was ever sedulously employed in improving in order and discipline. He renewed his alliance with Augustus at Brisen, in 1701. He exerted his endeavours to draw over the republic of Poland to him and his ally: but found it an extremely difficult undertaking, as even at that time the spirit of party prevailed generally in Poland, which in more recent times has brought such misfortunes on that country. It was given out by the adversaries of Augustus,

Auguſtus, who abounded in numbers, that by invading Livonia without the conſent of the republic, and thereby declaring war againſt the king of Sweden, by forming an alliance with the tzar, and by keeping ſaxon troops about him, he had violated the conſtitution of the country, and they became very clamorous for a peace with Sweden. To this Auguſtus and his party would not conſent, attempted to block up all entrance into Poland againſt the Swedes, placing their reliance on being ſupported by Peter with men and money, and ſtrained every nerve to move the ſtates, aſſembled in a diet, to a declaration of war againſt Charles. But in vain. No unanimity could be effected *. Charles had

already

* That Poland would be gradually on the decline, and at length, as the hiſtory of our own times has evinced, entirely vaniſh from the rank of governments, might have been even then foreſeen, as ſo little genuine patriotiſm was prevalent among the great. Every one of them was attentive only to his private intereſt, and, according as he ſaw the balance to incline, was ever going over from one party to the other. Johann Reinhold von Patkul, a livonian nobleman, who, with ſome others, was ſent in the name of the livonian nobility to Charles XI. king of Sweden, at that time ſovereign of Livonia, to repreſent to him the grievances of the livonian nobility, and to implore relief, but, inſtead of receiving an anſwer, was arreſted and taken into cuſtody, afterwards found an opportunity to eſcape out of priſon, entered thereupon

already a great many friends and adherents, who only waited for his appearance in the country to declare on his side.

Favoured, therefore, by the opponents of Augustus, and the irresolution of the Poles in the support of their prince, he pushed farther and

---

upon into the service of Peter, was by him appointed ambassador to king Augustus, and in that station was obliged to have much intercourse with the principal Poles, gave such a description in his accounts to the tzar of the then great men of Poland, that it is easily discoverable, that those things must befall that country which have since befallen it, as the patriotism and defence of liberty, of which they were ever talking, were so many idle words, and everything was to be had for money. Here follow some passages from this Patkul's letters: " Mere unsubstantiated words are not here of
" much avail; the Poles pay more regard to the hands than
" to the mouth; whoever has anything to do with them, will
" find that miracles are performed among them with ready
" money."—" A principal man of quality has given me to
" understand, that if presents were to be made to the com-
" mander and the treasurer (who were in opposition to king
" Augustus,) of 15,000 ducats each, and a yearly pension
" of 5000 ducats, all these affairs would be presently
" brought to a conclusion."—" No dependance is to be
" made on the Poles: they are to-day for the Swedes, to-
" morrow good royalists, and the day after know not them-
" selves what they are."—" Of the Poles nothing is to be
" expected but words."—" No reliance is to be made on
" the republic to the force of a hair," &c.

farther,

farther, advanced through Courland and Lithuania to Poland, and put in execution his plan of dethroning Auguſtus, cauſed Staniſlaus Leſchinſky, voivode of Poſen, to be elected king, proceeded from Poland to Saxony, and thence turned back to Poland, in order now, after vanquiſhing his ſecond enemy, Auguſtus, to compel the third, Peter, to a humiliating and diſadvantageous peace in Moſco. But for this Charles had loſt the proper moment; for while he had been humbling and dethroning Auguſtus, in which he conſumed ſeveral years, the formerly unpractiſed ruſſian troops, were learning to make an effectual ſtand againſt the Swedes, had even formed themſelves, by the very war with that exerciſed and valiant people, into hardy and veteran ſoldiers, and had gradually made themſelves maſters of a part of the ſwediſh poſſeſſions on the Baltic.

That Peter, as on the firſt unſucceſsful campaign againſt the Turks was not diſpirited, neither gave up all for loſt in conſequence of the unfortunate battle near Narva, I have already mentioned: his firſt object was to repair his loſſes, and to remedy his defects, in hopes that his troops, among whom he had always admitted and ſtill continued to admit many foreigners, would one day learn to overcome the Swedes,

though

though for the prefent they might be beaten by them, and probably by repeated ftruggles with them as well trained troops, difcover the way to victory. It was not long before his expectations were fully juftified.

As it was very eafy for the Swedes to proceed from Narva acrofs the Peipus lake into the territory of Novgorod, for preventing this, Peter caufed a number of fchooners to be built on that and the Ladoga lake, on one hand to refift the Swedes in cafe they fhould attempt a landing, and at the fame time to annoy Livonia, Efthonia, and Ingria, as occafion might require, by the debarkation of his own troops. Accordingly, frequent battles were fought in thefe parts between the Ruffians and the Swedes, both by water and by land; and, though the Swedes were generally the conquerors, yet it fometimes happened that the Ruffians had the advantage; and even on thofe occafions when the Swedes were victorious, the ruffian troops were at leaft gaining experience, and gradually becoming more expert in military affairs, and forming themfelves from day to day into good foldiers. Indeed it was unpardonable in Charles to remain fo totally unconcerned about the vifible progrefs of the Ruffians, and fo confident in the expectation that they would always continue to be the

fame

fame Ruffians that they were before Narva, and be everywhere as eafily beaten as at that place.

Peter was every day deriving advantage from Charles's negligence and fcorn. He took Marienburg, and Nœteburg an exceedingly ftrong fortrefs on the Ladoga lake, was now mafter of the Neva which flows into the Baltic, and was in a capacity therefore to fee his wifh fulfilled of having poffeffions adjacent to the fea, if he might prefume to hope that he could maintain the conquered country againft its old poffeffor. Another triumphal entry into Mofco rewarded the courage of the troops both by fea and land, while Charles thought the conquefts that had been made not of any concern. Peter redoubled his affiduity in the conftruction of fhips to be employed on the lakes Peipus, Ladoga, and Onega. In 1703 he captured Nyenfchantz, a fortrefs at the mouth of the Neva; and, in the neighbourhood of that citadel, in a region conquered from the enemy, the calm poffeffion whereof was by no means certain, but was ftill extremely liable to the verfatile fortune of war, laid the foundation of ST. PETERSBURG. The Swedes were at firft carelefs fpectators of the founding and building of a city, which, from the marfhinefs of its foil, they thought could never be brought to effect; but Peter removed or furmounted

mounted all difficulties, and a fortrefs was foon erected covered by another fort on an ifland, Kronfchlot. To eftablifh a commerce by means of the contiguous Baltic, and thus to procure for his empire a more extended reciprocal intercourfe with other european countries was Peter's main object in building Peterfburg; and fcarcely were the foundations laid, when a merchant-fhip from Amfterdam arrived in its harbour. Peter rewarded it richly. This firft was foon followed by others. Thus had Peter knit a new tie between his empire and the reft of Europe. By an ever vigilant and active attention to all the enterprifes of Sweden, who indeed now gradually but too well perceived how dangerous Peter's views might prove to her, he fruftrated her attempts to deftroy this new colony, employed the fortreffes he had raifed in thefe parts in continually making frefh acquifitions from the enemy, already in 1704 conquered Dorpat and Narva, and was now mafter of Ingria, over which he appointed prince Mentchikof, his favourite, to be viceroy, with orders to make the farther building of Peterfburg his principal concern, where not only ftructures were rifing in every quarter, but alfo navigation and commerce were increafing in vigour and extent.

In the meantime Peter continued to affist his ally Auguftus with men and money; and had not the latter been fo totally neglected by the polifh nation, had he on this occafion only met with fomewhat more fidelity, it is highly probable that he would have been able to hold out againft Charles, and not been obliged to fubmit to fuch hard conditions at the peace of Altranftadt in 1706. Ere this was concluded, with which Peter, however, was not fatisfied, the tzar's troops had penetrated into Lithuania; but they could do nothing for Auguftus, and it moreover ufually happened, that wherever Sweden and Ruffia fought in the open plain, the latter fubmitted, and were forced to leave the field to the former as victors. In October 1706, the united Ruffians and Saxons on one fide, and the Swedes on the other, came indeed to an engagement, in which the latter were defeated; but then the accommodation between Auguftus and Charles was already in train, and the latter fought only as it were by compulfion againft the troops of a monarch, with whom he had even begun to negotiate. The victory, therefore, was not followed up to any advantage. However, though Peter's troops and money were found inadequate to keep Auguftus on the throne, the ruffian arms were more and more fuccefsful on the fhores of the Baltic, where Peter was making a rapid, and for Ruffia an advantageous progrefs.

At length, when Charles in 1706 faw his wifh fulfilled, by having forced Auguftus to renounce the polifh crown, he thought it the moft important ftep he could take, to march with his army, now well recruited and provifioned, out of Saxony directly to Ruffia, for the purpofe of forcing [1707] Peter likewife in his turn to a peace, as he had acted before with Frederic and Auguftus. His neareft way for penetrating into the heart of Ruffia, lay through Poland and Lithuania. Peter, who was ftationed at Grodno in Lithuania, abandoned that city in hafte on the approach of Charles; and it appeared as though the Ruffians were able to bid defiance to the troops of that prince, fo long as he himfelf was not at their head; but, when led on by their king in perfon, would give no proof of valour, and would be as eafily vanquifhed by him as formerly before Narva. Peter indeed endeavoured to ftop Charles from piercing farther into Lithuania, by which country his own was covered, and the ruffian troops difputed all the pofts with the fwedifh foldiers; but Charles everywhere drove them back, forced them from

all

all their entrenchments [*], and opened to himself a way into Peter's provinces. Five hundred miles he had yet to Mosco. Certainly not too tiresome a march for him and his army, who had come the much longer road from Sweden to Saxony; especially as, Smolensk excepted, only few places of any consequence stood in their way. But the borders of Russia seemed at the same time to be the boundary of that military success which had hitherto accompanied Charles; and the failure of a plot concerted with that prince, not only rescued Peter, but procured him also a complete victory over his antagonist.

Mazeppa, hetman of the kozaks, was not well-disposed to Peter. He owed his dignity to prince Galitzin who had been banished by the tzar; and now entered into a negotiation with Charles. Induced to this either by a sort of gratitude towards his old patron, or by the hope of rendering himself, under the auspices of the fortunate Charles, sovereign of the kozaks and independent on Russia, or even from the apprehension that, amidst so many reformations,

---

[*] Thus it was at the battle of Holovtzin, in July 1708, where the Russians, notwithstanding their advantageous position, and their brave resistance, were obliged to submit to the Swedes.

Peter might also think of reforming the constitution of the kozaks; he therefore might probably resolve to prevent him, by contributing what he could to weaken this enterprising tzar. Whatever was the cause, thus much is certain, that Mazeppa invited Charles to push farther down to the south, where he would go over to him with his numerous kozaks, representing to Charles that he would afterwards have a much easier march from the Ukraine to Mosco, as the kozaks would join him and supply him with provisions, which indeed were with great difficulty to be obtained in Poland, ravaged and desolated as that country was by Swedes and Russians, and the two parties of Augustus and of Stanislaus. Charles found this proposal so agreeable, that, in opposition to the advice of his counsellor, count Piper, he turned out of the strait road to Russia, and proceeded to the Ukraine. At the river Desna, Mazeppa had engaged to meet him with his people. The Russians disputed with Charles the passage over this river; however, he surmounted even that obstacle. But, waiting here for Mazeppa's considerable body of auxiliaries, and their supplies, which he was no less in want of, he found himself miserably deceived. Mazeppa had promised far more than he was able now to perform; not quite five thousand kozaks went

went over with him to the Swedes, the rest retained their allegiance to Russia; and to add to the disappointment of Charles, a russian corps had attacked and carried off the greater part of the provisions destined for the Swedes *. Fortunately, as Peter had defeated Mazeppa's plan, and reduced him to a very insignificant ally of Charles, he was soon after not less successful in depriving that prince of another needful assistance, by entirely defeating the Swedish general Lœvenhaupt, who had been ordered to him by his king, not only to strengthen the army by his corps, but to convoy with him a great quantity of provisions and ammunition from Livonia; so that all the stores fell into Peter's hands; and of the 15,000 men of which Lœvenhaupt's army consisted, scarcely 6000 came to Charles †. The situation of that monarch now became every day more critical. His army was rapidly wasting away, numbers of his people were carried off by the frost, and the scarcity of provisions admitted of no remedy: yet he obstinately

* Mazeppa was afterwards proclaimed an outlaw, and hung in effigy.

† Three days successively was this corps six times attacked by the Russians, far superior to it in numbers, and yet refused to submit, but cut their way, sword in hand, to Charles.

persisted

persisted in his plan of subjecting the Ukraine to him, and thence of proceeding to Mosco. The inclemency of the weather had just sufficiently subsided for allowing him to act when he broke up his camp to lay siege to Pultava, a strong place in the Ukraine, where the Russians had several magazines. Peter, who now commanded in person, conducted himself like an able general, and likewise displayed great intrepidity. He had not been idle; had always accurately watched his enemy, placed the frontiers of his empire and the road to Mosco, in a good state of defence, and arrived now with a numerous army likewise at Pultava, where he gained so complete a victory over Charles, that he was obliged to save himself by flight. In this battle, the 8th of July 1709, the whole swedish army was either destroyed or taken prisoners; only a very small part of it escaping with the king to Turkey. This battle was certainly one of the most decisive that was ever fought. On it depended not only the fates of Peter, Charles, and Augustus, but those of Russia, Sweden, and Poland entirely rested on the issue of a battle between two armies, who both fought with bravery and true courage, and were sensible to the high prize that awaited the victory on one side or the other. Fortune declared for Peter. And in consequence of his being conqueror at

Pultava,

Pultava, all farther dread of Charles was put to flight, which had indeed been lately somewhat lessened by the latter's not proceeding directly from Lithuania to Russia; the Ukraine, of which Peter had greatly to apprehend the loss, was again free; the affairs of Augustus began to revive; he and Peter might now hope to increase their influence on the Poles, on having reduced Charles, whom they dreaded, to a situation in which he could do no harm; Peter's new possessions on the Baltic, for the preservation whereof he must hitherto have been under great apprehensions, his darling Petersburg, his conquered Ingria, seemed now entirely secured; he could now act more unmolested, and prosecute without impediment the reformations he had begun to make in his empire. Peter had been witness that his troops, in the eight years that had elapsed since Charles beat them before Narva, had very much improved; that they had shewn themselves uncommonly brave and well-disciplined, and highly merited the triumphal entry into Mosco which he had now decreed. On no former occasion of triumph likewise had the Russians reason for so great rejoicings as on the present, as they had been in dread and danger lest Charles might have made an hostile entrance by that very gate through which their

tzar

tzar now proceeded in triumph as victor of the warlike swedish king, and conducted the vanquished Swedes as witnesses of his glory *.

Augustus immediately profited by Charles's defeat, appeared again in Poland, reconciled himself at Thorn, in October 1709, with Peter, who, though he had not approved of the peace of Altranstadt, and, much as Charles had formerly supported his newly-elected Stanislaus, so much was Peter labouring to maintain Augustus now once more as it were seated on the throne. Denmark likewise again now publicly declared against Charles, and even Prussia combined with Peter and Augustus in opposition to the hero who had been unfortunate at Pultava. In the meantime, as Peter had successfully enforced the claims of his predecessors on Ingria, he now strove to subject to him likewise Karelia, Livo-

---

* On the day of the battle, about 9 in the evening Peter wrote to admiral Apraxin at Mosco: " Very early this " morning the furious enemy attacked our cavalry with " all his horse and foot; and, though they fought as " bravely as could be expected, yet they were forced to " retreat with great loss. However, in one word, the " whole hostile army has come to an end like Phaeton. " But what is become of the king we are not able to dis- " cover, whether he be with us or with the enemy. — " *Now, by God's assistance, the foundation stone for the building* " *of Petersburg is indeed completely laid.*"

nia,

nia, and Esthonia, upon which countries the tzar had earlier exhibited his pretensions; and his measures here also succeeded. The fortifications of Vyborg, Riga, and Reval, the capital cities and principal places of Karelia, Livonia, and Esthonia, together with Kexholm and the isle of Œsel, were already in Peter's possession before the termination of the year 1710, and he was therefore master of the principal ports of the Baltic. — Peter likewise took part in the enterprises against the possessions of Charles in Pomerania, and against the territory of the dukes of Holstein.

But, however great the advantage which the victory at Pultava had procured to the whole russian empire, and however Peter had profited by it that same year, as I have just been relating, yet, so soon after as 1711 (therefore only two years from that fortunate event) he was in danger of losing all that he had gained, and of seeing the fruits of his undeniably great exertions and his unwearied activity at once ravished from him.

It was not very difficult for Charles to raise an interest in his behalf in the divan of the sultan of Constantinople. They had heard of his exploits, and still regarded him as a great hero. That this hero was now unfortunate

could

could not leffen the veneration in which he was held; befides, it was the tzar of Ruffia who had fo totally defeated Charles, to whom the Turks, but a few years ago, had been forced to furrender Azof, a mortification which they knew not how to forgive. It did not indeed at firft appear that the porte intended to take an active part in the conteft between the two fovereigns, as in 1710 they renewed the armiftice with Ruffia. But Charles was enabled by his difcreet and active friend Poniatoffky, (the father of the late king of Poland,) to increafe his influence in the divan, and even to procure the difgrace of two fucceffive grand vizirs, who gave their advice againft the war with Ruffia, and at length attained his aim in the hoftile meafures now begun to be adopted by the porte againft Peter. Peter, who now faw himfelf fuddenly menaced by an unexpected enemy, had recourfe to the means of defence; but, by advancing againft the Turks, committed the fame faults which had proved fo difaftrous to Charles. As Charles had fhewn a contempt for the Ruffians for which he paid fo dearly at Pultava, fo Peter contemned the Turks. — Charles placing reliance on Mazeppa, and allured by his promifes, marched to his great misfortune into the Ukraine; Peter, becaufe Cantemir, the hofpodar of Moldavia, a

vaffal

vaffal of the porte, promifed him his fupport, marched alfo too far into the enemy's country, quite to Yaffy in Moldavia, where he foon experienced a want of provifions, as Charles had done; nay, he faw himfelf at length fo furrounded by the Turks, on the river Pruth, not far from Yaffy, that only three ways were open for his efcape, each more horrible than the other. — Either he and his people muft perifh with hunger, fince on one fide he was encompaffed by the turkifh camp, and on the other by the tartarian, fo that abfolutely no* provifions of any kind could be conveyed to him, or he muft furrender, or attempt to cut his way through the enemy, which in his circumftances indeed feemed an impoffibility, as he had at moft little more than twenty thoufand men, whereas the camp of his enemy contained upwards of two hundred thoufand foldiers. Peter, reduced to defperation, fat in his tent, reprefenting in his troubled mind all his labours at once deftroyed, all his hopes defeated, and thought himfelf at that moment more unfortunate than Charles was at Pultava. — In the

* The Ruffians could not even provide themfelves with water from the adjacent river Pruth, as the Turks were enabled by their fituation to fire upon them whenever they approached the water-fide.

midft

midſt of this diſtreſs, his conſort Catharine ſuggeſted to him that nothing prevented his aſking peace of the grand vizir; and, in order to obtain a gracious reception of him, to accompany the meſſage with conſiderable preſents; perhaps a voluntary propoſal of an accommodation might be preferable in the vizir's mind to any hopes ariſing from the uncertain iſſue of a battle. The project ſucceeded beyond expectation. All the valuables, all the money that could be ſpared, were got together, propoſals were made to the grand vizir, offers were made of ſome ſacrifices, the diſtreſſing ſituation was indeed as much as poſſible concealed, much was ſaid of courage and intrepidity, of cutting a paſſage through the Turks, and, in conſideration of the abandonment of Azof, the razure of the newbuilt Taganrok, and the promiſe of quitting Poland, the tzar obtained a peace of the grand vizir, who reſolved not to ſtake on the event of a battle the certain advantage which he had procured for his country in the peace, as the Ruſſians only the day before had given proofs of their valour, and he was not without apprehenſions that a ſmall army fighting deſperately might even contend to advantage againſt ſuperior numbers.

No wonder that Poniatoffky, Charles's friend, who was with the vizir in his tent, endeavoured by the moſt inſtant remonſtrances to diſſuade him from this peace; no wonder that Charles, who came into the turkiſh camp ſoon after it was ſigned, raved and ſtormed like a madman; knowing as they did that it was in the vizir's power to have entirely ruined Peter, or at leaſt to have dictated to him ſuch terms of accommodation as would have been of eſſential advantage to Charles: whereas he had ſcarcely done anything for him *. — However, as Peter was conſtantly finding reaſons for deferring his evacuation of Poland, and thereby ſeemed not inclined to fulfil the articles of the treaty, it was eaſy for Charles again to inflame the reſentment of the ſultan. Accordingly twice did the Ruſſians and Turks appear to be again on the point of coming to a rupture; but Peter both times had the art of appeaſing the porte, and to prevent it from far-

* Upon this Charles did not reſt till this vizir, who had been ſo regardleſs of his intereſts, was depoſed from his office and ſent into baniſhment. All that appeared concerning Charles in the treaty was: " as the king of Sweden " has put himſelf under the protection of the porte, his " tzarian majeſty promiſes, out of friendſhip, to allow him "'a free and ſafe return to his country, and to conclude a " peace with him — if the terms can be agreed on."

ther

ther espousing the part of Charles. [1712, 1713.] The Porte and Russia therefore continued to be friends, and Peter was every day carrying his arms farther into the country of the defeated monarch. Helsingoers and Abo, and by them almost all Finland, as well as the isle of Aland, fell, 1713, into Peter's hands; and fears were entertained in the capital and residence of Sweden, where the sovereign had not been for many years seen, of witnessing the victorious entry of the monarch of the neighbouring empire.

But the great successes of Peter, alarms arising from the prodigious increase of his territory, and jealousy at the rapid progress it was making in arts as well as arms, indisposed to him the powers confederated with him against Charles, so that, under the guidance of Goertz, a negotiation was even entered into between him and the swedish monarch, which however, was interrupted by the death of the latter after his return from Turkey; who, though once more victorious in Norway, was slain before Frederichshal in 1718. The new swedish government, to whom Peter applied for the termination of the negotiation that had been set on foot, were encouraged to hope, by the aid of Great Britain, to bring him to a compliance with their terms,

and

and in two campaigns he employed the time afforded him by the tediousness of the english fleet, in committing horrible devastations on the swedish coast *. His intention was to extort a peace; but Sweden obstinately held out till 1721, in which year on the 10th of September at Nystadt in Finland, a peace was brought to effect, by which the dreadful struggle for eighteen years between two sovereigns, and the war of one-and-twenty years between two neighbouring nations were happily brought to an end. The swedish government was on this occasion obliged to subscribe to the following hard condition: Sweden cedes to Russia, LIVONIA, ESTHONIA, INGRIA, A PART OF KARELIA, WITH THE TERRITORY OF VYBORG, THE ISLE OF ŒSEL, AND ALL OTHER ISLANDS IN THE SOUTHERN SEA AND THE BALTIC, FROM KUR-

* In one of the campaigns, according to Gordon's account, who was an eye-witness, six considerable towns, eleven stone palaces, 109 noblemen's seats of timber, 826 farms, 3 mills, 10 magazines, 2 copper and 5 iron forges, were demolished by admiral Apraxin. Major-general Lacy laid waste 2 towns, 21 noblemen's seats, 535 farms, 40 mills, 16 magazines, and 9 iron-works, whereof one was of so great value that the proprietors offered 300,000 dollars to preserve it — but in vain. The Russians destroyed not only what was upon the earth, but even what was under it; they ruined several iron and copper mines for ever.

LAND TO VYBORG * — receives back Finland, and two millions of dollars, and has the liberty to export duty-free, from Riga, Reval, and Arenfberg annually, corn to the amount of fifty thoufand rubles. — The tzar promifed to maintain the provinces ceded to him in their liberties, laws, and religion.

On occafion of this peace fo glorious to the empire, grand feftivities were appointed throughout all Ruffia, and the fenate and the fynod offered Peter, the conqueror of the Baltic, in behalf of his nation, to exchange the title of tzar for that of EMPEROR AND AUTOCRATOR OF ALL THE RUSSIAS, and to permit himfelf in future to be ftyled, FATHER OF THE COUNTRY. To thefe appellations were added the honourable furname, THE GREAT.

But it was not merely on account of the conquefts that Peter had made, that he obtained from his country the furname of THE GREAT, and which pofterity has confirmed; he acquired that glorious epithet by more important

---

* Peter did not expect that fo much would have been conceded to him; but his plenipotentiary, Oftermann, dexteroufly — by money — procured a fight of the fwedifh ambaffador's inftructions, and found that his court was difpofed to relinquifh everything, and therefore made his demands accordingly.

exploits,

exploits; it was conferred upon him as due to his merits in regard to the numerous and various institutions, enterprises, and regulations, which, even during this long war, amidst the din of arms, he planned and executed, with a diligence which has never been equalled by any sovereign in modern times, and which he intended, to the utmost of his inclination and ability, to be beneficial to his empire, and to the civilization and improvement of his people. But these his great and undeniable merits run so like a tissue through the war of twenty years, that I thought it most advisable to confine myself here entirely to the uninterrupted history of that war, which was of such consequence to the empire at large *, and to represent the progress of the russian nation in improvements of every kind, for the sake of its easier survey, in a connected representation afterwards. I therefore now proceed in the narrative of what relates to the extension and aggrandizement of the empire from without.

Shortly after the peace concluded with Sweden, which gave an entirely different aspect not only to the russian empire, but to the whole north of Europe, and by which Russia was con-

* Let us only consider, for instance, the connection thereby obtained with the Baltic.

siderably augmented, Peter had an opportunity for enlarging the borders of his empire likewise towards the south. Several disturbances had arisen in Persia so long since as 1709; and among others, at the capture of the persian town Schamachy in 1712, a number of russian merchants were partly killed, and partly despoiled of their property. Peter, in 1715, entered into a new treaty of commerce with the shah of Persia, and promised him at the same time assistance against the rebels. He afterwards took such advantage of favourable circumstances as to make it easy for him to gain the dominion of the Caspian, by marching into Persia in 1722, in order, as he declared in his manifesto, to protect the shah, who in fact was much reduced by repeated exertions; but at the same time to chastise the rebels who had behaved so injuriously to the russian subjects. He arrived with his army at Derbent, and made himself master of that city. Peter's new successes soon rouzed the attention of the Porte; and, alarmed at this progress in the adjoining country of Persia, threatened him with a war. However, the two powers came to an agreement by a treaty similar to that which in our times was entered into by Russia, Austria, and Prussia on the partition of Poland; and in virtue whereof the porte appropriated

priated to itself a part of Persia, Peter obtained several provinces, and the rest of the country remained to the shah. It was naturally to be supposed that the last did not heartily concur in this partition; as the sequel indeed confirmed. Besides, the inhabitants of the provinces occupied by the Turks and Russians looked upon these pretended patrons as enemies; and it cost Peter a great number of men, and, by reason of the distance of Russia, much money, to maintain himself in possession of the five districts that had been allotted to him.

In the very year, however, when this partition was effected, 1725, Peter died; and his second consort CATHARINE ascended the throne.

Peter, when no more than in his seventeenth year had married Eudokhia Lapukhin. But the character of that lady was too opposite to his own to allow of any lasting union. Eudokhia was descended from a very ancient russian family; and, imbued with the prejudices of her country and rank, could find no satisfaction in Peter's more liberal way of thinking in regard to religious ceremonies, his contempt for the clergy, his innovations, and his intercourse with foreigners, but made him frequent reproaches for his illicit amours, and created in him a dislike to her, which she seemed rather disposed to foster than

than to remove. Add to this, that Peter's favourites, who were often from the lowest orders, were slighted by her, and therefore took their revenge by alienating the tzar's affection from her; and, at length, after he had repudiated her, even made her suspected by him of keeping a correspondence with his enemies. This drew upon her the hard lot of being banished to a convent [1698]. On the subsequent condemnation of her son, in whose criminal transactions, it was pretended, but never proved, that she took part, Peter sent her to another convent, where she was doomed to live, like a prisoner, on hard diet, till she was afterwards set at liberty by her grandson Peter II.

Peter's early aversion to Eudokhia had a most pernicious influence on Alexey, the son she bore him in 1690, and was the ground of the deplorable series of sorrows which befel that prince. The dissentions between the father and the mother speedily diminished the father's affection for Alexey. Peter's vast and comprehensive plans, his campaigns, his concerns, entirely confined to the reformation and improvement of the empire, with his various journies to the remote parts of his dominions, prevented him from paying much attention to the education of his son. Alexey at first grew up under female tuition,

tuition, and then fell into the hands of some of the clergy; who, with most of the members of the spiritual order in Ruffia, were diffatisfied with Peter's reforms, with his toleration, and his notion of ecclefiaftical authority, which, though juft, was by no means agreeable to that body, and they therefore hoped to educate this fon as a future pillar of the church. Under their guidance the prince imbibed prejudices in abundance, and daily conceived a greater abhorrence for his father. This being obferved by Peter, he put an end to the fpiritual education, and appointed Mentchikof chief preceptor of the prince, a man who himfelf had never received the flighteft education; but by his attachment to the tzar had acquired his favour. Mentchikof was not fond of Alexey, and the latter had been early infpired by the mother with contempt and averfion for the favourite of his father. The tutors, who were now placed about the prince, were not able to eradicate the prejudices impreffed on his mind from his infancy, and now grown inveterate; befides, he had an unconquerable diflike to them as foreigners. The future fovereign of fo vaft an empire, that was now reformed in all its parts, and by profperous wars ftill farther enlarged; the heir of a throne, whofe poffeffor ruled over many millions of

people,

people, had been brought up from his birth as if designed for a russian bishop; theology continued to be his favourite study: with a capacity for those sciences which are useful in government, he discovered no inclination to them. Moreover he addicted himself early in life to drunkenness and other excesses. There were not wanting such as flattered his perverse dispositions, by representing to him that the russian nation was dissatisfied with his father, that it was impossible for him to be suffered long in his career of innovation, that even his life was not likely to hold out against so many fatigues, with many other things of a like nature. Alexey's way of life, particularly his indolence and sloth, were highly displeasing to Peter. Mentchikof, from political motives, to preserve himself and Catharine, was constantly employed in fanning the tzar's resentments, while Alexey's adherents, on the other hand, were embracing every opportunity for increasing the aversion of the prince, who, from his very cradle, had never known what it was to love, and had only dreaded his father. Alexey even at times gave plain intimations, that he would hereafter undo all that his father was so sedulously bringing about. Nay, when the latter, in 1711, went on an expedition against the Turks, and appointed the prince regent during his ab-

sence,

fence, though under his supremacy, the latter made it his first business to alter many things in behalf of the clergy; so as clearly to describe in what school he had been brought up. The next was in hopes to reform this intemperate conduct, by uniting him with a worthy consort; but even this attempt proved fruitless. The princess of Brunswic, who was selected for his bride, and with whom Alexey was married at Torgau, in 1711, notwithstanding all her eminent qualities of mind and heart, and her great beauty, could make little impression on him, and sunk under the load of grief, brought on by this unhappy connexion, soon after giving birth to a prince, who was called by the name of his grandfather, Peter. [1715.] By a continuance in his dissolute mode of life, by his bad behaviour towards his spouse, by his intercourse with persons who were notorious for their hatred of Peter and his reforms, Alexey seemed bent upon augmenting his father's displeasure; accordingly, now in 1715, Peter wrote to him: "If you do not "amend, I will exclude you from the succession "to the throne. If I spare not my own life for "the good of my people, why should I spare "you?" And in another letter, shortly after, on Alexey's declaring that he would renounce the succession: "If you were even at present
"inclined

"inclined to keep your promise, yet those long-
"beards* could at any time compel you to
"break it. Do you ever aſſiſt me in my ar-
"duous undertakings? Do you not always
"cenſure and condemn whatever I am able to
"do for the benefit of my people? Have I not
"reaſon to believe that you will ruin all if you
"ſurvive me? Strive, therefore, either to ren-
"der yourſelf worthy of the throne, or make
"choice of the monaſtic life." Alexey preferred the latter. Peter conſented, though not immediately: but, to give him time for conſideration, took a journey in the following year, 1716, to Copenhagen, and ſent for the prince to him, at the ſame time endeavouring to poliſh him by travel and ſociety. Alexey ſet out from Moſco, but, inſtead of proceeding to his father at Copenhagen, went to the emperor Charles VI. at Vienna, who was married to a ſiſter of the deceaſed conſort of Alexey. From Vienna Charles ſent him to a fortreſs in the Tyrol, and from thence to St. Elmo, a neapolitan fortreſs, in hopes that he could here remain undiſcovered under a borrowed name. This flight, as might naturally have been expected, greatly increaſed the indignation of the tzar. He cauſed diligent inquiry to be made. The emperor made formal

* The clergy.

remon-

remonstrances against delivering him up, but Peter made still more earnest remonstrances against his upholding and affording protection to a son in opposition to his parent: Alexey was accordingly given up, and returned to Mosco.

Peter now in a public proclamation declared him to have forfeited the crown. A court, consisting of 180 persons, among whom 55 were of the clergy, was appointed to try him. Many of the ecclesiastical judges would doubtless have willingly saved him, as they visited the tzar in private, addressed themselves to his feelings, confessed that he was deserving of punishment, but at the same time reminded the tzar of the pattern presented him by Christ in the parable of the prodigal son, but the temporal judges declared the prince to have incurred the penalty of death as guilty of crimes against the state. Many persons who were accomplices in his pretended plot, for the charge was never brought home to him, to get possession of the crown during his father's lifetime, or had assisted him in his flight, or accompanied him in it, were capitally executed. A manifesto was published, declaring, that the prince, on hearing the sentence of death, fell into violent convulsions, during which he expired. [1718.]

The

The reports that were spread concerning the real manner of his death, are extremely various [*]. From Peter's great activity, from his indefatigable zeal to rouze his people out of that sluggishness and ignorance in which he found them, and to new-model his empire in all its parts, it may reasonably enough be imagined, that, as Brutus the Roman formerly did, he might forget the father in the sovereign; the prince being by no other means to be disposed of, and as Peter must have been perfectly convinced, that, as soon as he should be no more, Alexey his successor, supported by the clergy, by the discontented among the great, and by the hatred, not yet entirely eradicated, of a great part of the nation towards foreigners and innovations, would completely demolish what he, with so much exertion, with such unwearied zeal for the welfare of the country had been striving to found, to establish, and to rectify. To free his mind from this sad prospect, he could think of no better

[*] Such as, that he was secretly beheaded, and the head then sewn on to the body, that it might be exposed to the public, and that he died naturally be rendered probable. Other accounts say, that a vein was opened, and that he was bled to death. Again, others talk of a death by the dreadful knoot.

means than by the death of a prince, who, though perhaps more weak than wicked, more misled than of himself capable of forming projects detrimental to the empire; yet, by his weakness and condescension in his future relations as sovereign of the russian empire, could not but be productive of harm to the country. Moreover, during the whole of the prince's trial, Peter proceeded openly, did not despotically pronounce sentence upon him, but the court declared him guilty.

In the room of the condemned Alexey, the tzar nominated a prince, named Peter, whom Catharine had borne to him, to be his successor; but he died in 1719. There was now remaining only Alexey's son, Peter's grandson, as male heir to the throne, and he was extremely young, being then [1719] only four years old. Peter, who felt that he was not likely to attain to any great age, and that he should not see his grandson grown up to maturity for the throne, was now the more anxious to appoint a fit successor. In order, however, to be quite at liberty to fix his choice upon whom he would, he published in February 1722 an extremely remarkable law*, regarding the succession to the throne.

He

---

* Among other things it is therein said, " that he pub-
" lished this law, that the children of future monarchs might
" not,

He abolished the hereditary succession, and ordained, that every future monarch should be at liberty to constitute as successor to the throne, the person whom he should deem most fit and worthy, but might revoke his choice if he saw that the person nominated was rendering himself unworthy of it. Peter's intentions in framing this law might be very laudable, but it was manifestly liable to be a source of discord among the members of the reigning family, and thus become dangerous to the empire. The learned bishop Theophanes was ordered by Peter to compose a work under the title of, " The right of the monarch in the " arbitrary appointment of a successor to the " empire." In the meantime Peter departed this life without having appointed a successor; and Catharine, taken prisoner by the Russians at Marienburg in 1702, became empress of Russia.

" not, from the dissolute example of Alexey, fall into simi-
" lar iniquities, but be restrained from imitating him, by
" knowing that it was in the breast of the reigning sove-
" reign to deprive them of the succession."

Having closed the former part of this History of Ruffia with a few obfervations on the civilization and culture of the ruffian nation, from the origin of the empire to the time of Mikhaila Romanof, I will now prefent the reader with an account of the progrefs which the Ruffians have made in a variety of refpects to the death of Peter the Great, and principally by his means. Accordingly, I fhall here attempt to give a compreffed reprefentation of all which that great fovereign performed and regulated. — The adminiftration of government and laws, army and navy, ecclefiaftical affairs and fciences, arts, manufactures, trade, commerce, handicrafts and means of livelihood in general, focial life and ordinary intercourfe, the cuftoms, and manners, nay, the whole turn of mind of the ruffian nation were within the fpace of little more than the twenty years which Peter reigned, either fo changed or fo entirely new created and formed, that it is well worth while to defcribe his influence on thefe feveral objects, for fhewing what the Ruffians as a nation have actually gained

gained by him. Previously, however, some few things farther concerning his predecessors.

Mikhaila, the first tzar of the dynasty Romanof, acquired great merit by promoting the russian commerce with England and Persia. France, likewise, in order, like England, to reap advantage from a nearer connection with Russia, sent an ambassador to Mosco, and in 1629 a treaty of friendship and commerce was settled between the two countries. Alexey was still more active in the extension of commerce, in the adoption of arts and trades, than his father had been; and, as his reign immediately followed on turbulent times, could possibly be. Under him Russia became much more acquainted with the rest of Europe. A russian embassy travelled to Spain, France, and Holland. In the last-mentioned country they were accosted with peculiar liberality and friendship; hence they therefore took away with them several ship-carpenters and sailors, as Alexey had already conceived the design of causing ships to be built for sailing by the Volga into the Caspian. Designing to carry on by means of that sea the trade with Persia so very important on account of its silk, which hitherto had been necessarily prosecuted by land, and which, besides that it was more expensive and troublesome, the roads

thither

thither were now become extremely unsafe, by the depredations of the kozaks. He, therefore, also concluded a treaty of commerce with Persia in 1667; but Radzin's rebellion, and his robberies in the vicinity of Astrakhan, and the piracies committed by him on the Caspian, defeated this enterprise, ere it came into play. Of longer duration, of incomparably greater and more beneficial influence on the nation, was the law-book (called Uloshenie, national-law,) which Alexey caused to be compiled; in which, though the code put together by Ivan*, as well as the later ordinances of the tzars, were the groundwork of it, yet a great number of the laws were altered and amended, adapted more to the then state of the nation, and several new ones were added. This statute-law affords abundant proof, that, from the time of Ivan, they had learned to decide more justly concerning right and wrong, and to ascertain the punishments on transgressions of the laws with more equity, discretion, and moderation. Thus, for example, it enacts, that, "Intentional murder shall be peremptorily "punished with death in the perpetrator, and "in those who have been assisting to him. "Yet no vengeance for blood, and in general

* See vol. i. p. 356.

"no self-revenge is allowed."—"If any one be at the same time indebted to Russians, and to foreigners, when it comes to a complaint, the foreigners shall have precedence in the payment." In regard to the impartial administration of justice many sound maxims are seen in it: "All matters between the inhabitants of the russian empire shall be decided with justice. Foreigners, and all settlers shall have the very same law, without regard to friendship or hatred. The judge shall not have respect to the face of the mighty, and shall deliver the oppressed out of the hands of the unjust. The partial judge, if his iniquity be clearly proved, shall pay to the complainant threefold the demand, besides a fine or penalty to the tzar; moreover, in case he be a boyar, a chamberlain, or of the council, he shall lose his rank; if he be an inferior he shall be knooted publicly in the market, and never thenceforward be employed in any business." Other laws must indeed be judged of, according to the then state of the russian nation, not according to the times in which we live: thus, for instance, instead of the penalty of death to be inflicted, as formerly, on the second act of theft, it was now ordained, that only the third theft should be a capital crime; but that the

the thief, for the first and second offence, should be severely corrected, and one of his ears cut off as a mark of his guilt, and for the more impressive warning to others.

Under Alexey a very considerable trade was opened with China, in which the siberian furs were delivered to the Chinese in return for silks and other stuffs, rhubarb, &c. The russian yufts, hemp, sope, potashes, as well as coarse linen, were already considerable articles of exportation: on the other hand, many necessaries were brought from other countries, particularly from Sweden the iron that was wanted, of which metal so much was afterwards discovered in Russia. That the Russians were now grown somewhat more active and industrious, was a natural consequence of the increasing trade with foreigners. Yet their activity and traffic bore no proportion with the activity and industry of the other european nations of that time. Foreigners resided among them, but the Russians held no intercourse with them, except from mercantile views; in all other regards they looked upon them with scorn. They had the greatest aversion to foreign manners, customs, and arts, and even the form of their clothes differed too much from the foreign modes of dress to allow them any near and familiar approach. The ambassadors and their retinue excepted, scarcely any Russian went abroad; and therefore nothing short of such a bold genius as Peter afterwards proved, could have operated efficaciously on the temper of that nation, and in a manner incorporated what was good in other countries into his own people. Of the clergy nothing was to be expected. The generality of that body of men were rude, unformed, and ignorant, and so illiterate, that many of them could not write. The superior clergy, it is true, stood in great respect; the patriarch was the first person in the empire after the tzar: but the spiritual dominion, so far as it extended to temporal matters, had been from the remotest periods so interwoven with the maxim that the people should be kept in ignorance, that nothing could be hoped for from the russian clergy, until they should be brought back to their proper destination of teachers appointed for the moral and intellectual improvement of the nation. A blind attachment to theological tenets, the attendance on church rites, a punctual observance of the fasts, crossing themselves before the sacred pictures, and things of like import, composed the whole essence of religion. The national character, however, of the Russians of those times bore undeniable marks of intrinsic worth. " If I keep not my word, may it turn

" to

"to my infamy!" This, which had heretofore been the customary confirmation of a promise *, was now indeed grown rather out of fashion, yet they still were much attached to fidelity and credit. Numbers of their customs could not be indifferent to the formation of character. Thus, for example, it was usual on Sundays for the younger members of a family to visit the elders of it, and to carry home with them many good lessons from the conversation of their parents and grand-parents †. There was a certain gravity peculiar to the nation, which indeed frequently degenerated into an indolent and gloomy behaviour, a formality, too great an attachment to everything traditionary, and an aversion to everything new, and not indigenous to their country. In the great towns of the empire, as Novgorod, Pscove, it was customary for all the men about noon to

---

* See vol. i. p. 367.

† Reverence and obedience of children to parents was universally much regarded; as is likewise seen from some of the laws of the land. For instance, "When children in-
"sult their parents, or even strike them with their hand,
"and the parents make complaint of it, the children shall
"be knooted."—"A child that brings a formal process
"against his parent shall not be heard, but punished with
"the knoot, and then delivered up to the parents."

assemble in a public place, and to discourse together on the various topics that occurred. In Mosco, the capital and the residence, this was done in what was called the beautiful or the red place in the vicinity of the tzar's palace. These meetings had much resemblance with the assemblies of merchants in large commercial towns, on the exchange, which perhaps might gradually arise from the intermixture of foreign merchants. So in Mosco a variety of mercantile business was transacted, yet company and mutual converse were the primary motive of these assemblies. Accordingly, here were not only traders, but likewise persons of all ranks, the humblest burgher, as well as the principal boyars. Their conversation turned on public and domestic affairs, they made acquaintance, imparted advice to one another, and young persons particularly might here pick up much good instruction for the future management of business and housekeeping, and a store of cautions confirmed from the mouth of experienced persons; they likewise had an opportunity of recommending themselves to some one or other, or of getting themselves introduced by a friend to such as in time might be of service to them. Tzar Alexey himself encouraged these public meetings very much,

much, and was pleased in hearing accounts of whatever passed in them that was worthy of notice.

Feodor, as has been before observed, principally effected some alterations in the notions that were current concerning the privileges arising from pedigree, and true or false honour and disgrace among the nobility.

A late russian author draws the following picture of the Russians of that time: " Their " knowledge was certainly not multifarious; " books were not the means by which they " gained information, but the example of pa- " rents and education. They were hospitable " and courteous without selfishness. To break " the word once given, was reputed infamous *. " Lies were severely punished even in children. " In regard to manners a certain uniformity " prevailed, and in general firmness of prin- " ciples, a naturally found understanding, and a " right judgment. Their industry was solely " confined to the country-products." The name of barbarians, therefore, cannot with

* In proof of this the same author observes, that masters and servants usually bound themselves by a written contract, deposited in a public office. The strelitzes, in their insurrection, burnt these contracts; but the servants remained true to their masters notwithstanding.

any propriety be bestowed on the Russians in general, previous to the time of Peter; though it cannot be denied, that, in comparison with other european nations of the same period, the English, French, Germans, &c. they were some centuries behind in point of civilization, and that, particularly in the inland provinces, profound ignorance, untractableness, sloth, and, in part also, real barbarism prevailed.

I come now to the age of Peter, to speak of what his people gained by him in point of culture. As far as related to the GOVERNMENT, the alterations that Peter made in it were certainly advantageous to the improvement of the nation. The entire government in all its parts had hitherto ever been despotic. The boyars, who sat at the helm of the state in the capital, as well as the viceroys in the provinces, decided, commanded, and acted according to their own humours. Peter abrogated what was called the boyarskoi dvor, or court of boyars, which had hitherto constituted the ministry of the tzar, and without the consent whereof nothing could be enacted; appointing in its place a *SENATE

---

* All the decrees of government, accordingly, began with these words: By command of the tzar, and with the approbation of the boyars.

dependant

dependant on the monarch, and at the same time ten imperial colleges, each having its own proper business within its peculiar department. In these no determination could be made by any one person, but the members were to deliver their sentiments in general consultation, and to pronounce upon the question by the majority of voices.

The ADMINISTRATION OF JUSTICE likewise was an object that Peter was very desirous of correcting for the benefit of his country; for, as many of his predecessors had already found themselves under the necessity of preventing injustice in the courts by laws and penalties, so Peter also was well aware that this species of iniquity was extremely frequent. He therefore abolished most of the fees and perquisites of the courts, that the poor might not be prevented from having recourse to law for obtaining their right, for fear of the expence. He published an amended mode of proceedings. He insisted inflexibly that strict and impartial justice should be administered; and when any judge was found guilty of taking bribes, of pronouncing sentence from favour or affection, or of oppressing the poor, he punished him with great severity and without respect of person *. — It was his en-

deavour

---

* 'Thus,' for instance, Mentchikof, that all-powerful favourite of the tzar, on account of his underhand dealings,

deavour therefore to secure the common man from oppression, to protect the poor among the people from their superiors, and to provide that even in the most indigent inhabitant of the empire humanity should be honoured and be screened from injustice and arbitrary power.

There had been great deficiences in the REVENUES OF THE EMPIRE till his time; as, from the bad method employed in raising them, and from worse management afterwards, a considerable part remained in the hands of those who had the superintendance, so that at last very little came into the tzar's treasury; he made it his business to reduce this important concern of government into better order. Whereby likewise the people were gainers, by being less burdened, as a greater regularity prevailed, and the receivers were under closer observation.

' That even the LAW-BOOK, which had been compiled in the reign of Alexey, from which I have already quoted a few specimens, was still in want of many corrections; that chicanery was not by far sufficiently guarded against in it, and

---

ings, forfeited his fine estates in the Ukraine, and moreover was obliged to pay a fine of 200,000 rubles. 1722. Peter caused other partial judges to be knooted, turned them out, banished them to Siberia, and confiscated their estates.

that

that it was not decisive in all cases, had long been manifest. Peter here too made it his endeavour to promote the interests of his people. He framed several statutes and ordinances that do honour to him as a lawgiver; but they related only to particular objects. He afterwards, however, was desirous of giving out an entirely new collection of laws, completely adapted to the wants and condition of the nation, appointed a commission for that purpose in 1718, with instructions to get it ready, and to take for the basis of it the law-book that had been hitherto in use. He encouraged and assisted this commission by every means in his power, and among other things commanded, that the judges should in all cases strictly adhere to the letter of the law. But it is probable that the commissioners were not actuated by the same zeal and ardour with the great sovereign for the benefit of the country. They were at work five whole years, and then declared, [1723,] that the old lawbook could not serve as a foundation, and that the basis of it must be laid on a plan entirely new. Peter, to this end, selected the danish code, adverting to the alterations necessary to be made for his empire and his nation. But — just as the commission were on the point of resuming their labours — he died, and left the continuation

ation and completion of the reform of laws, which he had so much wished, and towards which he had done so much, to his successors.

Thus therefore the affairs of government acquired a more orderly form, better suited to a civilized people, the subjects now directed their obedience rather to the laws, than to the will and caprice of their superiors, even the poor and lower orders had some pretensions to right and justice, the taxes came with fewer subtractions into the treasury of the sovereign, and in the collecting of them there was less opportunity for acts of oppression. All which must have had great influence on the rational formation of his people.

The improvements introduced into the russian ARMY I have already several times had occasion to mention; and in this respect likewise Peter put his nation on a different footing. If war, if standing armies be once admitted as necessary evils, then certainly it is meritorious in that ruler who endeavours to give his subjects a more thorough knowledge of military art. Tumultuous and irregular attacks ceased in Peter's time to be the method by which the fate of a battle was decided. He introduced the knowledge of artillery, the construction and defence of batteries, fortifications, and entrenchments, regularity and order in the attack, in the battle,

and

and even in retreat; and, by the art of fighting now practised, the number of the killed is not so great as formerly it was from the irregular manner of combat. Peter, therefore, was in reality providing for the culture of his nation, by taking experienced foreign officers into his service, and by the Russians, whom he sent to travel abroad, he encouraged and promoted the true art of war among his people. From all experience it appears, that those troops are the bravest where the strictest subordination prevails. Such troops, for example, were the swedish under Charles XII. and they were on that account extremely formidable. The russian soldiery, prior to Peter, were but little acquainted with this quality so necessary to an army; and the lamentable consequences were clearly seen even before Narva. Where genuine valour subsists, a well-disciplined army never exercises cruelties against a foe, not even in the enemy's country. But how furious and savage were the russian soldiers previous to Peter! how ungovernable the strelitzes! Patkul even frequently complains in his letters, that the russian soldier never knows how to behave in the enemy's country, acting cruelly even to the unarmed. At the taking of Narva, [1704,] it was in vain that Peter attempted by words to put a stop to

the

the plundering, the ill usage, and the violences committed by his soldiers, he was forced to cut down some of them with his own hand — as a warning to others. Peter was particularly careful to correct his soldiers of their savage cruelty, a relict from the wars of the Russians with the Tartars, that they might be brave but at the same time humane. For the better guidance of their conduct, he therefore published a system of martial law. — Even his triumphal processions were calculated to spread among his soldiers a spirit of true courage, shewing that they ought not to behave like robbers and assassins, but regard themselves as the defenders of the country, and after this just notion form themselves into valiant, but humane and generous warriors. That Peter fully attained this end I shall not pretend to affirm, but it cannot be denied, that such devastations as were committed by the ruffian troops in Sweden, must rather incite and nourish ferocity and savage cruelty than courage among the soldiers. Yet certainly the Russians, considered as soldiers, were rendered by Peter not only more bold and courageous, but also, which is doubtless of greater value, far better disciplined, and of more civil manners than they were before him.

One

One thing that Peter had in view by his wars was to introduce a greater degree of activity among his people; it was also a primary object with him in creating a NAVY, and in founding St. Petersburg, as a new commercial town in the vicinity of the Baltic. Were it true, as has been asserted, that in his early youth he was uncommonly afraid of the water, and had therefore to conquer his disposition before he could bring himself to go on board of a ship, it would be still the more admirable, that the conviction that a fleet would be of great benefit to his country, and contribute to their moral improvement, should bring him to the resolution of getting the better of that aversion. On his accession to the government, he found not the slightest preparations towards a navy, but created himself a fleet and an admiralty, as well as by the harbours which he conquered in the Baltic, and by his newly founded city, he conferred upon his country a far greater opportunity for commerce and dealings with other nations, as a vent for the products and manufactures of it, and, therefore, at the same time rouzed their activity still farther.

In regard to RELIGION, Peter unquestionably had clearer perceptions than any of his predecessors on the throne of the tzars. His good

natural

natural underſtanding, his ſound judgment, probably too his travels, and his intercourſe with foreigners, and with men of all ranks, and of the different creeds, taught him very ſoon to diſtinguiſh religion from church-rites, to diſcriminate between the leſſons of Chriſt and the doctrines of the ſchools, and to form juſt ideas of what conſtitutes the true eſſence and ſpirit of religion *. It had ſtruck him forcibly, while yet very young, that eccleſiaſtical authority could have no good political tendency, unleſs it were entirely ſubordinate to the temporal power. The ruſſian prelates, eſpecially the patriarchs at Moſco, ſhared with the tzars the ſupreme command. The patriarch Philaretes, as I have ſaid before, was held in the higheſt veneration by tzar Mikhaila his ſon, and, though not in name, was actually co-ſovereign. The ſucceeding pa-

* As an inſtance of his firmneſs of mind, the following anecdote is related. Once as he lay very ſick, it was repreſented to him, that he ſhould now, according to the practice of the former tzars, grant a free pardon to ſeveral capital delinquents, in order by this pious act to obtain from God the ſpeedier reſtoration of his health. Inſtead of following this ſuperſtitious advice, he commanded theſe culprits to be immediately brought to trial, and if they were found guilty, to loſe no time in executing ſentence upon them, as he hoped that this would be more agreeable to God than the letting ſuch raſcals looſe again upon the world.

triarchs were never by their own consent of less consideration than Philaretes. — This was particularly the case with Nicon, patriarch of Russia under Alexey (from 1652 to 1658). Undoubtedly he had the principal share in quelling the novgorodian insurrection *, and his conduct on that occasion was highly laudable †. But as soon as the title of patriarch was conferred upon him, he wanted to be something more than primate of the clergy, he required that his voice should be of greater weight in matters of government than that of others; and, on finding that his advice was not followed in all things, he voluntarily resigned the patriarchate and retired into a monastery which he had previously built. But even here he would not be quiet; by his spiritual pride he offended tzar Alexey, and was continually affronting the great men of the court, till at length he was formally deposed

* See before, p. 18. of this volume.

† It is said of him, that during a scarcity at Novgorod, he let no poor person go from him without a good bellyfull, that he distributed every day money and bread among the necessitous, founded four poor-houses, visited the prisoners, punished their vices, set the innocent at liberty, and was the common protector of the poor against their hard masters. At Mosco, likewise, Nicon made it his business to receive all petitions addressed to the tzar, and on a certain day in the week to deliver them to him.

from the patriarchate, and degraded to what he had originally been, a simple monk [1666]. Nicon was the author of much good while archbishop of Novgorod; and he afterwards attempted some reforms in regard to devotional books, introduced the greek church-music, hitherto only used in Kief, into the rest of Russia, and thus, as chief religious teacher of the empire, shewed himself active for the improvement of what is called divine service; he even frequently delivered sermons, (at that time a practice extremely rare,) and, as he was a very eloquent man, and highly reverenced by the people, effected much good.

But Nicon's history throughout was a very important example to sovereigns of what an inordinate spiritual power may lead to, and a convincing proof that the patriarchs might very easily become rivals of the authority due only to the tzar*. Peter, therefore, from this example, deduced the maxim, that it would cer-

* To what length the patriarchs had extended their power, may be judged of by this among other circumstances, that, on Palm-sunday, when a procession was held, the tzar not only went on foot, while the patriarch rode, but was even obliged to lead the horse of the spiritual cavalier by the bridle. — Can it be a question, whether, at least on that day, the patriarch was not greater than the sovereign in the eyes of the populace?

tainly

tainly be better not to leave any longer the supreme spiritual power in the hands of a single person, left, by insensible degrees, a pope might grow up in Russia, sharing the sovereignty with the monarch, or even set him at defiance and directly oppose him. It was necessary for him, however, to proceed slowly and warily in the execution of his plan: so, therefore, he did, and in that particular likewise shewed himself, though an enterprising, yet a sagacious monarch, knowing how to prepare his people for the regulations he was meditating to introduce. The patriarch Adrian had died in 1700; and, though Peter was even then already firmly resolved not to confer that dignity again, yet he did not proceed immediately to put his resolution in force. He excused himself for the present, from the multiplicity of business brought on him by the war, as not being able to attend with proper earnestness to so important a matter as the appointment of a person to fill the patriarchal throne. — Having thus gained time, he now gradually brought on the intended alteration. He began by constituting an administrator of the patriarchal functions, with power, however, of deciding in very indifferent matters alone, to consult on more important affairs with other bishops, and ultimately to refer everything to

the

the determination of the tzar. Thus the nation was by little and little accustomed to live without a patriarch. And when at length he thought it now time to be able to go through with his alteration, he proclaimed, in January 1721, that the patriarchal dignity was abolished, and in its stead, for the future, the government of the church was to be conducted by a spiritual consistory composed of several members. This consistory, at the sittings whereof Peter himself frequently attended, obtained the title of THE HOLY DIRECTING SYNOD, was immediately under the tzar, who appointed the members of it. In this manner Peter recovered to the sovereigns of Russia the supremacy of the church, and made his people independent on the despotism of the spiritual power; and all this was effected by Peter, who owed nothing to others for the forming of his mind, at a time when Lewis XIV. was entirely governed by his clergy, and suffered a great part of his subjects to be hunted out of the country on account of religion, a proceeding not less impolitic than unjust, and therefore contrary to religion. Peter also determined to reform the monasteries, to diminish the number of monks and nuns, and so render the religious houses less hurtful to population, and at the same time to assign useful employments to their inhabitants, of whom he expressly says, in his decree, that the majority are lazy drones. All those monks who entered the convent not to study there, and hereafter to become bishops (as in Russia the offices of the superior clergy are filled by regulars), were now to employ themselves in nursing and waiting on the poor as well as disbanded soldiers, who, for that purpose were to be distributed among the monasteries. The nuns were to keep schools for poor girls, to teach them female works, and likewise to admit and succour the poor of their own sex. — Unfortunately, however, these regulations of Peter, in regard to religious houses of all denominations, produced but little effect, as he died the same year in which he decreed them.

His TOLERATION had still a greater influence on the intellectual improvement of his people, by which he allowed christians *, who were not of the greek persuasion, to build churches in several parts of his empire, and Russians of either sex to marry with persons of other communions. This indeed excited the zealous fury of the major part of the clergy. Peter, however,

* Only he would by no means tolerate the jesuits in his country. He was not pleased while at the court of Vienna, because, as he said, he met jesuits everywhere.

would not be disturbed at it, but pursued his course, associating with heretics, though for so doing he had the name of Antichrist bestowed on him, and biblical passages concerning Antichrist directly applied to him. He nevertheless attained his aim, by habituating his nation gradually to think more reasonably, and even to consort familiarly with the professors of a different creed. In order, likewise, to make his people acquainted with what was contained in the bible, and consequently with the doctrines of religion and what has been in aftertimes added to them, he caused the Bible to be translated and printed in the sclavonian language. This however went on so tediously, from the continued opposition of the clergy, that only the new testament was finished before his death, of which he had the copies fetched from the press as fast as they were ready, and dispersed among the people. — Even the clergy were benefited under Peter, as he held worthy persons of that denomination in high esteem. Theophanes, a learned and eloquent divine, who had spent three years at Rome, and had improved himself by travel, attended him in his campaign against the Turks, gave him very active assistance in his reforms of the clergy, and was appointed conjointly with the archbishop of Novgorod, vice-president of

the

the synod. — Besides this meritorious prelate, Peter's reforms produced several rational and learned members among the clerical order.

From all this it may be inferred, that Peter not only removed what was detrimental to the state in it, while the ecclesiastical authority was distinct from the temporal, but that he likewise contributed much to eradicate the extravagant and pernicious opinion of the sanctity of an inactive monastic life, to accustom his people to toleration for persons of a different faith, and to open their eyes concerning what was religion and what had been grafted upon it.

Arts and sciences in Russia were still in their infancy previous to the reign of Peter. That prince in these likewise began to do something for his country, and to lay the foundation in this respect to farther improvement. He endowed at Petersburg a seminary for future navigators, as well as a mathematical school at Mosco. He caused some public libraries to be set up, instituted a museum at St. Petersburg, for which he collected productions of nature and art himself on his travels, fetched other collections from abroad, and at the same time made it a repository for all kinds of natural products found in the russian empire. This institution he devoted to the nation at large. Every one had free entrance here, and by the contemplation of nature, or the works of human induſtry, might acquire juſter conceptions and an encouragement to activity. He provided a ruffian printing-office, cauſed uſeful books * to be tranſlated from foreign languages into ruſs, and, by means of the preſs, diſperſed them among his people. The academy of ſciences at St. Peterſburg, founded by him, and which has always contributed in an uncommon degree to extend the knowledge of Ruſſia among foreigners as well as natives, was enjoined by his plan to write learned books, afterwards to tranſlate them into the vulgar tongue, that they might be put into the hands of the common people, particularly of the youth. The obſervatory which he had inſpected at Paris on his ſecond journey through a part of Europe, raiſed in him a wiſh to have a like beneficial eſtabliſhment; and preſently after his return an obſervatory was built at St. Peterſburg. He himſelf took great pains to acquaint himſelf with the courſe of the heavenly bodies, and when he had acquired ſome

* Writings in the departments of hiſtory, of fortification, of the engineer; on mechanics and arts in general; calendars, almanacs, &c. were the firſt works that were printed at this printing-office, moſtly at the inſtance and ſelection of the tzar.

knowledge

knowledge of aftronomy, frequently converfed on it with the great men of his court, in order to expand their ideas a little; telling them, for inftance, that an eclipfe of the fun or the moon was an appearance altogether as natural as rain or funfhine, of which it was then as difficult to perfuade the Ruffians, as it has, even more recently, been found to convince the natives in other countries. Peter, who was ever ready as much as poffible to combat and deftroy fuperftition, ordered it to be publicly announced, in 1715, that an eclipfe of the fun would happen on fuch a day, in order to make it apparent that this event was not ominous of any difafter, or an awful menace of divine judgments. As the obfervatory of St. Peterfburg was a fruit of his travels, he had likewife, on his firft and fecond journey, procured artifts and men of letters in England, Holland, Germany and France, whom he fent into his empire on terms very agreeable to them, that they might contribute by their writings, or by the exercife of their arts, and by inftruction imparted to the young Ruffians, to the improvement of the nation. For the fame reafon youths were felected and fent to travel at his expence in foreign countries. And as, by means of his good natural underftanding, he very foon acquired a knowledge of feveral arts

and

and sciences, he prescribed to the young persons whom he had sent abroad, what they were particularly to study, examined them himself on their return, observed whether they had properly employed their opportunities of learning, or had passed the time in idleness; the expert he put into places that suited their attainments, encouraged and promoted them, and punished the unimproved by taking no farther notice of them, or by assigning to them posts in which they could get neither honour nor profit. For the more general cultivation of the Russians, it were indeed to be wished that their famous sovereign Peter had bestowed greater care on the first education, on the elementary institution of the youth in schools. Though both his father and his brother had already done something in this respect by erecting some schools and institutions for the information of youth; yet it was but a very small beginning. On the whole, most of the schools in Russia, even in the time of Peter, were upon a very miserable footing; and Peter, who gave himself so much concern on a variety of objects, did here far less than could have been wished, and than he perhaps would have done if he had attained to a greater age. Under him, indeed, it must be owned, though without his concurrence, and only by accident,

some

some scattered rays of reason and moral light pierced even to the inclement regions of Siberia: as the swedish prisoners who were sent thither by Peter, and particularly the officers, erected schools in those frozen climes, and instructed the natives in many useful branches of knowledge [*]. Even these unfortunate persons, who did not obtain permission to return to Sweden till the peace of Nystadt, contributed, therefore, in some measure, to drive ignorance out of Russia.

MANUFACTURES, TRADES, MECHANICAL ARTS, BUSINESSES, AND OBJECTS OF INDUSTRY OF ALL KINDS, were the principal aim of Peter's active mind; and doubtless in these respects he cultivated his nation greatly more, and advanced it higher than it had been before. His having himself acquired a knowledge of the generality of matters of that nature, his having always been, while on his travels, an inquisitive and attentive observer of everything that related to them, not unfrequently himself putting a hand to the

[*] As one instance, among the rest, von Vreech, a swedish captain, in 1713 founded a school at Tobolsk, where the scholars were taught christianity, writing, reading, and arithmetic, the german, latin, and french languages, geography, geometry, and drawing. In this school were seen children from all parts of the empire.

work *, and concerning himself in general about the minutest trifles, as well as about the greater parts and the whole, must unquestionably have had a vast influence on the progress of his people, among whom it was his endeavour to transplant whatever was good and useful among foreigners.

And, while a traveller, he observed, examined, and informed himself thoroughly of everything that fell under his notice, in order to employ and to apply what he had seen for the benefit of his empire †, he also sent young Russians into foreign countries

---

* It is well known that both in Holland and in England he not only caused himself to be shewn what was most material in the dockyards, but even worked at the several businesses with his own hands. According to our countryman, captain Perry, whom Peter took with him from London to Russia as an engineer, there was no kind of work, from the casting of cannons to the making of ropes, that furnished anything to ship-building, in which Peter had not acquired the clearest notion of every particular, and had even set his hand to work at. Even in Russia he executed something or other in every workshop that he visited; onewhile hammering iron as a smith, at another employed as a carpenter; he once even built a whole wall with bricks: but his favourite business was that of a shipwright.

† He even sent a model of a coffin to Russia. In general, nothing appeared to him so insignificant as that he did not vouchsafe it his attention, as soon as he thought that any benefit might arise out of it to his country. Thus, shortly before

countries to study and follow the art of ship-building, and other useful occupations, that at their return they might teach others; and for the same purpose took into his pay many foreigners, emigrant Frenchmen, Scotsmen and Germans, among whom were several very able men. He put the manufactory of small arms upon an excellent footing, set up forges for anchors, and built a number of mills, instituted manufactories for linen, sailcloth, cordage, silk and woollen stuffs, built in the neighbourhood of St. Petersburg a multitude of brick and tile kilns; and acting differently from Charles XII. who conquered Poland without deriving from it any benefit to Sweden, nay, which was indeed injured by it, caused sheep and shepherds to come from that country, for the sake of improving the breed of sheep in Russia. He also zealously promoted

---

before the conclusion of the swedish war, he had brush-makers, basket-makers, even butter-women with butter-firkins, nay rat-catchers and dutch cats brought to Russia. He had heard that the dutch cats were famous for preventing the mischief occasioned by mice and rats in ships and houses. So attentive was he to the minutest objects, that, perceiving the russian boors made better mat-shoes than the finnish peasants in the neighbourhood of St. Petersburg, he distributed russian mat-shoemakers in Finland, that they might communicate their art to the Finns.

inquiries

inquiries into the manner of exploring and working mines, particularly in Siberia; and, in order to render it more methodical and regular, constituted a peculiar mineral-college, to which he gave the inspection over the works to be carried on. He greatly improved the docks and yards at Archangel, and formed new ones at Petersburg and Voronetch. He took delight in assisting such persons as were inclined to undertake manufactories and workshops, by advancing them money, and granting them privileges. Thus industry and trade were continually gaining by him in an extraordinary degree; and what I remarked above of the swedish prisoners in Siberia, that they strewed the seeds of some improvement even in that part of the russian empire, is applicable also in a particular manner, in regard to useful handicrafts. Even the swedish officers employed themselves here, partly for want of other means of support, in a variety of mechanical arts and trades. In their distressful situation, being reduced to the necessity of applying themselves to consider and to imitate what they had seen in Sweden and other countries, they became the teachers of the inhabitants of the country, disseminated their knowledge among them, and instructed them in several profitable employments.

Not

Not less important was the progress which the Russians made under Peter in regard to COMMERCE. Inconsiderable and confined as it was, prior to his reign, so much did he contribute to the advancement and extension of it, and thereby rouzed and formed his nation to greater activity, by procuring them more traffic, more connections with Europe and Asia than they formerly had.

The trade with the bordering empire of China seemed to secure many advantages to Russia, as each of the two countries possessed those natural products of which the other was in want. Peter soon turned his attention to this matter. A peace concluded between China and Russia in 1689, by which the numerous disputes concerning the boundaries of the two empires were finally adjusted, had determined the chinese government to adopt an amicable behaviour. Peter immediately took advantage of the opportunity to settle the trade between the Russians and the Chinese on a more firm and lasting establishment; and afterwards, when, on account of complaints that had arisen concerning some disorders that had been committed by the Russians in China, sent a new embassy to that country to settle all misunderstandings, and to revive the trade. The acquisition of the peninsula of

Kamtshatka

In the reign of Alexey [1663] a german merchant at Mosco made some attempts at the introduction of a POST-OFFICE. Till then all letters were obliged to be sent by messengers, or as opportunity served; the former method being as expensive as the latter was unsafe. Travellers could proceed from one place to another only in their own carriages and sledges, for which they were forced to hire horses of the boors. This was much altered by Peter. He instituted, what had been done in France in the fifteenth, and in Germany at the beginning of the sixteenth century, regular posts between the principal towns of the empire, and a packet boat between St. Petersburg and Lubeck.

For the more effectual facilitation of communication between the several parts of the country, Peter employed his care to the maintenance and reparation of the ROADS. He caused them to be greatly improved, and, by a police, on a similar plan with that in France, cleared them from

---

pleted by Peter the Great, was resumed in 1768, and prosecuted with great vigour till 1774, when the mathematicians appointed to conduct the work were murdered in the rebellion of Pugatshef. Since which the whole business has been at a stand.

beggars and vagrants, and erected inns at various stations.

The great advantage of LIKE WEIGHTS AND MEASURES in all parts of the empire to trade, to buyers and sellers, Russia owes likewise to Peter the Great; who also provided the country with a proper MINT, by taking several french mint-masters and assayers into his service.

The BOARD OF TRADE instituted by Peter, the members whereof consisted in one half of native Russians, and the other half of foreigners, undoubtedly contributed much to the encouragement of trade; as formerly it often happened, that when foreigners had a process with natives in the ordinary courts, the russian judges shewed great partiality to their countrymen. Tzar Alexey had indeed already attempted by several laws to put a stop to this injustice*; but Peter's provision concerning the assessors of the board of trade was certainly a more effectual remedy to the evil, than any laws could be.

The WAY OF LIFE, and in general the whole face of society, as well as the MANNERS and CUSTOMS of Russia, underwent a very great revolution in the time of Peter, and were in various respects new moulded.

* See before, p. 114.

In order to render the Russians more like the other civilized nations of Europe, Peter, at the commencement of the year 1700, abolished the old russian calendar and introduced the corrected style. The ancient Russians, in common with all the slavonian nations, began the year with the month of March. In the year 1343 the greek mode of computation of time was adopted in Russia, according to which the beginning of the year fell in the month of September. This Peter now likewise altered, and decreed that, as in the rest of Europe, in Russia the first of January should for the future be the first day of the year; in this change however he did not adopt the gregorian*, but the old julian calendar which is still used in Russia. — The people indeed murmured not a little at this innovation; but Peter, regardless of it, on the first of January 1700, appointed great solemnities to be held, at

---

* Pope Gregory XIII. reformed the julian calendar formerly used; and from 1583 the gregorian calendar was observed in the catholic countries. In Germany, Holland, Denmark, and Switzerland, this computation was not introduced till 1700, in England not till 1752, and in Sweden not before 1753. The russian calendar is eleven days behind ours; so that, e. gr. the first of January in Russia falls on our twelfth of the same month. Hence the date is sometimes doubly expressed, as: on the 16/27th of May Peter laid the foundation of Peterſburg.

which

which the new regulation was proclaimed, which was also ordered to be notified from the pulpits in the courts of justice and in the public places of the several towns of the empire. By these and other methods the Russians were brought gradually to a familiarity with this and the rest of his alterations.

Nothing of acknowledged utility in other countries escaped the notice of so attentive an observer as Peter; and accordingly he endowed two HOSPITALS in St. Petersburg on the plan of those at Amsterdam, for superannuated or infirm soldiers and sailors, and an infirmary at Mosco. ORPHAN and FOUNDLING-HOUSES were either new-built or enlarged and improved. The police in France had, during his stay in that country, met with his entire approbation; immediately, therefore, on his return [1718] he instituted a POLICE-OFFICE in Petersburg, to which he committed the care of the internal security of the empire.

To guard against the ruin of families he prohibited all games of hazard, and at the same time prescribed bounds to extravagance in dress.

By a TABLE OF PRECEDENCE, which extended to all persons in office, whether military, civil, or at court, dividing them into fourteen classes, he endeavoured to check the frequently ridiculous

ridiculous pretensions and disputes in regard to rank and pre-eminence, and likewise abolished the court of nobles *. In conformity to this table even the sons of russian princes, counts, barons, &c. have indeed, in respect of their descent and the merits of their fathers, access to the assemblies at court, but not the least degree of rank till they have done service to the country in some department. Married ladies enjoy the rank of their husbands; but unmarried ladies must go back four classes †.

Society was a thing almost unknown to the manners then prevalent in the russian nation. Peter accomplished much likewise in this respect, convinced as he was that intercourse and society could not be inefficient in the cultivation of a people, but must contribute to a greater expansion of the faculties, to bring truths, opinions, judgments, and ideas into more rapid circulation; and that therefore a sociable people would be more sensible than an unsociable. In order, therefore, to set the fashion, as he knew that the example of the higher orders invites the lower

* See before, p. 119.

† By this regulation he intended to discourage parents from giving their children, especially daughters, an education above their rank, whereby many young women are made unhappy.

ranks to imitation, set on foot [1716] societies under the name of assemblies, and even gave out a particular set of rules for them. They were kept three times a week in the houses of the principal persons of quality in rotation. Peter and Catharine frequented them in person; but all formality and constraint were banished [*]. All persons of rank, noblemen, superior officers, respectable merchants, ship-builders, and other people of condition had free admission with their wives and children. That ladies too should take part in such companies was a thing as yet unheard of in Russia. Hitherto even married women, only on certain great holidays and in company with their husbands, could venture to visit their nearest relations. They lived retired in the back part of the house, and were

[*] "The assemblies," it is said, in the orders that were published concerning them, "shall not begin earlier than four o'clock in the afternoon, and continue only till ten in the evening. The host is not obliged to receive or to wait upon the guests, or to give them his company; but must provide chairs, lights, liquors, and a variety of entertainments. The guests may divide into the apartments, in one of which may be dancing, in the other cards, chess, or draughts may be played; in a third tobacco may be smoaked, &c. Every one may come and go when he pleases, may be a spectator, or take part in the diversions," &c.

very

very much confined*. Unmarried ladies were kept in still greater constraint. These severities Peter did his utmost to remove, by declaring that women ought not to be excluded from the comforts of social intercourse; and they testified their gratitude to him for it. He wanted to alter the asiatic dress of the Russians, and to introduce that generally worn in the other parts of Europe. He therefore made it one of the rules to be observed in the forementioned assemblies, that every one must appear in the light modern dress; and the female sex, who had obtained more liberty by Peter's means, carefully and with chearfulness adhered to this rule. It was far more difficult to bring the men to an alteration in their dress, which, however, in Peter's opinion, might much contribute to lessen the hatred entertained by his countrymen against foreigners. — He commanded all his subjects (the clergy, boors, Tartars, Kalmuks, and tribes of their class excepted,) to shave their beards — An order to which violent opposition was made. For enforcing this regulation he laid a tax on long beards, and great numbers submitted to pay it rather than part with their beard which was universally held to be an ornament to the

* See before, vol. i. p. 367.

person.

person. Superstitious Russians even thought it an outward characteristic of the orthodox faith, (for in what trifles has not orthodoxy been made to consist?) and, if too poor, or too parsimonious, to pay the tax for retaining the beard, they religiously preserved the beard shorn off, and had it deposited in the coffin with them on their decease, that they might present it to St. Nicholas, on his refusing to admit them, as beardless christians, into the kingdom of heaven.— Peter wanted likewise to effect an alteration in the DRESS of the men. Accordingly, whoever was in his service must appear in clothes of a foreign cut, and under all the gates of the town patterns of these clothes were even hung up*.

Peter also resolved to give his people a taste for the DRAMA. Before his time, at Kief and Mosco spiritual plays were performed occasionally in the monasteries. Under his patronage a national theatre was formed at Mosco, which, however, it must be owned, was bad enough.

* Whose coat was not agreeable to this pattern must pay a fine, or submit to have so much of it cut off as exceeded the standard. Many likewise had their beards cut off in the streets. In regard to dress, the clergy, boors, &c. were also excepted.

More

More was done in this matter by his female successors.

In the times anterior to Peter it was usual for parents to conclude marriages for their children; and the young people never saw one another till they were to be betrothed. A custom which was certainly attended with many inconveniences. Peter made a law that every young couple should frequent one another for six weeks at least previous to the betrothing.

In order to discredit in the eyes of his people the old usages, many of which were indeed highly ridiculous, Peter had recourse to various methods. At times he appointed an entertainment, at which every thing was to proceed on the old footing, in which his design was to display the difference between the ancient and modern manners, and to shew the superiority of the latter in a way irresistibly striking. Thus, for example, he once celebrated the nuptials of one of his court-fools in a most magnificent manner; but entirely in the style of the sixteenth century. The guests were obliged to appear in the dress after the fashion of that time. No fire was lighted, though the weather was intensely cold; because it was an old superstitious notion, that the kindling of a fire on the wedding day was unlucky.

unlucky. The old Ruffians were fond of mead and brandy, but drank no wine — this particular was therefore punctually obferved. The guefts fhewed themfelves highly difcontented at it. "This was exactly the cuftom with our forefathers," Peter anfwered them fmiling; "and furely old cuftoms are preferable to new ones." Thus jeeringly giving them a good leffon. It was then ufual to keep fools for the diverfion of the court; and, indeed, till very lately the nobility always had one about the houfe: nor is the practice yet entirely left off in the country. The court-fools ufed frequently to make themfelves merry with the old fafhions, cuftoms, and manners, mimicking many of the ftiff obftinate fticklers for the antiquated ftyle; and, on their complaining to Peter of the affront, he generally anfwered them: They are FOOLS, what can be done with them?

From what has been faid, it plainly appears that Peter in many refpects gave a new turn to the manner of thinking and acting of the ruffian nation. I fhall only fubjoin a few obfervations. The extraordinary and indefatigable activity of this monarch: one while undertaking a fiege at a diftance from his empire, or fighting at the head of his army, then fuddenly appearing in the refidence, and frequenting the fittings of the
senate,

senate, or presenting himself in the courts of justice, or consulting with the clergy on ecclesiastical reforms, or selecting ingenious persons to send out on travels; now undertaking a journey himself; working in foreign countries in the dockyards and workshops; becoming an attentive scholar in the studies of literary men, at Amsterdam with the naturalist Ruysch, or, as at Paris, visiting an academy of sciences; then re-appearing in his empire, and there making dispositions for establishing a manufactory; in one place causing a canal to be dug, in another ordering ships to be built; to-day publishing an ordinance relating to processes in the courts, to-morrow issuing a table of precedence; one moment severely punishing a judge who had suffered himself to be corrupted, the next rewarding another for services performed to the country; now holding a triumphal entry, then passing the whole day in the museum of the works of nature and art of his own institption, in the contemplation of nature, and the great performances of human industry and contrivance — in short, that in all his undertakings for the good of his country he was obliged to work and act himself, as he was in want of able persons to whom he should need only to trace out a plan, and then could leave the execution to
their

their care — such a vast activity must surely have rouzed in some degree the Russians, who were apt to let their faculties lie dormant, from their inaction, animate them to the employment of their abilities, and teach them to consider industry as a good and useful property.

Peter, by prizing and rewarding merit whereever he found it, by shewing that the man of the lowest station, if he were but expert and useful, was in higher estimation with him than the dull and indolent, though of the first family of the empire, must have tended greatly to banish the idle pretensions to anceftry and hereditary consequence out of the heads of the russian nobility, to diffuse juster notions of the true worth of man, and at the same time to encourage and animate the talents of a number of young persons of the inferior ranks of society.

Peter, by serving upwards through the several stations in the army and navy, gave likewife a fit lesson to the nobles of the empire, as on the other hand it must have flattered the common soldier and sailor, to see his humble station honoured so far as that even the sovereign did not disdain to fill it, and thereby to confess that it was serviceable to the state.

Peter, by working himself at the ordinary mechanical trades, must have confiderably weakened

ened the prejudice, then very common in Russia, that they who passed their days in a luxurious ease were happier than they who were doomed to work, and helped to disseminate the maxim, that industry brings content.

Peter habituated his Russians to adopt what was profitable in others, and not to despise and neglect a foreigner, because he was a foreigner; consequently altered in this respect the national way of thinking, as the people had hitherto always entertained an aversion for all foreigners.

Such is the brief account of what the russian nation gained by Peter the Great; who, though as a man, was not certainly free from some of the vices of his nation, such as drunkenness and cruelty, yet raised himself so far above his countrymen, that he was not improperly termed a wonder of his times, that posterity has unanimously acknowledged him to be one of the greatest of mankind, as well as of monarchs, who for the most part formed himself, that the russian nation with gratitude proclaims his great merits both towards the empire and towards the people, and allows that this one sovereign advanced and improved them farther than the whole series of former princes had done.

Peter indeed has been blamed for bringing so many strangers into his country, and for having

operated

operated upon it, and generally ruling it more by strangers and foreigners, than the improvement of the people by their own powers rendered necessary. But it is to be supposed that he was so well acquainted with his countrymen, as to know that their abilities were only to be called forth by the method he made choice of; a method which had ever been adopted by the wisest of his ancestors, Ivan, Boris, and Alexey; and if he had frequently recourse to harsh or cruel measures, we may imagine he thought them necessary in Russia. Nothing but the unalterable will of a sovereign could have executed here those arduous tasks. Peter had nothing but that to oppose to superstition, prejudice, selfishness, and an utter abhorrence of all innovation, for effectually carrying those alterations which to him appeared necessary.

Of all the tzar's innovations, that which was attended with the greatest difficulty, and occasioned him to shed the most blood, was the alteration of the habit that had been for ages worn by his subjects. It was with extreme reluctance that the Russians submitted to wear the german dress, and to be shaved; and they several times rebelled for the sake of retaining their long garments and their beard. But Peter had in view, by giving his people the fashions of the other nations of Europe, to introduce among them their manners, without foreseeing, perhaps, that he was calling up a taste for luxury, of which he was not fond. That prince was always very plain in his dress, kept a very frugal house, was not more than a quarter of an hour at dinner, and would frequently laugh at his favourite Mentchikof, who, from nothing more than a pye-boy at the corner of a street, being now a prince, displayed a pomp and magnificence hitherto unequalled; and never sat down to dinner without the music of trumpets and cymbals and various other instruments.

In regard to the simplicity of his attire, the following is related in the manuscript memoirs of a diplomatic agent, who resided a long time at his court. " On all the solemn festivals, he
" only wore the uniform of his préobajenskoi
" regiment of guards. I saw him in 1721 give
" a public audience to the ambassadors of
" Persia. He entered the hall of audience in
" nothing more than a surtout of coarse brown
" cloth. When he was seated on the throne,
" the attendants brought him a coat of blue
" gros-de-Naples, embroidered with silver,
" which he put on with great precipitation, be-
" cause

"caufe the ambaffadors were waiting for ad-
"mittance. During this he turned his eyes
"towards a window where the tzaritza had
"placed herfelf to obferve the ceremony. Ca-
"tharine was heard repeatedly to burft out into
"fits of laughter, as the tzar feemed to her to
"be aftonifhed at feeing himfelf fo finely
"dreffed; and the tzar laughed at it himfelf, as
"alfo did all the fpectators. As foon as the
"ambaffadors were gone, Peter I. threw off
"his embroidered coat, and put on his
"furtout *."

His violence can never be excufed, and his cruelties admit of no palliation. He not only chaftifed with his own hand the courtiers, his generals, his minifters, for any flight fault they had committed; but he himfelf was often the executioner of the wretches whom he had caufed to be fentenced to death.

His rage, it is true, was not always fo fatal; but, whether this monarch was really not mafter of himfelf, or whether he intended to make his fubjects believe that nothing in nature ought to refift his will, he fometimes did things which in any other man would have paffed for acts of infanity.

* The blue-filk embroidered coat is the identical one which is now on his wax effigy in the academy of fciences, and it was made for his marriage with Catharine.

After being returned from his travels, designing one day to exhibit a proof of his skill in navigation, he took the exercise of sailing in a small vessel on the lake Ladoga, which is often very tempestuous, and just then was more agitated than usual. Peter, being frightened, regained the shore; but being angry that the waves had no more respect for him, he sent for the executioner of the town, and ordered him to give the knoot to the intractable lake.

And what are we to think of that endless comedy in which Peter I. caused himself to be represented by knæz Romodanoffky, the most vulgar and brutal of all the Russians, while he himself affected to play a subaltern part? He conferred on Romodanoffky the title of tzar of Mosco; made a public report to him of all his undertakings and his most important successes; all petitions, memorials, and other documents, addressed to the sovereign, were presented to this phantom of a tzar, who privately dispatched them to the council; and when the persons concerned, on not obtaining what they desired, complained to Peter, he answered coldly: " It " is not my fault; all depends on the tzar of " Mosco."

A refusal was not the only inconvenience they had to apprehend from the insensible and capricious Romodanoffky. He kept in his palace

palace a bear of enormous magnitude, and broke to a very curious trick. The animal prefented to every one who wifhed to fpeak with his mafter a great glafs of brandy, in which there was a ftrong dofe of pepper. Whoever did not drink off this liquor was fure to have his cloaths torn to pieces by the bear, and to be feverely fcratched into the bargain.

After having abolifhed the office of patriarch, Peter I. in confequence of his refolution to crown his confort Catharine, in 1725 applied for that purpofe to the archbifhop of Novgorod, primate of all Ruffia. The prelate, thinking this a favourable opportunity for getting the patriarchate re-eftablifhed in his favour, obferved to the tzar, that fo auguft a ceremony would acquire far greater folemnity by the prefence of a patriarch. The tzar anfwered him no otherwife than as he was wont to do fuch of his fubjects as he was difpleafed with, that is, by a fhower of ftrokes with his cane. The archbifhop afked pardon; the tzar was pacified; the coronation was performed, and nothing more was faid of a patriarch.

Mentchikof was the fon of a pye-man, and paffed a part of his youth in felling little pies about the ftreets. One day, felling fome of his paftry in a houfe where feveral perfons had met to breakfast; one of the party having drank pretty freely, let some words escape him, that intimated a plot against the tzar. Mentchikof ran in all speed to the palace, requested to reveal a secret to Peter, and informed him of what he had overheard. The tzar wrapped himself in a cloak, and hastened to the house pointed out to him by Mentchikof; here, leaning his ear to the door of the room where the people were breakfasting, he distinctly heard what confirmed to him the report of his conductor. He immediately entered and found himself in the midst of the conspirators. Whether they imagined that his guards were at the door, or whether they were intimidated at his presence alone, all of them fell at his knees, and threw themselves on his clemency. From that moment the tzar took Mentchikof to be about him; and the pye-boy shortly after became a prince.

The first insurrection occasioned by the general order to all Russians to leave off the custom of wearing the beard, was followed by the execution of about eight thousand persons. For containing such a great number of victims, the tzar made choice of a spacious square adjoining to his house of Préobrajinsko, three versts from Mosco. The place was surrounded by palisades, through which it was easy to see what was passing within the inclofure; where, after placing a great number of balks and blocks, the wretches condemned to lose their lives were made to kneel at them.

Several executioners were immediately employed in cutting off heads. Peter himfelf, with an axe in his hand, fet the example to the executioners. Moft of the tzar's courtiers were eager to imitate him; and Mentchikof boafted afterwards that it was he who had cut off the greateft number of heads. A boy about twelve years old came and laid his neck on the tzar's block. The prince, inftead of chopping his head off, took him by the arm and fhoved him away. The boy, without faying a word, went and placed himfelf at another block. The tzar, perceiving this, advanced towards him, raifed him up and put him away again. Prefently after the boy returned to fubmit his neck to the axe. The tzar then angrily afked him, why he perfifted in wifhing to have his head cut off? "Thou haft cut off my father's head, my "brother's, and the heads of all my relations, "who were no more guilty than I am," faid the boy; "why fhouldft thou not cut off "mine?" — Peter made no anfwer, but ordered the boy out of the inclofure, threw down his axe, and went away.

That

while his base courtiers were getting drunk with him, and applauding the ferocity of such sanguinary pastime *!

Endowed with a fine figure and a superior understanding, invested with sovereign power, and though passionately fond of women, Peter I. was never beloved by one; or at least he was duped by all with whom he formed an attachment. While yet very young he married Evdokhia Lapukhin, who was mother of the unhappy Alexey. Not long after his marriage with Evdokhia, the tzar fell desperately in love with Anna Moëns, a handsome Fleming, the daughter of a brewer settled at Mosco.

* This anecdote, though not mentioned by Voltaire in his history, was well known to him, as the king of Prussia, Frederic II. then prince royal, sent it him, with other accurate memoirs concerning the life of the tzar, and to which Frederic subjoined: "The tzar had not the slightest tincture of humanity, of magnanimity, or of virtue: he had been brought up in the grossest ignorance, and only acted by the impulse of his unruly passions." In another of his letters, Frederic writes to Voltaire: "The tzar will appear to you in this history very different from the figure he makes in your imagination..... A concurrence of fortunate circumstances and favourable events, in conjunction with the ignorance of foreigners, have transformed the tzar into an heroic phantom, concerning the grandeur whereof no one has ever thought proper to doubt."

Evdokhia

Evdokhia at firſt was apparently grieved at the defertion of her huſband: but prefently after confoled herſelf in the fociety of a young boyar, named Glebof; and, to the misfortune both of herſelf and her lover, neglected to make a fufficient fecret of her amour. The tzar, who thought he might be inconſtant with impunity, would not allow another to be fo with him. He ſhut up the tzaritza in a convent, and afterwards repudiated her in form. His vengeance towards Glebof was far more cruel: he impaled him alive; and it is confidently afferted, that the wretched victim of his fury remained upwards of four-and-twenty hours on the ſpike before he expired *.

The tzar went in all eagerneſs to enjoy this horrible fight. He did more; he got upon the pediment of brickwork in which the pale was fixed, and exhorted the fufferer to confeſs to him the facts which he had hitherto refuſed to avow. "Come nearer, that thou mayeſt hear "me the better," anſwered Glebof; which the tzar having done, Glebof collected his re-

* The diplomatic agent, already cited, affirms in his manuſcript memoirs that more than a hundred witneſſes of this fact related it to him; and that, on his arrival at Moſco, he himſelf ſaw the head of Glebof ſtill affixed on the pale.

maining

maining forces for an inſtant, and ſaid to him: "Thou tyrant, the moſt cruel that ever hell produced, if what thou imputeſt to me were true, thinkeſt thou, that, not having confeſſed it before my puniſhment, while yet ſome hope remained of obtaining mercy by the avowal; canſt thou think, I ſay, that I am ſuch a fool or ſuch a coward as to ſatisfy thee now that it is no longer in thy power to ſave my life. Go, horrible monſter," added he, as he ſpit in his face; "begone!"

The tzar had ſerious thoughts of placing Anna Moëns on the throne. That young woman, who regarded it as the greateſt of all misfortunes that her ſovereign was fond of her, and to whoſe paſſion ſhe only ſubmitted through fear, dextrouſly eluded his offers of marriage. Peter, however, continued his viſits to her; but, either diſguſted at the coldneſs with which ſhe repaid his ardour, or the natural fickleneſs of his temper led him elſewhere, he ſoon left her to follow her inclinations in marrying a leſs illuſtrious lover with whom ſhe had long held an amorous correſpondence *.

* Her firſt huſband was Kayzerlinguen, miniſter from Pruſſia to the tzar; after his death ſhe was married to lieutenant-general Balk.

Peter became enamoured of a young woman of Livonia, who, after having been married to a swedish dragoon, is generally reported to have been succeffively miftrefs to the generals Bauer, Scheremetof, and Mentchikof, became emprefs of Ruffia under the name of Catharine I.*

---

* A french author, who writes from goood authorities, gives the following account of Catharine. She bore the name of Martha till she quitted lutheranifm for the greek religion. She was born in a petty village of Livonia, of poor parents who laboured for their livelihood. While yet very young she was taken by a lutheran clergyman, who lived at Marienburg, named Gluck, to wait upon his daughters. No fooner was she marriageable than the beauty of her figure drew upon her the attention of feveral young men. She had even a fort of intrigue with a Livonian, named Tiezenhaufen, who taught latin at paftor Gluck's; and this latter, on perceiving the forward difpofition of Catharine, married her to a fwedifh dragoon, by whom fhe was courted. The dragoon and his wife were fhortly after made prifoners by a party of Ruffians; and, as at that time prifoners of war were treated as flaves, Catharine was conducted to general Bauer, who very foon made a prefent of her to Scheremetof. Scheremetof refigned her to Mentchikof; and, at the end of two years, the tzar having accidentally feen her, took her away from Mentchikof. It is affirmed by fome writers, that the hufband of Catharine had been fent to Siberia: others pretend that he lived many years at Riga upon a penfion that was fecretly conveyed to him.

Though

Though Catharine owed every thing to the tzar, who had seated her on the throne, she was not always so faithful to him as he had a right to expect. Catharine had chosen for her chamberlain the young Moëns de la Croix, whose sister, madame Balk, was about her person, and had, as we have just now seen, rejected the hand of the tzar. Moëns being of a handsome figure, it was not long before he made a lively impression on the heart of the empress, and the intercourse was soon perceived by count Yagujinsky, who was then in full confidence with the tzar, and had the cruelty to communicate the discovery he had made to his master. Peter's jealousy took fire. He vowed vengeance; but resolved first to convince himself by ocular proof of Catharine's treachery. Accordingly, he pretended to leave Petersburg in order to pass a few days at one of his country-palaces, but repaired secretly to the winter-palace; then sent a page, on whom he could depend, with his compliments to the empress, and to tell her that he was at Strelna, a few leagues from the residence.

The page, who had orders to take notice of everything, hastened back with a strong confirmation of the tzar's suspicions. Peter went in all haste to Catharine, and surprised her in the

the arms of her lover. It was two o'clock in the morning, and madame Balk was watching at some distance from the apartment of her majesty. Peter, in his fury, overset a page who stood in his way, and struck Catharine with his cane; but said not a word to Moens, or to madame Balk, intending to punish them in a manner more severe than by some strokes of his cane.

On leaving Catharine, Peter, still in a transport of rage, ran abruptly into the chamber where prince Repnin was asleep [*], who, starting up, and seeing the tzar, thought himself undone. "Get up," said the tzar, "and hear me. Thou "haft no need to dress." Repnin rose, trembling at every joint. Peter related to him what had happened, and added: "I am determined "to cut off the empress's head as soon as it is "day-light."—"You have sustained an in- "jury, and you are absolute master," answered Repnin; "but permit me, with due respect, to "make one observation. Why divulge the fatal "adventure at which you are so much irritated? "You have been forced to destroy the strelitzes.

[*] Prince Repnin has often related these particulars. He was the grandfather of prince Nicholas Repnin who was some years ago ambassador at Warsaw and governor of Livonia.

"Almost

"Almost every year of your reign has been marked by bloody executions. You thought it behoved you to condemn your own son to death. If you cut off the head of your wife, you will tarnish forever the glory of your name; Europe will behold you in no other light than as a prince greedy of the blood of your subjects, and of all your kindred. Revenge the outrage; put Moëns to death by the sword of the law. But as to the empress, your best way will be to get rid of her by means that will not sully your fame."

During this speech Peter was violently agitated. After fixing his eyes for some moments on Repnin, he left the room without uttering a word. The ruin of Moëns was already resolved. He was arrested as well as madame Balk. They were both confined in the winter-palace, in an apartment where none had admission, except the emperor himself, who carried them their victuals. At the same time a report was spread, that the brother and the sister had been bribed by the enemies of the country, in hopes of bringing the empress to act upon the mind of the tzar prejudicially to the interests of Russia.

Moëns was interrogated by the monarch in presence of general Uschakof; and, after having confessed

confessed whatever they pleased, he lost his head on the block *.

Madame Balk, his sister, received the knoot; and it is pretended that it was the tzar himself who inflicted it on her: after this she was sent into Siberia.

Moëns walked to meet his fate with manly firmness. He always wore a diamond bracelet, to which was a miniature of Catharine; but, as it was not perceived at the time of his being seized, he found means to conceal it under his garter; and when he was on the scaffold he confided this secret to the lutheran pastor who accompanied him, and under cover of his cloak slipped the bracelet into his hand to restore it to the empress.

The tzar was a spectator of the punishment of Moëns from one of the windows of the senate. The execution being over, he got up on the scaffold, took the head of Moëns by the hair, and expressed with a brutal energy how delighted he was with the vengance he had taken. The same day, that prince had the cruelty to conduct Catharine in an open carriage round the stake on which was fixed the head of the unfortunate sufferer. Catharine was sufficiently

* The 27th of November 1724.

mistress of herself not to change countenance at the sight of this terrible object; but it is said, that on returning to her apartment she shed abundance of tears *.

Not only the internal frame and constitution of the russian empire received from the hand of Peter a great and almost general reform, but even its relation to the rest of the european, particularly the northern states, was now, in comparison with former times, entirely changed. Sweden and Poland, lately the formidable foes and neighbours of the empire, saw themselves now weakened and humbled by Russia, and the former even despoiled of a great part of her possessions. Russia became, in the space of a few years, so powerful as to be the most dangerous neighbour to both. The ottoman empire, at the close of the foregoing century, had already beheld the effects of Peter's enterprising spirit, and did not dare to violate the treaty to which the tzar had been compelled by adverse circum-

* These particulars are taken from the above-mentioned manuscript memoirs written at the time.

stances to accede at Pruth, though instigated to the breach of it by the earnest solicitations of Charles XII. or to oppose, by force of arms, the conquests of the Russians in Persia. Peter had thus, therefore, raised his country to a pitch of eminence, which the neighbouring kingdoms saw with jealousy, and that within the short period of not quite thirty years. Yet all his labours might have been rendered altogether vain, all his undertakings and their important consequences have been entirely frustrated, unless his successors should prosecute the edifice of which the foundations were laid by him. Nothing more was requisite than that the succeeding sovereigns should tread in Peter's footsteps for producing the effect, that the consequence to which the tzar had raised the empire should not only be undiminished, but even the circumference of it from time to time considerably increased; and that at present, at the close of the eighteenth century, Russia's importance in the political scale of Europe, is not only as great, but much greater than that which Peter endeavoured to procure it, and to which, a hundred years ago, he made the beginning by his successful war against the Turks. It is very remarkable and singular, that Peter's system of policy was preserved, prosecuted and enlarged, under the government of women; for his two succeffors who bore his name, fat not long upon the ruffian throne.

The modern hiftory of Ruffia is alfo principally marked by feveral revolutions, and thefe revolutions are again extremely different from events of that nature in the hiftory of other countries. In other countries thefe great changes have been attended with bloodfhed and civil wars; but in Ruffia they were all the work of one night or one day. The nation at large took little or no fhare at all in them; the court and the great men alone feem to have been anyways concerned; and the foldiers, efpecially the GUARDS, were always the principal actors. Now, though thefe revolutions in the throne produced no alterations in the body of the empire, yet I have thought it not proper tranfiently to pafs them over, not only becaufe it is in the nature of man to take an intereft in the fate of thofe who ftand fo high as fovereigns, particularly if it have any thing unufual in it; but likewife becaufe the ftudents of hiftory may form conclufions from fuch events concerning the character of the nation as well as of the fpirit of the government.

Peter died of a painful difeafe in 1725, without having appointed a succeffor, as he had a

right

right to do in virtue of the law of succession enacted by himself and ratified by the oath of his subjects. It seemed now to rest entirely on the nation, or its chiefs, to supply the vacancy of the throne, as the great men in Russia had constantly asserted their influence on the succession of their monarchs. Accordingly, on this, occasion several plans were framed concerning the succession. The principal personages had taken every possible precaution to have the emperor's death immediately announced to them; having, during the last days of his life, caused one of their servants to wait in the Imperial palace, in order to have notice of the event the instant it should happen. It was foreseen that Mentchikof would employ every effort to raise Catharine, the tzar's second consort, to the throne; that, in quality of her favourite, he might rule the helm of the state; but this Mentchikof was spurned at by most of the great men on account of his humble origin, and hated for his unbounded arrogance and avarice [*]. It was therefore

---

[*] Mentchikof was led by his avarice to frequent embezzlements and to commit many acts of oppression and injustice, which the tzar punished as well as he could by beating him heartily with his stick: but notwithstanding this he retained him in his employments. Peter I. when angry

fore the wiſh of theſe to remove both him and Catharine from the government, to aſſign the latter a convent, and the former Siberia for their abode, to proclaim the young prince Peter emperor, now nineteen years of age, and grandſon of Peter the Great, and during his minority to have the entire management of the adminiſtration, to diſmiſs the foreigners, of whom a great number, favoured by Peter, had been appointed to various ſtations in all the departments of government, to reſtore a variety of cuſtoms aboliſhed by the tzar, and in that view to repeal many of his ordinances and ſtatutes. This, I ſay, was the wiſh of moſt of the great men who

---

angry on ſimilar occaſions with the perſons in office, would ſay, that he thought it abſolutely impoſſible to prevent his countrymen from ſtriving to cheat; ſometimes adding, to a foreigner, " If you want to find a Ruſſian of honour and " probity, examine cloſely whether he has hair growing in " the palm of his hand; and, if you find none, ſay boldly " that he is a raſcal." — Peter I. at his death was only 53 years old. It is generally ſaid that he died of a ſuppreſſion of urine. Voltaire affirms, that he was deſirous to make a will, but that he was unable either to write or to dictate. The manuſcript memoirs of Magnan, on the contrary, inform us, that it is highly probable that he actually made that will; but, as it was agreeable neither to the tzaritza nor to Mentchikof, they came to the reſolution to ſuppreſs it.

conceived

conceived they had a right to speak their opinion on the subject of filling the vacant throne. It is probable, likewise, that this plan might have been brought to bear, if the authors and abettors of it had not been restrained by the excessive awe which all men had for Peter, while he breathed, from taking the smallest step to the execution of this project; being apprehensive, that if he should recover, and be informed of the design, they might be punished in his usual severe and inexorable manner. So much the more artful were the measures pursued by Mentchikof and his adherents for securing the succession to Catharine. The clergy and the soldiers were all that were necessary to be gained by them for promising themselves the desired success; and these were gained — by money, for Mentchikof had wisely in time availed himself of the opportunity of getting possession of the imperial treasure. Catharine likewise had, the day before Peter's death, an interview with Mentchikof and some other men in power, at which they promised her every assistance in her undertaking.

Immediately on the death of the tzar the great men of the nation assembled in the imperial palace at Petersburg; and scarcely were they met than Catharine appeared, with Mentchikof,

chikof, the duke of Holſtein, and ſome others in her train, and propoſed herſelf as EMPRESS. Indeed ſhe preſently after withdrew, in order, as was ſaid, to give the aſſembled nobles time to deliberate on the legitimacy of her claim to the throne; when much was ſaid on the circumſtance that Peter had left no will, and therefore that they might proceed to an election. But a part of the aſſembly, and particularly the heads of the clergy, had been won over; another part complied with the propoſal from fear *; and againſt the few who oppoſed it an appeal was made to the oral declaration of the late tzar, by which it was pretended, that he affirmed that he had cauſed Catharine to be ſolemnly crowned only that ſhe might hereafter ſucceed to the government. At length Mentchikof interrupted the conſultation by a word of command, at which the guards, whoſe concurrence had been for the greater part ſecured, for which no money had been ſpared, marched out, exclaiming: Long live our empreſs Catharine. During which ſhe preſented herſelf at the window to the populace; and now there was

* The officers of the guards, in the pay of Mentchikof, and diſperſed by him about the place of meeting, openly threatened to poignard any who ſhould endeavour to prevent the proclamation of Catharine as empreſs.

not one of the whole assembly who would have dared to shew any opposition in her presence. She was therefore declared empress; on which she promised to be the mother of the country, as Peter had been the father; and Mentchikof, to the great mortification of many of the nobles, who wished themselves in his place, had the satisfaction to see his project crowned with success [*]. Thus, for the first time, since Olga, who reigned in the tenth century, a woman sat upon the throne of Russia, a woman of obscure descent, by the most singular turns of fortune, raised to the exalted rank of an unlimited sovereign [†].

The history of Catharine's infancy is still covered with darkness and uncertainty; and the

---

[*] According to field-marshal Munich's account, Mentchikof, at the head of the guards, burst into the hall where the senators were sitting with the doors locked, consulting about the succession, and ordered Catharine to be proclaimed empress.

[†] Mentchikof at first shared the sovereign power which he had obtained for her with the empress; and it is a very striking circumstance, that in a period justly styled an enlightened age, the two personages at the head of the most extensive empire of the world could neither write nor read. The artful and treacherous Tolstoï managed almost all the affairs of the russian cabinet.

various and contradictory accounts of it would of themselves compose a volume; as even the year and place of her birth are not accurately ascertained *. Only thus much is extremely probable, that she was born a Livonian, and sprung from vulgar parents †, that she lost them when very young, was afterwards taken into the house of the provost Gluck at Marienburg, where she served as housemaid and nurse to the children, got acquainted with a soldier, with whom she was soon after married. But whether this soldier was obliged on the very wedding-day to join his regiment and make an abrupt departure, as the Russians were every day more closely investing Marienburg as enemies, and consequently whether Catharine as a bride fell into the hands of the conquerors, or whether she had already lived some time in wedlock, remains equally undecided. More authentic, however, is the account, that, after the conquest of Marienburg by the Russians, the provost Gluck presented himself to the russian

* By some accounts she was born in 1682, by others later, and even not till 1689.

† Some statements make her the daughter of a swedish quarter-master. By others we are told that she was an illegitimate daughter of a swedish lieutenant-colonel and a livonian female vassal.

general

general Scheremetof, the first in command, to beseech him to mitigate the calamities that threatened the town. Catharine was in company with Gluck, and by her beauty attracted the general's notice, who immediately took her with him home, furnished her with better cloaths, and treated her with great kindness. Mentchikof, who here saw Catharine, by his authority appropriated this part of the spoil to himself: but he enjoyed her not long. Peter, who happened once to see the fair stranger at Mentchikof's, was so struck with her, that he took her to himself, forbade Mentchikof to have any farther intimacy with her, gave her servants to attend her, and conferred on her the title "her grace." She was now baptized into the russian church [*], and was highly pleased with her new situation, made it her principal business to study Peter's character, that his love for her increased from day to day. She likewise frequently blessed Peter with children; and it is probable that he privately married her in 1707, but first publicly declared her to be his wife in 1711, instituted an order of knighthood in her honour, appointed her a

[*] She was originally brought up in the lutheran confession. In the opinion, however, of those who make Catharine a native Lithuanian, she was a catholic.

coronation with pompous ceremonies in 1724, and with his own hands placed the crown upon her head*. Such were the fortunes of this extraordinary woman. Catharine, as a fruitful mother, by sharing all dangers with the tzar, accompanying him on his travels, as in his second journey to Holland, and even attending him in war, taking the tenderest care of his health, which was none of the strongest, never betraying any symptoms of jealousy when other ladies were found amiable: in short, by gaining a thorough knowledge of his character, and bearing with his humours, by never meddling with government affairs, only desirous of being wife and mother, secured to her Peter's affection as long as he lived; and it is by no means improbable, that Peter himself, if he had been granted a longer life, would have declared her for his successor. The generality of the nation found not the least impropriety in Catharine's acceding to the vacant throne, as she had been Peter's wife for many years, and had been solemnly crowned empress. By a condescending, mild, and obliging deport-

* While Peter was performing this ceremony, Catharine embraced his knee, and kissed it. Peter immediately raised her up.

ment towards every one*, which she constantly preserved, a great part of the nation was moreover much prepossessed in her favour. The soldiers were particularly her friends, from her having been present in so many campaigns, from her having had a considerable hand in making the peace which the army, surrounded near the Pruth, obtained of the grand vizir, and having been the physician and saviour of great numbers of the wounded. Accordingly, the soldiers, on receiving the tidings of Peter's death, one and all cried out, If, however, our father be dead, our mother is still alive. Indeed, discontented persons were not wanting, who saw with extreme dislike, that a woman of such vulgar descent, who was not even a native Russian, had ascended the throne; yet the dissatisfaction of numbers of the great arose less from dislike to Catharine than from hatred to Mentchikof.

This man, too, born in a mean station, and elevated to be Peter's favourite †, enjoyed, indeed,

---

* Accordingly she endeavoured to provide for her fosterfather Gluck, and procured him a good situation, as well as conferred a number of benefits on all the persons of his family.

† If Mentchikof in his youth was not a pastry-cook, he was certainly one of the lowest menial servants at the tzarian court. Peter observing him to be a shrewd lad, took him among

deed, during the reign of this empress, the greatest respect, which was only in some degree lessened by the duke of Holstein.

CATHARINE, from the very commencement of her reign, conducted herself with the greatest benignity and gentleness, whereby she secured to herself still more the love and veneration of the generality of her subjects. She reduced the annual capitation-tax by one eighth, ordered the gibbets to be cut down which had been erected by Peter in great numbers throughout the country, had the bodies of the numerous persons he had executed, still lying unburied, interred; recalled the greater part of those who had in the late reign been banished to Siberia [*], paid the troops their arrears, restored to the Kozaks several of their privileges and immunities which had been wrested from them by Peter, and made

---

among the potefchnii, and Mentchikof was artful enough to gain so complete a knowledge of his master's humours and temper, that though Peter often treated him very harshly, by beating him, and several times imposing on him heavy penalties, yet Mentchikof contrived to keep himself in the tzar's favour to the day of his death; and this he did chiefly by admiring foreign customs, and helping to render the russian usages and manners ridiculous.

[*] Excepting the relations and friends of Peter's former wife.

no changes among the officers of ſtate. She thus attached to her the people, the army, and even moſt of the great families of the nation *. The attempts of two impoſtors, who ſeverally gave themſelves out for Peter's unfortunate ſon Alexey, were ſpeedily defeated, and the pretenders to the throne beheaded. The empire enjoyed during her reign the bleſſing of peace, which it had ſcarcely ever been able to do under Peter. But in the enjoyment of peace, neither the army nor the navy were neglected; on the contrary, both were put in the beſt condition †; and it was ſettled by treaty entered into by the government [1726] with the german emperor, that, in caſe of an attack, they ſhould reciprocally aſſiſt one another with an army of 30,000

---

* Catharine, however, who, during Peter's lifetime, had ſhewn ſo much courage, activity, and ardour, in the greateſt enterpriſes, ſoon diſdained to trouble herſelf with public buſineſs, and gave herſelf up entirely to luxury and pleaſure. She took on at once two new favourites, the young prince Sapieha, and a livonian gentleman named Lœwenwolden. Theſe two rivals equally ſtrove to pleaſe her, and alternately received proofs of her tenderneſs, without ſuffering their happineſs to be interrupted by the interference of jealouſy.

† The former was augmented to nearly one hundred and eighty thouſand men, and the latter conſiſted of twenty-ſix line of battle ſhips, fifteen frigates, one hundred and forty gallies, ſeveral ſmall tranſport veſſels, and fourteen thouſand ſailors.

men,

cerning the succession, was, that Peter Alexiévitch* should be her successor, and, till he attained his sixteenth year, to be under the tutelage of the princesses Anna and Elizabeth; the duke of Holstein, and the other members of the council †; making provision also for the casualty of the young emperor's dying without heirs. A second article of the will was, that the regency should endeavour to bring about a marriage between the young emperor and a daughter of prince Mentchikof. The will, moreover, even contained several proofs of Catharine's concern for her son-in-law the duke of Holstein.

The bounds of the empire were also enlarged under Catharine, by the homage paid her by the kubinskian Tartars, and the submission of a georgian prince to Russia.

That Catharine, notwithstanding she could neither write nor read, had a great natural understanding, a very high degree of prudence, and a perfectly sound judgment, is manifest from the whole tenor of her reign. Yet, perhaps, if she had lived longer, that would have happened

* Alexey's son, and grandson of Peter.
† This council, or college of private advice, as it was called, was established under Catharine, and consisted originally of seven members, whose business it was to look after foreign affairs.

which has often been afferted, namely, that fhe would have been detruded from the throne. At leaft, there was never wanting a great number of malcontents all the while fhe reigned. The impenetrable veil of obfcurity that concealed her origin, the hiftory of her earlier days, ere fhe was acknowledged by Peter as his wife, were a ftumbling-block to many; and papers were frequently handed about, in which fhe was very irreverently mentioned. Already, in the fecond year of her reign, fhe felt herfelf under the neceffity of threatening to punifh with death all fuch as fhould fpeak of her family in difrefpectful terms*. The following judgment, therefore, paffed upon her by a german author of that time, who was well informed of the circumftances of Catharine's life, feems accurately to fuit her. " The gratitude and kindnefs," fays he,

* All at once arrived at Peterfburg a brother of Catharine, whom fhe ordered to take the name of count Skavronfky. He brought with him his wife and three children. What made this circumftance the more aftonifhing was, that it had always been believed that the emprefs had no knowledge of any of her relations. His children were two boys and a girl. The emprefs married the latter to her favourite Sapieha. Several authors have mentioned that the tzar knew the brother of Catharine; but, according to the manufcript memoirs already often cited, this is a miftake.

VOL. II.   o   " which

" which this princess discovers towards all man-
" kind, particularly towards her former acquaint-
" ance, her resignation in adverse affairs, her
" unabating sollicitudes for the health of her
" spouse, and her humanity in always advising
" the tzar to gentle and temperate measures *,
" are such laudable qualities, as in some degree
" to efface the blemish on her birth, and to
" atone for *other fatalities.*"

The succession and the marriage of Peter II. †
with Mentchikof's daughter, were the two sole
items of Catharine's will which Mentchikof was
anxious to execute. Indeed, numbers of the
great would have been glad to see Peter deprived
of the succession, partly because it was highly
probable that Mentchikof would continue to act
the same part under the new monarch which he
had begun under the former, partly because
they were afraid that Peter II. would make his
resentment fall heavy on those who had assented
to the sentence of death passed on his father.
Mentchikof, however, took his measures with

* She wished to persuade Peter not to proceed with such
severity even against Alexey. She kept Alexey's son, the
young Peter, whom she nominated her successor, as her own
son, and took care of his education like a mother.
† He was born in 1715.

so much prudence, that the imperial heir, now twelve years old, immediately received homage as emperor. If, while Peter I. was alive, he stood close by the throne, and had a great influence in the government during the reign of Catharine, as his sphere of operation was only somewhat bounded by the duke of Holstein, still greater opportunities now presented themselves to him of having the entire management of the administration during the emperor's minority, as the expected marriage of his daughter with the young monarch would probably place him and his family for ever in close relationship with the reigning house. The most sanguine wishes could require no more. He even thought himself so sure of his business, that he now threw off all restraint, and in his whole behaviour shewed himself as already the father-in-law of the emperor. In order to have the prince constantly about him, to conduct him absolutely by his will, and in the monarch of the empire to form to himself an obedient son-in-law, he took him home to his mansion. No one seemed able or bold enough to oppose in the smallest degree what Mentchikof did and resolved to do. But he stood not long on this pinnacle of power. Just when he thought himself most secure, the

hour

hour of his fall arrived *. Several of the first families of the empire had ever viewed his prosperity with envious eyes; and as Mentchikof's pride and arrogance constantly kept pace with his advancement, as he exercised his power with the most absolute despotism, the number and the hatred of his enemies increased in an equal degree.

* The duke of Holstein and his minister were not the sole enemies of Mentchikof: he had a great number of such as were implacable and secret, among whom was Ostermann, the most assiduous of his flatterers. Ostermann, born in Westphalia, the son of a lutheran pastor, had acquired the confidence of Peter I. and arrived at the high post of vice-chancellor; but, although he had time enough to accustom himself to the manners of the Russians, he could never forgive Mentchikof for addressing him always in an arrogant and supercilious tone, and often threatening him with the knoot, and with Siberia. Being resolved to have his revenge, he had seized the favourable moment for prompting the favourite to take the imprudent step that accelerated his downfall, that of declaring the young grandduke heir of the empire, to prevent the duke of Holstein from acceding to the crown on the death of the tzaritza. Ostermann had been secretary to count Shafirof, the most able minister of Peter I. He had the ingratitude to cabal against Shafirof, and to cause his dismission; as he likewise procured that of marshal Munich. In short, in 1741 Elizabeth banished Ostermann to the borders of the Frozen-ocean, and there he died in 1747. His son was vice-chancellor under Catharine II.

Attempts

Attempts had often been made, but in vain, to work his downfall: they now succeeded *. A youth of one of the most respectable families of the empire, Ivan Dolgoruki, the daily companion of the young emperor, very soon found an opportunity to instil prejudices against Mentchikof in the mind of Peter, by representing to him that this man was allowed to assume too much of the monarch, the latter having properly no will of his own, but was entirely ruled by that of

* The chiefs of the party were Tolstoï, Butturlin, and the count de Vier, a portugueze adventurer, made minister of police in Russia, and brother-in-law to Mentchikof, much against his will. The count de Vier, more known in Russia under the name of Antone Manuelovitch, was midshipman on board of a merchant-ship when Peter I. took him into his service. That prince placed him afterwards at the head of the department of police, in which post de Vier acquired great reputation. It was not safe to travel in any part of Russia, except by caravans, the roads were so infested by robbers, often protected by the lords of the domain. De Vier found means of repressing these disorders; in reward for which service Peter I. gave him the title of count, and made him marry the sister of Mentchikof. The secret meetings of the party were held at the house of a Piémontese, named count Santi. This count Santi had been involved in France in the conspiracy of the prince of Cellamare. Being thrown into the bastile, whence he had the dexterity to escape, he went over to Russia, and there became master of the ceremonies at court.

Mentchikof. Dolgoruki's infinuations operated with the fpeedier effect, as Peter felt no fondnefs for Maria Mentchikof, who was defigned to be his bride, and openly confeffed that he wifhed to be rid of her. Mentchikof, who had happily outftood even the boifterous temper of Peter the Great, had been all-powerful under Catharine, notwithftanding the duke of Holftein's machinations againft him, and was afterwards the auftere and imperious father-in-law of Peter II. was now overthrown, and obliged with his whole family, of which even the betrothed wife of the young emperor formed a part, to depart for Berefof in Siberia*, 1727. By this ftroke of fortune all his plans of greatnefs were at once defeated, and the treafures he had accumulated † poured into the imperial coffers, from which the greater part had been furreptitioufly taken.

The

---

* Tolftoï was exiled to Siberia, where he died. De Vier had the fame lot, after having received above a hundred ftrokes of the knoot. Butturlin and fome others were banifhed to various places. Mentchikof died in his exile at Berefof in 1729.

† Confifting of nine millions of rubles in bank notes and obligations, one million in cafh, 105 lb. of gold utenfils, 420 lb. of filver plate, and precious ftones to the value of about a million. If we reckon, befides, the confiderable eftates in land which he poffeffed, his palace and the furniture of

it,

The family of Dolgoruki now took the place of the degraded favourite; and so completely, that even a young lady of that house was selected to be the young Peter's bride instead of Maria Mentchikof, who was forced to share in her father's lamentable fate, and from the expectation of ascending the greatest throne in the world, was plunged in the deepest distress. Catharine Dolgoruki made so strong an impression on Peter the very first time he saw her, that he asked her hand of her father, and Catharine was soon after publicly affianced to the emperor.

The coronation was fixed for the beginning of the year 1728, and Peter travelled from Petersburg to Mosco for that purpose. Mosco and the adjacent country, which he frequently traversed on the hunting parties, with which the Dolgorukies amused him, pleased him so much, that he had an intention to transfer the residence hither from Petersburg: a design by which he attached to him all the Russians of the

---

it, we shall be the more surprised at the treasure which Mentchikof was able to amass, as Peter was very far from being liberal to his favourites, and had often punished Mentchikof for his embezzlements by confiscating a part of his property.

old ftamp, who had an antipathy to the new city, the building whereof had been very burdenfome to them, and by its becoming the refidence had detracted much from Mofco.

Peter was much beloved by the nation in general; and at firft he greatly raifed their expectations. His capacities were indeed far above the ordinary level; Catharine I. had taken as much care of his education as if he had been her fon; and Oftermann drew up a plan for the conduct of it*, which, as is the cafe with all

---

* It will be worth while to infert here fome particulars of this plan. Oftermann made it a main concern, and to be kept conftantly in view, that it was a *reigning fovereign* to be inftructed. National hiftories, politics, legiflation, functions of the magiftrate, the rights of nations in war and peace, as well as the military art itfelf, were the main objects of this inftruction; together with which, mathematics, natural knowledge, &c. were to be taught: the leffons were to be rather in the didactic method, that the emperor might be fpared much reading and writing. — For the religious part of his education Theophanes laid down the plan; and it is indeed more excellent than could have been expected of thofe times. "Let the being of God," he fays, "be proved to the emperor from the exiftence of the creatures, the foul, the confcience; and the neceffity of a life after death from the divine juftice, as the fortunes of men in this world cannot always be made fuitable to their actions. Let at leaft as much attention be paid to the *duties of life* as to the dogmas of faith."

plans and projects of this nature, if in many respects it had been but half executed, Peter must have been modelled into one of the most active, enlightened, and best sovereigns that ever added lustre to a diadem. It must be freely confessed, however, that it was not the intention of those who wanted to have a hand in the business, especially the Dolgorukies, to make of him a sovereign who saw with his own eyes and was guided by his own sentiments. Their aim was to draw off the young monarch from the serious affairs of his station; and they succeeded in their endeavours, by inspiring him with an immoderate passion for the sports of the field. Peter frequently suffered many days to pass successively without ever being seen in Mosco, but was continually at one or the other of his hunting-seats; and his eagerness for this pastime was increasing from day to day. It is easily conceivable that this frequent and violent exercise was not propitious to the health of the young emperor, his bodily strength not being yet arrived at maturity, that it weakened him too much, and was the cause that the disease by which he was attacked brought on the dissolution of his frame*. Peter II. departed this
life

---

* Ostermann, with tears in his eyes, observed once to Munich: " The course they pursue with the emperor
" might

life in the night between the 29th and 30th of January 1730, at Mosco, of the small-pox, in the arms of Ostermann. With him was extinct the male race of the family Romanof, with him the fairest hope of the nation, the hope of hereafter being governed by a wise and benign sovereign*, for which in reality he discovered particular dispositions, sunk into the grave. — All Russia since has termed his reign its happiest period for a hundred years. No war with any neighbouring country, during his reign, wasted its men and money. Every one might quietly and securely enjoy what belonged to him. Mosco particularly had great expectations from this reign, as Peter seemed so much disposed to

---

" might tempt one to think they intended to kill him." A ukase that appeared in 1739 in express terms charges the Dolgorukies with having undermined the young emperor's constitution by the fatigues of hunting.

* The day after his accession to the throne he wrote to his sister: " It having pleased God to call me in my tender " youth to be emperor of all Russia, my principal care shall " be to acquire the reputation of a good sovereign, by " governing my people in righteousness and in the fear of " God, by hearkening to the complaints of the poor and " innocent under oppression that fly to me for refuge, by " granting them relief; and, after the laudable example " of Vespasian, letting no man go sorrowful from me." What a happiness for Russia, if this emperor, always thinking and acting in this manner, had attained to an extreme old age!

make

make this residence of the ancient tzars the place of his abode. But whether his predilection for Mosco and his indifference to Petersburg might not perhaps have occasioned under his government less attention to have been had to the fleet and maritime affairs with which Petersburg was so closely connected, and whether the national consequence which Russia now maintained among the states of Europe might not thus have been lost, was much to be dreaded, since both the army and navy are said to have been sensibly affected by the emperor's absence. It was likewise easy to foresee that the influence and importance of foreigners, which had risen very high in Russia from the time of Peter the Great, would have greatly diminished under Peter II. Peter himself was indeed by no means indisposed towards foreigners; he promised several advantages to such as were willing to come to Russia; but the native Russians, in conjunction with the Dolgorukies, would, by insensible degrees, have wrought an alteration in his mind, and have inspired him with a stronger partiality for the russian nation, and for russian manners: for the great of the old russian families always regarded with jealousy the authority which some of the foreigners had acquired in the country.

The

The Dolgoruki family would undoubtedly have entirely guided the helm of state, if they had once fully effected the projected union with the reigning prince by the marriage of Catharine with Peter. But their hopes and schemes were presently defeated by the premature death of the monarch. Indeed, after that event the young Dolgoruki made one more attempt to ensure to himself and his family the influence on the affairs of the empire. He had forged a testament, which he pretended to be the last will of Peter II., in which the Catharine Dolgoruka, betrothed to Peter, was declared successor. With his sword drawn he left the imperial chamber, proceeded to the hall, where the great men were assembled, and exclaimed: Long live the empress Dolgoruka — but, finding that no one joined him, he sheathed his sword, and — concealed the testament. Even his father, on seeing that Ivan had fetched a party of the guards to him, in the hope of effectuating his design, called it a foolish trick, and sent him home.

This testament, therefore, being declared invalid, the succession to the throne was to be decided by that still extant of Catharine I. and not annulled by Peter II. In this it was ordained that, in case Peter should die without heirs,

heirs, Anne Duchefs of Holftein, and her pofterity; on failure of them the princefs Elizabeth * and her pofterity fhould fucceed. Anne,
indeed, had been dead ever fince 1728, but had
left behind her a prince. He therefore would
be now, according to the purport of that will,
the legitimate heir. But the duke of Holftein
and his confort had fhortly after Catharine's
death thought fit to take their leave of Ruffia,
where Mentchikof rendered their abode extremely irkfome, and return to their poffeffions
of Holftein-Gottorp in Germany; and the council, which on Peter the fecond's death directed
the fucceffion and was averfe to foreigners,
would have paid no regard to the young prince
of Holftein, even if his father had been ftill in
Ruffia, much lefs was any notice taken of him
now that he lived in Germany †. — Next to
Anne

* Second daughter of Peter I. and Catharine. The eldeft was married to the duke of Mecklenburg. Anna Ivanovna was a widow without children. Oftermann was the means of bringing about her election; becaufe, as he had formerly taught her to read, he was in hopes of having confiderable influence with her.

† Indeed he was only mentioned for the fake of calling to mind that both he and the princefs Elizabeth were the offspring of a double adultery, and therefore both of them ought for ever to be excluded from the throne. It was ob-
fer

Anne and her posterity, by Catharine's last will, the princess Elizabeth was to succeed: but that princess remained entirely inactive on the vacancy of the throne, though her physician Lestocq took all possible pains to persuade her to put in her claim to the succession. It had hitherto been her sole desire to live at her ease, exempt from all concern in the affairs of government, and only to pursue her pleasures.

The council, the senate, the general officers, and other persons of distinction had assembled immediately on the demise of the emperor, in order to consult on the proper measures to be taken in regard to the succession. On this occasion no notice at all was taken of Catharine's testament. The council proceeded to appoint an election. The male line of the Romanofs was extinct in the person of Peter II.; yet, besides Elizabeth, Peter the first's daughter, three daughters of tzar Ivan, step-brother and partner in the government with Peter I. were still alive. The eldest lived at Petersburg in a state of separation from her troublesome husband, the duke of Mecklenburg; the second, who

---

served that when Peter I. married Catharine, the first husband of that princess and the empress Evdokhia Lapukhin were still living.

had been married to the duke of Courland, lived as a widow, from 1711, in Mittau; the third was at Petersburg, still unmarried. Of these three princesses the council was to elect one *. The eldest sister was not agreeable to them on account of her having a foreign and turbulent prince to her husband; and therefore the second, ANNA IVANOVNA, dowager duchess of Courland, was nominated empress of Russia.

In the meantime, though the hopes of the Dolgorukies of getting the government into their hands under Peter had proved abortive, they nevertheless continued to form a powerful party in the council and in the senate, as the chief counsellors of the empire, and were therefore striving to procure themselves an influence during the future reign. As now not only they but several other of the great nobles viewed with jealousy the respect in which foreigners were held; and apprehending, moreover, that they might retain their consequence likewise in Anna's

---

* Peter's first wife, Evdokhia, who had been banished by her husband to a cloister, out of which she was liberated by Peter II. her grandson, seemed to have a right to the throne. But she discovered not the smallest inclination to make it appear. The conventual life and her misfortunes had given a turn to her mind that rendered her altogether unfit for swaying a sceptre.

reign, a plan was formed to tie up the hands of the future sovereign: by a capitulation, that all things now might proceed according to the inclination of the council, and the sovereign be in a manner merely the executrix of its resolutions, the sitting was closed. " The general welfare," said Galitzin in a speech delivered on the occasion to the assembly, " requires that *the supreme au-*
" *thority*, and the unlimited power of the sove-
" reign, by which Russia has hitherto suffered
" so much, and which is supported by the fo-
" reigners that are brought in, should be *cir-*
" *cumscribed*, and that the crown should be
" conferred upon the new sovereign Anna only
" *under certain conditions.*"

His proposal was received with approbation; and the following conditions were agreed to:
" The high privy council continues, and the
" new empress governs solely by its resolves;
" she cannot of her own motion either wage
" war or make peace; cannot of herself lay any
" new tax on the people; cannot alone dispose
" of any important office; cannot inflict capital
" punishment on any nobleman or confiscate
" his estates, unless he be convicted of the
" crime laid to his charge; cannot arbitrarily
" give away and alienate any lands pertaining
" to the crown; cannot marry or nominate an
" heir,

" heir, without firſt obtaining the conſent of the
" council." — To theſe this ſingular article was
added, that Anne ſhould bring her favourite,
the chamberlain von Biren, with her into Ruſſia:

By this means, therefore, a great revolution
in the form of government in Ruſſia was in‑
tended. The authority of the ruſſian ſovereigns
hitherto perfectly abſolute was to be exceedingly
diminiſhed and confined. Ruſſia's ruler, ſo far
from being ſamoderjets or autocrator, was now
to be reduced to a ſimple executor of the reſolu‑
tions of the council, and Ruſſia's monarchy
converted into an ariſtocracy.

An embaſſy compoſed of three members of
the council * was diſpatched to Mittau to inform
the ducheſs of her election, and at the ſame
time of the capitulation annexed. Anne would
probably have heſitated at ſubſcribing to the capi‑
tulation, and would perhaps have abſolutely re‑
fuſed to accept the crown upon ſuch terms, had

* Of whom one was prince Vaſſilly Lukovitch Dolgoruky,
who had been the ſucceſsful lover of Anna Ivanovna, and
was doubtleſs in hopes of becoming ſo again. — On enter‑
ing the apartment of Anna Ivanovna, Dolgoruky found
with her a man rather meanly dreſſed, to whom he made
a ſign to retire. As the man did not ſtir, Dolgoruky took
him by the arm to enforce his hint. Anne ſtopped him.
This man was Erneſt John Biren, and thus it was that
the ruin of the Dolgoruky family was occaſioned.

she not been already made acquainted with them from the account sent her by lieutenant-general Yagujinsky. In this message he at the same time advised her to sign the capitulation for the present, and when she should once be empress to revoke what she had done, and that he would from that moment take measures accordingly. Tranquilized by this letter, Anne put her signature to the instrument, and was declared empress. In the mean time the rumour spread concerning a capitulation proposed to the empress, excited no small sensation in the public mind, which the opposite party exerted themselves to increase and to employ to their purpose. It was reported that the Dolgorukies wished to confirm, by this capitulation, the influence they had acquired under Peter II. to the detriment of the nation. The other noble families, who had no relation in the council, were naturally afraid that the government would now pass into the hands of some families who would only take care to provide for their relations, whereas it might reasonably be expected that an unlimited monarch would look chiefly to merit in his promotions, as Peter had all along done. This argument operated particularly on the guards, among whom were several of the country nobles. The nation in general,

hitherto

hitherto accustomed to be ruled by an absolute sovereign, soon made it plainly understood, that they had rather obey one emperor than eight masters. At length a petition was presented to the empress, signed by several hundred noblemen, in which she was prayed to accept of the government in such manner as her predecessors on the russian throne had always possessed it, to unite the council with the senate, by being absolute and unlimited ruler. Anne was never so much inclined to acquiesce to any petition as to this, which, in such complete conformity with her wishes, promised to free her from the controul of the council. She therefore ordered the council to be convened; and, in the presence of those who had presented the petition, audibly and deliberately read the capitulation, asking at every separate article: Is this the will of the nation? — No, was unanimously answered by all who were not members of the council. Upon which Anne tore the act of capitulation to pieces in the face of the whole assembly, saying: " Then there is no farther need of this paper." A manifesto was immediately published, declaring, that the empress ascended the throne of her ancestors, *not by election but in virtue of her hereditary right.* It had formerly been the practice to promise in the oath of fealty to be

true

true to the empress and the country; in the new oath * now framed, and required to be taken by the subjects, not a word was said of the country, but allegiance was sworn to Anne as *unlimited sovereign*, with full maintenance of all the rights appertaining to sovereignty that were already introduced *or should be introduced in future*.

Thus Anne in a short time freed herself from the ties in which she was intended to be bound†.

Biren

* " On our arrival in Mosco," it is said in the preamble to the form of the second oath of allegiance, " though all our subjects took the oath of fidelity to us and the empire, yet, as afterwards these same faithful subjects all unanimously besought us to take upon us the sovereignty in our empire as our forefathers from time immemorial had done, we, therefore, in compliance with this humble and loyal request, have ordered a new form of oath to be prepared and printed, by which all our subjects are to swear fealty to us as their sovereign lady, and thereupon to kiss the cross."

† Ostermann had the greatest share in annulling the capitulation. Under the pretext of indisposition he neglected to attend the council assembled on Peter's death, refused his assent to the capitulation, complimenting at the same time the great men, by telling them that they best knew what was for the benefit of the country, while he was exerting every effort to counteract the council, and thus acquired the favour of Anne to a superlative degree.— It proved, likewise, of great assistance to Anne, that

the

Biren came to the russian court, and took possession of the place near her which Mentchikof had filled near Catharine.

The newly erected council, distinct from the senate, was now abolished, and again a directing senate appointed, as under Peter the Great. Anne, however, afterwards established a cabinet to superintend the affairs of greatest importance, consisting of no more than three persons, and in which Ostermann's voice was of peculiar weight. The senate had now only to decide upon less important matters, and had in fact very little to do.

The election of a king of Poland, a treaty to be concluded with Persia, and a war with the Turks, were the affairs that occupied Anne in the first years of her reign.

Peter I. had supported the election of Augustus II. to the crown of Poland; and the Poles experienced already under Anne, that their *free* choice might henceforth be very much *limited* by the neighbouring courts, particularly by that of Russia. Though the french ministry [1733] made great exertions to reinstate on the

---

the clergy were not drawn in to approve of the project of the capitulation; and, as their opinion had not been consulted, they declined to support it.

polish throne Staniflaus Lefchinfky father-in-law to Louis XV. and though Staniflaus also found a great number of friends and supporters of his election in Poland, yet Ruffia and Auftria so powerfully affifted the caufe of the other candidate, Auguftus elector of Saxony *, that he at laft got the better of his rival, and became king of Poland, under the name of Auguftus III. The partizans of king Staniflaus, who had retreated with him to Dantzik, were obliged to fubmit to the Ruffians; Staniflaus himfelf was reduced to the neceffity of faving himfelf by flight, and Ruffia took a decided fuperiority in conducting the election of Auguftus. France, who faw with great difpleafure a power arifing in the north of Europe that in time might render doubtful the confequence fhe had hitherto maintained in this quarter of the globe; France, whofe plan to give Poland a king devoted to her interefts was now entirely defeated, fought to ftir up a dangerous neighbour to Ruffia in Sweden, and that the influence of France was great at Stockholm has frequently fince been feen.

* In this view Anne fent troops to the Rhine againft France — but before they could difplay their courage there a peace was made.

Peter

Peter the Great, as we have already observed, had extended the confines of his empire on the side of Persia. But it was very soon found that this enlargement of the borders was no substantial acquisition to the country. In the first place, in order to preserve them, it was involved in an expensive and tedious war, and these scenes of devastation must probably be often renewed; secondly, the newly acquired provinces, even in peace, required a very considerable garrison; and, as the climate of those parts did not agree with the Russians, a multitude of soldiers were constantly falling victims to disease *. Anne therefore opened a negotiation with the shah of Persia, promising to restore to him the conquered countries, if in return he would accord to her subjects some advantages to their commerce. They at length came to terms; and Russia [1735] made a formal surrender of all her persian possessions, for which the russian merchants obtained mercantile privileges to a considerable extent in the territories belonging to Persia. — On this occasion the empress also concluded a defensive treaty with the shah against the Turks,

* It is computed that, from the first taking possession of these persian provinces, in 1724, no less than 130,000 men had perished there.

with whom Russia was desirous of forming an alliance.

The peace which Peter, when surrounded by the Turks, had been obliged to sign on the borders of the Pruth, the evacuation of Azof, the demolition of the fortifications at Taganrok, by which Russia was excluded from all the benefits of trade on the Euxine, the refusal of the porte to grant the imperial title to the monarch of Russia, the incursions of the krimean and other Tartars, acknowledging the turkish supremacy, into the russian dominions, in which they ravaged large districts, and carried away many captives into bondage: all these circumstances together had already occasioned Peter to meditate a new war with the porte. In prosecution of this design, he strongly fortified the principal places of his empire in the neighbourhood of Turkey, furnished them with provision and military stores, and thus completely armed for war. But he died on the eve of it; and under Catharine I. and Peter II. the execution of the plan was no farther attempted. Anne, however, revived the idea; entertaining the greater hopes of succeeding in this enterprize, as she now could rely on 30,000 auxiliaries from the emperor of Germany, and had, besides, drawn the Turks, now at peace with Russia, into a war against Persia, and

and therefore already employed them on that side.

The Tartars, under the protection and supremacy of the porte, had recently again given occasion for fresh complaints on the part of Russia, by their predatory inroads upon the russian territory, in which they carried off men and cattle. The porte replied with the ordinary excuses, that it was utterly impossible to keep a restraint on these Tartars: an excuse which, indeed, could only be offered by the turkish government; and Russia, therefore, thought herself justified in chastising herself this breach of good neighbourhood. In 1735 a russian corps marched into the Krim, and ravaging a part of the country, killed a good number of Tartars; but, having ventured too far without a sufficient stock of provisions, were obliged to retreat, and sustained so great a loss in men, that what they had accomplished bore no proportion to this misfortune.

However, the almost total failure of this first attempt, which had cost the Russians ten thousand men, by no means deterred that court from adhering to the plan of subduing the Turks and Tartars. Count Munich, afterwards so famous in the modern history of Russia, was appointed to assert the honour of the russian arms against the Turks, who, since the peace of the Pruth,

had

had no very favourable opinion of ruffian valour, and to chaftife the Tartars. After he had conquered Dantzik, in quality of field-marfhal, and thereby fecured the crown to Auguftus III. he was fent into the Ukraine with the commiffion to take meafures for chaftifing the piratical Tartars for their ravages committed on the ruffian territory. From the Ukraine he proceeded [1736] into the peninfula of the Krimea. The Tartars, lefs fitted for fighting in the open field than for predatory excurfions and fudden attacks, fuffered the ruffian troops to advance unmolefted, thinking themfelves fafe behind their entrenchments, denominated the lines of the Krim *, from any

* Thefe lines extend about fix englifh miles in length from the fea of Azof to the Euxine, and are intended to protect the Krim from any attack on the land-fide. There is but one paffage through them, and that is the road from Perekop, which city and fortrefs lie within the line. Along the line are towers furnifhed with cannon. The ditch is of confiderable depth, the height of the ramparts from the bottom of the ditch to the top of the breaftwork is 70 feet, and the breaftwork is of proportionable folidity. The Tartars held thefe ramparts, in the conftruction of which fome thoufand men were employed for feveral years, to be impregnable. Peter had already intended to erect a fimilar line of forts in the Ukraine, againft the frequent attacks of the Tartars; but the defign was not completed till 1732. It terminates on one end at the Dniepr, and on the other at the Donetz.

attack

attack of the Ruffians. But entrenchments of that kind were unable to refift the impetuofity of ruffian troops. They were furmounted; the Tartars repulfed; and a great part of the Krimea lay at the mercy of the conquerors. In the month of June they entered the krimean fortrefs of Perekop. That the ruffian troops now repaid the devaftations committed by the Tartars in the empire, by defolating and carrying off whatever fell under their power, needs no particular mention. It was not, therefore, furprifing that they found it impoffible to remain in a country where thofe that fled endeavoured to fpread defolation as they went, for the fake of difabling their purfuers to overtake them; and where it is ufual for the conqueror himfelf, to make the whole of his warfare to confift in plundering, devaftation, and fpoil. Accordingly, whatever the army was in want of, muft be fetched from the Ukraine, which was attended with extreme difficulty; for which reafon, Munich at length found himfelf under the neceffity, towards autumn, of withdrawing with his troops by the fhorteft way to the Ukraine, in order there, where provifions at leaft were to be had, to go into winter-quarters, in which, however, they were very frequently infefted by the Tartars. While Munich was in the Krim, endeavouring

to

to chaſtiſe the Tartars for their depredations, Laſcy had proceeded with another army againſt Azof for ſeizing the protecting ſovereignty of the Tartars from the paramount Turks. The attack proved ſucceſsful; and on the firſt of July the fort of Azof had already ſubmitted to his arms.

The grand vizir had himſelf courteouſly treated the ruſſian ambaſſador recalled from Conſtantinople by his court, and the porte in general wiſhed to be able to avoid a war with Ruſſia; as Ruſſia, however, would not liſten to any accommodation, the Turks began to arm, recruited the garriſons in the ſeveral forts, cauſed a fleet to be equipped in the Euxine, and put the army in a proper condition. The porte continued, neverthelefs, to employ every means, even by having recourſe to the mediation of Auſtria, for preſerving peace with Ruſſia; but as ſhe could not be brought to make voluntary ſacrifices, the mediation of Auſtria proved of no avail, and Ruſſia demanded of the latter 30,000 men, as auxiliaries in virtue of the treaty ſubſiſting between the two powers. Auſtria, however, at preſent thought it better to contend with her whole force againſt the Ottomans, than merely to ſend auxiliary troops to the Ruſſians, and thereby ſtrengthen their power. She expected in the former caſe that it would be

more

more easy for her to conquer something from the Turks, whereas in the latter it seemed only furnishing Russia with the means of extending her conquests. The porte, already apprehensive that Austria would supply its inveterate enemy with auxiliaries, was now thrown into consternation on learning that the former power intended to become a principal in the war, by which she had to engage with another adversary, whose forces, under the conduct of prince Eugene, had been so formidable to her only a few years before.

As, however, Russia and Austria spoke in a lofty tone to the porte, the latter thought it was at any rate better to stake on the fortune of war what her enemies wanted her to surrender to their ambition, than voluntarily make such sacrifices as were inconsistent with her honour and safety; and as Russia, withal, shewed so little disposition to peace, the porte began to arm for a campaign [1737]; and the Russians and Austrians, with combined forces, threatened to shake the ottoman empire.

The russian army, having now supplied the loss it had sustained in the former campaign by forty thousand new recruits, undertook, in the course of this year, the conquest of Otchakof, under the orders of count Munich, while the

troops

troops commanded by Lascy entered the Krimea. Otchakof submitted, in which a garrison was placed by the conqueror; the Krim was desolated; and this was all the advantage that accrued from the campaign, for which Russia sacrificed about fifty thousand of her veteran troops; and the army was obliged to return to take up its winter-quarters in the Ukraine. Wars that are attended with no alteration in the state of nations should occupy but a short space in history. The Russians, on all sides victorious, conquerors of Moldavia, masters of Azof on the Palus Mæotis, and of Otchakof on the Euxine, were glad to purchase peace by the sacrifice of their conquests.

The great expectations that had been raised from the united efforts of two such empires as Russia and Austria were entirely disappointed. It seems to be ordained, that the russian and austrian arms, in conjunction against one common foe, should perform no mighty deeds. This was confirmed in the turkish war of which we are speaking; it often afterwards proved to be the case in the seven years' war, as well as in that which Catharine II. and Joseph II. carried on in alliance against the porte. It must be owned, however, that field-marshal Munich's hatred to Austria contributed in no small degree

to

to the little fuccefs of the auftrian arms in this conflict, which hindered him from acting on the fame plan with the auftrian generals. Indeed, excepting in the capture of Otchakof, he remained inactive during the whole campaign. Thus the Turks were enabled to prefs with their entire force upon the Auftrians, and even there to break their ranks with the greater eafe, as the commanders were at variance among themfelves, and jealous of each other. The confequence of all this, therefore, was, that the two combined courts prefented mutual complaints, each of the generals of the other, and particularly from the cabinet of Vienna accufations were conftantly coming forth againft Munich. But he as often eafily juftified himfelf to his fovereign, by making it appear to her, that if the campaign had not been attended with any brilliant fuccefs, the blame was due to the auftrian generals. The Turks took advantage of this difunion between the leaders on either fide, as well as of the inactivity thence arifing of the hoftile armies, by gaining various advantages over the Auftrians. The turkifh foldiery afcribing thefe, which in truth had their fource in thofe diffentions, to their own bravery alone, were therefore rifing in fpirits from day to day, and more zealous and active for the continuation of the war. The porte

porte recalled the ambassador whom they had sent to the congress which was to be held at Nemirof in Poland, though at the same time giving to understand, that they might hearken to terms of pacification with Russia, if she would agree, without the concurrence of the emperor, to put all things in their former state, by evacuating Azof, and Otchakof, the conquests she had made. As Russia, however, was not inclined to accede to either the one or the other, the controversy was again left to the decision of arms. Munich, in the ensuing campaign [1738] was assiduous in his marches, convinced the Turks of the superiority of the russian troops over theirs; but on the whole effected little.

General Lascy had again undertaken a hostile expedition into the Krimea. But here, likewise, no real advantage was gained; men and cattle were harrassed by tedious marches in a ravaged, desolated country, in which numbers of them died by fatigue; the people were even frequently in danger of perishing with hunger; and, after committing horrible depredations and havoc, were forced to retreat. The russian arms did not seem actually tending to success till the following campaign. [1739.] Marshal Munich, having drawn the whole army together at Kief, crossed the Bogue, completely routed the Turks in a pitched battle

near

near Stavutſhan, took in Auguſt the fortreſs of Khotyim, paſſed over the Pruth, made himſelf maſter of Yaſſy, the capital of Moldavia, and had the ſatisfaction of compelling the whole of that territory to ſubmit to the empreſs Anne. Leaving Moldavia, he repaſſed the Pruth, and made preparations for the capture of Bender; but, while he was ſending diſpatches to Peterſ- burg, with accounts of one victory after another, and all his enterpriſes ſeemed favoured by fortune, circumſtances had ſuddenly changed. Though Munich's campaign had this time been ſo brilliant, and the injury he had done to the Turks by the conqueſt of the fertile Moldavia ſo great, that even his ſoldiers thought themſelves ſufficiently paid for the toils of the campaign by pillaging the country, yet little or nothing was atchieved by the auſtrian allies. Reciprocal rivalſhips among the commanders, and envy at the ſucceſs of the ruſſian arms, fruſtrated all their enterpriſes. In addition to this, contagious diſeaſes broke out in the auſtrian camp. Moreover, the emperor Charles VI. lay dangerouſly ill, ſo that his recovery was doubtful; and his daughter Maria Thereſa wiſhed for nothing more earneſtly, than to ſee an end to the turkiſh war, that peace might be preſerved on that ſide, ſince it was extremely probable that ſhe would ſhortly have

ſeveral

several enemies to encounter. The auſtrian chieftains, therefore, made overtures of peace to the Turks; and, contrary to all expectation, the articles agreed on between the porte and Auſtria were ſigned at Belgrade on the firſt of September 1739. Every thing remained on the former footing; and the grand expectations which Auſtria had entertained from this war, were rendered entirely abortive. Inſtead of having made new conqueſts, ſhe was obliged to reſtore Belgrade, her rampart of Hungary againſt the Turks, together with almoſt all the conqueſts of the former war, happily terminated under the auſpices of prince Eugene.

With this partial peace, however, the cabinet of Peterſburg was by no means ſatisfied; and though Auſtria had ſtipulated that ſhe ſhould be allowed to give to Ruſſia the 30,000 auxiliary troops, as bound by treaty to do; though at preſent there was every appearance that Ruſſia might be victorious; yet, as the vizir ſhewed a diſpoſition to enter into a negotiation even with Ruſſia, compliance was not refuſed on the part of the empreſs; and thus, ſo early as the 18th of September, a peace was effected between the court of St. Peterſburg and the porte. Ruſſia had ſacrificed in this war ſo great a number of men, and been forced to expend ſuch vaſt ſums

in

in the profecution of it, that nothing better could be done than to confent to terms of accommodation, efpecially as the Turks were enabled by the treaty with Auftria to direct the whole of their force againft Ruffia. The conditions of peace were, that Azof fhould be evacuated, and, together with its territory, fhould lie wafte and uncultivated, as a boundary between the two empires. Neverthelefs, it fhould be lawful for Ruffia to build a fortrefs on the Don, as likewife for the porte to conftruct another in the Kuban. The greater and the lefs Kabardia were likewife to remain unoccupied, as a frontier; both governments agreed, however, to take a certain number of hoftages from the inhabitants of the country, for their greater fecurity that this liberty might not be abufed. The Ruffians were not permitted to keep a fleet either in the Palus Mæotis or in the Euxine, and ruffian merchants had licence only to carry on commerce in turkifh bottoms in the latter. Not only the Moldau, but likewife all the other conquefts that had been made by the Ruffians, were reftored to the Turks. Such were then the unimportant confequences of this war, which had coft Ruffia greatly above a hundred thoufand men, and prodigious fums of money; fince the army was obliged to carry with it all the provisions and ammunition necessary for the whole campaign: so that at the commencement of an expedition, about a hundred thousand waggons were requisite for this conveyance, as a supply must also be taken of water and wood, on account of the waterless steppes through which they must march. Indeed the Krim was laid waste in this war; but the Tartars were not quite exterminated; the Russians suffered much from their attacks while in winter-quarters: and, even after the peace, they were still powerful enough to infest the russian borders. On the other hand, the Turks no longer possessed the fortifications of Azof, but — neither did Russia retain them. Some few commercial advantages were all the gain that accrued from these successive years of desolating and murderous war.

One of the reasons why Russia was so ready to follow the example of the house of Austria, in concluding a peace, was undoubtedly because she was afraid lest Sweden, encouraged by the porte and France, which latter power was now of almost sovereign influence in the councils of Stockholm, might have recourse to arms, and endeavour to make a diversion in the north of Russia, in favour of the porte, while it was engaged in the south by the ottoman troops. It
is

is to be observed, that Russia and Sweden had in 1724 entered into an alliance for the term of twelve years, by which they mutually guaranteed their dominions; and, in case of an attack, to assist each other with ships and soldiers. At the expiration of these twelve years, this treaty was again renewed, [1736,] when Russia even made herself responsible for the payment of a debt due from Sweden to Holland of 750,000 dutch guldens. But the amity of the two countries continued to stand on a very tottering basis. The generality of the Swedes could not bring themselves absolutely to forget the considerable sacrifices which they were reduced to make to Russia at the peace of Nystadt; and the french court, which was friendly to the Ottomans, and consequently hostile to Russia, exerted herself, by means of her ambassador, to fan the discontents against the latter, by reiterated efforts. Under the form of government that then obtained in Sweden, by which the national council in fact directed everything, while the king was but the shadow of a monarch, the french cabinet found no difficulty in forming to itself a strong party, by presents properly bestowed. Sweden now was in hopes that, while Russia was occupied with the Turks, she might venture some enterprises against that empire, with little danger of miscarriage; and, notwithstanding that many true patriots remonstrated against a war with Russia; notwithstanding that the peace so recently concluded between Russia and the porte rendered it now more hazardous to attempt any thing against that power, the warlike party at length triumphed in the diet; and war against Russia became not only the wish of that body, but also of the whole swedish nation and the majority of the estates of the kingdom, when an event occurred by which every Swede thought himself insulted by the Russians.

A swedish major, named Sinclair *, who had been made prisoner at the battle of Pultava, then sent into Siberia, and, with the other prisoners his countrymen, was not set at liberty till the peace of Nystadt, had been sent by the swedish government to Constantinople, to negotiate concerning the debts which Charles XII. had contracted there, but at the same time to bring about a closer connection between Sweden and the Porte. Sinclair, a determined foe to the Russians, on his way home through Poland had at times spoken not very advantageously of the empress Anne, and had suffered occasionally to escape him some intimations about an ap-

* See Life of Catharine II. vol. iii. p. 252. fourth edit.

proaching humiliation of the ruffian pride by the combined power of the Swedes and Turks. Munich, who was then ftationed at the polifh frontiers, being informed of this, directed a particular attention to the fwedifh officer, and laid a plan to entrap him on his journey back from Conftantinople. In order to this, his picture was engraved, and numerous impreffions of it were difperfed among the ruffian officers commanding on the frontiers.. Sinclair fet out from Conftantinople in April 1739, travelled through Poland to Breflau, thence continued his journey; but, not far from Naumberg in Silefia, was attacked by feveral perfons, among whom were fome ruffian officers, and cruelly murdered. His fellow-traveller, Couturier, was then conveyed to the ruffian fort of Sonnenftein, but afterwards was fet at liberty, with a prefent of 500 ducats from the ruffian ambaffador, and arrived in September at Stockholm, where in the meantime Sinclair's difpatches had been received by the poft. This murder was generally reputed to have been perpetrated by an order from the ruffian court. The emperor of Germany complained heavily of the tranfaction as a violation of his territory; but Anne caufed a declaration to be drawn up, afferting her entire ignorance of the whole affair: and Mannftein,

who was adjutant-general to field-marshal count Munich, affirms likewise in his memoirs, that Anne actually knew nothing of it; adding, that this murder was solely the contrivance of her favourite Biren, count Ostermann, and marshal Munich, in order to come at the contents of the papers which Sinclair had about him. In the meantime the horrid transaction excited no small attention in Sweden; the french party took advantage of it for inflaming the resentment of the nation against the Russians; the populace of Stockholm, in testimony of their indignation, broke the windows of the russian ambassador's house; and the party in favour of war now found it more easy to attain the accomplishment of their wishes, a declaration of war against Russia. That government, quickly aware of the designs of Sweden, had, however, in the meantime got her hands at liberty by the peace concluded with the Turks, but wished nevertheless to avoid engaging in a new war, as the wounds inflicted by that lately terminated were still sensibly felt, and accordingly entered into a negotiation with Sweden, in which, however, the year 1740 was entirely taken up. Preparations were made notwithstanding on the part of Russia, by securing the frontiers of Finland, filling the magazines, providing the harbour of
Cronstadt

Cronstadt with a competent garrison, causing the fortifications to be repaired, and getting everything in readiness for the commencement of hostilities. Ere the storm could burst from these threatening appearances, the empress Anne died at St. Petersburg [1740] after a reign of ten years.

Anne had not sat so long on the russian throne without acquiring some portion of fame, by executing and completing many things that had been begun by her uncle Peter I. — Though the turkish war, in which she engaged, proved of very little benefit to the empire on account of the peace rashly concluded by Austria; yet the russian troops had shewn themselves bold and intrepid in the course of it, and the Turks on the other hand had learnt to consider them as formidable adversaries; for it was not the bravery of the Turks, but the frequent direful want of provisions, the strangeness of the climate, and the fatiguing marches, that prevented the russian army from making farther progress. Thus Anne succesfully executed Peter's project of again convincing the porte of the superiority of the russian arms. — Then, the canal along the Ladoga-lake, begun under Peter I, a work of extreme utility to the easier transport of provisions to St. Petersburg, was completely finished

under

under Anne in 1738, after the navigation on it had been opened in the reign of Peter II. Munich had the principal merit in the conſtruction of this canal. — Peter, not long before his death, ſent out ſeveral able perſons, to ſail from Kamtſhatka towards the north, in order to learn whether North America was connected with Siberia or not. But the enterprize terminated without gaining any clear information on the ſubject. Anne ſet on foot a new voyage in the ſame deſign, and thereby advanced the more accurate knowledge of thoſe hitherto unexplored regions. — It had been one grand object with Peter I. from time to time to improve the ſtate of the ruſſian army: Anne here alſo followed his footſteps; and Munich was the man whoſe advice and propoſals ſhe adopted in the reform of the military. Marſhal Munich introduced not only a better and ſtricter diſcipline, which was very much wanted among the Ruſſians, wherein he was mightily aſſiſted by the generals Laſcy and Keith, likewiſe foreigners, but alſo projected a completely new military exerciſe, and made in general a variety of uncommonly uſeful regulations in the army. Thus, for example, he conſtituted a corps of engineers, unknown till then among the Ruſſians; and, as there was particularly a want of good officers, he

moved

moved the empress to establish an institution for the forming of able commanders. Anne, therefore, at his instigation, endowed the noble land-cadet corps, for the education of young men of noble families in the several branches of knowledge necessary for an officer, of which Munich drew up the plan. An institute that still subsists, continuing to be improved and perfected from time to time, and serving as a seminary of expert commanders. — As in the russian army the singular custom prevailed, that men who held the same rank, had yet a difference in their salaries, as they were either foreigners or natives; the former being far better paid than the latter, Munich procured an order that the pay of the officers, having the same rank, whether foreigners or home-born, should be perfectly alike; on the whole, however, higher than had hitherto been the practice. By this alteration all cause of envy on the part of the native Russians against foreigners was in a great measure done away. — For the sake of giving a sort of counterpoise to the two regiments of guards, which had already shewn that their influence, even in determining the succession to the imperial diadem, was by no means small, Anne added to them a regiment of foot-guards, and another of horse; to the army was also given a few regiments of cuirassiers, cuiraffiers, which it had never had before. — Munich had the fatisfaction to fee his imperial miftrefs teftify her concurrence with his plan by putting it in execution, and the honour of finding that it even met the approbation of that great commander prince Eugene of Savoy.

Befide the changes by which Anne endeavoured to put the army in a better condition, fhe was particularly attentive to the benefits that might accrue to her empire from new or renovated treaties of commerce. In a view to the extenfion of trade, and thereby to better the condition of a great proportion of her fubjects, fhe was induced to relinquifh the perfian provinces. Her ambaffadors at foreign courts had her commiffion to look out for induftrious and able perfons in thofe kinds of trades and profeffions in which Ruffia was ftill behind, and fent them into the empire: fhe particularly procured for the country a great number of manufacturers in woollen ftuffs and filk. She executed a new treaty of commerce with Great Britain, and was in general no inactive ruler, taking upon herfelf the affairs of adminiftration, and governing with gentlenefs and equanimity, except in thofe cafes when fhe thought it behoved her to punifh, and then fhe was fevere. Her long refidence in Mittau, her intercourfe with the courifh nobles,

bles, in general remarkable for their urbanity and franknefs, had communicated to her character a certain fweetnefs and affability, which eafily gained her the affection of all that approached her. The manners of the peterſburg court, during her reign, took a fofter and politer turn. Drunken perfons, formerly frequent among the courtiers, made their difgufting appearance at court much feldomer, under her, as ſhe detefted drunkennefs. Delighting in the more decent and tranquil pleafures of mufic and dancing, ſhe encouraged them by not only taking foreign fingers and performers into her fervice, but alfo provided that young Ruffians of both fexes ſhould be inftructed in thofe arts.

The number of the fubjects received a great increafe under Anne, by the return of the zaporogian Kozaks to their obedience to the ruffian fceptre, which happened ſhortly after the breaking out of the turkiſh war. Thefe Kozaks in the time of Peter I. adhered to Mazeppa; and, on the latter being forced to flee with Charles XII. had put themfelves under the fupremacy of the khan of the Krimea The territory of the empire was alfo enlarged, on the fubmiffion of the Kirghifes, a very numerous nomadizing nation on the chinefe borders, to the protection the person elected, or free will in the electors, had certainly any share; but was as much influenced by the russian troops, then stationed in Courland, as the presence of the same troops, in more recent times, operated on the election of Staniflaus king of Poland *. The courish nobility, accordingly, had very soon cause to lament that their choice had been obliged to fall upon Biren †, as the new duke commonly resided in St. Petersburg, concerning himself not at all about his country, but even there dooming to punishment every one who by any means had

* Afterwards, Staniflaus Lackland. See Life of Catharine II. vol. iii. p. 330, &c.

† He was elected on the death of Ferdinand, last prince of the house of Kettler. The Courlanders were forced to accept for their sovereign him whom they knew to be grandson of a groom to their duke James III. and whom they had refused to associate with their nobility. The emprefs had already made Biren marry a courish lady of the family of Treden. A brother of Biren's wife had the insolence one day to attempt some familiarities with the princefs Elizabeth, whom he met walking alone in the gardens of Peterhof. Elizabeth complained of it to the emprefs Anne, who only laughed at the brutality of Treden, and told Elizabeth that she might surely allow a courish nobleman to take what she every day granted freely to a grenadier of the guards. This grenadier, it is well known, was Alexius Razumoffky.

drawn

drawn upon him his difpleafure, as defpotically as the conftitution of Ruffia allowed *.

In the government of the ruffian empire, under Anne, Biren had an abfolute influence; and it is very poffible to conceive that the turkifh war, which Oftermann and Munich were at firft decidedly againft, was profecuted by that monarch chiefly at the inftigation of Biren, as by that means he had it in his power to keep marfhal Munich at a diftance from Peterfburg. Munich had been fo fortunate as to gain the confidence and efteem of his fovereign in an eminent degree; and Biren was afraid of him as a dangerous rival, in knowledge and experience undoubtedly his fuperior.

Anne, though a widow, was ftill young when fhe came to the imperial throne; and, as it was probable that fhe might marry again, the council had very wifely inferted a claufe in the capi-

---

* At the very time when this barbarous favourite was fhedding torrents of blood, the ruffian courtiers, as well as the foreign minifters, were lavifhing upon him the vileft adulations. It was no uncommon thing, even at the public feftivities, to fee the minifters of Vienna, Berlin, and Saxony, kiffing the hand of the favourite, and drinking his health on their knees, after having given this toaft: " Per-
" dition to whoever refufes to do the like, and is not the
" true, fincere, and faithful friend of his highnefs mon-
" feigneur the duke de Biren!"

tulation,

tulation, that she should not take a consort without the consent of that body. By nullifying the capitulation, Anne indeed became entirely free in this respect; but Biren, who generally took great care to remove whatever might in the least degree have a tendency to limit his influence, cut off therefore every opportunity to a second marriage of his mistress. A prince of Portugal, who came to St. Petersburg for the purpose of solliciting her hand, was obliged to go back without his errand. For similar reasons Biren exerted all his talents to oppose the marriage of the princess Anne, daughter of the duke of Mecklenburg, and of Catharine Ivanovna, elder sister to the empress Anne. Her majesty, who had no intention to enter again into the state of wedlock, was desirous at least that her niece should take a husband*. Her design was to consider the children proceeding from such marriage in all respects as her own; and, by settling upon them the succession, to prevent the

* Several princes had made offers to marry this princess, who was afterwards so unfortunate. The king of Prussia, Frederic William I. was ambitious of having her for his son Frederic, in order to see him heir of the crown of Russia, and at liberty to leave that of Prussia to prince William Henry. If that project had succeeded what immense advantages would not Frederic II. have drawn from the great means thus put at his disposal!

disorders

diforders and tumults, which were naturally to be apprehended, if she should leave the world without having nominated an heir. Count Lœvenvolde, master of the horse, was accordingly sent to the court of Vienna to make choice of a spouse for the princess Anne. Charles, margrave of Brandenburg, and prince Anthony Ulric of Brunswick, were the two princes whom Lœvenvolde, on his return, declared worthy of soliciting a marriage with Anne; and Anthony Ulric, duke of Brunswick, was at length the person pitched on for her spouse. The duke therefore came to Russia. Biren saw this with dislike, fearing, as he must, that the father of the future successor might stand in the way of his authority, and therefore endeavoured by every effort to break off, if possible, the projected match. Perhaps, as he has been accused, and indeed not without grounds, he might have had a plan of bringing about a union between his son and the princess. — However, in spite of all his exertions, the marriage was consummated in the month of July 1739; and, on the 12th of August 1740, the princess, to the great joy of the empress Anne, became the mother of a prince, whom the sovereign immediately took under her tuition, and in the October following declared him her successor to the throne.

The empress about this time felt that probably she had not long to live. — This apprehension moved her to cause the oath of fealty to the newborn Ivan as successor to be taken by all her subjects. At the same time the prospect of the speedy dissolution of the empress set the heads of the administration, Biren, Munich, and Ostermann, in motion. Ivan, the successor, was only a few weeks old; and must, therefore, if Anne should presently die, have a guardian. The choice of this guardian was that in which Anne on her death-bed and the great men at court were not a little employed. Though his parents seemed to be the natural guardians of his infancy, and had the foremost claim to that charge, yet Biren, Munich, and Ostermann had formed very different plans, and never rested till they had got a paper signed by Anne, appointing duke Biren guardian of the young emperor Ivan, and regent of the empire during his minority [*]. It

[*] The artful Ostermann, who, in concert with the favourite, had fabricated the will of Anne, in which, excluding the duchess of Brunswick from the succession, she left the throne to Ivan and the regency to Biren, now framed a petition in the name of the several orders of the state, requesting Biren to accept the place of regent, which his ambition had already anticipated; and, what one would scarcely believe, notwithstanding all we have read, the principal members of the clerical order, the prime nobles, the ministers, and the senators were base enough to sign this request.

was certainly Biren's wish that the business should take this turn, though he directly after pretended to deny it, giving out that he had only yielded to Munich's importunity. However, it is possible that he might not at first have ventured to propose himself as guardian, fearing too violent an opposition; and afterwards, by an affected reluctance, as if it were difficult for him to resolve, he caused himself to be much importuned ere he would comply with the request of Ostermann and Munich to take the regency upon him. But these two politic ministers had concurred in bringing this matter about, in hopes that Biren would shew his gratitude to them, by undertaking, as regent, nothing of importance without them, but consult them on all occasions, so that they also would have been a part of the regency; in which Ostermann would have directed the affairs of state, while Munich was at the head of the military department: whereas if duke Anthony Ulric should have the regency and the guardianship, they were afraid that he might look upon it as a thing due to him of right, and therefore not think himself under any sort of obligation to them, though they should procure it for him, and accordingly not leave them so much scope for acting as they pleased. The project of conveying

veying the administration of the empire into the hands of duke Biren of course succeeded, particularly since the parents of the emperor happily observed a perfect silence in the business; and, when the last will of Anne was opened in the presence of the minister, the senators, the chiefs of the army, as well as of duke Anthony Ulric and his lady, it was found to contain the following injunction, already known to several, to others totally unexpected: " Biren shall be the
" administrator of government till the emperor
" Ivan shall have attained his seventeenth year,
" at which period he shall be declared of age.
" Should Ivan die before that time, then Biren
" shall continue guardian to Ivan's brethren
" born after him who shall succeed him on the
" throne. Should neither Ivan nor any one of
" his brethren afterwards born remain alive,
" then shall Biren, with the concurrence of
" the cabinet, the senate, and the generals of
" the army, elect and confirm a new emperor,
" who shall conduct all the affairs of the em-
" pire, foreign and domestic, as unlimited and
" absolute monarch of Russia."

Though nobody dared openly to oppugn this dying injunction of the empress Anne, by which a foreigner was placed, for many years to come, at the head of the government; as whoever had
presumed

presumed to do so would have infallibly brought upon himself either death or perpetual exile, yet the public was by no means satisfied with this testament. The parents of the emperor must have felt themselves most hurt at seeing a man who had made his fortune chiefly by personal gratifications with the deceased empress, entrusted with a guardianship which they naturally had reason to expect, and to which no person had a nearer claim than they. Anne thanked duke Biren for consenting to take upon him the weighty cares of government; but probably these thanks did not proceed from the heart, only serving as a delicate concealment of her mortification at the testamentary injunction of her aunt.

Biren was now mounted on the highest pinnacle of grandeur to which his imagination could have ever prompted him to aspire: if he was not addressed in the style of emperor, he had however the prospect of being for several years the ruler of the russian empire. He took his residence in the imperial summer-palace, giving the parents of the emperor, who would by no means be persuaded to quit their son, the winter-palace for their dwelling, with a yearly pension of 200,000 rubles, while his own amounted to 500,000. Instead of being called, as before, illustrious

illustrious prince, he assumed the title "of his highness, regent of the russian empire;" at the same time, however, granting to duke Ulric the title of "his highness."

The discontents excited at the new regency very soon and plainly appeared. There were not wanting persons who thought it an act of injustice to the parents of the emperor, to whom both the guardianship of Ivan, and the regency of the empire, ought properly to have been commited; while others were irritated at seeing Biren at the head of the government. The regent had his spies, who informed him immediately of all that was said; and he thought he provided in the best way for his safety, by severely punishing such as expressed their displeasure: so that a great number of persons were plunged into irretrievable distress for having imprudently delivered their sentiments on Biren's elevation; and the natural consequence of it was, that the discontents, instead of being suppressed, spread more and more, and duke Ulric now perceived that it would be no difficult matter to seize the regency out of Biren's hands.

He plainly told the regent that he would protest against the will of the late empress, as invalid, and that he even should not be displeased pleafed if it brought about an alteration in the regency. Expoftulations and quarrels fucceeded between him and the regent, which at length grew to fuch a height, that the duke threw up all his employments. While this difunion lafted between duke Ulric and the regent, count Munich was always the middle perfon, through whom the regent caufed the duke and his fpoufe to be told many difagreeable things. Munich employed this opportunity for gaining the confidence of thefe two neglected perfonages, hearkened to their complaints againft duke Biren, affented to the reafonablenefs of many of them, and in this manner the franknefs and intimacy between them grew greater from day to day. At length the duke and his fpoufe let fall, in the prefence of Munich, fome words, intimating that they had a defign to force the guardianfhip from the regent, and the marfhal in the fame undifguifed manner gave them to underftand that they might rely on his affiftance in the execution of their plan. Munich, whofe ambition and vanity knew no bounds, recreated his mind with the profpect of lording at court, under the aufpices of duke Ulric and Anne, if they by his affiftance fhould attain their end; and he might alfo hope that his project to depofe Biren would be attended with fuccefs,

particu-

particularly as the regent was far from being beloved, while Munich was much honoured, especially by the army; and thus he who, but a few weeks before, had contributed so much to Biren's appointment as regent, was now the most active promoter of his disgrace, the most zealous adherent to Biren's antagonists, the princess and her spouse. The enterprise admitted of no delay; and therefore they waited no longer than to the nineteenth of November for putting their plot in execution, by which the young emperor's parents were to take upon themselves the government of the empire, as guardians of the monarch. The regent Biren, his consort, his family, and his firmest partisans, being without trouble taken into custody in the night, all the great men then in town assembled before day-break at the palace, and the princess Anne received homage on the same day as grand-duchess of Russia, and guardian of her son, the infant emperor [*].

Only

---

[*] Biren lodged in the summer-palace. During supper he seemed thoughtful; and all at once said to Munich, "M. le marechal, have you never gone upon any important "enterprise in the night-time?" The marshal immediately thought his scheme was discovered; he, however, maintained sufficient composure to answer: "I cannot call to mind "any extraordinary matters that I have undertaken during
"the

Only two and twenty days had Biren poſſeſſed his ſtupendous fortune; and from the many cares and diſquietudes that attended it, even that ſhort ſpace was without enjoyment. From the caſtle of Schluſſelburg, where he was confined as a priſoner, he was brought to a trial, condemned, and exiled in June to Pelim in Siberia *,
where,

" the night; but I make it a rule to ſeize all opportunities
" that ſeem favourable to my views." After ſitting ſome time longer, he took his leave, and went ſtrait to the winter-palace, which was occupied by the young emperor and his parents; and, after having engaged the ducheſs of Brunſ-wick to admit of her party the officers and the hundred and forty ſoldiers on guard about the tzar, he returned to the regent, whom he arreſted by a detachment of twenty men, commanded by the aid-de-camp Mannſtein.

* The charges that were brought againſt him, and recited as the reaſon and juſtification of the ſentence of baniſh-ment paſſed upon him, in the imperial manifeſto that was publiſhed in that behalf, were the following: That the duke, during the laſt illneſs of the empreſs Anne, had thought of nothing but how to obtain the regency, to the excluſion of the emperor's parents; that he had ſquandered away extraordinary ſums from the imperial treaſury, and moſtly employed it to his own emolument out of the empire; that he and his family had ſcornfully neglected to ſhew a proper reſpect to the parents of the emperor; and, in order to deprive them of the public affection, had ſpread various ſorts of calumnies againſt them; that he had chal-
lenged

where, in addition to his misfortune, he was obliged, in banishment and misery, to associate with the numerous wretches who owed their banishment and misery to him *.

Thus, Anne having obtained her aim, by procuring the guardianship of her son and the regency of the empire, the ambitious Munich, who expected now to be all in all under the new administration, gave no respite to his efforts till the present regent had conferred on him the title of minister, the post enjoyed by Ostermann, who still remained at the head of affairs. But

---

lenged the father of the emperor to fight a duel with him (1), and obliged him to give up his places; that he acted of his own mere motion, contrary to statutes and ordinances, and conceived such plans as would have thrown the empire into the greatest confusion. "He hath, therefore," concludes the manifesto, " by the laws of God, of nature, and " of the empire, merited death." The emperor, however, freed him from capital punishment, but condemned him with his family to perpetual imprisonment.

* Biren was so dreaded, that when he rode on horseback through the streets, people, on seeing him come at a distance, exclaimed, " It is Biren, let us run!" Persons on foot made as fast as they could for the first gateway. Those who were in carriages stopped, got out and prostrated themselves before him.

(1) At a particular altercation, matters indeed did go so far, that Biren, in the heat of his passion, put his hand to his sword.

what

what Munich in reality ſtrove to obtain was the ſtation of commander in chief of the army and navy; however in this attempt it was impoſſible for him to ſucceed, as thoſe places were already poſſeſſed by duke Ulric: he therefore contented himſelf with extorting the former title from the regent. At this, however, count Oſtermann did not fail to take umbrage, and accordingly attached himſelf more cloſely to the duke, who alſo was ſenſible to the affront put upon him by Munich's application for his poſts*. Thus aroſe two parties; one headed by Anne and Munich, and the other by Oſtermann and the duke. Oſtermann, undoubtedly one of the moſt able and acute politicians of his time, ſoon found opportunities of diſplaying his extenſive views in politics, as well as his comprehenſive knowledge of the ruſſian empire, in ſo ſtriking a manner, that even Anne placed more confidence in him than ſhe did in count Munich.

* How could he help being offended at the following ukaſe, in which the duke is appointed generaliſſimo, and which was drawn up by Munich? It runs thus: "Though " field-marſhal Munich, on account of the great ſervices he " has rendered the empire, might claim the poſt of gene-" raliſſimo, yet he has waved that right in favour of duke " Anthony Ulric, as the father of his imperial majeſty, and " has *been contented* to accept the place of prime miniſter."

The

The king of Pruſſia, Frederic II. had juſt then begun his reign; who, not pleaſed at ſeeing the amity that ſubſiſted between the courts of Peterſ- burg and Vienna, endeavoured to make Munich his friend; and Frederic found it not very difficult, by flattering letters, ſo to work upon his vanity; that this miniſter, already not well diſpoſed to Auſtria, now made it his principal buſineſs to bring about a more intimate con- nection between the ruſſian court and that of Berlin. By this means the cloſe union that had hitherto ſubſiſted between Auſtria and Ruſſia was diſſolved, and the whole political ſyſtem of Europe totally changed.

A defenſive treaty had before been concluded between the ruſſian and pruſſian courts. Munich effected the renewal of it; and both parties mutu- ally bound themſelves to furniſh an aid of 12,000 men, in caſe of an attack. Anne, however, ſecretly determined to adhere to the terms of this treaty only ſo long as Pruſſia ſhould be at peace with Auſtria, the remonſtrances of Oſter- mann having inſpired her with a partiality for that houſe: and Frederic having now adopted meaſures for taking poſſeſſion of Sileſia, as a part of the inheritance of Maria Thereſa, the court of St. Peterſburg intimated to him that it never would conſent to that act. Accordingly,

at

at the commencement of the year 1741 a new alliance was formed with the imperial court, with an engagement to furnish auxiliaries. Munich, extremely diffatisfied at this procedure, ftrove to retard its execution, but in vain: he requefted his difmiffion; hoping by that means to induce Anne to lend a more favourable ear to his reprefentations; but this too had no effect: an honourable difmiffion was granted him, under pretence that, from the ftate of his health and his age, he could no longer be ufeful to the fervice. Munich, it is true, remained at St. Petersburg, in the hope of being employed again; but he was miftaken — the protracting his ftay there foon after brought upon him an involuntary journey to Siberia.

One of the moft remarkable events that happened during the regency of the duchefs of Brunfwick was the arrival at Mofco of an embaffy from Thamas Kouli khan. After having ufurped the throne of the fophis, and conquered the empire of the Mongoles, Thamas Kouli khan, who had heard much concerning the beauty of the princefs Elizabeth, fent to afk her in marriage, at the fame time promifing to introduce the greek religion into Perfia. His ambaffador was attended by fixteen thoufand men and twenty pieces of cannon. But this formidable troop

was

was invited to stop at Kitzliar on the borders of the Terek, and the ambassador made his entry into Mosco with a train of only three thousand persons on horseback. He presented to the regent, on the part of the shah, fourteen elephants and a great quantity of jewels, among which were very large diamonds[*]. The presents were accepted, and the proposals of marriage rejected.

Russia, however, took no active part in the war between Prussia and Austria, as the king of Poland and the elector of Saxony, who themselves raised pretensions to Theresa's patrimony, protested against the march of the russian troops through Poland; and Sweden at the same time threatened to open the campaign against the Russians on the frontiers of Finland, in consequence of a formal declaration of war against Russia, at Stockholm, in the month of August.

---

[*] These diamonds came from the Mongoley. Thamas Kouli khan brought away from that empire to the value of 146 millions of pounds sterling in precious stones, in gold, silver, and other valuables. The throne of the peacock alone, which he conveyed away from Dehli, was estimated at 202,500,000 francs, or nine kiurures. The kiurure makes a hundred laks, each lak a hundred thousand rupees. The rupee varies in value, but may be generally estimated at 2 s. 3 d. sterling.

It

It was well known in Sweden, that the ruffian nation in general was by no means satisfied with the present government, and that, therefore, some alteration in it was shortly to be expected. The court of France too was at no small pains, by its ambassador at Petersburg, to effect a revolution there, from which Sweden hoped to derive advantage. The latter reckoned so certainly that she should come off conqueror in the approaching war, and the Russians be vanquished, that in the diet of Stockholm, previous to the opening of the campaign, no less than three sets of articles were framed, on which she would hereafter make peace with the *conquered* Russians.' Should the arms of Sweden be completely successful, then Russia should give back Karelia, Ingria, Esthonia, and Livonia, and, in short, all that had been ceded to her at the peace of Nystadt; were she no more than partially successful, it was expected that at least Karelia, Kexholm, Vyborg, Petersburg, Nœteburg, Kronstadt, Kronschlot, the whole extent of the river Neva and Esthonia should be restored. In case, however, contrary to all probability, Russia might not be so far humbled as to surrender all these territories, then she should be allowed to retain Esthonia; but the rest of the countries just mentioned must be in any case evacuated

evacuated by her, without permission to keep a single ship on the livonian and esthonian coasts, and with an obligation from her to grant the free exportation of corn. It has rarely happened that any national council ever extended its plans of aggrandisement so far, with so great a deficiency in the necessary means for carrying them into execution, as Sweden did on this occasion. She deliberately settled the conditions of the future peace, though utterly unconcerned about a proper arrangement for the conduct of the war by which these terms of accommodation were to be secured. It is even said by a swedish historian, that "No man "knew of any generals, who by skill and expe- "rience had gained the public esteem." The two generals Levenhaupt and Buddembrock, who were the greatest advocates for the war, when hostilities were begun conducted them but miserably. The fleet was not in a condition to put to sea. The army, though brave and zealous, was poorly supplied with provisions; and, for want of good plans for the campaign, and intelligent officers, could effect very little.

Russia, resolving not to be behind hand with the Swedes, sent Lascy to march against them in August 1741, before they had time properly to collect their forces, and defeated them

near

near Vilmannſtrand. The ſurrender of that fortreſs to Ruſſia was the conſequence of this victory; and though the Swedes now rallied in ſuch manner that the Ruſſians, who were greatly inferior in numbers, could proceed no farther, yet they did nothing more through the whole of that campaign. As the Swedes, in entering upon this war, had principally laid their account in the ſuppoſition that things could not remain tranquil in Ruſſia, they diſperſed a manifeſto, in the view of inciting the Ruſſians to attempt a revolution; hoping at the ſame time that it would not paſs over ſo quietly as the former had done, that the troops then wanted in the interior muſt be drawn away from the borders, and the Swedes would thus have free ſcope to act with effect againſt Ruſſia. " The ſole intention " on the part of Sweden," ſays the manifeſto, " is to defend herſelf by arms againſt the op- " preſſions exerciſed againſt her by the arrogant " foreigners *, the miniſters of the ruſſian court, " and at the ſame time to deliver the ruſſian " nation from the yoke which theſe miniſters " have impoſed on it, by aſſiſting the Ruſſians " to regain their right of electing for themſelves " a *lawful ruler*."

* By theſe foreigners were meant Munich and Oſtermann.

It was, therefore, not from a want of good will in the fwedifh government, that no rebellion arofe againft its prefent rulers, and that a civil war, with all its horrors, did not enfue; for it thus exprefsly declared the regency unlawful. Happy, however, it was for Ruffia, that the revolution which happened this very year, in November 1741, and was not brought about by the fwedifh manifefto, but by very different motives, was effected without bloodfhed, that the alteration of the perfon of the ruler produced no farther changes, excepting among the heads of the adminiftration, and that it was attended with no confufion or difturbance in the empire.

What facilitated, however, in an eminent degree, the revolution by which Elizabeth became emprefs of Ruffia, was the behaviour both of Anne and her confort the duke. There was no harmony nor confidence between them. The regent fhut herfelf up entirely with a countefs Mengden, with whom fhe lived on the moft intimate footing, entirely eftranged from her hufband, paffing whole days and weeks in a total neglect of government affairs; and thus, no lefs than by the influence which fhe allowed that lady to exert, created to herfelf many enemies. The envy and jealoufy of the native Ruffians were every day increafed by the partiality uni-

verfally

versally shewn to the german party: hence it proceeded, that no more concord subsisted between the ministers Ostermann and Munich, than between the duke and the regent; one party being constantly employed in thwarting and counteracting the other. Thus, though Anne abhorred severity, and her government was extremely mild; though she was ever prompt to bestow favours and exercise her liberality: yet thus in short it was, that the enterprise of Lestocq, the physician to the princess Elizabeth, for seating her on the throne of her father, was attended with success.

For abating the influence of foreigners in the administration of the empire, the plan of a convention had been framed on the demise of Peter II. by which the supreme authority was to be placed in the council, whereof the greater part were Russians. This was annulled by Anne; and Biren a foreigner was all-powerful under that princess: Ostermann being the soul of the administration, and Munich the first man in the army; the foreigners therefore remained at the head of affairs.

Anne died; but the foreigners still continued in the chief offices of state: Biren being little less than emperor and autocrator of all the Russias; and, after his downfall, which followed on the heels of his success, the government remained, nevertheless, in the hands of Ostermann and Munich. The emperor Ivan himself was but a very remote descendant of the tzarian house of Romanof; his father was a german prince, his mother the daughter of a german prince, only his great-grandfather on the mother's side, Ivan, brother to Peter I. was descended from the Romanofs: in appearance, therefore, it was rather a foreign than a russian family that was now in possession of the throne; and the more, as the various offices of the state were given with increasing partiality to foreigners. This was taken very much amiss by the country at large, and the desire of an alteration on their part greatly facilitated that which presently after happened. As the plot for the overthrow of Biren had succeeded without resistance, it was easy to foresee that it might prove no less feasible to displace Anne; who, from her inconsistent behaviour, by her contempt of the russian customs, by the exorbitant favours she lavished on her adherents, mostly foreigners, had but little hold on the hearts of the people, and especially as a candidate for the crown had started up, who must naturally be more agreeable to the nation, being a true-born Russian, than the present emperor.

The

The person thus aspiring to the crown was no other than the princess Elizabeth, daughter of Peter the Great, residing at St. Petersburg, in the very bosom of the court. On the death of Peter II. she might, perhaps, have preferred her pretensions to the throne of her father not without success; but at that time she made not the smallest stir in this design. She even remained quiet during all the reign of Anne, though the Dolgorukies were accused of an intention of advancing her to the imperial seat *, continuing to live with that empress on the most amicable terms, exciting no surmises of that nature, either

* Towards the end of the year 1739, the Dolgorukies were arrested and put to the torture. They confessed that they had concerted an insurrection for carrying off the empress, the princess Anne and her consort, together with the duke of Courland, to drive all the Germans out of the country, to proclaim Elizabeth empress, and to marry her to one of the Narishkins. How much truth was at the bottom of this confession, how much of it was to be imputed to the torture, by means of which, whatever is wanted may be extorted, cannot now be ascertained. Biren hated the Dolgorukies, as the principal authors of the capitulation, and the clause that he should not be permitted to come to Russia. Add to this, that, as one of the first families of the empire, they were always dangerous; accordingly, one of them was broke alive upon the wheel, three others were decapitated, and two thrown into a dungeon for life. This may serve as an instance of Biren's usual manner of acting.

in her or her partizans, and as, from her whole behaviour she seemed more disposed to enjoy the pleasures of life in full measure, than to take upon her the weighty burden of such a government as that of Russia. Besides, Elizabeth had very few intimacies among the great men at court; and there was not the slightest appearance of any party at all devoted to her: she attached herself more to the soldiery, particularly to the guards; and there seldom passed a week, in which she did not once or twice stand sponsor at the christening of the children of some of those soldiers. If, therefore, it might occasionally occur to the empress Anne that it would be preferable to place Elizabeth in such a situation as would render it impossible for her to form any design upon her father's throne, perhaps by sending her into a convent; every anxiety was soon dispelled by the manner of life and the whole deportment of Elizabeth: indeed Biren himself was always against the idea of attempting anything to the prejudice of that princess. It is also probable that, under the empress Anne, Elizabeth laid no plan for ascending the throne, and that the project first entered her mind, on the demise of that monarch, at seeing an infant emperor, under the tutelage of a foreigner, accede to the sceptre; and, shortly after, the

parents

parents of the emperor, who likewise were to be regarded rather as foreigners than as Ruſſians, get poſſeſſion of the guardianſhip, and hearing it even reported that the princeſs Anne, Ivan's mother, had reſolved, at the inſtigation of count Oſtermann, to declare herſelf empreſs on her birthday in the enſuing December [1741], and to ſettle the ſucceſſion in the line of her daughters.

Now it was that the advice of Leſtocq, Elizabeth's phyſician and favourite, found ready admiſſion; and he exerted all his zeal and addreſs in collecting a body of partizans, by whoſe aſſiſtance he might put the reins of empire into the hands of his patroneſs. Bringing together by degrees a number of the ſoldiers of the guards who were devoted to Elizabeth, they promiſed to ſupport her in the attempt to ſeat herſelf on the throne of her father, and likewiſe to perſuade their comrades to engage in the ſame cauſe *. The money neceſſary for the enter-

---

* A broken merchant, now corporal in the preobrajenſki guards, named Grunſtein, and one Schwartz, a trumpeter, were the firſt whom Leſtocq prevailed upon to liſten to his propoſal. The hopes of making their fortune induced theſe people to enter into the ſcheme themſelves, and to gain accomplices. After the enterpriſe had ſucceeded they were both amply rewarded.

prife was furnifhed partly by Elizabeth and partly obtained by Leftocq from M. de la Chetardie, the french ambaffador at St. Peterfburg, who offered his affiftance in bringing about this revolution, in hopes that the new emprefs would, from gratitude to France, no longer take part with Auftria; and as Sweden might, perhaps, likewife on this occafion be fomewhat a gainer. In the meantime Elizabeth's courage drooped as the execution of her plot drew nigh, and fhe put it off from day to day. The foldiers moreover, who had been induced to take up the bufinefs, were not people to be trufted with a fecret of that magnitude; and there was already fomething of a rumour abroad concerning fome project of the princefs. It even reached the ears of the regent; and fhe would not have been to blame if fhe had employed the means fhe had in her power of confining Elizabeth. But Anne, notwithftanding all fhe had heard of the bufinefs, was unaccountably carelefs, taking no more fteps about it than if nothing was paffing to alarm her fecurity: a conduct, for which, afterwards when it was too late to rectify her miftake, fhe was feverely reproached by her hufband. But, inftead of confulting him on the beft meafures to be adopted on fuch a ferious occafion, fhe concealed everything from him.

Count

Count Ostermann warned her of her danger; the british minister prophesied her certain ruin, unless she took the proper means to prevent it; she received an anonymous letter, in which she she was conjured to beware of an approaching shock; and indeed it was difficult to conceive how she could entertain the least doubts on the matter: yet, instead of resorting to any methods of counteraction, such as by the seizure of Lestocq, to deprive the prime mover and most zealous promoter of the plot from all power of mischief, as the duke proposed, she disclosed to Elizabeth, in full court *, the whole contents of the admonitory letter she had received, and the reports that were spread. Certainly this was not the way to come at the truth. Elizabeth confessed nothing, protested that she was entirely innocent; and, by dissimulation and even tears, effectually dispelled all ideas of suspicion in Anne. Lestocq had previously appointed the day of the consecration of the waters † for Elizabeth to make her appearance publicly as claimant of the throne, to put herself at the head of her followers, to assert her right to the succession by a public declaration, and to cause herself to be proclaimed empress.

* On the 4th of December.
† The 6th of January 1742.

But

But no sooner did he learn from Elizabeth the subject of this conversation, than he would hear of no farther delays, redoubled his activity, got daily more partizans for Elizabeth, by means of french gold, and inculcated it more forcibly than ever upon her that there was now no time for hesitation unless she would give up all for lost. He told her that the guards were soon to march towards Sweden, and that she would thus lose those on whose assistance she reckoned most; adding, that this alone was reason sufficient for accelerating the cataftrophe. Elizabeth, appearing to be still irresolute, Lestocq the next morning pulled out of his pocket-book a card, on one side whereof he had drawn Elizabeth in a nun's habit, surrounded by a number of gibbets; on the other, that princess with the crown on her head attended by a circle of nobles: a contrivance by which he meant tacitly to suggest to her the choice of one or the other of these situations for herself and her friends; that all depended on a moment, and if that moment were suffered to escape no choice would remain, but the former would inevitably be their portion. Upon this, Elizabeth seemed resolved to put all to the hazard for obtaining the crown; and, as the revolution occasioned by the apprehending of Biren by night had been quietly effected

without

without bloodshed, the nocturnal silence it was thought would be favourable to the present attempt; and the following night, between the fifth and sixth of December, was fixed upon for the execution of this important project, in which Lestocq undertook the principal part, in the expectation, if all succeeded, of honours and rewards, but in case of a miscarriage, of certain death. He now prepared his accomplices and adherents, went in the evening and fetched some thousand ducats from the french ambassador, in order to obviate or to conquer all opposition and resistance by that powerful application, money; then repaired to the apartments of the princess Elizabeth, and intreated her to follow him to take possession of her father's throne. Even now Elizabeth betrayed her want of fortitude; Lestocq, however, at length got the better of her fears. She threw herself prostrate before a crucifix, repeated a long prayer, got up perfectly composed, after having made a solemn vow that no blood should be shed in this attempt, put on the riband of the order of St. Catharine, and placed herself in a sledge with a chamberlain by her side, behind which two grenadiers stepped up as guards. Lestocq and Schwartz followed in a second sledge. They drove directly to the barracks of the preobrajenski guards. At some
distance

distance from the gate-way the sledges stopped short, and Elizabeth proceeded on foot, attended by her sledge-party, that they might excite the less attention. Holding the cross in her hand — by which such great things had already so often been performed — she made a speech to the soldiers, in justification of her enterprize, to place herself on the throne. She had certainly much to advance in her behalf; and it must naturally have made great impression on the native Russians, when she mentioned, that, as the daughter of the immortal emperor Peter the Great, she had resolved to wield the sceptre of her father; that though she had been unjustly forced aside from the throne by a foreign child, and though there was even a design on foot to bury her in a convent, yet the faithful guards were they by whose assistance and support she now cherished the hope of ascending the paternal throne. — A part of the guards were already made acquainted with the business, and had been gained over to espouse it by money, fair speeches, promises and rewards on one side, and on the other by denunciations of cruel punishments in case of opposition; the force of surprise, which was increased by the distribution of inflammatory liquors and Elizabeth's affable and captivating demeanor, soon brought over most

of

of the remainder. A few of them, however, absolutely would not be either bribed or persuaded to hearken to Elizabeth's pretension to the throne, as the young emperor was still alive. But, being greatly overpowered by numbers, they were manacled, and the party proceeded towards the palace inhabited by the emperor and his parents. The armed suite by this time consisted of several hundred men. All they met on the way were pressed to join the train that nothing might be betrayed, and in this manner they reached the palace; where the sentinels were easily brought to compliance, as the soldiers belonging to the conspirators threatened to use violence unless they voluntarily surrendered. Elizabeth reiterated her remonstrances, and — she was obeyed as monarch.

The duke and his spouse were now rudely awaked from the profound sleep in which they lay, and dragged out of bed — the latter being scarcely allowed time to cover herself with a gown, while the former, having had recourse to weapons, was carried by the soldiers, wrapped in the bed-clothes, put in the sledge, into which they then threw some garments, and both were now conveyed away, as prisoners of Elizabeth, into the palace of that princess, where they were strongly guarded. Ivan, the innocent unconscious

conscious boy, in whose name already so many manifestos had appeared, of which he could neither understand nor know anything; who, with no ambition to flatter, had been raised to the imperial purple, and was now without consternation dethroned, was gently sleeping in his cradle, during this transaction, which doomed him to a life of misery. Elizabeth had given orders not to disturb his repose, and several soldiers assiduously stood watching his cradle; but immediately on his awaking Elizabeth took him with her to her palace, that she might shew him to his father and mother. — Not only the young emperor and his parents, but also the two grand promoters of Ivan's succession and the regency of Anne, Ostermann, and Munich*, were carried off without much noise that same night, and on the marshal was literally retaliated what he had done to Biren duke of Courland. The same lot befel several other persons, as, the brother of the duke, prince Lewis Ernest of Bruns-

* Munich called to the prisoners, who wanted to take him prisoner: " Put up your swords, you scoundrels, or " you shall all fall victims to your insolence " Only the day before every soldier would have trembled at this menace of the field-marshal — at present they laughed at it; and, on his shewing a reluctance to submit, they pushed him forward, and even repeatedly struck him.

wick,

wick*, the first lord of the bed-chamber baron Munich †, the feldt-marshal's son, and some other adherents to the regency.

Thus, under favour of the darkness and silence of the night, this great revolution was effected at Petersburg. The emperor Ivan and his parents were now in captivity to a princess, whose clemency was their only hope. The inhabitants of the residence heard early in the morning of the important, though not altogether unexpected, revolution; and, as only one year before,

---

* In the month of June, in this year, he had been elected duke of Courland, and thereupon went to St. Petersburg, there to wait for the ratification of his election by the king and the republic of Poland. In the mean time the revolution happened, by which his brother and his family were reduced to misery. Lewis too was treated at first like a prisoner; but this lasted not long. In February 1742 he quitted St. Petersburg, and went back to Brunswick.

† Marshal Munich was brought to his trial on a charge of having expended too much money on the army, and of having been the death of a great number of soldiers in gaining his victories. This is exactly similar to the process brought by cardinal Richelieu against the marshal de Marillac. Munich, irritated at the interrogatories of his judges, said to them: " Draw up yourselves the answers " you would have me to make and I will sign them." — They took him at his word; he signed the paper, and was condemned to be quartered.

they had taken the oath of allegiance firſt to Ivan as ſucceſſor, then to Biren as regent, and ſhortly after to Anne in the ſame quality, ſo now they were called upon to ſwear fealty to the new empreſs Elizabeth; which was done this very day by all the troops ſtationed in and about St. Peterſburg *, after Elizabeth had preſented herſelf to the ſenate and the great officers of ſtate as empreſs, and had been acknowledged by them as ſuch without contradiction. In the manifeſto publiſhed on this occaſion it is ſaid:
" The empreſs Anne having nominated the
" grandſon of her ſiſter, a child born into the
" world only a few weeks before the empreſs's
" death, as ſucceſſor to the throne; and during
" the minority of whom various perſons had
" conducted the adminiſtration of the empire
" in a manner highly iniquitous, whence diſ-
" turbances had ariſen both within the country
" and out of it, and probably in time ſtill
" greater might ariſe; therefore all the faithful
" ſubjects of Elizabeth, both in ſpiritual and
" temporal ſtations, *particularly the regiments of*

---

* As the ſoldiers were ſhouting *hourrah* before the palace of the empreſs, the little Ivan endeavoured to imitate the vociferation, on which Elizabeth tenderly ſaid: " Poor " babe, thou knoweſt not that thou art joining the noiſe " that is raiſed at thy undoing!"

" the

" *the life-guards*, had unanimously invited her,
" for the prevention of all the mischievous con-
" sequences to be apprehended, to take pos-
" session of the throne of her father as nearest
" by right of birth, and that she had accordingly
" resolved to yield to this unanimous request of
" her faithful subjects, by taking possession of
" her inheritance derived from her parents the
" emperor Peter I. and the empress Catharine."

Another manifesto appeared shortly after of greater length, in which the legitimacy of Elizabeth's accession to the throne was chiefly grounded on the testament of the empress Catharine I. her mother. In this it was said, " that on the de-
" mise of Peter II. when she ought to have
" succeeded *, by Ostermann's malice against
" her,

---

* This, however, is not in strict conformity with truth. This testament has been mentioned above, p. 204. Had Elizabeth now intended to act in complete pursuance of it, she would have caused the young duke of Holstein, Peter, to come to Russia and had him crowned emperor, and she might have remained his guardian and regent of the empire till his majority, he being now only thirteen. This, however, she did not, but reserved the throne, which it would have been dangerous for her to have ascended; though the next year [1742] she invited the same duke, Peter of Holstein, her sister's son, to Russia, and appointed him successor. — Besides, Elizabeth's accession to the throne was

" her, Anne was elected; and afterwards, when
" that sovereign was attacked by a mortal dis-
" temper, the same Ostermann appointed as
" successor the son of prince Anthony Ulric
" of Brunswick and the princess of Mecklen-
" burg *, a child only two months old, *who
" had not the slightest claim by inheritance to the
" russian throne;* and, not content with this, he
" added, to the prejudice of Elizabeth, that
" after Ivan's death, the princes afterwards born
" of the said prince of Brunswick, and the
" princess of Mecklenburg, should succeed to
" the russian throne, whereas even *the parents
" themselves* had not the smallest right to that

---

even a proof that Peter the Great's law, by which the sovereign was at liberty to appoint a successor, would become only a source of alterations in the succession and of revolutions in the government. Elizabeth therefore appealed to Catharine's testament. — The empress Anne had come to the crown contrary to the purport of this testament, but as empress had also the right to nominate her successor. It is said, indeed, in Elizabeth's manifesto, that Anne, from extreme weakness, signed a testament forged by Ostermann; but Ivan was certainly appointed successor by Anne, a few weeks before her death.

* This must, however, have sounded very outlandish in the ears of a true born Russian, and shewn the case of Ivan and his parents as strange, and their claim to the throne as invalid.

" throne.

" throne. That Ivan was, therefore, by the
" machinations of Oſtermann and Munich,
" confirmed emperor in October 1740; and
" becauſe the ſeveral regiments of guards, as
" well as the marching regiments, were under
" the command of Munich and the father of
" Ivan, and conſequently the whole force of
" the empire was in the hands of theſe two per-
" ſons, the ſubjects were compelled to take the
" oath of allegiance to Ivan. That Anthony
" Ulric and his ſpouſe had afterwards broke
" this ordinance, to which they themſelves had
" ſworn, had forcibly ſeized upon the admini-
" ſtration of the empire, and Anne had re-
" ſolved, even in the life-time of her ſon Ivan,
" to place herſelf on the throne as empreſs.
" That in order then to prevent all dangerous
" conſequences from theſe proceedings, Eliza-
" beth had aſcended the throne, and of her
" own imperial grace had ordered *the princeſs
" with her ſon and daughter to ſet out for their
" native country.*"

However this was not done; neither Anne, nor her huſband, nor her ſon Ivan ever ſaw Germany again: and this appears to be the pro-pereſt place briefly to relate the ſubſequent for-tunes of this unhappy family.

On the twelfth of December they were conducted from St. Petersburg, and arrived at Riga the 6th of January 1742, from which place it was their most earnest wish to proceed to Germany, preparations having already been made at Berlin for their reception[*]. Elizabeth, however, had in the interim changed her mind, and detained them there in custody; in order by their means, as was reported, to obtain an elucidation of several matters which she wanted to have explained. The princely captives made two several attempts to escape: but both were frustrated; and, as was reasonable to expect, were followed by a closer confinement in the citadel of Riga, where they now could only enjoy the open air in the garden, and were kept under the inspection of a numerous command. Applications were made to no purpose by the courts of Berlin, Vienna, and London for their enlargement: though Elizabeth would have yielded to their sollicitations to set the duke at liberty, but Anne and the children she was absolutely determined not to liberate; and only on that condition would Anthony Ulric accept of a deliverance. Some attempts being afterwards

[*] The king of Prussia was brother-in-law to the duke.

discovered, even at St. Petersburg, to dethrone Elizabeth, and to recall the former administrators of the government, the empress was still more embittered against the ejected family. They were conveyed [1743] to Dunamund, where their imprisonment was still closer and more severe: from this fortress they were removed to Kolmogory, an island at the mouth of the Dvina in the White-sea, about fifty miles from Archangel. Here Anne died in child-bed in 1746, a prey to grief and melancholy, principally owing to the privation of her eldest son Ivan, who had been taken from his parents and shut up in a monastery at Oranienburg. Her husband survived till 1775, when he finished his calamitous career in prison. The death of Anne seemed for a moment to assuage the resentment of the implacable monarch: she caused the corpse to be brought to St. Petersburg, where it was deposited with due rites in the imperial sepulchre, and she herself attended the interment.

The dethroned Ivan continued to live from 1744, far from his parents in the monastery at Oranienburg, where he was brought up in such seclusion that his mental powers were left totally unemployed. He was not allowed either to write or to read. A monk of the convent thought

thought to make his fortune by carrying off the unfortunate prince; but the attempt was attended by ruin to himself, and additional horror to the doleful situation of Ivan. Being taken at Smolensk, they were brought back, and poor Ivan was made dearly to expiate the project that had been undertaken without his knowledge or consent. A dungeon in the castle of Schluffelburg was now assigned him for his dismal abode; and he was here so closely immured, that he might be said to be literally buried alive in a subterranean vault into which no beam of the sun could ever stray, passing his time in total inaction, by the gloomy light of a lamp, which so far from cheering his mind seemed calculated only to plunge it into deeper despair, by shewing him somewhat more distinctly the horrors of his situation. He rarely knew whether it was day or night, any more than what was the hour; seldom could the officers and soldiers that were on guard, for the sake of mitigating a little the cruelty of his situation, transiently converse with him on the most indifferent topics: for all discourse with him was utterly forbidden. He could scarcely ever obtain permission to behold for a few moments the blessed light of heaven, and to breathe the free air in the inclosed court of the fortress. How can the least

doubt

doubt be entertained, that the mind of this prince, by such a course of life, must take a direction peculiar to itself, bordering on despondency, sullenness, misanthropy, absence, and confusion*? He occurred frequently to

the

---

* Catharine II. likewise conversed with him once unknown, and the following was the result of this visit, as published in a manifesto of that time: "After we had "ascended the throne, and offered up to heaven our just "thanksgivings, the first object that employed our thoughts, "in consequence of that humanity which is natural to us, "was the unhappy situation of that prince, who was de- "throned by the divine providence, and had been unfortu- "nate ever since his birth; and we formed the resolution "of alleviating his misfortunes, as far as was possible. We "immediately made a visit to him, in order to judge of his "understanding and talents; and, in consequence thereof, "to procure him an agreeable and quiet situation, suitable "to his character, and the education he had received. "But how great was our surprise, when, besides a defect "in his utterance, that was uneasy to himself, and rendered "his discourse almost unintelligible to others, we observed "in him a total privation of sense and reason! Those who "accompanied us, during this interview, saw how much our "heart suffered at the contemplation of an object so fitted to "excite compassion; they were also convinced, that the "only measure we could take to succour the unfortunate "prince, was to leave him where we found him, and to "procure him all the comforts and conveniencies that his "situation would admit of. We accordingly gave our "orders for this purpose, though the state he was in pre-
" vented

the thoughts of Elizabeth, who caused him twice to be brought secretly to St. Petersburg, where she talked with him, without letting him know who she was; but, for his liberation, for the alleviation of his horrible — *unmerited* — doom, she did nothing. Peter III. who shortly after his accession, went and made him a visit likewise, without being known to Ivan, in the determination somewhat to better his condition, by granting him the small boon he requested, the enjoyment of the free air within the castle. Peter accordingly gave orders to build a small house, for the accommodation of the prince, in an angle of the fortress; but his own death defeated this laudable purpose. Two years afterwards, Ivan also was cruelly assassinated, and thus suddenly delivered from a life that had afforded him, from his very birth, so few satisfactions, being rather one continued tissue of calamities and sorrow.

"vented his perceiving the marks of our humanity, or
"being sensible of our attention and care; for he knew
"nobody, could not distinguish between good and evil, nor
"did he know the use that might be made of reading, to
"pass the time with less weariness and disgust; on the con-
"trary, he sought after pleasure in objects that discovered,
"with sufficient evidence, the disorder of his imagination."
See Life of Catharine II. vol. i. p. 504. fourth edit.

A lieu-

A lieutenant, named Mirovitch, thinking himself neglected as an officer, conceived a plan to revenge himself on the emprefs Catharine II. by delivering the captive Ivan from his dungeon, and replacing him on the throne. A plan, which, besides the extraordinary difficulties with which it must be attended, seemed utterly unlikely to succeed; as the manner of life to which that prince had all along been condemned, disqualified him for ever for the station of a ruler. Yet Mirovitch, capable of any attempt, however inconsiderate, to which he was prompted by his vindictive spirit, found means to gain over a few accomplices to his rash design. The emprefs being gone on a journey into Livonia in 1764, and he happening then to have a command at Schluffelburg, for strengthening the guard at that fortrefs, whereby he had frequent opportunities for making himself thoroughly acquainted with the place of Ivan's confinement, caused the soldiers of his command to be rouzed in the night, and read to them a pretended order from the emprefs commissioning him to set the prince at liberty.

The soldiers thus taken by surprife, were induced by threats, promises, and intoxicating liquors, to believe, what however on the slightest reflection must have struck them as the groffest abfurdity.

Headed

Headed by Mirovitch, they proceeded to the cell of Ivan. The commandant of the fortress, waked out of his sleep by the unexpected alarm, immediately on his appearing, received a blow with the butt end of a musket, which struck him to the ground; and the two officers that had the guard of the prisoner were ordered to submit. Here it is to be observed, that the officers whose turn it was to have custody of him, had uniformly, from the time of Elizabeth, secret orders given them, that if any thing should be attempted in favour of the prince, rather to put him to death than suffer him to be carried off. They now thought themselves in that dreadful predicament: and the prince, who when an infant of nine weeks, was taken from the calm repose of the cradle to be placed on an imperial throne, was likewise fast locked in the arms of sleep when that throne was taken from him only one year afterwards, and now also enjoying a short respite from misery by the same kind boon of nature, when he was awakened — by the thrust of a sword; and, notwithstanding the brave resistance he made, closed his eyes for ever by the frequent repetition of the stroke. Such was the lamentable end of this unfortunate prince! of this russian monarch! The event excited great animadversion throughout the residence, every

unbiassed

unbiaſſed perſon bewailed the youth ſo innocently put to death; and inceſſant crowds of people flocked to ſee his body in the church of the fortreſs of Schluſſelburg. The government was at length obliged to ſteal it away by night for inhumation in a monaſtery at a conſiderable diſtance from town. Mirovitch paid the forfeit of his enterpriſe with his head *.

We ſhall now reſume the thread of our hiſtory.

Whatever ſeverity the empreſs Elizabeth ſhewed againſt the depoſed regent, her ſpouſe, and their family, and though ſhe had baniſhed the chiefs of the late adminiſtration, Oſtermann and Munich, to Siberia; yet, on the other hand, ſhe recalled many thouſands who had been ſent to pine out their days in thoſe dreary regions, under the late regency; among whom were even two Dolgorukies, whom ſhe reinſtated in their poſts. What Munich and Oſtermann had been, under the foregoing governments, Beſtu-

---

* Ivan had ſtill two brothers and two ſiſters, who remained in priſon with their parents, three of them being born during their impriſonment. It was not till the year 1776 that they were permitted by Catharine II. to go to Horſens in Yutland, to their aunt the dowager queen Juliana of Denmark, on which occaſion the empreſs ſettled on them a penſion.

chef

chef was now. As the friend of Biren he had been exiled with him, but, on Munich's disgrace, was liberated and recalled by the regent Anne. Elizabeth appointed him now vice-chancellor, and soon after promoted him to the high office of grand-chancellor; in which station he for many years successively directed the affairs of the russian government, almost entirely at his own will.

Elizabeth, desirous of making herself beloved throughout the nation, by restoring all things as they had been under Peter I. reinstated the directing senate established by that monarch, but whose province had been very much contracted by the council erected by Catharine I. and afterwards by the cabinet under Anne, in its full privilege of conducting the affairs of the country, and fixed the number of its members at fourteen. The foreign concerns were mostly managed by the chancellor Cherkaskoy and Bestuchef, afterwards by the latter alone: she also erected a council of conference. [1756.]

It was expected that Elizabeth would proceed to fulfil her second promise, of keeping, as much as possible, all foreigners from holding offices under government: but this had like to have been attended with very sad consequences, as a more extensive interpretation was given to it, than was intended by that princess. The guards, for the moſt part natives, were particularly incenſed at the foreign officers. Elizabeth, to ſhew her gratitude to the preobrajenſki guards for the aſſiſtance they had given her in mounting the throne, had honoured the troop of grenadiers with the name of the life-company, increaſed them to 300 men, appointed herſelf their colonel, aſſigning at the ſame time to every common man the rank of nobleſſe and of lieutenant, and to the petty officers and officers of this company an equality with thoſe of higher rank in the army. Intoxicated with theſe marks of favour, they conſidered them as the bare reward of their great ſervices; and ſuppoſing themſelves now the favourites of the empreſs, they rioted in all kinds of exorbitances, extorting money from wealthy perſons, maltreating every body who did not act juſt as they would have him, and behaving with the greateſt rudeneſs and inſolence, particularly to the foreigners in the army. Nay, while the empreſs was at Moſco, they proceeded ſuch lengths that they even formed the mad reſolution to murder all the foreigners; which, indeed, they began to put in execution, by attacking and wounding ſeveral. Elizabeth, therefore, was under the neceſſity of uſing harſh methods, and of making declaration, " that ſhe was ſo far from tolerating

" this

"this *senseless* conduct, that she never should
"forget how much the foreigners had contri-
"buted to the beneficial changes that had taken
"place in the russian empire. That, though
"her subjects should at all times enjoy her
"graces in preference to foreigners, yet the
"foreigners who were in her service were as
"dear to her as her subjects, and might rely
"on her protection." The hatred against foreigners manifested itself even afterwards still more frequently in the army, but was as often happily suppressed.

The war with the king of Sweden, which had been begun under the late regency, was not yet terminated, and at present only interrupted by both armies retiring into quarters for the winter. The Swedes, indeed, entertained great hopes from the new empress, to whose accession they thought they had greatly co-operated by their manifesto. The french ambassador at St. Petersburg, whom the empress very much esteemed, likewise employed every effort to work upon Elizabeth in their favour, and a cessation of hostilities was obtained at the opening of the year 1742, during which it was intended to negotiate a peace. But Elizabeth proved far more uncomplying than Sweden had expected. Sweden required the treaty of Nystadt to be annulled, or at least have all Finland and Vyborg given back. Elizabeth, however, having but just acceded to the throne of Peter the Great, her father, was not inclined to give up those countries, which he, after toilsome exertions, had ravished from Sweden. She easily perceived that, in so doing, she would have badly recommended herself to the nation; and would have acted just as unwisely as Peter III. afterwards did, when, at the very commencement of his reign, he shewed his magnanimity towards the king of Prussia. But, as Sweden might possibly have been requested by Lestocq to support Elizabeth's pretensions, in case of necessity, with an armed force, and as it was, therefore, now intended to gratify her in this matter, in return for her complaisance, though that necessity did not occur, yet Elizabeth offered to pay her a considerable sum of money, if she would consent to make peace, without insisting on any restitution of country. To this proposal Sweden would not comply; thinking, though on what grounds it is impossible to imagine, unless she was in expectation, perhaps, of a counter-revolution, that she had a right to demand more: and, therefore, hostilities, which had been interrupted by the armistice till the first of March, on the expiration of that term were renewed. Though the Swedes had acted with such inconceivable

ceivable stupidity in the former campaign, they proceeded in the same manner now; and the total ignorance in the art of war, that had been shewn by their commanders then, was no less flagrant on the present occasion. The swedish troops were so carelessly dispersed in winter-quarters, at great distances from each other, that they were not nearly all assembled, when Lascy had again made an incursion into Finland; and even after they had completed their junction, the Swedes behaved with so little bravery, that they abandoned one fortified place after another, to the pursuing Russians, till they were at length surrounded by the enemy near Helsingfors. They had even, according to custom in these campaigns, resolved to retreat from thence to Abo; but a boor of Finland betrayed to the russian general another way to Abo, by which he might reach that place before the Swedes. The Russians took that road; and the Swedes, now cut off from Abo, were obliged to turn back to the walls of Helsingfors. Here they for some time kept up a communication with Sweden; but of this likewise they were soon deprived by the russian fleet.

During this campaign Elizabeth also made an attempt to draw off the Finns entirely from Sweden. In a manifesto which she caused to be

dispersed,

dispersed, she accused the swedish government of
" having begun an unjust war; and though the
" empress had consented to an armistice, and
" offered to come to terms of accommodation,
" yet the court of Sweden insisted on war.
" Though certainly the whole kingdom was
" not pacifically inclined, yet she was persuaded
" that the inhabitants of Finland, who suffered
" most by the war, were heartily desirous of
" peace. The empress, therefore, made them
" the proposal, that they should remain quiet
" during the war, neither acting inimically
" against the Russians, nor giving succour to
" the Swedes — if they agreed to this, then
" Elizabeth would assist them in becoming *a*
" *free and independent nation*, living in future
" under the *protection* of Russia." Russia
indeed might hope, and have reason to expect,
that if Finland were once under russian protection, it might soon be converted into a russian province, and then its independence would not certainly be alarming to its neighbours, or its liberty dangerous to itself. In consequence of this, the king of Sweden published a counter-manifesto, admonishing the Finns " not to
" suffer themselves to be misled by empty pro-
" mises of future independence, but to continue
" happy in the enjoyment of their present con-
" stitution

"stitution under swedish supremacy," aiming thereby, and by the declaration, that Elizabeth herself had broken the truce, to efface the impression of the russian manifesto.

In the meantime, that manifesto had not been so diligently dispersed, without making some impression; and, though the Finns took no measures, yet Sweden could not be altogether secure that they might not hearken to the offers of Russia. However, the ravages and devastations committed by the russian troops in Finland, were by no means calculated to give the Finns a very pleasing idea of the russian supremacy. Upwards of two hundred villages, besides single houses, were burnt by the russians.

The swedish army being surrounded near Helsingfors, and deprived of all means of forcing a passage through the russian troops, both by land and water, no hope of deliverance was left, but by negotiation. The two swedish generals, Levenhaupt and Buddembrok, who were reputed at Stockholm to be the authors of the unfavourable position of the army, were dismissed by the government, and the command was given to another officer, who thought he could do nothing better than capitulate. Thus, the swedish troops, lately so confident of vanquishing the Russians, were now satisfied with being

allowed

allowed to return with their arms to Sweden, under promise of taking no farther share in the war, so long as it should last. This was certainly an event, least of all expected by the Swedish government, though their whole conduct during the war rendered it most probable; and Sweden was at present compelled to make peace whenever Russia should be inclined to consent to it. Finland being in the hands of the Russians, the Swedish army in part tied up from serving, the Finns obliged to remain inactive, and the Dalecarlians refusing to enlist, it was easy for the Russians to press forward into Sweden; Elizabeth, however, was more disposed to a pacification than to continue the war, but, availing herself of the advantages gained by her soldiers, would hearken to no other terms, than the evacuation of a great part of Finland by the Swedes.

The Swedes were now reduced to no small perplexity, as Russia had a right to insist on the hardest conditions: they saw no means of evasion. Fortunately for them, just at this juncture, an accidental circumstance arose, which occasioned Russia to agree to an equitable accommodation; and this was no other than a sudden resolution adopted in Sweden, as the king was entirely childless, to settle the succession during his lifetime. For the sake of gaining favour

favour with the empress Elizabeth, the diet made choice of the young duke of Holstein Gottorp, Anthony Peter Ulric, as heir to the swedish throne. Prior to this, however, Elizabeth had invited that prince into Russia, for the purpose of making him her successor. Peter received a deputation from Sweden, with an offer to him of the throne of their country — but he had already undergone the ceremony of conversion to the orthodox greek church, and Elizabeth was not inclined to let him quit Russia: he, therefore, thanked the swedish nation for their kind intentions, and remained in Russia. Could he but have had a glimpse into futurity, how different must have been his resolution! In consequence of this refusal, Elizabeth recommended the Swedes to choose her relation, the bishop of Lubeck, uncle to Peter III. for their king; and the Swedes had reason to expect a peace on moderate terms, if they complied with the wish of Elizabeth.

The majority of the Swedish nation, however, had no inclination for this candidate proposed to them by Russia. There was, on the contrary, every appearance that Denmark and Sweden would again be united, as most of the Swedes were desirous of having the hereditary prince of Denmark on their throne; and the Dalecarlians even broke out in open insurrection on that account,

account, rushed into the capital, and furiously insisted on the election of the danish prince. Denmark, who wished for a renewal of the treaty of Kalmar, made a number of apparently advantageous proposals; and Russia, therefore, seeing the negotiation for peace was likely to be delayed, took up arms again in the year 1743, in order to prosecute the war with vigour. In this campaign it was resolved to attempt some great exploit with the fleet; but, as an armament was also fitted out by Sweden, the Russians contented themselves with making a few inconsiderable descents on the enemy's coasts. In July the election of the future king was to come on at Stockholm; and a swedish ambassador, who was negotiating a peace with the russian commissioners at Abo, at length, by a stratagem, took advantage of the approaching election, to determine the Russians for peace, by pretending that Denmark was using efforts to frustrate the measures of the present congress, in order to carry on her own designs; and, as the Russians were absolutely bent on making no compliances, he broke up the meeting. This the russian delegates had not expected; but now, for the sake of gratifying the wishes of their sovereign, concluded a peace, by which Elizabeth restored the greater part of Finland, occupied by her troops, on condition, that the bishop of Lubeck should be appointed successor. The news of the peace arrived at Stockholm just before the election; the Dalecarlians were driven by the soldiers to Pasren; on the 4th of July Adolphus Frederic, duke of Holstein and bishop of Lubeck, was elected king of Sweden, and the succession settled in his posterity; and, in August, the peace between Russia and Sweden was fully ratified. Though the conditions of peace were now, after the war was terminated, of a very different kind from those, which only two years before had been framed previous to the commencement of it; yet the Swedes had reason to think themselves very fortunate that, by the pleasure which Elizabeth shewed at the election of her kinsman to the succession, they were enabled to procure to themselves better terms than they had otherwise reason to expect. The treaty of Nystadt, which the Swedes were so earnest to have annulled, was now adopted as the basis of the present, and they moreover agreed to give up the province of Kymmenegard in Finland, with Frederickshamm and Vilmannstrand, besides several other places, and all the harbours at the exit of the Kymmene, together with the islands to the south and to the west of that river. On the other hand, Sweden obtained the restitution

of

of all the places occupied by Ruffia during the war, and the boundaries of both territories were fettled anew. The inhabitants of the part of Finland ceded to Ruffia, were fecured in their privileges and immunities, as well as in the exercife of their religion, and the Swedes were allowed to export, years of fhort harveft excepted, to the value of 80,000 rubles of corn in the harbours of the gulf of Finland, to thofe of the Baltic, duty free. Thus Elizabeth, immediately in the firft years of her reign, enlarged the borders of the empire; and, as Anne had promoted the election of king Auguftus III. fo Elizabeth very clearly difplayed her influence in the choice of a fovereign for the neighbouring kingdom of Sweden.

Whatever pains the french ambaffador at St. Peterfburg had taken to draw off Ruffia from the auftrian party, and how furely foever this was to have been expected, as the auftrian ambaffador was implicated in the abovementioned connection, which had for its object to replace Anne upon the throne, yet Beftuchef, who was devoted to the houfe of Auftria, had the addrefs fo to guide the inclinations of the emprefs, that fhe continued in her adherence to its interefts; and, in 1747, fent troops to Germany to the affiftance of Maria Therefa, by which means the peace of Aix-la-chapelle was brought on. The friendfhip ship subsisting between the two imperial courts, was now gradually becoming more firmly cemented from day to day: so that, notwithstanding the efforts of the king of Prussia to preserve a good understanding with Russia, yet the party devoted to Austria at the russian court found means to defeat all his endeavours; and the empress of Germany, Maria Theresa, experienced in Elizabeth a friend and ally, no less faithful to her interests than the empress Catharine I. and both the Annes had proved to her predecessors.

It is true that Elizabeth and Frederic formed an alliance in 1743, and harmony seemed to prevail between them; it was, however, of very short duration, being continually undermined by Frederic's opponents at the court of Petersburg, till by their unwearied efforts it was at length totally annihilated, and aversion and hostility succeeded to its place. No longer time after than 1745, when the king of Prussia requested the empress to guarantee the treaty of Dresden, she rejected his application, under the flimsy pretence, that she had already too many guarantees on her hands. If hence it was to be concluded, that Frederic was not on the best terms with Russia, he had reason to think himself still more hurt by a treaty entered into between the courts of Petersburg and Vienna

in

in 1746, which though it was communicated to him as nothing more than an alliance for the purpose of mutual affistance, and by no means relating to meafures of aggreffion or offence to a third; from which, however, it was very foon eafy to infer what the king of Pruffia had to look for from Ruffia. — Rumours were now much abroad concerning an approaching rupture between Pruffia and Auftria. They were, however, publicly contradicted by both courts, who declared that no mifunderftanding had arifen between them. It was undeniable neverthelefs, that Ruffia, the ally of Auftria, was fecretly making difpofitions for war, and that both courts were ufing their efforts to draw the king of Poland and elector of Saxony into the confederacy, which might prefently, from a defenfive, be converted into an offenfive alliance, by means whereof Auftria indulged the hopes of regaining Silefia. Auguftus, however, hefitated to accede, as the hazard to him was by far the greateft.

Leftocq, who had been the moft forward of all that affifted Elizabeth in obtaining the crown, whom fhe had appointed to be director-general of the medicine-department throughout the empire, with a falary of 7000 rubles, ufually interfered in matters of ftate; and thereby, but

particularly

particularly from his predilection for Pruffia, drew upon him the hatred of Beftuchef, which at length involved him in the fame cataftrophe by which fo many favourites in Ruffia had finifhed their parts — a banifhment to Siberia *. All the time he was at court he had uniformly diffuaded the emprefs from breaking with Pruffia. No fooner was he difgraced but all poffible means were employed afrefh to excite difcord between Elizabeth and Frederic.

A paffage in the writings of the king of Pruffia, where he makes the mother of the emprefs to have been the wife of a petty officer, a free remark on Elizabeth's manner of life which once efcaped him while fitting at table with the ruffian ambaffador, and being, as ufual, magnified by report, made Elizabeth the per-

---

* Under pretence that Leftocq was in correfpondence with two foreign courts to the detriment of the empire, he was put in prifon; he was even accufed of having formed the defign to dethrone Elizabeth, and to make the grand-duke Peter emperor. — Leftocq, as was cuftomary in thofe cafes, was tried before a commiffion, where the accufers and the judge were the perfonal enemies of the culprit, and — condemned to death. But Elizabeth abfolutely could not be moved to affent to *this* fentence, but even deferred the execution of the punifhment of exile for four years and a half, for which it was commuted; Leftocq being arrefted in 1748, and not fent to Siberia till 1753.

sonal enemy of Frederic; and, as he was generally suspected of aiming to get possession of Courland and Polish-Prussia, it was certainly not surprising that Elizabeth was ever drawing closer the connection with Austria against Prussia, notwithstanding the numerous endeavours of the prussian party at St. Petersburg, to maintain the bond of amity between Frederic and the russian monarch. — In the year 1750 the empress recalled her ambassador, without many apologies, from the court of Berlin, and Frederic followed her example with his minister at Petersburg. In 1753 it was agreed between Russia and Austria, not only *to resist all farther augmentation* of the prussian power, but also to use efforts to reduce it; and in 1755 they resolved to put themselves in such a condition as should enable them at all times *to attack* Prussia, or in case of an attack from that quarter, to resist it with energy.

It is well known that Frederic, from whom this combination against him could not long be kept secret, thought it the best course he could take to go resolutely to meet his foes and anticipate their attack; that in 1756 he gave the signal of war by an incursion into Saxony; and Elizabeth, for five years, took a very active part in the wonderful contest of seven years which was entered into in behalf of Maria Theresa,

Theresa, and would have been more sensibly, and perhaps fatally felt by Frederic, had not the grand-duke, appointed by Elizabeth as her successor, been his friend, which had this consequence, that Elizabeth's orders, which tended to the ruin of Frederic, were not all so punctually fulfilled as they otherwise would have been, that likewise many who were employed in military affairs were very tender of hurting that monarch, in order to gain the approbation of the future sovereign Peter III. and accordingly rather chose to act in conformity with the secret instructions of the grand-duke than to adhere to the commands of the empress.

In the first year of that war [1756] the Russians had taken no share whatever in the contest between Frederic and Maria Theresa, begun by the former, and in which Saxony was so unfortunately involved. They first began to march in the following year [1757] to humble Frederic in the name and by the orders of their empress; and, which was thought to be highly possible, to gain possession of the kingdom of Prussia. From a variety of impediments[*] it was not till the month of July that the russian

---

[*] The army was extremely ill-provided, and many articles were wanting for putting it in a proper condition, as Austria, from whom the sums for that purpose had been expected, was unequal to the supply.

troops appeared before Memel, and made themselves masters of that city. From the moment of their entering on the prussian territory, this army not only betrayed a great want of discipline, but particularly their light corps, consisting of Kozaks, Kalmuks, and Tartars, behaved like real barbarians *. The cruelties which they committed on the inhabitants of that kingdom, were such as had never been heard of in the military history of Europe for upwards of a thousand years. The russian commanders themselves were sensible that it was no honour to them to be at the head of an army which brought on them the guilt of such proceedings. Several of them used every means in their power to put a stop to these enormities; but it was not possible to succeed: and, as in consequence of these barbarities, all persons fled at the approach of so unprincipled an enemy, it was extremely difficult for the Russians to prolong their stay in Prussia from the total want of the necessary means of subsistence in a country where the husbandmen deserted the land before them.

* The little town of Goldap on the frontiers was first plundered of everything and then burnt. The officers themselves set a very bad example. An adjutant wantonly set a village in flames through which the troops were to march, thereby subjecting the Russians themselves to the utmost danger in case the sparks had fallen on the powder-waggons.

An

An army of 24,000 men under the command of field-marshal Lehvald was all the force that Frederic had been able to leave behind him in Pruſſia for oppoſing his new enemy, the Ruſſians, whoſe ſtrength conſiſted in upwards of 100,000 combatants; and yet the marſhal had the boldneſs to quit his camp at Vehlau, where he was ſo uncommonly well entrenched and ſecure, that the enemy would not have ventured to attack him with all their ſuperiority of numbers, to go and give battle to the Ruſſians on the 30th of Auguſt at a place called Norkitten, not far from Groſyægerſdorf. Revenge for the inhuman devaſtations everywhere perpetrated by the Ruſſians now inſpired the pruſſian ſoldiers with valour and intrepidity. The pruſſian army, animated, not by the thirſt of conqueſt, but by a genuine patriotic zeal to defend their country, ruſhed like angry lions on the ſavage hordes, who thought they had no reaſon to fear that the little pruſſian army would ſeek an opportunity for coming to an engagement with them. Fortune ſeemed at firſt to declare in favour of the brave defenders of their country; towards the end of the battle, however, the Ruſſians gained the advantage, and the Pruſſians were forced to leave them maſters of the field. The Ruſſians were therefore conquerors; but, as they neglected to follow up their victory,

chuſing

chusing rather to repose upon their laurels, they left the Prussians to retreat unmolested. General Lehvald therefore retired in excellent order, without being pursued, having killed five times more of the enemy than he had lost of his own men, and more formidable after his defeat than the Russians after their victory; besides, it was impossible for the latter to stay longer in a country which they themselves had ravaged and laid waste, they were also obliged to retreat in their turn, in order to escape that most dreadful of all foes to an army, famine. Nay, by a strange concatenation of circumstances, field-marshal Apraxin, whose troops had occupied a very great part of Prussia, was at length induced entirely to abandon that kingdom, after leaving behind him a single garrison in the frontier-fort of Memel. The same barbarities and cruelties, as those with which the Russians had tarnished their honour on their entrance into Prussia, they now exercised at their departure; and smoking or burnt villages, mangled carcases, and crippled people marked the road they took. This extraordinary retreat, however, of so great an army, so lately victorious, and being still possessed of a good sea-port in the country, was an event so totally unexpected that it astonished all Europe, and drew complaints not

only

only from Austria but also from the other courts coalesced against Frederic, since it was not forced on by the superiority of the prussian troops, but voluntarily determined by the Russians, and so quickly and hastily executed that they even left behind them in Prussia a part of the baggage and a great number of cannon. The true motives of this retreat having never been hitherto assigned, they shall here have a place. Count Bestuchef, grand chancellor of Russia, who had for several years been Elizabeth's right hand, was no friend to the grand-duke, afterwards Peter III. but entirely devoted to Austria, as Peter on the other hand always espoused the party of Frederic. Elizabeth, just at this time, lay so dangerously ill, that her physicians began to doubt of her recovery. Bestuchef thereupon conceived the plan, in case Elizabeth should die, to exclude the grand-duke from the government, and to place upon the throne his son the present emperor Paul Petrovitch, under the guardianship of his mother the late empress Catharine II. To this end, however, it was necessary that he should have the troops at hand in order to use them in case of need, and the rather as their commander Apraxin was entirely at his devotion. In the meantime Elizabeth recovered; and, on inquiring after her army in Prussia, was not a

little

little exasperated on hearing that it was entirely withdrawn from that country. The austrian and french ambassadors preferred heavy complaints to the empress concerning the orders for retreating, which Bestuchef had transmitted unknown to her; the grand-duke Peter likewise did what he could to incense the empress against Bestuchef: and thus the combined efforts of the two several parties, with the great delays at the opening of the campaign, and this unaccountable retreat, gave the empress ground to suspect that she had been betrayed by her ministers or her generals. Marshal Apraxin was therefore removed from the command and put under arrest. He justified his conduct by the express orders of count Bestuchef. Bestuchef was removed from his office and put under arrest also. Count Vorontzof succeeded Bestuchef in his employment, and the generals Brown and Fermor took the command of the army in the place of Apraxin, who was sent as a prisoner to Narva*. The empress also appointed a commission

* On being informed of the overthrow of his friend and patron Bestuchef, he was so affected at the news that he fell down and expired. Bestuchef, in the manifesto that was issued against him, was charged with having, merely from

mission to inquire at large into the conduct of the field-marshal during the whole of the campaign, as the court of Vienna expressly declared that the russian commanders had not shewn such a behaviour as ought to have been

---

from ambition and the lust of dominion, meddled in matters that did not concern him; with having at various times neglected to obey the orders of her majesty when they were not agreeable to him; with frequently issuing decrees without previously consulting the empress; with having slandered the grand-duke and grand-duchess to her, and endeavoured to incense the empress against them. He was banished to a village belonging to him 102 miles from Mosco, and thus became another striking example of the instability and lubricity of fortune in courts. The modern history of Russia in general presents a series of discarded favourites who were all repaid the measure they had meted to others. All of them, as long as they stood beside the throne, as long as their will and their sentence could honour or condemn, made free use of that privilege, and all of them at last met the same condemnation. Here we cannot but recollect, that Mentshikof was turned out by the Dolgorukis, and these in their turn experienced a more terrible fate at the instigation of Biren. But also exile awaited Biren; and Munich, who procured it for him, escaped it not himself. Lestocq and Bestuchef exulted in the fall of Munich; Bestuchef found means to bring about the downfall of Lestocq, in spite of Elizabeth's attachment to him; but neither did he enjoy his triumph long, and fell at the very time when he thought himself most secure!

expected from *faithful* allies, and from an army which fought the glory of its monarch*.

The

* A gentleman of Weymar, who at that time served as quarter-master-general under marshal Apraxin, and likewise was summoned to Petersburg to give evidence concerning the sudden retreat, and on the behaviour in general of the Russians in Prussia in the year 1757, says, in his justificatory memorial, on the points presented to him: " It cannot be
" denied that the Prussians had uniformly an account of all
" that was passing among the Russians — that the barba-
" rities exercised, particularly by the russian light troops,
" had exasperated the inhabitants against the Russians to
" such a degree, that they never shewed them the right
" road, but on the contrary assisted the enemy by every
" means in their power — that the soldiers, as usual, even
" on the day of the battle near Grosyægersdörf, were much
" more intent upon pillaging and making booty, than on
" pursuing the enemy and profiting by the victory; and
" that in the russian army throughout very little subordi-
" nation was observed. Indeed, the field-marshal was very
" severe and frequent in punishing; the knoot was liberally
" administered, noses were slit, and ears cut off in abun-
" dance; but forasmuch as all capital punishments were
" absolutely forbidden, every other punishment was insuffi-
" cient to deter them. As all the countrymen had fled,
" they were reduced to the utmost distress for want of pro-
" visions, and the inhabitants in general paid no regard to
" the orders for delivering their quota of contribution.
" The insubordination that prevailed among the troops
" was so great, as to oblige the field-marshal, on his retreat,
" to cause the villages before him to be burnt, for depriving

" the

The Russians having thus in the first campaign burnt and destroyed every place to which they came, and pillaged and ravaged wherever they went, carrying off numbers of the inhabitants of Prussia, murdering and maiming others, and gained a battle without reaping any benefit from it, but rapidly retreated out of the hostile country occupied by them, thereby furnishing the enemy with an opportunity of employing the force opposed to them elsewhere: the whole of this year's campaign, therefore, was in no respect to their honour as european warriors of the eighteenth century.

Bestuchef's fall, however, produced no alteration in the sentiments of Elizabeth in regard to the king of Prussia; she rather resolved to make up in the following year for what had

---

" the soldiers of the opportunity of running about in par-
" ties to rob and plunder, so much to the separation and
" weakening of the army, that it would have been easy for
" the pursuing enemy, by encountering and defeating the
" detached corps, to do them great mischief. It is not,
" however, to be denied," continues Weymar, " that in
" this campaign a certain pusillanimity and fear was con-
" spicuous among the Russians; and, though the light
" troops particularly, were very adventurous in pillaging,
" they did not behave gallantly in battle against the
" enemy."

been

been neglected in the hasty retreat of 1757; and, so early as January [1758] the Russians marched again into Prussia under the command of general field-marshal Fermor. Not only Kœnigsberg, the capital, but the whole kingdom of Prussia, had submitted to them before the end of that month, and continued in their possession during the remainder of the war. In the conquest of which, however, they found no difficulty, as Frederic had not been able to cover that part of his territory. The Russians now began to think that the kingdom of Prussia would soon be incorporated into the dominions of the empress, and form a part of Russia. On this occasion, so far from repeating the outrages and barbarities of the foregoing campaign, they, contrary to all expectation, behaved with the greatest gentleness, now that they considered it as already a part of their country, and regarded its inhabitants as their future countrymen*. The inhabitants, who were obliged to swear fealty to the empress of Russia, were even in doubt themselves, whether it would ever be possible for their king, pressed as he was on all

---

* It was even read from the pulpits, that whoever had any complaint against a russian soldier should present it to the military-chancery at Kœnigsberg, where he would infallibly have redress.

sides, to replace himself in the possession of the country; and accordingly strove by every means to render themselves agreeable to the Russians, in order to restrain them from a renewal of those calamities under which they had suffered the year before. — This lenity, however, shewn by them to the kingdom of Prussia, which they already looked upon as their own, they soon laid aside, and resumed the old russian deportment when once they were got into the other countries of the king, Pomerania and the Mark. Fermor advanced through Pomerania, and made an assault on the fortress of Kustrin in the Neumark, and bombarded the town, contrary to the usages of war observed by all civilized nations, before he had sent a summons to the commandant, laying all the houses and other buildings of the town, within the space of a few hours, by a dreadful conflagration, in one smoking heap of ruins: then, not till two days after, attacked the citadel; and, at length, on the fourth day, summoned the commandant to surrender. This was rejected with disdain by the governor; and Fermor raised the siege on receiving intelligence that the king was advancing in person to the defence of his country. The Prussians, rushing from Silesia, under the conduct of their king, would doubtless have taken bloody revenge

venge on an army of whose inhuman devastations and cruelties so much had reached their ears, and of which they now, on their arrival in the territories of their king, beheld the melancholy proofs in the consumed villages and towns, the desolated fields, the maimed, ill-treated, or impoverished inhabitants presenting themselves at every step. The king himself was so enraged at the vestiges he perceived on all sides of the barbarous ravages of the Russians, and at the accounts that were brought him of the terrible havoc they had committed, that he gave orders not to spare the life of a single Russian in the battle that was daily expected to come on; an order which the russian general, on being informed of, threatened to retaliate. Marshal Fermor was encamped at Zorndorf, six miles from Kustrin, where he was attacked by the king at the head of his army on the 25th of August. The russian ranks stood like walls, and fought valiantly: but the military skill of the Prussians, the valour of a host fighting for their country and for the martial glory they had hitherto maintained, and glowing to revenge themselves on a barbarous enemy, displayed their amazing effects on the day of that bloody fight; and the generals, Seidlitz and Ziethen in particular, performed miracles of

prowess

prowess with the cavalry. After the battle both armies claimed the victory, but the greatest loss was manifestly on the part of the Russians; they therefore founded their claim on the circumstance of having kept the field * : however this be, the army-chest, and most of their artillery, fell into the hands of the enemy, who likewise took an extraordinary number of prisoners, amongst whom were several officers of the first rank; and, in consequence of this, they soon retreated. Frederic was still able to shew himself the father and benefactor, as well as the protector of his people. In the midst of the devouring waste of such an expensive war, from the funds of his œconomy he was enabled to remit the taxes to those parts of his dominions which had suffered from the russian barbarity: he even advanced money to those whose distresses had been the greatest. It should be remembered too, that all this was done while the whole kingdom of Prussia still remained in the hands of the Russians.

* It is highly probable that it was their intention to have withdrawn across the Oder, had not the king previously caused all the bridges to be broken down, in the hopes of giving them an entire defeat, and by the demolition of the bridges depriving them of every means of making good their retreat.

The

The court of Petersburg still adhered to its old system, in spite of the late ill success of her arms, and all the efforts of the british minister to withdraw her from her alliance. If she had some loss of men, it was the least loss she could feel: and she thought that, while the war was carried on at the expence of others, the reduction of so near, so dreaded, and so hated a rival as the king of Prussia, and the opportunity of forming her troops to service, and perfecting her officers, were objects of consequence enough to keep her closely attached to her first sentiments. Fermor now undertook the siege of Colberg, for the purpose of obtaining a commodious deposit for provisions and ammunition; but all in vain: seven hundred of the country militia bravely defended that town against a russian corps of several thousand men, and the Russians retired, without making this conquest, to their winter-quarters in Prussia and Poland: even there they were harassed by the prussian troops, who destroyed several of their magazines.

Poland was henceforth to be the country where the exploits of the next campaign were to be atchieved. Hither, therefore, the Russians marched, and hence they afterwards spread themselves over all the prussian territory, [1759] under the command of count Soltikof, who had

been

been appointed chief of the army, in the room of marshal Fermor*. Frederic's german dominions, and Silesia, became now the scene of action. Fortified, in some measure, by the reinforcements he had received, and in pursuance of his orders, general Wedel resolved to attack the Russians on their march. They had got to Zulichau towards the latter end of July, and directed their course to Krossen in Silesia, to get before the prussian army, and to make good the passage of the Oder. The situation of the Russians was very advantageous; posted upon eminences, defended by a powerful artillery, and near seventy thousand strong. The prussian army fell short of thirty thousand; and they had greater disadvantages to get over than what arose from the inferiority of numbers. They had a bridge to pass, and such a narrow defile to struggle through, that scarce a third of a battalion could march in front. The ground was such, that the cavalry could not support their infantry. Yet with all these difficulties, the attack was long and resolute. But this resolution made their repulse, which all these disadvantages had rendered inevitable, far more bloody and distressful. Four thousand seven hundred were killed or taken

* Fermor now served under him.

prisoners;

prisoners; and the wounded were, at least, three thousand. The Prussians were obliged to retire, but they were not pursued; and they passed the Oder without molestation. The Russians seized upon the towns of Krossen and Frankfort on the Oder.

Frederic now marched with ten thousand of his best troops to join the broken army of Wedel, in order to drive this formidable and determined enemy from his country. Prince Henry commanded the remainder of his army, which was too well posted to fear any insult during his absence. The eyes of all were fixed upon his march, and his soldiers who remembered Zorndorf, eagerly longed to try their strength once more with the same antagonists.

Marshal Daun, the austrian general, was not unapprised of the motion of the Russians, or the designs of the king of Prussia. He knew that the great defect of the russian troops, was the want of a regular and firm cavalry, which might be depended upon in the day of action. This defect had been a principal cause of their misfortune at Zorndorf the last year; a misfortune which disconcerted all the operations of that campaign. As this was the only want which the Russians were under, so it was that which Daun was best able to supply at a short warning.

With

With this view he selected about twelve thousand of his horse, and there is no better horse than that of the Austrians; which, with about eight thousand foot, he placed under the command of general Laudohn, one of the ablest officers in that service. This body was divided into two columns, one of which marched through Silesia, and the other through Lusatia. By extreme good fortune and conduct, with little loss or opposition, they both joined the russian army, and were received with transports of joy.

In the meantime, the king of Prussia, who was unable to prevent this stroke, joined general Wedel at Muhlrose, and took upon him the command of the united armies. But, still finding himself too weak for the decisive action he was preparing to attempt, he recalled general Finck, whom he had sent some time before into Saxony with nine thousand men, in order to oppose the Imperialists in that country. With these reinforcements he was not able to raise his army to fifty thousand complete. That of the Russians, since the junction of Laudohn, was upwards of ninety thousand. They had besides taken a post, which they had so strongly entrenched, and defended with such a prodigious number of cannon, that it was extremely difficult and hazardous to attempt them; yet, under these

accumulated

accumulated disadvantages, it was absolutely necessary that he should fight. The detachments from count Daun's army already menaced Berlin; Saxony, which he was obliged to leave exposed, had become a prey to the Imperialists; and the Russians, united with the Austrians, encamped before his eyes in Silesia, the best and richest part of his dominions. In short, his former reputation, his present difficulties, his future hopes, every motive of honour and of safety, demanded an engagement; the campaign hasted to a decision, and it was evident, that nothing farther could be done by marches and choice of posts. The sanguine temper of other generals has often obliged them to fight under disadvantages; but the king of Prussia's circumstances were such, that, from the multitude of his enemies, he was neither able to consult times nor situations. Rashness could hardly dictate anything, which, in his condition, would not have been recommended by prudence.

When the attack was resolved, the king's troops put themselves in motion on the 12th of August, at two in the morning; and, having formed themselves in a wood, advanced towards the enemy. It was near eleven before the action began. The principal effort of the king of Prussia was against the left wing of the russian army.

army. He began, according to his usual method, with a fierce cannonade; which, having had the effect he desired from it, he attacked that wing with several battalions disposed in columns.

The russian entrenchments were forced with great slaughter. Seventy-two pieces of cannon were taken. But still there was a defile to be passed, and several redoubts to be mastered, which covered the village of Kunnersdorf. These were attacked with the same resolution, and taken one after another. The enemy again made a stand at the village, and endeavoured there to preserve their ground, by pushing forward several battalions of horse and foot: but their resistance there proved not more effectual than it had done everywhere else; they were driven from post to post quite to the last redoubts. For upwards of six hours fortune favoured the Prussians, who everywhere broke the enemy with an unparalleled slaughter. They had driven them from almost all the ground which they had occupied before the battle; they had taken more than half their artillery: scarcely anything seemed wanting to the most complete decision.

The king in those circumstances wrote a billet to the queen, to this effect: " Madam, we have
" beat the Russians from their entrenchments.
" In

"In two hours expect to hear of a glorious "victory." This news arrived at Berlin just as the post was going out, and the friends of the king of Prussia throughout Europe, exulted in a certain and conclusive victory. Meantime, fortune was preparing for him a terrible reverse.

The enemy, defeated in almost every quarter, found their left wing, shattered as it was, to be more entire than any other part of the army. Count Soltikof therefore assembled the remains of his right, and gathered as many as he could from the centre, reinforced that wing, and made a stand at a redoubt, which had been erected on a very advantageous eminence. No more was wanting to terminate matters in favour of the king, than to drive the Russians from this their last hope. But this enterprise was difficult. It was confidently said, that the prussian generals were unanimous in their opinion, that they should not endeavour at that time to push any farther the advantages they had obtained. They represented to the king, that the enemy was still very numerous, their artillery very considerable, and the post which they occupied of great strength; that his brave troops, who had been engaged so long a time, in the severest action perhaps ever known, and in one of the hottest days ever felt, were too much exhausted for a new attempt;

an attempt of such extreme difficulty, as might daunt even troops that were quite fresh. That the advantage he had gained would be as decisive in its consequences, as that at Zorndorf; and, whilst the enemy filled the gazettes of their party with frivolous disputes of the field of battle, he would be reaping, as he did then, all the effects of an unquestioned victory. That the enemy would be obliged to retire immediately into Poland, and to leave him at liberty to act in other quarters, where his presence was full as necessary.

These reasons were very cogent, and for a few moments they seemed to have some weight with the king. But his character soon determined him to a contrary resolution. He could not bear to be a conqueror by halves. One effort more was alone wanting to that victory, which would free him for ever from the adversary which had leaned heaviest on him during the whole of the war.

Once more he put all to the hazard. His infantry, still resolute, and supported by their late success, were readily brought to act again. They drew on their bodies, fainting with heat and labour, to a new attack. But the enterprize was beyond their strength. The situation of the enemy was impregnable; and their artillery, which began to be superior to that of the Prussians,

Prussians, on account of the difficulty of the ground, which made it impossible for the latter to bring up any other than a few small pieces, repulsed these feeble battalions with a great slaughter. With an astonishing, perhaps with a blameable perseverance, the prussian infantry were brought to a second attack, and were a second time repulsed, and with a loss greater than at first. These efforts being unsuccessful, the affair was put to the cavalry. They made redoubled, but useless attacks; the horses were spent, as well as those they carried.

It was just at that time, when the prussian horse was wasted by these fruitless exertions, that the greatest part of the russian and the whole body of the austrian cavalry, which had been hitherto entirely inactive, and was therefore quite fresh, rushed down upon them, broke them to pieces, forced them back upon their foot, and threw the whole into irreparable disorder. The army was universally seized with a panic; and in a few minutes those troops, so lately victorious and irresistible, were totally dispersed and defeated. The king did everything to restore the field, hazarding his person, even beyond his former daring, and prodigal of a life he seemed to think ought not to be separated from conquest. Thrice he led on his troops to the charge; two horses were killed under him; several balls were in his clothes. The utmost efforts of skill, courage, and despair were made, and proved ineffectual: a single error outweighed them all. Scarcely a general, hardly an inferior officer in the army was without some wound. That of general Seidlitz was particularly unfortunate; for to that wound the failure of the horse, which he commanded, was principally attributed. It was to the spirit and conduct of this able officer, that a great part of the success at Zorndorf had been owing, in the last campaign. It is known, that if it had not been for a seasonable movement of the horse, the whole prussian army had then been in great danger of a defeat.

The night, and the prudent use of some eminences, which were defended as well as circumstances, would admit, preserved the prussian army from total destruction. However, their loss was far greater than any which they had sustained from the beginning of the war. All their cannon was taken. The killed, wounded, and prisoners, by the most favourable accounts, were near twenty thousand. General Putkammer was killed on the spot. Those generals, whose names were so distinguished in that war, Itzenplitz, Hulsen, Finck, Wedel, and Seidlitz, were among the wounded; as was the prince of
Wurtemberg,

Wurtemberg, and five major-generals. The enemy could not have fewer than ten thousand killed on their side. For hardly ever was fought a more bloody battle.

When the king of Prussia found himself obliged to quit the field, he sent another dispatch to the queen, expressed in this manner: "Remove from Berlin with the royal family. Let the archives be carried to Potsdam. The town may make conditions with the enemy." It were vain to attempt to draw the picture of the court and city, on the receipt of such news, in the midst of the joy which they indulged for the accounts they had received but a few hours before. The terror was increased by the indistinct relation that soon followed, which gave them only to understand, that their army was totally routed; that there was no account of the king, and that a russian army was advancing to take possession of their city.

The day after the battle the king of Prussia repassed the Oder, and encamped at Retvin. Thence he moved to Furstenvalde, and placed himself in such a manner, that the Russians did not venture to make any attempt upon Berlin. He continually watched their army; a part of which, instead of turning towards Brandenburg, marched into Lusatia, where it joined that of the

Auſtrians. Here the victorious Soltikof, for the firſt time, met marſhal Daun, and amidſt rejoicings and gratulations, conſulted about the meaſures for improving their ſucceſs.

The Ruſſians profited no more by the advantages obtained at Kunnerſdorf, than they had done the preceding year by the victory at Yægerſdorf, but remained ſtationary in that diſtrict, and demoliſhed, according to cuſtom, being ever intent on ſpreading ruin and deſolation arourd them, all the ſluices of the Frederic-William canal, which connects the Spree with the Oder. Marſhal Daun was for paſſing the Oder: but he was over-ruled; and thus furniſhed another inſtance, that the auſtrian and ruſſian generals do not readily act in concert *. Soltikof excuſed himſelf by alleging, that he had already done much: having in this year alone twice routed the Pruſſians, and thereby extremely reduced his numbers, while the great auſtrian army had remained totally inactive; and that therefore he ought not

* This diſlike to the Auſtrians might probably be in part aſcribed to the complaints which, in the ſeven year war, the court of Vienna was perpetually making againſt the ruſſian generals at that of Peterſburg. This being at length perceived by the former, attempts were made, by flattery and preſents, to repair the union that had been thus diſſolved — too late.

to remove far from Poland, for fear of being distressed by the want of provisions for his troops. Daun promised to send him provisions: a promise which, as the Russians kept advancing, he was unable to perform, especially since prince Henry endeavoured everywhere to destroy the austrian magazines. Daun, who therefore had enough to do to provide for himself, now offered the Russians money: but Soltikof sent him word that his soldiers could not eat money; and as, moreover, the king was doing his utmost to prevent the junction of the Russians with the Austrians, Soltikof retired to winter-quarters in Poland, without performing anything farther. His army also on this retreat committed incredible outrages and cruelties, burning villages, the seats of noblemen, and several towns in Silesia and Brandenburg, so that smoaking ruins now likewise marked the way by which they abandoned the prussian territory*.

In the year 1760 the Russians marched into eastern Pomerania, where they invested Colberg

---

* They were resolved, it was said, to leave the prussian subjects nothing but air and earth, and were actually making preparations to put their inhuman threats, unjustifiable even in war, into execution. Frederic on this occasion said, "We have to do with barbarians who are digging the grave of humanity."

both by land and sea, and pressed that city with a close and unremitted siege; but again without effect. In the meantime another corps, under the orders of count Chernichef entered Berlin; and the king of Prussia at last saw his capital taken by his most cruel enemies, and put to ransom; his native country was wasted; they took up their quarters in his palaces, ruined all the royal manufactories, emptied the arsenal, and would have carried their wild outrages still farther against the city and its inhabitants, had not general Tottleben, who had been formerly in the prussian service, and lived sometime in Berlin, acted the part of a mediator between them and their enemies, and exerted himself to the utmost to procure them a reprieve. The Russians, however, no sooner heard that the king was on his march to the succour of his distressed capital, than they turned about and withdrew to Poland, after the command had been given to count Butturlin, in consequence of an opinion that prevailed even at St. Petersburg, and which had been corroborated by accounts from Vienna, that it was the fault of the *russian* commanders, that the combined forces of the two imperial courts had atchieved no more.

Again in the following year [1761], the Russians succeeded in effecting a junction with
the

the Austrians near Strigau. But the want of provisions separated the two armies; when the Russians, having re-crossed the Oder, now made themselves masters of the fortifications of Colberg, which, though badly garrisoned, had been no less than ten times summoned to surrender in vain, and took up their winter-quarters in Pomerania, and the Neumark. The affairs of the king of Prussia were certainly at present in a far more calamitous situation, than they had been at any period during the whole course of the war. The Austrians had spread themselves over all Silesia, while the Mark and Pomerania were submitted to the ravages of the Russians: nothing remained to him but Saxony. Frederic too felt his distresses more heavily than ever; he became suddenly reserved, speaking but little, even with his most confidential officers; and seemed now to apprehend that it would be extremely difficult, if not utterly impossible, for him any longer to make head against his enemies. But at the very moment when his condition seemed the most hopeless, the death of the empress Elizabeth, which happened on the 25th of December 1761, opened to him all at once a brighter prospect, and rescued him from a labyrinth, out of which he could perceive no escape, and from which it is

hard

hard to conceive a possible means of being extricated by any human combination of events. So unfortunately circumstanced were the affairs of the king of Prussia, that his wisest schemes and happiest successes could hardly answer any other end, than to vary the scene of his distress; when exactly in this critical conjuncture, that unexpected removal of his inveterate foe took place; and the very change thus effected in the person of the russian sovereign, which suddenly snatched him from his lamentable condition, at the same time laid the basis of that honourable peace, which two years after crowned his toils, and completely annihilated the plans and machinations of his numerous enemies.

Elizabeth, as empress, governed but little of herself; it being properly her ministers and favourites who dictated her regulations and decrees. Of this number, besides Bestuchef, was also Razumoffky, to whom, as was said, the empress was even privately married. At the beginning of her reign, it is true, she went a few times to the sittings of the senate; but the matters transacted there were by much too serious for her mind; and, accordingly, she very soon left off that practice altogether, contenting herself by confirming with her signature the resolutions

tions of that assembly, and the determinations of her minister, or the *conference*, which supplied the place of the council.

Her character in general was mild, as was evident from the tears it cost her whenever she received accounts from Prussia even of victories gained by her own army, on account of the human blood by which they must necessarily have been purchased. Yet even this delicate sensibility did not restrain her from prosecuting the war which she had entered into from a species of revenge, and for the purpose of humbling the king of Prussia, and even on her death-bed from exhorting the persons about to the most vigorous continuation of it. It also proceeded from this sensibility, that immediately on her accession to the government she made the vow never to put her signature to a sentence of death. A resolution which she faithfully kept; though it cannot be averred to have been for the benefit of the empire: since in consequence of it the number of malefactors who deserved to die was every day increasing, insomuch that even the clergy requested the empress to retract her vow, at the same time urging proofs that they could release her from it. All the arguments they could use, however, were of no avail to move the conscientious monarch;
she

she would not give effect to any sentence of death*, although the commanders in the army particularly would have been glad that her conscience had yielded a little on that point. They declared that the soldiers were not to be restrained from their excesses by the severest corporal punishments they could employ; whereas such was their dread of a solemn execution, that a few examples of that nature would have effectually kept them in awe.

Commerce and literature, arts, manufactures, handicrafts, and the other means of livelihood, which had been fostered by the former sovereigns, continued their course under Elizabeth with increasing prosperity. The country-products were obtained and wrought up in greater quantities, and several branches of profit were more zealously carried on. The sum appointed for the support of the academy of sciences founded by Peter I. at St. Petersburg, was con-

---

* It is true, that, in lieu of capital executions, punishments were inflicted far more terrible than death, as for example, the tearing out the tongue by the roots. The commandant at Rogervyk had usually ten thousand malefactors under his care, all of them shockingly mutilated, either by having the tongue torn out, or the sides of the nostrils cut away by red-hot pincers, or their ears cut off, or their arms twisted behind them by dislocation at the shoulders, &c.

fiderably augmented by Elizabeth, and she moreover established in 1758 the academy still subsisting for the arts of painting and sculpture, in which a number of young persons are brought up as painters, engravers, statuaries, architects, and the like. At Mosco she endowed an university and two gymnasiums.

The empress Elizabeth herself having a good voice, music, which Anne had already much encouraged, found under her administration a perpetual accession of disciples and admirers; so that even numbers of persons of distinction at St. Petersburg became excellent performers. The art of acting plays was now also more general among the Russians. Formerly none but french or italian pieces were performed on the stage of St. Petersburg, whereas now Sumarokof obtained celebrity as a dramatic poet in his native language, and in 1756 Elizabeth laid the foundation of a russian theatre in her residence. — Architecture, likewise, found a great admirer and patroness in her, Petersburg and its vicinity being indebted to her for great embellishments and numerous structures.

The magnificence which had prevailed under Anne at the court of St. Petersburg was not diminished during her reign, and the court establishment

blishment therefore amounted to extraordinary sums. Elizabeth, indeed, in this respect did not imitate her great father; and accordingly in the seven-year war the want of a well-stored treasury was already very sensibly felt.

The population of the empire was considerably increased under her; and so early as 1752, according to the statement in an account published by an official person it was augmented by one fifth.

Elizabeth continued the practice of her predecessors in encouraging foreigners to come and settle in her empire. Emigrant Servians cultivated a considerable tract of land, till then almost entirely uninhabited, on the borders of Turkey, where they built the town of Elizabethgorod, and multiplied so fast, that more recently [1764] a particular district was formed of these improvements, under the name of New Servia. Only the jews Elizabeth was no less resolute not to tolerate than her father had been; insomuch that so early in her reign as 1743 they were ordered to quit the country on pain of death.

The army was augmented under Elizabeth; improved, however, certainly not. There were now no longer at the head of it such men as the

foreigners

foreigners Munich, Keith, or Lœvendal*; who, besides their personal courage and intrepidity, possessed the soundest principles of the art of war; and, what is of no less consequence in a commander, kept up a strict discipline, and took care that the laws of subordination were punctually observed. The excessive licence which the regiments of guards, particularly the life-company of the preobajenskoy guards, presumed to exercise, under the very eyes of the empress in St. Petersburg, afforded no good example to the rest of the army; and Elizabeth, in appointing those soldiers of that life-company, who had been most guilty of flagrant disorders and the basest conduct, to be officers in the marching regiments, gives us no very high idea of what was required in an officer, but rather serves easily to explain whence it arose that such frequent complaints were made of insubordination. — A great number of excellent regulations that had been introduced into the army, and

---

* Munich was in Siberia; Keith was gone into the prussian, and Lœvendal into the french service. The empress greatly regretted the loss of the two latter; and unquestionably they were the best generals of her army, but they were often obliged to put up with affronts from the native Russians under Elizabeth, and had no friend in Bestuchef.

always

always enforced by foreigners, especially by Munich, were suffered by the russian generals to fall into total disuse; the bad effects of which negligence were very soon perceived: and it was undoubtedly a circumstance highly favourable to the russian troops, that for several years successively in the war which we have had occasion so often to mention, they had to engage with such a master in the military art as the king of Prussia, and by their conflicts with him, as well as by their connection with the austrian, and in the sequel with the prussian soldiery, they had an opportunity for learning so many things and of forming themselves into regular combatants *. As soldiers, the Russians, even in the seven-year war, displayed great personal bravery, generally opposing the enemy with the utmost obstinacy. "These fellows may be killed, it is true," Frederic once observed, "but they can never

---

* Thus, for example, in an engagement with the Prussians, they drew up in the same order of battle as they observed in their wars with the Turks and Tartars, forming the whole army into a quadrangle, in the centre of which was the baggage. But the cannon balls made dreadful havoc with troops so closely compressed; one single shot is said to have either killed or wounded 42 men of a regiment of grenadiers. — In fighting against Tartars, who have in part no other arms than arrows, this order of battle may perhaps be advantageous.

" be conquered;" for they stood like ramparts, defended themselves valiantly at their posts, and frequently would suffer themselves to be cut in pieces rather than fall back an inch. But when once they were thrown into disorder, it was out of the power of any officer to bring them to rally and stand their ground; they then began to fall upon the brandy casks among the baggage, with which they made themselves so beastly drunk that they fired and cut at their officers who were endeavouring to restore order among them, or they dispersed themselves over the scene of action to ransack the villages and rob the inhabitants, where they often met death as a reward for their imprudence. Thus it was usual for them, by their behaviour in the field of battle, in the camp, and in their quarters, to give a striking example of what a disciplined army ought not to be. The art of engaging with heavy artillery was moreover that particular branch of military science, wherein the Russians had always been most expert, and the fire of their cannon struck terror into the enemy. One of their generals, count Shuvalof, had, shortly before the seven-year war broke out, invented a new kind of howitzer which produced the greatest effect, and in the several engagements with the Prussians, was employed greatly to the disadvantage of the latter.

Elizabeth tarnished her reign * by the institution of a political court of inquisition, under the name of a secret state-chancery, empowered to examine into and punish all such charges brought before it as related to the expression of any kind of displeasure with the measures of government. This, as is usual in all such cases, opened a door to the vilest practices: the lowest and most profligate of mankind were now employed as spies and informers, who were paid for their denunciations and calumnies, for bearing witness against the most virtuous characters, if they happened by a look, by a shrug of the shoulders, by a few harmless words, to signify their disapprobation of the proceedings of the sovereign, as was frequently the case, especially on the part which Elizabeth took in the war

---

* The barbarities of the russian troops in the territories of the king of Prussia were committed indeed during her reign; but in this respect she may perhaps be thought in some degree excusable, as these horrors were perpetrated without her knowledge. It was at least not her will that her troops should behave in such a manner. She had given proper orders for a more honourable treatment of the inhabitants of the hostile countries — only these orders met with the same fate that many thousands, both before and since, have had, that of not being obeyed.

againſt Frederic II. Sons might impeach their fathers, debtors their creditors, and thus the priſons were frequently inſufficient to contain the number of thoſe who were accuſed of a want of reſpect for the government, and of ſome ſeditious ſpeech, as every ſlight ſtricture was immediately called. — Elizabeth evinced, eſpecially in the latter years of her life, great apprehenſions and alarms, as if afraid that ſhe ſhould meet a ſimilar fate with that ſhe had brought upon Anne; and is ſaid therefore to have more than once curſed the memory of thoſe who firſt conceived the thought of chacing princes from their thrones. — She is univerſally reported to have indulged, but more particularly for ſome years before her death, in the moſt unbounded intemperance and ſenſuality: however, ſhe continued in the undiſturbed and tranquil enjoyment of her exalted ſtation to the laſt day of her life. At that period Charles Peter Ulric, or, as he is ſtyled in his quality of emperor, Peter III. peaceably and legitimately acceded to the ruſſian crown as her declared ſucceſſor.

PETER III. was the only ſon of Charles Frederic duke of Holſtein, by the princeſs Anne, eldeſt daughter of Peter the Great and Catharine I. He was born at Kiel, in 1728; his parents having thought it prudent to quit Ruſſia on the death of Catharine I. their affectionate mother. Soon after Peter's birth his mother Anne departed this life. — His father on the demise of Charles XII. had every reasonable expectation of being king of Sweden. Had the life of Charles been protracted, and, as from his little propensity to the female sex there was room to expect, had not married, then probably the duke would have been his successor; but that monarch being suddenly killed by a shot before Frederikshall, the views of Charles Frederic on the swedish throne immediately vanished, though, as the son of Charles's elder sister, he had the nearest right. Ulrica, younger sister of Charles, took the crown of Sweden, and the disappointed duke repaired to Russia. Peter I. would gladly have helped him in the recovery of his right; but his exertions were fruitless; and that sovereign was even obliged, at the treaty of Nystadt, to promise not to meddle either directly or indirectly in the succession of Sweden. The duke was however husband of the princess Anne, and had some hope to see, on the death of Catharine I. his wife, perhaps, Catharine's eldest daughter, empress of Russia: but this hope also was defeated. Mentshikof, in order to keep up his consequence in the administration, had so contrived that the young

Peter

Peter was named as successor in Catharine's will, to whom, only in case he should die childless, Anne was to succeed; and, that this case might not easily happen, Mentshikof resolved to marry Peter early. Nevertheless, as Peter actually died unmarried and without heirs, Anne might certainly have appealed to Catharine's testament in support of her claims to the vacant throne. But she was now no longer alive, and her husband the duke, who lived in perfect retirement, seeing the pretensions also of his son Peter now totally frustrated by the election of Anne dowager duchess of Courland, brought him up in a manner befitting a prince of the petty domains of Holstein-Gottorp, as fortune seemed to have cut him off from all hopes of acquiring a grander throne. Peter's education, therefore, at Kiel, first under the care of his father, and then under that of his uncle, duke Adolphus Frederic, bishop of Lubeck[*], was such as promised to qualify him for an able and worthy ruler of his little patrimony; when all at once in his fourteenth year, the most brilliant prospect, that of being one day monarch of the vast russian empire, opened upon him. Elizabeth, the maternal aunt of Peter, sent for the

---

[*] Afterwards king of Sweden.

young prince to St. Peterſburg; and, on his arrival there, after he had publicly made profeſſion of the greek communion, proclaimed him grand-duke of Ruſſia, and her ſucceſſor to the imperial diadem. The ſame year, likewiſe, the Swedes had elected him their king: an honour which he declined to accept; and remained in Ruſſia. Thus therefore the ſon preſumed to reject that crown for which the father had contended in vain; and in lieu thereof obtained the reverſion of a ſtill mightier realm, which the father had ſuppoſed to be loſt to him for ever.

Elizabeth then acted ſo far entirely as became a relation to her nephew; and ſhe really had a cordial affection for the young prince. But certainly much more was incumbent on her than ſimply the calling of him to Ruſſia, if ſhe intended to form him for a ſovereign, capable of being one day a bleſſing to himſelf and to his people as her immediate ſucceſſor. Here, however, ſhe was unpardonably negligent. Inſtead of giving Peter an opportunity for ſtudying the train of ſtate buſineſs in ſo extenſive a monarchy as that of Ruſſia, ſhe kept him at a diſtance from whatever related to the affairs of government. Diſtruſt and jealouſy which evil-minded perſons endeavoured to excite and to foment

foment very soon begot a coolness between the aunt and the nephew; and Elizabeth more and more narrowed the sphere of Peter's activity, instead of guiding it, as she ought to have done, to objects worthy of a future sovereign. She even suffered him frequently to be in great want of money. No employment was therefore left for Peter, except the military. He was diligent in exercising the guards; but occupied himself principally with a small body of holstein troops that were quartered in Oranienbaum, and to whom he was more attached, as his countrymen, than to the Russians, and they in return shewed greater fidelity and devotion to him.

This reciprocal want of confidence between Elizabeth and Peter continued with increasing effects, but more particularly in the first years of the war of 1756. Peter, who had been personally acquainted with the king of Prussia, entertained an unbounded reverence for that monarch: he could imagine nothing more valuable than his friendship; of which Frederic also gave many testimonies to Peter, and the grand-duke suffered no opportunity to pass, in which he could evince his veneration for his royal friend. These sentiments, so entirely opposite to those of Elizabeth, necessarily engendered parties in the court; and it could not be agreeable to the emprefs, who wifhed from her heart to render all her fubjects the implacable enemies of the Pruffians, that even her fucceffor fhould fet the example of difapproving her proceedings againft Frederic: When the ruffian army gained a victory over the Pruffians, and a thankfgiving was kept for it in Ruffia, Peter never appeared at the folemnity; but endeavoured, by publifhing more authentic accounts of the loffes fuftained by the Ruffians, to abate the joy of the fubjects: on the other hand, when the king of Pruffia defeated the Ruffians, he celebrated the day in feftivity with his foldiers and companions at Oranienbaum. This ftriking partiality of the grand-duke for the pruffian hero may very eafily be fuppofed to have raifed apprehenfions in the mind of Elizabeth left Peter fhould, perhaps, by putting all to the ftake, as fhe had done before, get poffeffion of the throne; to which fhe was inclined to fufpect that Frederic might furnifh him with the beft advice. But Peter was not a man to bring fuch a defign to bear, if the plan of it had been fuggefted to him: he had neither courage nor refolution enough for it, as was afterwards feen at his detrufion from the throne. Thus much, however, may fafely be affirmed, that Elizabeth's diffolution caufed him no extreme regret, though certainly not fo

much

much becaufe he was delivered by it from his very confined fituation, as becaufe he now obtained the opportunity of giving the king of Pruffia a more explicit and unequivocal proof of his friendfhip and efteem, by putting an end to the war carried on againft him, than he had been hitherto able, by the important fervices he had rendered him during the war, and in endeavouring in various ways, and as far as poffible, to alleviate the preffure of it.

He fent to inform Frederic of his acceffion to the throne; and the king, not content with barely felicitating him on the event, communicated to him his earneft defire to enter on a negotiation for peace with him. Though Peter inherited the crown from Elizabeth, he did not inherit with it her animofity againft Pruffia, and therefore immediately fettled an armiftice with Frederic: he next addreffed himfelf to the allies of his empire to bring about a general peace with Pruffia; and, on their refufing to hearken to his propofals [*], he prefently after concluded a feparate peace between the courts of St. Peterfburg and Berlin, by the terms whereof Frederic had reftitution of all that the ruffian troops had captured in his dominions.

[*] For the anfwers given by the feveral courts and other ftate papers during this reign, fee Life of Catharine II. vol. i. Appendix.

Though

Though this was already much more than the prussian monarch could have expected, yet Peter stopped not here, but directly proceeded even to declare himself the friend and ally of the king of Prussia, and at the same time sent orders to his troops to join the Prussians, where they were to act under the immediate orders of the king. Thus the two powers, from the most inveterate enemies, were now not only friends but even allies. A change which indeed excited universal astonishment, and at first seemed incredible even to the contending armies, though it presently impressed itself on them as an undeniable fact. Frederic, however, did not make use of the Russians at this time: they once afforded him signal service, though not till after Peter's death, and then not so much by participation as by their inactivity, as may be seen from the history of his successor.

By this peace the emperor did not acquire many thanks from his country, as they conceived he had acted too generously, and given away too much. The rejoicings were infinitely greater on account of the abolition of the secret state-chancery, and the recall of all those who had been banished under the former * administrations

* Thus Biren, Munich, and Lestocq now obtained their freedom.

as the victims of policy, or of the selfish passions of the rulers, and the intrigues of their ministers.

The activity of Peter's mind seemed now to expand with his elevation; and the state of inaction in which Elizabeth had kept her nephew, was succeeded by a vigilance and energy highly honourable to the monarch. He enacted several new statutes, and made many salutary regulations. Thus, in alleviation of the burdens of the people, he lowered the price of salt; gave the russian nobility, whom he considered as still in want of some farther polish, permission to enter into foreign service to improve themselves in military exercises, and to visit foreign courts to correct and enlarge their notions; for the encouragement of commerce he lessened the duties in the livonian ports, and instituted a loan-bank to abate the pressure of excessive usury. He diligently visited the several official departments of government, was industrious in his application to state affairs, received petitions with his own hand — by all which he excited the general hope that the empire would be prosperous during his reign. Yet, notwithstanding his activity, through which a certain hearty goodwill to be useful to his country was manifestly apparent, he shewed, by his behaviour towards his wife, who greatly excelled him in intellectual endowments, by his prominent partiality for

the

the Germans, by the hasty regulations he introduced among the troops, particularly the guards, by his attempts to reform the church and the clergy, by his perfect indifference for popular opinions and prejudices, by his inveterate hatred to Denmark, and by the war he projected for the pacification of it, that he had not the art of calculating the consequences of his actions as a sovereign, and of combining with his activity the necessary qualities of wisdom and prudence. It was this want of prudence, which appeared on so many occasions, though it was doubly necessary to him as a german prince on the russian throne, that involved him in his subsequent misfortunes, and finally brought on his ruin; so that he was dethroned without the least opposition.

Elizabeth had taken care early to provide a fit match for her nephew the grand-duke Peter. Her first choice, as she was then in peace and amity with Frederic, was directed to the princess Amelia of Prussia, sister to the king, as a consort for her successor. Frederic, however, declined this honour; and, in return for the confidence reposed in him, took the liberty to suggest, that the princess Augusta Sophia Frederica, of Anhalt-Zerbst, a relation of the grand-duke would be a suitable match: the connection was accordingly brought about, Lestocq having a

principal

principal share in the negotiation. This princess, therefore, came to Russia in 1744, was baptized into the greek church, receiving at the ceremony the name of Ekatarina Alexievna, and was married to Peter on the first of September 1745. The new-married couple agreed together very well at first; but this marriage certainly was not crowned with that complete and permanent union, which is founded on a similarity of sentiment and character. Peter was rather unpleasing and coarse in his manners; and had fallen into habits of intemperance: as these were highly disagreeable to Catharine, it was no difficult matter for the court-cabal to weaken still more the little affection that subsisted between them, till at last a mutual coldness and aversion ensued. Peter had ceased to shew any indulgence, especially since he became emperor, and indeed to observe any decorum towards his spouse; affronted and insulted her both in public* and in private, thereby continually more and more alienating her from him, and even talked openly of repudiating her, and of disinheriting her son. His enemies, of whom he had a great many at court, failed not to represent his behaviour to

* She was obliged, for instance, to confer the order of St. Catharine on the countess Elizabeth Voroutzof, with whom he carried on an intrigue.

the empress in the most odious light, to fan her dislike to him, to inspire her with a dread of him, and by these means to prepare her for adopting those measures, which they represented to her as the only ones left to procure a deliverance.

Peter was a German, and was so little acquainted with the art of concealing his predilection for his countrymen, so plainly manifested on all occasions his contempt for the Russians, that it was utterly impossible for him ever to gain the attachment and affection of the nation he governed. By his general conduct, and particularly by his inordinate admiration of whatever was prussian, he injured himself most with the troops, and especially with the guards. The russian army had in the last year several times defeated the Prussians: and though these victories were always more to be ascribed to the superiority in numbers of the russian forces, than to their greater dexterity in the art of war, yet it was obvious to every man, that the Russians, considering themselves as conquerors of the Prussians, would naturally boast of being better soldiers than the Prussians. But Peter, notwithstanding, conducted himself as the disciple, as a general of the king of Prussia, paraded frequently in the prussian uniform, having already, while

grand-

grand-duke, exercised his holstein troops in the prussian methods, and resolved now, on being emperor, to form the whole russian army on the model of the prussian, made a beginning with the guards, gave his uncle, prince Lewis of Holstein, the chief command of them, intending through him and his holstein officers to effect a thorough reform in the military. The regiments of guards, finding their pride hurt by these proceedings, murmured not a little. In addition to this, Peter disbanded the life-company of the preobragenskoi guards, who had been so highly favoured by Elizabeth, that his holstein soldiers might do the duty of a life-guard about his person; ordered out the guards, (who were always kept in Petersburg, as the garrison of the residence, and for guarding the imperial palace,) to take the field against the Danes. Was it then a matter of surprise, that the guards were not favourable to Peter III. and that they did not stand by him at the revolution that followed?

The clergy likewise took umbrage at the conduct of Peter, and became his enemies, pretending to discern, from the whole of his behaviour, that he was not a true greek christian. He had been brought up in the protestant communion; and, though in his fifteenth year he had conformed to the orthodox greek church, yet the change had been not so much from conviction, as for form, and from the necessity of the case; so that, notwithstanding he might have made himself master of the observances and rites of the greek church, yet in his heart he had probably retained his attachment to protestantism; and was too little acquainted with the arts of hypocrisy, to conceal his principles. But, alas, he wanted to bring about a reformation, expressed a desire to limit the worship, and lessen the number of the figures of saints, and required that the revenues of the sacred order, particularly the church-lands, should be better managed. But how dangerous a thing it is for a ruler to set about the extirpation of religious prejudices, and to give new limits or regulations to the authority of the national clergy, all history shews. Peter the great, who made reforms in almost every department, was obliged in this to give up several plans which he had adopted; and it was reserved for Peter III. to feel the fatal effects of hastily proceeding to such alterations. The archbishop of Novgorod resisted him openly; Peter deprived him of his dignity: but, this raising a clamour among the people, he, for the sake of preserving peace, restored the prelate, and thus at once injured his own cause, shewed

the

the clergy the extent of their influence, and drew upon himself the hatred of that body, and with it the appellation, of heretic: an opprobrious epithet, which has never failed to deprive every prince who bore it of the love of his subjects, by rendering them insensible to his other merits, were they ever so great.

As Peter seemed but little inclined to accommodate himself to the sentiments of the nation in ecclesiastical affairs, which are apt to be confounded with religion, he shewed no less contempt for the public opinion in other respects, particularly in regard to his coronation. He delayed this ceremony from time to time, though, in the eyes of the people it was not till the coronation had been performed that he was the legitimate ruler of the empire. Even Frederic, his royal friend, advised him to be crowned as soon as possible: but Peter was deaf to all remonstrances, considering it only as an indifferent ceremony; though, as being necessary and important in the judgment of the nation, it would have greatly added to his consequence and dignity.

Another circumstance, by which Peter incurred the displeasure of his people, was his projected campaign against the Danes. He resolved to enforce the claims of his family to the territory of Schlefvig which Denmark had entirely appropriated, as Catharine I. had formerly resolved to do in favour of his father. But certainly this was a rash undertaking, unnecessarily involving Russia in a new and expensive war; and seeming to be not so much the concern of the emperor of Russia, as of the duke of Holstein, rather as a private controversy than a state affair. Frederic dissuaded him much from this war and offered his mediation: but Peter was immovable. "I will get possession of " the heritage of my fathers," said he; " it is " of more value to me than the half of the " russian empire." This declaration, however, was not calculated to satisfy the Russians, who had already shewn their discontents in various ways *. They were angry that Peter had given up the con-

---

* General Brown, to whom Peter had granted the patent of field-marshal, that he might carry on the war against the Danes in that character, told him bluntly, that this war was contrary to the maxims of sound policy, and the political constitution of Europe. Peter on this snatched the patent out of his hand, and ordered him to quit Russia; three days after he sent for him back, took him again into favour, and dispensed him from serving in a military capacity against Denmark, saying, "I will fight alone for my rights." Besides, Denmark had long been afraid of a rupture with Russia, and some of the russian nobles were even pensioned by that court for looking after its interests at Petersburg.

quests made by their troops in Prussia, without the slightest compensation, and for wanting to rush into a new war; that he had voluntarily surrendered what he had acquired there, and wished to put it to the fickle chance of war whether he should make any new acquisitions. It was no difficult matter for the party in opposition to Peter to take advantage of these hostilities, for which preparations were already begun, for representing him as always ready to sacrifice the country's welfare, the blood and property of his subjects, and the treasure of the empire, to his stubborn will and selfish resentments.

At the head of those who now united in a conspiracy to dethrone Peter III. were the brothers count Orlofs, count Razumofsky hetman of the kozaks, count Panin chief tutor of the heir apparent, and the princess Dashkof. It afterwards appeared that the empress was likewise privy to the plot. This conspiracy was as little concealed from Peter, as formerly Elizabeth's enterprise had been from Anne; and Peter shewed the same unaccountable carelesness as Anne had displayed. Both the english and prussian ministers warned him frequently of it, and Frederic gave him several hints in his letters; but he slighted every caution of this nature,

as

as if perfectly satisfied that he was in no danger. It is true that some of the persons who were about him, particularly Razumoffky, contributed much to his carelessness at first, in regard to the plot, and to the irresolution he afterwards shewed when it was put into execution, by pretending to be his friends, while they kept up an intelligence with the opposite party, and therefore dissuaded him from embracing proper precautions.

It is probable that the foundation of the scheme for removing him from the government was already laid while Elizabeth was yet living; and, not being able to succeed in preventing him from the accession on the demise of that princess, it was determined now to dethrone him. It was at first settled to take the time when Peter should set out with the army, which he had caused to be raised in Pomerania in order to employ them against the Danes, to have declared him to have forfeited the crown by his absence. This plan, however, was attended with great difficulties, as Peter might then gain over the troops, return at the head of them, and take his throne by conquest. The party, therefore, deemed it better not to let him depart at all; and, accordingly, the 9th of July 1762, was the day on which they suddenly and successfully put their design in execution.

execution. Peter was at his favourite feat, the imperial country-palace of Oranienbaum, the empress being at another, that of Peterhof. From this place Catharine repaired early in the morning, attended by count Gregory Gregorievitch Orlof, who commanded the ismailoffky regiment of guards, to Petersburg, and presented herself as empress, not only to that regiment, the generality of whom had been already gained over, but also to the other regiments; and, after making a few scruples, was acknowledged as such! an acknowledgment which was soon followed by the greater part of the nobility of St. Petersburg, and the public in general. Peter's uncle, prince Lewis, was preparing to adopt hostile measures, but he was presently put out of condition to effect anything. About ten o'clock in the forenoon, Catharine took the oath as empress *, in the church of our lady of Kazan, swearing to defend the liberties and the religion of the Russians; on which the nobility, the soldiery, and the populace, did homage, by taking the oath of fealty to the new

* The archbishop of Novgorod, whom Peter had deposed, and then restored, chanted the Te deum on this occasion. How greatly must the concurrence of such a man have justified and sanctioned the enterprise of Catharine in the eyes of the people!

autocratrtix, who juftified her acceffion to the throne in a manifefto * prepared for that purpofe.

Notwithftanding the care that had been taken left Peter fhould have too early information at Oranienbaum of what was paffing in St. Peterfburg, an officer attached to him found means to let him know betimes, that an infurrection threatened to break out in the refidence againft him. Peter — ftill incredulous — inftead of thanking the faithful officer for his kind intelligence, ordered him to be arrefted, remained in perfect compofure, fuffering the firft precious moments, in which, perhaps, by adopting vigorous meafures, he might have averted the misfortunes that threatened him, to pafs unemployed, calmly giving orders for his carriage to take him to Peterhof, there to celebrate the feaft of Peter and Paul †. On the road he received the dreadful confirmation of what had happened, learnt that his confort was not at Peterhof, fent meffengers forward to bring him accurate intelligence of every tranfaction; but — none of them coming

---

* Much was faid in it about the dangers which threatened the empire and religion from the peace with Ruffia, by which the glory of the country was tarnifhed, and of the injuries done to the internal conftitution of the empire.

† This falls on the 28th of June; which, according to our calendar is the 9th of July.

back,

back, he now first began to open his eyes on the fate that awaited him. Irresolution, perplexity, plans and projects, formed one moment, and hastily rejected the next as impracticable, now swayed the minds of Peter and his male and female attendants at Peterhof. His truest friends were unquestionably his holstein troops quartered in Oranienbaum, amounting to about three thousand men, who were all ready to sacrifice their lives for him and his preservation, if he would only head them and march to Petersburg. Marshal Munich, being then with him, offered to conduct the troops; and from a man of his stamp much was to be expected. Peter, it is true, adopted one resolution after another, but in a few minutes rejected them all; wavering to and fro in such a manner, that the time for execution with any probability of success was past; and so, as he did not accept of the offers of the Holsteiners to fight for him, another proposal to embark with all speed, and sail for Prussia or Sweden, fell to the ground. Without, therefore, having determined on anything, he returned in the morning of the tenth of July, extremely dejected in mind, to his palace at Oranienbaum; while his consort, on the same morning, accompanied by her partizans and the guards, whose uniform she wore, set out for

Peterhof,

Peterhof, now as empress, to put a finishing hand to the dethronement of the late emperor her husband. Finding Peter no longer there; and, as he had entirely given up all hopes of escaping with his life, or at least of being able to effectuate anything by force; nothing was left for him but to try what gentle means would do: accordingly, he attempted a negotiation by sending proposals to Catharine; requesting, among other things, that if she would allow him to go to Holstein, he would make a full renunciation of the imperial throne. But even this submission seemed, to those who conducted the revolution, not to promise sufficient security; it was required that Peter should come immediately to Petersburg, to receive instructions concerning what was farther expected of him. He came, hoping probably to see his spouse, and to obtain by oral negotiations what could not be granted him in writing; but — his expectations were too great — here he saw nothing of Catharine: he never saw her again. Count Panin seized him as her prisoner, delivered to him a paper containing the orders of the empress; and Peter subscribed the following act of renunciation — with what sort of emotions may easily be conceived! " During the short space of my absolute " reign over the empire of Russia, I became " sensible,

" fenfible, by experience, that I was not able to
" support so great a burden, and that my abili-
" ties were not equal to the tafk of governing fo
" great an empire, either as an abfolute fove-
" reign, or in any other capacity whatever. I
" alfo forefaw the great troubles which muft
" have thence arifen, and have been followed by
" the total ruin of the empire, and covered me
" with eternal difgrace. After having, there-
" fore, ferioufly reflected thereon, I declare,
" without conftraint, and in the moft folemn
" manner, to the ruffian empire, and to the
" whole univerfe, that I forever renounce the
" government of the faid empire, never defiring
" henceforward to reign therein, either as an
" abfolute fovereign, or under any other form
" of government; never wifhing to afpire
" thereto, or to ufe any means, of any fort, for
" that purpofe. As a pledge whereof, I folemnly
" fwear, before God and all the world, to this
" prefent renunciation, written and figned this
" 29th of June 1762, O. S."

On the fame day Catharine returned with her retinue to St. Peterfburg, where, by the gracious and condefcending deportment fhe adopted, even in the verieft trifles *, fhe the more eafily gained

* Such as the kiffing the hands of the principal clergy who were waiting in the apartments of the palace, as a mark of her veneration for them.

the

the hearts of the populace, in the same proportion as Peter by his negligence had lost them. The degraded monarch was now dismissed to Ropscha, a small rural seat, about forty-eight miles from Peterhof, where, on the eighth day following, he was deprived of life.

The government endeavoured to stifle the various conjectures and reports to which his sudden departure, under such circumstances, naturally gave rise, by publishing a manifesto, stating the cause of his death *. The body was, two days afterwards, deposited without funeral pomp in the monastery of St. Alexander Nessky; nor did the empress appear at the obsequies †. The death of Peter dissipated all those apprehen-

* In this it was said that he died of an hæmorrhoidal colic, to which he had been subject at times; that though the empress, in obedience to the injunctions of christianity, and the command to preserve the life of our neighbour, had endeavoured by medicines to prevent the effects of this accident, but to her great affliction she learnt, that the Almighty had called him out of this mortal life. She then invited all her subjects to forget all past calamities, to shew the last honours to the corpse, to pray for the repose of his soul, and to regard this *unexpected* event as a peculiar dispensation of the Most High.

† Out of regard to her health, as it was expressed in a notification published by the senate, she having already taken the death of the emperor so much to heart, that she was continually dissolved in tears.

sions, that the commiseration for the unhappy monarch, which presently appeared, after the bustle of the accession was over, might be attended with any dangerous consequences to the new government.

Thus Catharine II. ascended the throne of her husband; and, through a reign of thirty-eight years, raised the empire she governed to such a degree of respect and consequence, so greatly enlarged its borders, and made in every respect such progress in civilization, that her reign forms one of the most memorable periods in the history of Europe for the eighteenth century.

THE END.

SKETCH

OF

MOSCO.

CHAP. I.

Magnitude of Mosco. — Streets. — Lanes. — Gates. — Rivers. — Bridges. — Antient divifion. — Divifion by the police regulation. — Population. — Difference in the number of people in fummer and winter. — Climate. — Geographical fituation.

Mosco, or more properly Mofkva, the metropolis of the ruffian empire, is one of thofe ftupendous works of time and human induftry, which mankind, by whom they were produced, behold at length with aftonifhment, as doubting whether in reality they are the work of their hands.

From an eminence before the Dorgomubof gate, the eye furveys this coloffal city. The whole face of the horizon feems covered with houfes; and deep beneath, where the fky appears

to

to touch the earth, ſtill gorgeous palaces and lofty towers project their ſummits, preſenting themſelves to the deceived eye as little cottages and thin poles. The perimeter of Moſco amounts to ſomewhat above forty verſts, or nearly ſix geographical miles. Three and fifty main ſtreets, ſome whereof are ſeveral verſts in length, and four hundred and eighty-two collateral ſtreets and lanes, interſect this prodigious maſs of houſes, conſiſting of more than ten thouſand buildings. Twelve ſaſtavas or gates lead into it; and two rivers, the Moſkva and the Yauſa, with the rivulet Neglinnaiya, run through it. The MOSKVA riſes in the Moſchaiſk circle of the government of Moſco, and falls into the Okka near Kolomna. It abounds in fiſh, and in the ſpring bears conſiderable barks that come from the Okka laden with corn. It divides Moſco into two unequal parts, of which the citerior is the largeſt, the moſt populous, and, in regard to the number of fine ſtructures, the principal. Near the foundling-hoſpital the YAUSA takes it up, which riſes at Taininſkoï, twelve verſts from Moſco, and near the Kreml the NEGLINNAIYA, which takes its ſource in Moſco itſelf, on the Samoteka. Three and twenty bridges keep up the communication between the parts of the town divided by theſe rivers,

rivers, whereof the chief are the stone-bridge over the Moskva, and the court-bridge across the Yausa. Of the antient division of Mosco into five main districts, Kreml, Kitaigorod, Bielgorod, Zemlenoigorod, and the Slobodes, too many vestiges still remain to allow us to pass them by unnoticed, though they are no longer observed.

The KREML, a word of tartarian origin, signifying the fortress, is parted from the Kitaigorod by a rampart and a fosse running in a semicircle round it.

KITAIGOROD is likewise surrounded by ramparts and a ditch, and BIELGOROD too had formerly its walls and fortifications, but they have been long demolished. At present an allée runs round this quarter of the town, which forms an agreeable promenade for the inhabitants.

ZEMLENOIGOROD is bordered by an earthwall, whence it probably has its name — at present, however, only rudera of this wall are remaining. Lastly, the SLOBODES or suburbs, which inclose all these quarters, are encompassed by the kammer-college wall, which forms the extreme boundary of Mosco.

According to the police regulation, Mosco is partitioned into twenty chief divisions, denominated from the principal streets they severally comprehend, e. gr. the Bosmanskoi, the Verskoi,

skoi, &c. Each of these main divisions are again divided into several quartals.

The POPULATION of Mosco differs greatly according to the season of the year. In winter, when the numerous nobility, with their hosts of retainers, flock into the metropolis, the number of the inhabitants amounts to upwards of three hundred thousand; whereas in summer, when they are allured back to the country, it does not exceed two hundred thousand. Accordingly, in the former season, all is much more lively and bustling than during the summer. Trade, amusements, companies, are then inspired with new life, and the streets are crouded with carriages, whereas in summer the rolling of a coach is but rarely heard.

The CLIMATE of Mosco is certainly to be reckoned among the most salubrious. The situation is high, and the soil on which it stands dry, a few morassy parts about the Yausa and the Neglinnaiya excepted. Add to this that the atmosphere is generally clear and bright, and the weather regular and wholesome. The winter is particularly remarkable for settled and bright weather. It is absolutely impossible for an inhabitant of warmer countries to form a conception of a fine winter's day in the northern climes. The atmosphere is then so pure that we

feel

feel the genial virtue of it at every breath. The sky is so bright that the eye is scarcely able to bear it; and all the objects around have a superior and grander look than usual. The strong impulse to take exercise in the cold bracing winter air is not to be described, and a better method can hardly be imagined for the confirmation and establishment of health than by such a bath in the invigorating æther of the winter.

Besides, the streets of Mosco are broad, the squares are spacious, and in various parts are extensive gardens; the houses are mostly of only one story, and not contiguous, but separated by insterstices from each other, so that the air and the sun diffuse their benign influences in every part of them, and noxious vapours can nowhere stagnate. — Advantages in which other large cities are commonly deficient. All this contributes to render the result of the lists of births and deaths always favourable to population. Contagious distempers but seldom prevail, and still seldomer are they dangerous and ravaging. It is common to see aged persons of all ranks, though the rules of salutary diet are so often trangressed. It is to be observed, likewise, that the geographical position of Mosco, in 35° 45' 4" north lat. and 55° 12' 4" east long.

long, is doubtless one of thofe that are moft propitious to the health of man. For neither fcorching heats nor intenfe frosts impede the growth and expanfion of animal nature. On the contrary, the degree of cold which marks the winter here, contributes rather to harden and fortify the body. Hence arifes the ftrong and nervous ftructure of the men who properly compofe the Mofcovites, whofe families have been long fettled in this city, and are particularly met with among the mercantile people of the place.

CHAP. II.

More particular defcription of the Kreml. — Situation. — Profpect. — Prefent appearance of the Kreml. — The ancient palace of the tzars. — The beautiful fteps. — Churches. — Tombs of the tzars. — The great filver luftre. — Portrait of the Virgin Mary by St. Luke. — Religious ceremonies and feftivals. — The monaftery of Tfchudof. — The convent of nuns of Vofnefenfkoy. — Tombs of the tzarevnas. — The fynodal houfe. — The fynodal library. — The great Ivan. — The fenate houfe. — The arfenal. — The gates.

JUST in the centre of this great city ftands the KREML on a confiderable elevation on the bank

of

of the river Mofkva. The prospect hence on the side of the river is not to be paralleled. Far beneath flows the Mofkva, the windings whereof may be pursued by the eye to a great distance. To the right is the stone-bridge, and to the left that of timber, on which the rattling of carts and carriages of all sorts is inceffant. Beyond this bridge the stream is covered with barks, and from it may be surveyed a great part of the city. Here rife lofty palaces, worthy of adorning either Florence or Rome: there stand miferable huts that would be a disgrace to many a german village — a contraft which diftinguishes Mofco from all other great cities in Europe. Gothic monafteries, with their gilded turrets on charming elevations, decorate both fides of the river; and the beneficent foundling hofpital with its elegant modern buildings, in a lower fpot at the confluence of the Yaufa and the Mofkva, contribute not a little to diverfify and embellifh the grand picture that prefents itfelf to the fpectator.

Of a quite different kind are the objects in the foreground, but by no means lefs interefting to the view.

Here ftands the ancient palace of the tzars, in which the brave Ivan, the magnanimous Mikhaila Romanof, the wife Alexey Mikhailovitch,

the

the gentle Feodor, and the great Peter formerly refided. It is built in the pure gothic ftyle, but has nothing majeftic or impofing in its appearance, as by reafon of its numerous angles and corners only a fmall part of it can be feen at once; what it wants, however, in actual magnificence is amply fupplied by the imagination and the recollection of the great perfonages who have here laboured at the growth and formation of Ruffia. At prefent all here is filent and void: only Time with his ever-working fcythe feems to have made it his abode; and in various parts the marks of his all-deftroying fway were already manifeft, when the emperor Paul gave orders to reftore this venerable feat of the ruffian monarchs, and to fit it up as a dwelling place for himfelf and his family.

Some of the apartments of the tzarian palace ferve as a treafury, in which the filver and gold veffels, and other valuables of former times are preferved. Several others are made into armories, containing arms, horfe-caparifons, and accoutrements of days of yore, and of various european and afiatic nations. The afcent to this palace is by the grand flight of fteps eminently called *the red or beautiful ftairs*, krafnoe kriltzo. In it is the great hall of audience, granovitaiya palata, and the potefhnii dvoretz,
(pleafure

(pleasure house), which is now the kremlian post-office.

The present view of the Kreml is serene and solemn, to which the multitude of churches and monasteries undoubtedly contribute.

The Sobores, or cathedrals, are: Uspenskoi, to the ascension of Mary; Blagovefchtfchenskoi, to the annunciation, with four chapels; Archangelskoi, to the archangel Michael, with two; Spalskoi, to the saviour; Stretenskoi, to the purification: Spafkoi and Nikolskoi Galtunskoi: all richly provided with gold and silver church ornaments; and in the third, besides the relics of the tzarevitch Dmitri, who was murdered at Uglitsh, and is worshipped as a saint, are the tombs of several russian grand-princes and tzars. The tombs of these monarchs are of stone, covered with red cloth, velvet, or some costly stuffs. At the foot of the tomb, in shape like our table monuments, only rounded like a trunk instead of being flat at top, is a silver tablet inscribed with the name of the prince who lies beneath, with the year of his birth and that of his decease.

The curiosities of the cathedral dedicated to the ascension of Maria are: the monuments of the patriarchs, the great silver chandelier, and the portrait of the holy virgin, by the hand of the artist and evangelist Luke. The chandelier, a present from the Venetians to Boris Godunof, weighs 2800 pounds, and is in fact a wonderful piece of workmanship. The portrait bears every appearance of very high antiquity. It hangs at the entrance to the sacristy in a silver shrine, and is ornamented with a profusion of precious stones.

This church is in general one of the richest in the empire in gold and silver decorations, and the sacerdotal vestments that are here preserved are of surprising magnificence.

In this cathedral the russian sovereigns are crowned. Several other grand religious ceremonies are likewise here performed; as the foot-washing on holy Thursday, when the metropolitan washes the feet of twelve priests of the inferior order. Easter eve is in no church so solemnly attended as in this; and extraordinary festivals, such as the name-days of the imperial family, the celebration of successful events, victories, &c. are kept with peculiar solemnity in this church.

The other churches of the Kreml are either those belonging to monasteries or of the common order, all less remarkable than the two already mentioned. The whole number amounts to two-and-thirty.

The

The two monasteries of the Kreml are the Tſchudof for monks, in the wings of which the ſpiritual confiſtory meets, and the Voſneſenſkoy nunnery, in which latter are the tombs of ſeveral tzaritſas and tzarevnas. The mother of tzar Mikhaila Feodorovitch here terminated her life.

The ſynodal houſe, adjacent to the cathedral, in which formerly the patriarchs dwelt, contains the ſynodal library, remarkable for having the greek manuſcripts brought from mount Athos.

All theſe churches and monaſteries have a conſiderable number of ſteeples ſtanding near them, with gilt or ſilver cupolas and croſſes. Among theſe the belfry called the great Ivan, Ivan Veliki, accounted the higheſt turret in Moſco, is moſt conſpicuous. It was built in the reign of tzar Boris Feodorovitch Godunof, has 22 bells of various ſizes, and in a pit lies the largeſt bell in the world, which was caſt by order of the empreſs Anna; it weighs 12,000 poods, and a piece was broke out of the rim by its fall occaſioned by a fire in the year 1737.

Adjacent to the Voſneſenſkoy nunnery ſtands the palace of the Metropolitans, a modern edifice, built in the reign of Catharine.

Two other handſome large ſtructures adorn the Kreml. One the ſenate-houſe built by Catharine

tharine II. a grand imperial work, in a noble modern style. Here the senate and the sacred college hold their sittings and keep their archives. A circular hall of this edifice, in which the assemblies of the moscovian nobility are held, is particularly remarkable for the excellent works in stucco with which it is decorated. All round the hall are statues and groups in gypsum, that are certainly to be reckoned among the most exquisite performances of the kind. They are allegorical representations in honour of the late empress, replete with beautiful and lofty sentiments, and executed in a masterly manner. It is only to be lamented that this work is so fragile, and so little calculated to bid defiance to the destructive effects of time. The roof of this hall terminates in a cupalo, likewise enriched with stucco decorations, completing the magnificence of the whole.

The other grand building is the arsenal, standing opposite to the former — a solid and compact edifice; but since it was damaged by a fire it remains in an imperfect state. However a beginning has lately been made towards its restoration.

The Kreml palace was originally built of timber by prince Daniela Alexandrovitch in the year 1300; the grand-prince Dmitri Ivanovitch

vitch Donski re-constructed it of stone in 1367, and Ivan Vassilievitch, in 1488, employed some italian architects to enlarge the building, and give it the form in which it now appears. On the south side it is watered by the Moskva, and on the north by the Neglinnaiya. It is an irregular polygon with superb turrets in the gothic style, being surrounded by a deep fosse and lofty ramparts. It has a communication with the town by means of the Nikolskoi and Spaskoi gates on the east side, the Troitzkoi and Borovitzkoi on the west, and the Tainatzkoi on the south. On the Spaskoi and Troitzkoi gates are chime-clocks which Peter the Great caused to be made in Holland.

CHAP. III.

The Kitaigorod. — Origin of this name. — Gates. — Custom house. — Exchange. — Number of shops. — The government-house. — Police office. — The Zaikonospaskoi monastery. — The academy for slavonian, greek, and latin. — Sermons. — Merits of the metropolitan Plato in regard to the clergy. — Private houses. — Streets. — Description of Bielgorod. — Origin of the appellation. — The allée. — Public edifices. — The paskoffskoi house. — Principal streets. — Bird market.

From the bank of the Moskva to the Neglinnaiya, the second division of Mosco, called
KITAI-

KITAIGOROD, runs in a semicircular form round the Kreml. The origin of this appellation is uncertain. The word Kitai still signifies in russ China; and as the commerce with that country was formerly in a very flourishing state, it is probable that the name Kitaigorod attached to this quarter of the city, as there, among other commodities, chinese goods were principally sold. Tzar Ivan Vassillievitch caused the buildings between the Neglinnaiya and the Moskva in 1538 to be surrounded with a rampart and an earth wall.

This division is also in an eminent sense usually styled gorod, THE CITY. It is surrounded by a wall and a ditch, with four gates; the Voskresenskoi, the Nikolskoi, the Ilyinskoi, and the Varvarskoi, by which it communicates with the other districts of the town.

Kitaigorod is almost entirely filled with shops or warehouses, and the whole has the appearance of a perpetual fair. In the lower story of the gigantic buildings the numerous shops are huddled together; the upper stories serving as lodging rooms, eating-houses, taverns, and warehouses. They form the famous mart of Kitaigorod, which is too singular in its kind for not deserving a more accurate description.

The outside is surrounded by arcades, within which the principal tradesmen have their shops.

Beneath

Beneath these, that is, under ground, are wine cellars, and here and there are gangways leading to the interior of this structure amidst the intricate labyrinth of smaller shops of every species. Here streets and rows intersect one another without number, in which foreign commodities as well as inland products and manufactures are exposed to sale. Each class of goods has its peculiar row. Here are the silver-shops, sere-brennoye-riad; the iron shops, jelesnoye riad; the tin shops, the leather shops, the clothes shops, &c. all that either luxury or necessity can require is here to be had in abundance. The tradesmen lurk in these darksome allies eagerly watching such as come to buy, and as soon as a passenger enters them he is instantly beset by a whole mob of them; some offering and recommending their goods to him, others forcing him into their shops with polite address and importunity. In these obscure rows caution and circumspection are particularly necessary if you are determined not to be cheated; for in this place artifice and knavery have fixed their darling abode.

Of these large nests of shops there are properly no more than two. Besides these, however, are several prodigious buildings in Kitaigorod — monstrous convolutions of shops, warehouses, dwelling-houses, and eating-houses, as for example that of Grasnikof, that of Nikity Pavlof, that of Yublef and the exchange, which last is an elegant modern structure, lately rebuilt from the ground, and perfectly corresponds with the magnitude of Mosco, and the opulence of its merchants.

The number of all the shops and warehouses amounts to upwards of 6000.

The other remarkables in the Kitaigorod are the government-buildings, the police-office at the Voskresenskoi gate, in which the several courts of judicature are held; and the Zaikonospaskoi monastery in which is the academy for the slavonian, the greek, and latin languages. This institution is destined to the education of persons for the church. The specimens delivered annually at public exercises on appointed theses, and in latin, greek, russ, and german poetry, which are printed in honour of the name-feast of its founder and patron the metropolite Plato, display the spirit of this establishment and the degree of excellence to which it has attained: yet while we acknowledge that both teachers and students strive with great application and industry to penetrate into the sanctuary of the sciences, we are obliged to confess that they have chosen the path which is not exactly

exactly the right. The scholastic method of disputation, the practice of making insipid poetical anagrams, epimonies, and acrostics answers no end but to cramp the genius, and which have long been rejected in other countries as idle amusements and the productions of a false taste. This seminary will never properly flourish and prove a blessing to Russia, till it shall strenuously adopt the more liberal and enlightened modes of instruction which so usefully distinguishes its younger sister the university of Mosco. One excellent regulation here, however, is conspicuous for its good effects, and that is the exercise of preaching. A sermon is delivered every Sunday in the church belonging to this monastery. A practice very much wanted in Russia, as it is only at court, or in cathedrals, and then but on very particular occasions that pulpit discourses are given. The present institution owes its origin to the archbishop and metropolitan Plato, who has acquired great merit by his endeavours at the general improvement of the russian clergy; though a school was erected here in A. M. 7168 by the patriarch Joachim Savelof at the command of tzar Feodor Alexievitch.

Besides these public edifices the Kitaigorod contains a considerable number of private houses which are mostly inhabited by merchants and artificers, the palace of count Sheremetief excepted.

cepted. Here is also the cathedral Pokrof, where the grand ceremony was anciently held of the entrance of the patriarch on palm Sunday *. The other cathedral is dedicated to the mother of God of Kazan. Other buildings are, the printing-office of the holy synod, where church-books are printed, and where a collection of very old ones is kept. From an inscription over the gate it appears that this house was built in 1645. Also the house appropriated to the choristers of the synod, the custom-house, the corn magazines, and others. At the krasnaya ploschtschad, red place, 270 shops of two stories have been recently built. The whole number of shops in Kitaigorod is 4021 of brick, and 54 of wood. Opposite the Spaskoi gate is the place Lobnon, where on occasion of processions public prayers are performed. It has lately been new faced with granite.

The principal streets of this quarter are the Nikolskaia, the Ilinkaia, the Varvarka, and Moskvaretzkaia, so denominated from St. Nicholas, St. Elias, St. Barbara, and the river Moskva.

Bielgorod lies also on this side the river Moskva, and consists mostly of brick, and some of them elegant buildings. This quarter em-

* See Life of Catharine II. appendix to vol. i. No. I.

braces

braces the Kitaigorod in a semicircular form from the influx of the Yausa into the Moskva, to the bank of that river again. It was formerly called Tzaref, and probably obtained its present appellation Bielgorod or White-town, from the white wall or rampart which was built round it by order of tzar Feodor Ivanovitch in 1586, and at length pulled down on account of its ruinous condition. The vacant place is now furnished with an allée of trees and a canal which takes its rise at a spring two versts beyond the parish of Bolschoi Muititschtsch. This walk of birch and linden trees is certainly better calculated for utility as affording an agreeable promenade, which is the more valuable as the majority of the inhabitants of this enormous city live at the distance of several versts from any means of so wholesome an exercise.

The most remarkable public buildings of this district are: the monasteries Vuisokopetroffky, the Krestovosdvishenskoy, the Slatostenskoy, and the Stretenskoy. Nunneries: the Rosteftvenskoy, Ivanoffkoy, and Alexieffkoy; the Nikitskoy, and the Yegorieffkoy. Seventy-two churches, and an armenian church built in 1781. The university of Mosco founded in 1755 by the empress Elizabeth, with two gymnasiums, one for noble and the other for children of various classes. Here are taught the ancient and modern languages, mathematics, philosophy, medicine, theoretical and practical jurisprudence, and theology. It has 11 stated and 5 extraordinary professors, 49 tutors, 64 students at the expence of the crown, and 18 at their own, 79 noble scholars at the crown's expence, and 487 at their own; 71 of various classes on the foundation, and 373 at their own expence. The late empress Catharine II. devoted 125,000 rubles to the enlargement of the buildings.

The other structures are: the foundling-house, the grammar-school, the post-office, the salt-magazine, the archives, the assignation-bank, the artillery-court, the printing-office of the senate, the chief apotheke, the mint, &c.

The house of the noblemen's club has a magnificent hall able to hold about 2000 persons. In the galleries and halls of the public theatre masquerades are frequently given.

A silk-manufactory of 24 looms and 65 master workmen, and 4 manufactories of playing cards.

Among the private buildings Paschkof's house, of which more will be said presently, is undoubtedly the principal.

The

The largest and finest streets are: the Pokrofka, the Masnigkaia, the Stretenka, the Petroffka, the Tverskaia, the Nikitskaia, the Mochovaia, and the Pretschistenka.

The BIRD-MARKET, ochotnoi riad, deserves to be briefly mentioned. Here are sold singing-birds, dogs, rabbits, squirrels, and all sorts of domestic animals. This trade is by no means inconsiderable, as in no place are there such numbers of fanciers of this kind as at Mosco. Nightingales, quails, doves, pigeons, and particularly dogs, are frequently purchased at incredible prices. Canary-birds are imported in great quantities by the Tyrolese. The lowest price for a common canary-bird is five rubles; but when they are well taught, it is not unusual for them to cost from 50 to 100 rubles each.

In this quarter are 378 shops, 6 stone-bridges, and one of timber.

CHAP. IV.

The Zemlenoigorod. — Principal streets. — Slobodes. — Public edifices. — Infirmaries. — Surgical institution. — The hospital for invalids. — The apothecary-garden. — The german slobode. — Its inhabitants. — Churches. — Schools. — The new lutheran church. — Dr. Jerbzinsky. — Heideke. — The old church. — The imperial palace and garden. — Corruption of language. —

Sonorous expressions. — Attachment of foreigners to Russia, and its causes. — German physicians. — Professors. — Domestic tutors. — Artificers. — Grusinian and tartarian slobodes.

ZEMLENOIGOROD and the SLOBODES encircle the three quarters beforementioned, as well on this side as on that of the river Moskva. Here by the side of massy and elegant structures are seen wooden houses, and among them wretched hovels. The origin of the name Zemlenoigorod has been already mentioned. In the years 1591 and 1592, during the reign of tzar Feodor Ivanovitch, it was surrounded by a wall, which was entered by thirty-four gates of timber, and two of stone; of all these, only the two last are now remaining, the others being either burnt or decayed. Over one of them a tower in the gothic style, called Sukhareva, was erected under Ioann Alexievitch, and Peter Alexievitch, from the year 1692 to 1695, where is now the admiralty-office. The principal streets in this district are, the Patnitzkaiya, the Kusnetzkaiya, the Yakimanskaiya, the Kosmodemianskaiya, the Ordynka, the Arbatskaiya, the Ostoschenka, the Povarskaiya, the Ragoshkaiya, and the Taganka.

The SLOBODES or suburbs, are surrounded by the kammercollege wall, through which the zastaves or outer-gates are passages. This wall
incloses

inclofes likewife a number of wafte and empty places, which have probably been left in a view to the future enlargement of Mofco. And in fact the number of houfes augments from year to year; fo that feveral of thefe unoccupied places have within no long period of time been converted into populous ftreets.

The public edifices moft deferving of notice in the fuburbs, are the three infirmaries, the Pavlſkoi, the Katarinenſkoi, and the great hofpital. The laft is devoted to fick and infirm foldiers, as the former two are to other patients, of whatever clafs, nation, or religious profeffion. The plan of conduct in all of them is exemplary. To the great hofpital a chirurgical eftablifhment is annexed, in which a confiderable number of young men are maintained as ftudents of medicine at the public expence.

The HOSPITAL OF INVALIDS, an elegant building, with a garden properly attended, in a pleafant fituation, may be matched againft any beneficent inftitution of this nature.

The botanic or APOTHECARY-GARDEN, belonging to the imperial apotheke, is kept in an excellent ftate. This apotheke is appointed to fupply all the inferior apothekes of the lazarets of the empire with drugs and medicines. In the garden are reared almoſt all the officinal herbs in great abundance.

The principal and moſt remarkable ſuburb is undoubtedly the german ſlobode; and it is, therefore, by way of eminence, generally called the Slobode. It lies on the eaſtern ſide of the city, and forms the ſuburb as one comes hither from Vladimir. It is entered by three of the fineſt ſtreets, the Pokrofka, the new Boſmannaiya, and the old Boſmannaiya. This ſuburb is inhabited not only by Germans, as foreigners might be apt to ſuppoſe, but likewiſe many Ruſſians live here, either in their own, or hired houſes; nor do all the Germans in Moſco reſide in the ſlobode, but a great proportion of them dwell in other ſtreets and parts of the town. Theſe are chiefly phyſicians, apothecaries, tutors, merchants, and ſome tradeſmen, ſuch as taylors and ſhoemakers, who chooſe their ſituation according as it ſuits with their buſineſs. The german inhabitants of the ſlobode, beſides a few merchants, and ſome of the learned profeſſions, are moſtly artificers. The Germans have here four churches; two lutheran, one catholic, and one calviniſtic. The congregation of the new lutheran church is the moſt numerous. Theſe churches are ſupported by the voluntary contributions

butions of the several congregations. Each has its preacher with a tolerably good appointment. In connection with each of the two lutheran churches is a school, governed by a rector, who at the same time performs the office of organist and chanter during divine service. These schools would, perhaps, be better conducted, if the pay of the teachers was not so very small.

The new lutheran church is advantageously distinguished from the rest by several rational and prudent alterations. The introduction of the excellent petersburg hymn-book, containing the hymns of Klopstock, Gellert, Cramer, &c. and a noble and edifying liturgy, on pure evangelical principles, redounds greatly to the honour of the minister.

For these improvements the church is mostly indebted to its present pastor Dr. Jerbzimsky, a man who, among other virtues, possesses that of hearkening to reasonable remonstrances and of following the advice of the wise and pious. The dregs of the old leaven have in short been thoroughly purged out by Mr. Heideke, the pastor adjunctus, a young man of uncommon endowments, and eminent erudition. His sermons inculcate a sound morality, blended with a clear and convincing doctrine, with which he successfully combats religious prejudices and unchristian conduct;

conduct; animating his hearers to a virtuous life by the warmth of his compositions, and the elegance of his delivery. He has all the graces of diction at command, possesses a rare personal eloquence, a full and modulated utterance, and a dignified ease which never forsakes him. In short, he seems born for an orator.

In the old church the Kœnigsberg hymn-book is still retained, and the sermons are more in the taste of the old scholastic theology, so that those poor sheep of the lutheran flock in Mosco, who yet adhere to the antient formulary of dogmas, may here find their pasture.

The lutheran congregations in Mosco, as well as in Petersburg, have the privilege of choosing their own preachers; an advantage which the other german congregations in Russia have not. They receive their preachers at the appointment of the college of justice, by whom they are also paid; whereas the preachers at Mosco and St. Petersburg are salaried as well as elected by the congregations.

The generality of the Germans born at Mosco discover but few traces of their german origin; in manners and customs forming themselves chiefly on the Russians. Numbers of them understand not a word of German; and many who speak it, employ a jargon very difficult to be compre-

comprehended; bringing into their speech not only applications and properties of the russian language, but giving currency to whole words, with or without german terminations: and what is here said of the Germans may be applied to all foreigners. They say kriltzo, instead of the steps at the house-door; gulianie, instead of taking a walk; tscherdak, for the garret; dvornik, instead of servant; rasnoschtschik, instead of the man who sells things about the streets, &c. " be so good and tell me;" " do all what I could;" " I ordered the taylor to sew me a " coat;" " who sews your clothes?" instead of, " who makes your clothes?" and many other such instances verbally translated from the russ or german.

On the other hand it must be confessed, that the pronunciation of the Germans here, is incomparably softer and more sonorous than that of the native Germans, of whatever province they be. Their tongue becomes more pliant, as in their youth they learn several languages, and their ear is better capable of discriminating whatever is harsh, as they learn almost all the dialects of Germany from the new comers, who meet together in Mosco from the various provinces of that empire; and the provincialism of language cannot possibly have any charms to an unbiassed mind.

The German, as well as every other foreigner, comes to Russia in the design of making a fortune, and then quietly to enjoy the fruits of his labours in his native country. For a year or two he adheres firmly to this sentiment, as he finds no attractions to the contrary. Foreign manners and a strange language render his life uncomfortable, and he sighs for home. By insensible degrees, however, he becomes more familiar with these manners and this language. He experiences, on the part of the government, a generous and indulgent treatment, which the more gratefully affects him, the less he has been accustomed to it in his own country. While he enjoys almost all the benefits belonging to the natives of the country where he lives, he bears none of their burdens so long as he chooses to remain a foreigner, and the return to the place of his birth is always open to him, with whatever he has acquired by his industry, his abilities, or his good fortune in Russia. Only when he is determined by inclination, or his particular concerns, to declare himself a subject, in order that he may be a burgher, or purchase estates in land, he shares the burdens of the natives, as well as their signal advantages. This liberty enjoyed by foreigners in Russia is so inviting and alluring, that it almost always obscures the darling idea

of

of home, and seduces many a stranger to be unfaithful to his first-love. To this must be added, the luxurious way of life in which men are so apt to indulge, who make easy and considerable profits. Now, if we only consider that the foreigner is under no constraint from forms and ceremonies of any kind, that no vexatious corporation-laws obstruct or confine the artificer in his works, that the physician and the artist, after due examination, may exercise their art and skill, and the merchant employ his capital in what way he pleases, it will be easily conceived, that very few foreigners, who have lived a long time in Russia, have any aspirations to return to their own country; and that those few who have firmness enough to resist all the charms of their second home, and go back to their paternal seat, yet soon make their re-appearance in Russia's happy borders, confessing that it is difficult to accustom themselves again to the yoke of partialities, respectable only from their antiquity, and prejudices hereditarily derived, without examination, from age to age, which formerly appeared less hard to be borne, only from habit and the inexperience of early life.

The prime class of the Germans here, undoubtedly, is made up of PHYSICIANS. Over all Russia the medical department is almost exclusively

exclusively in the hands of german physicians. But few Russians, and still fewer Englishmen and Frenchmen, form an exception to this observation, and these have in all respects so assimilated with the Germans, that they may be easily mistaken for them. In general, the physician finds a very ample subsistence in Russia; but his richest veins of gold are Petersburg and Mosco. In London alone, perhaps, is the mine of diseases so productive as here. Several physicians make annually 10,000 rubles by their practice. The most eminent at present are, Frese, Yenisch, Keresturi, Doppelmayer, Pfahler, Richter, Maschmeyer, &c.

The rest of the learned Germans in Mosco are some professors of the university, the pastors, and the domestic tutors, though among the latter some unlearned occasionally creep in. The salary of the professors is not very high; and, in order to gain a decent livelihood, they find it necessary to have recourse to collateral occupations, as private tutors, writers, translators, &c. After having been ten years in office they get a title, usually that of hofrath, or court-counsellor, and regularly every ten years they are promoted in rank.

The domestic tutors, in the principal and most opulent families, are, since the french revolution,
mostly

mostly Germans; yet it is always required of them to possess the french tongue to a certain degree of perfection, as it still continues to be the language of conversation among the superior ranks.

Among the german tradesmen, the taylors are the most numerous as well as the most substantial. It would be thought a violation of the first rules of good taste to wear a coat made by any other than a german taylor; and these artificers in drapery are extremely well skilled in the art of turning this prejudice to their advantage. They bring in long bills, and are well paid for their work. The other german handicraftsmen, shoe-makers, glovers, joiners, smiths, &c. all make handsome profits, and are generally likewise in very good circumstances.

Besides the german slobode there is also a GRUSINIAN, where the princes, who fled from Grusinia, or Georgia, have settled with their followers; and a TARTARIAN. They lie on the opposite sides of the city.

CHAP. V.

The university. — Professors. — Curators. — Kheraskof. — Gallitzin. — Turyenief. — Faculties. — Students. — Sword students. — Half yearly examinations. — The gymnasium. — The academy of nobles. — The foundling-hospital. — Increase of this institution. — Structures. — Internal establishment. — Direction. — Funds. — Distribution into several ages. — Number. — Facility of gaining admission for children. — Benefit of this institution. — Commercial school. — Beneficent care of her majesty the present empress. — Excessive mortality. — Causes thereof.

YOUNG as the university is, being founded in the year 1755 by the empress Elizabeth, it already evinces many marks of confirmed maturity, and the solidity of the settled age; and, surprising as it may seem at so early a period, she rises from year to year to greater excellence. While the university reckons among its professors such men as Barsof, Matthæi, Schwartz, Schade, Rost, Tschubataref, Antonsky, Bause, Heym, and curators of such liberal and enlightened minds as Schuvalof, Melissino, Kheraskof, and Gallitzin, who have contributed greatly by their talents to bring it to its present respectable state, no doubts can be entertained of its farther

ther progress. Of these latter KHERASKOF shines foremost as one of the most distinguished authors in Russia, in the department of belles lettres. He is at present the senior curator. In the same rank with him stands prince GALLITZIN, a kinsman of the actual founder of the university, the first lord of the bedchamber, Schuvalof. He was educated abroad, chiefly in France. The director TURYENIEF understands several foreign languages, and is an active laborious man, who has the prosperity of this seat of learning much at heart.

The university has only three faculties: philosophy, jurisprudence, and medicine; as for the study of theology there are particular seminaries, in Mosco, in the Troitzkoë monastery, in Kolomna, Kief, &c. The number of young men who follow their studies at the expence of the crown amounts to fifty: these students, as well as most of the professors, reside in the university, which is a large elegant edifice situate on the Mochovaïya, occupying, with its collateral buildings, a very considerable space. The students are divided into two classes, one called simply STUDENTS, the other SWORD-STUDENTS, the sword, with which certain privileges are connected, being distributed as a reward to the more deserving. Nor has there

hitherto

hitherto been an instance of this mark of honour having been misapplied, as frequently happens at the german academies, where every one wears it on being matriculated. The distribution of the swords, as well as the gold and silver medals, and the books, which are conferred as recompences for industry and good conduct, is made at the great half-yearly examinations, when the students are obliged to give various proofs of their proficiency; a practice indubitably productive of beneficial effects, and which might be advantageously introduced into other universities.

The GYMNASIUM, which is connected with the university, serves it as a seminary; the most advanced of the superior classes being admitted therein as students. The number of scholars at the gymnasium amounts to some hundreds, of whom 150 are maintained by the crown; the rest have likewise their instruction free of expence. The sons of decayed noblemen, ecclesiastics, scribes, stewards, and petty merchants attend this school on account of its cheapness. But wealthy nobles and rich burghers send their children to what is called the NOBLE ACADEMY: an institution originally not within the plan of the university, but which was set up by a few professors as a collateral employment, but is now united with the university. It is in a very flourish-

flourishing state, and numbers about 150 pupils. The inspector of this institution is professor Antonsky, in all respects a very diligent and fit person for that station.

The FOUNDLING-HOUSE forms an elegant counterpart to the university. This beneficial foundation is continually increasing in stability and extent: a circumstance partly owing to the wise and well-digested plan on which it is framed, but partly likewise to the rare felicity of having had at its head, almost without exception, prudent and upright governors.

The habitations of the foundlings, their overseers, teachers, and nurses, the church, the magazine, breweries, bake-houses, kitchens, bathing-rooms, hospital-wards, &c. compose all together a little town; as the circumference of all these buildings comprizes above three versts. These several buildings are substantial, commodious, and handsome. Only the district in which they stand, at the confluence of the Yausa and the Moskva, is damp and marshy. The internal disposition is excellent. The greatest cleanliness and order everywhere prevail; due instruction in everything necessary for a burgher to know; the utmost attention and care, in regard to the health of the children, are the striking characteristics of this institution.

The

The empress takes upon her the chief inspection of the foundling hospital, and under her count Sievers directs the whole; an active and liberal nobleman, known in Europe chiefly by his embassy in Poland during the diet at Grodno. Under him is a council consisting of the chief director and three wardens. This council expedites everything relative either morally or physically to the establishment. In subordination to it are the censor, the œconome, and the principal accountant. The censor is the chief inspector over the education and instruction; the business of the œconome and the principal accountant, is sufficiently clear from the names of their office. The funds of this institution are a lombard, a tax upon all public entertainments, as plays, Vauxhalls, &c. and upon cards, which are stamped by the foundlinghouse. These two taxes are very productive. The house too has several manufactories, in which the work is performed mostly by foundlings.

Over the girls is a chief inspectress, under whom are the other inspectresses and nurses, as the girls and boys are kept carefully separate. Both the one and the other sex are divided into different ages. Each of these ages has its peculiar employments, pastimes, and lections. The instruction in sciences and languages is conducted

ducted by tutors both with the boys and the girls; but always apart. The latter are taught the feminine arts by women, and every age has an inspectress and a nurse, as the divisions of the boys are provided with their overseers and nurses. The whole number of the foundlings is upwards of 5000. At every hour of the day and the night, children are admitted, without the least objection or inquiry. Nothing but a ticket is required, intimating whether or not the child has been baptized; and, if it has, signifying the name it received. Here are also wards properly fitted up for lying-in women, who are delivered by expert midwives free of all expence.

It is not to be described how much this convenient institution is frequented. Not only the fruits of forbidden intercourse are here deposited by high and low, but also numbers of indigent married persons, fearful that they may not be able to provide food and education for their children, commit them to the care of this charitable establishment, where they are not only maintained, but brought up to become useful members of society. Since the first institution of this hospital, a period of more than forty years, not one instance of child-murder has been detected in the whole circuit of Mosco.

A school of trade and commerce is connected with this establishment, which owes its foundation to the generosity of a wealthy proprietor of iron-mines, the late Prokopy Dimidof. A capital of two hundred and five thousand rubles was the fund which he presented to its endowment. In this school, a hundred sons of poor merchants are maintained, and taught from their earliest youth the business of the counting-house, and the languages of Europe. Several mercantile houses in Mosco have already been furnished with able clerks from this institution.

The foundling house has been principally benefited, since her majesty the present empress Maria Feodorevna has bestowed such great care and attention in removing the abuses that had crept in, and for the restoration of order in its several departments. She has particularly exerted her endeavours to put a stop to the causes of that excessive mortality, which indeed was a great reproach to this useful institution. For, though no bills of mortality were ever published of the foundling-house, which, by the way, was a strange neglect, considering the general regularity that prevails in this place, and the number of physicians belonging to it, yet it is easy to conclude, from a variety of circumstances, that the

the mortality in the foundling-house must be exceedingly great. The causes of it, besides the damp and unwholesome situation of the place, appear to be the following. First, a great part of the new-born children are consigned to nurses in the country till they are weaned. However rational and proper this practice may seem, it is attended with dreadful effects; as the poor children are entirely trusted to negligent, generally hard and insensible women, and no farther concern is taken about them. Having once received their pay for nursing, their end is answered, whether the child live or not. Perhaps scarcely a third of the babes given to them ever came back. It is now ordered, that a surgeon shall go round the villages where the children are kept. In the next place, it seems impossible, that a wet nurse should give proper suck to several children at once; and yet it often happened that one wet nurse had three or four children to nourish. The empress has reformed this abuse likewise. And lastly, the inspectors and physicians were perhaps in many important respects rather too careless. They seemed to think that they had nothing to do with the poor children, except when they were ill in the sick wards; whereas certainly a concern for the health of the children in such an institution ought to be incessant and universal.

CHAP. VI.

The theatre. — Maddox. — Rooms for masquerades and concerts. — The inside of the theatre. — Boxes. — Pit. — Price. — Actors. — Comparison of the ruffian actors with the german. — Personal qualifications of the actors. — Afchokin. — The Melnik. — The Sbitenfchtfchik. — Pomerantzef. — Schufcherin. — Ponamaref. — Actreffes. — Siniefíky. — Naffova. — Kolagribova. — Plays. — Original. — Tranflations. Kotzebue's pieces. — Ballet. — Decorum of the pit. — Clapping. — Noife at the reprefentation of uninterefting pieces.

AN Englifhman, named Maddox, is the proprietor and manager of the theatre. He came to Mofco about five-and-twenty years ago, as a rope-dancer, pofture-mafter, and performer of fleight of hand. Without money, without knowing the language of the country, unacquainted with the manners and difpofitions of the Mofcovites, he ventured to open a theatre; and from his induftry, his verfatile genius, and perhaps likewife by that fortune, which is faid always to favour the bold, his undertaking was crowned with fuccefs. He foon obtained fo much credit as to enable him to erect a new theatre from the ground; a ftructure which for

elegance

elegance of architecture, as well as for dimensions and solidity, may vie with any in Mosco. Besides the theatre it contains concert and assembly-rooms, in which the new masquerade-room is particularly distinguishable for its magnificence. This hall, which is of uncommon magnitude, and conveniently holds several thousand persons, alone cost fifty thousand rubles.

The THEATRE is perhaps one of the largest in Europe. Besides four stories of boxes, it has two spacious galleries. The pit has two series of benches, extending to the main entrance down the middle, having at the sides inclosed seats; and yet there is a considerable vacant space remaining. The boxes are mostly decorated with sumptuous damask hangings, and furnished with mirrors and pendant lustres. The generality of them have silk curtains, forming altogether a superb and brilliant view. They are annually let for a certain number of representations; they are however to be had at a stated price on other days, for particular occasions, at the performance of a new play, or of one that is eminently admired. The annual rent of a box is from three hundred to a thousand rubles, and upwards. Admittance to the pit a ruble, — Prices which sufficiently shew the expensiveness of the amusements, as well as the luxury of Mosco. For it seldom happens that a box is unlet; and the pit is generally full.

The actors and actresses here are not held in that high esteem which they enjoy in Germany, and other countries of Europe by the admirers of their art: on the other hand, however, no prejudice is entertained against them, so as to exclude them from genteel company, or at least to bring them into contempt with certain classes of society, as is still the case in some parts of Germany. The actor, like any other artist, is esteemed by both the quality and the commonalty here, according to his merit; though neither himself nor his art is idolized to the disadvantage of other talents. On the contrary, he is generally classed lower than the poet, the painter, and the elegant scholar. However, he need nowhere be ashamed of his profession, and it is never made a matter of reproach to him. If he be otherwise a good and peaceable member of society, he enjoys all the advantages of it, and stands as high in the public opinion as any other man. His profession is no obstacle in his way. No popular prejudice keeps him down. In all civil relations he finds credit and confidence if he be otherwise deserving of them. He can quit the theatre, and may expect every suitable
provision

provision to which his talents give a right to pretend. I know not which has the best of it, the german actor, who is on one side extolled to the skies, and on the other sunk down to the bottomless pit, or the russian performer who quietly makes his way among his friends and countrymen like the rest of mankind.

The performers in Mosco are not so numerous as they might be. The principal parts are but moderately filled, and some that are not insignificant lie entirely fallow; for instance, the parts of the artful parasite. The most eminent actors are Aschokin, Pomerantzef, Schuscherin, and Ponamaref.

Aschokin, a very good comic performer, is particularly great in the national-comic scene, and his usefulness is the more considerable, as he sings. His capital parts are undoubtedly the miller in the MELNIK (the Miller), and the old guardian in the SBITENSCHTSCHIK*. Both pieces are national operettas. The chief part in the former is the MILLER, from whom the piece has its name. Together with his proper

* Sbiten is a liquor made of honey, pepper, and water, which in winter is carried about the streets, as mead is in summer. It is contained in a large glass decanter, and served in tumblers to the customers. The vender of this drink is called Sbitenschtschik.

trade he exercises the art of fortune-telling and of go-between. Nothing can be more natural and true than Afchokin in this part. The guardian in the Sbitenfchtfchik is an old covetous merchant, who resolves to marry his young and rich ward; but she, as usual, is snatched from his clutches by a poor but young and deserving officer. This character is not unfrequently met with on the theatre of other countries, and in some is well performed; but here so much of the national peculiarities is interwoven with it, that it is in some degree new. Afchokin plays it incomparably.

POMERANTZEF's parts are generous fathers. He is in the highest reputation of all the actors, as to his professional talents he adds a profound knowledge of the drama, and an excellent theory of his art. His triumphant part is the Painter in the german play of the Father of the Family. Pity that his organs of utterance are too weak for this large theatre.

SCHUSCHERIN, a well-shaped man, plays the principal lovers and heroes. Figure, powers of declamation, talents, all concur in rendering him an accomplished actor. His favourite part of all is Wilhelm in the Kind der Liebe* by Kotzebue.

* Acted in London under the name of Lovers' Vows.

He is rivalled by Plabilſchtſchikof, who plays alſo kings and heroes.

PONAMAREF, a comic actor. His parts are intriguing and diverting ſervants, droll tutors, ridiculous pedants, &c. A ſly and officious intermeddler in the above-mentioned Sbitenſchtſchik is one of his principal parts. He likewiſe plays excellently Ghita in the opera Coſa Rara.

Of the actreſſes the moſt diſtinguiſhed are madame Sineſſky, Naſſova, and Kolagridova.

Madame SINEFSKY (now Zakharof) performs the parts of the principal female lover with tolerable ſucceſs; but ſhe is deficient in voice. In general ſhe ſhews more ſcience than talent. Beſides, ſhe is no longer in her prime. Madame NASSOVA plays the parts of the romp and the ſimple country girl; and this department is exactly ſuited to her. She is, perhaps, the beſt female performer at this theatre; her excellence, however, ariſes more from nature than from art. Laſtly, madame KOLAGRIDOVA excels in Mrs. Siddons's line of parts, and leaves all her ſiſter performers far behind her, in what relates to art and acquired abilities.

It is not neceſſary to particularize the inferior actors. It muſt not be forgotten, however, that the number of excellent players has lately had an acceſſion of two by the engagement of SANPUNOF and his wife. Madame SANDUNOVA is

peculiarly

peculiarly ravishing in her performance of Ghita in the Cosa Rara. She sings to admiration, and is in general a complete actress.

Among the pieces represented, the originals are but few: most of them being translations from the germans and english, particularly the former. The most favourite, besides the Melnik and the Sbitenschtschik, which have been already mentioned, are the Nedorosl *, and the Brigadier, both by Van Wisin, and Dmitri Samosvanetch, the False Dmitri, by Kheraskof. This last is a tragedy, of which the plot is taken from the russian history. The two pieces by Van Wisin are comedies, and admirably paint the national manners.

The translations that have been attended with most success at this theatre, are Emilia Galotti, Miss Sarah Samson, Minna von Barnhelm, Clavigo, Beverley, Mariana, and above all the dramatic productions of Kotzebue: Menschenhass und Reue †, the Papagoy, the Kind der Liebe, Armuth und Edelsinn, i. e. Poverty and Generosity, and Die Lasterschule, or the School of Vice, which are become the favourite pieces

---

* Nedorosl signifies a minor, a pupil, or a lad; but throughout this play it seems to be the Spoiled Child.
† Performed on the English stage under the title of the Stranger.

of the moscovite public. These have all had a great run, and are still performed to such crowded audiences, that numbers cannot gain admission when a play of Kotzebue's has been announced. No dramatic poet, whether native or foreigner, has here ever attained such a height of celebrity as Kotzebue. His name is never mentioned in the politer circles without enthusiasm, and if that be the surest test of excellence, this writer must be a paragon of perfection. At any rate, it may suffice as a specimen of the taste of this capital in the department of the drama.

The BALLET is deserving of particular notice, as being by no means of an inferior quality. It has gained considerably under the management of the ballet-master PINUCCI, who has had it for some time. Both the male and female dancers are admirable; the scenery and decorations are good, and some by the famous scene painter Gonzaga, are real master-pieces. Occasionally, however, we are not entirely satisfied with the wardrobe.

The pit is here, perhaps, in many respects, one of the most polite that can be anywhere seen. The ears are never rent with those noisy marks of disapprobation, which do not correct bad actors, and which distress and overpower the inexperienced and timid. The bad or negligent performer

performer is here never clapped; which is surely punishment enough for a sinner not quite incorrigible. He will doubtless take all possible pains to improve himself, that he may obtain a share in the triumphs of his colleagues, unless he be lost to all sense of honour and disgrace; and in that case all the hooting and hissing in the world will never amend him. He is either incapable or shameless, and consequently unfit for the stage. Even the clappings of approbation do not so frequently distract the attention as in many other theatres, and, which deserves to be noticed, are much oftener directed at the poet than at the performer. A shrewd remark, a witty repartee, or an affecting sentiment, is sure of being clapped, even though coming from the mouth of a very indifferent performer.

There is one thing for which both boxes and pit are extremely censurable; and that is, when the piece is not one of the most admired, so much talking is heard among the company, that nothing can be understood of what is passing on the stage. On similar occasions silence would be demanded in a peremptory tone at an english or a german theatre; but the Moscovites are far too polite for that.

CHAP. VII.

Literature and bookselling. — University bookshops. — Bookshops in Kitaigorod. — The senate-printing office. — That of the synod. — Russian original compositions. — Kheraskof's works. — Gollikof's life of Peter the Great. — Karamsin. — Literary periodical publications. — Political newspapers. — Schirach's political journal. — Translations. — Heym. — Bause.

LITERATURE, in general, not being as yet arrived at that degree of estimation, which it has attained in other cultivated nations of Europe, it is no wonder that authorship and bookselling are in less consideration here than elsewhere. Besides the university-shop, which is the most considerable, there are indeed a number of book-stalls in Kitaigorod, but the generality of them contain only spiritual writings, collections of popular ballads, and some old romances, which have been long in possession of the public admiration. The privileged printing-offices are three in number, namely, those of the university, of the senate, and the synod; of which the first is particularly employed in works of literature, as the senate-presses print little else than ukases, and those of the synod are confined to books of devo-

tion

tion and spiritual edification. Some private printing-offices have been abolished by the late ukase of censure, in pursuance whereof only privileged printing-offices are tolerated.

The chief original works in russ, that have appeared within the last ten years from the university-press, are the following:

KHERASHKOF's works; containing romances, poems, and plays. They compose several volumes, and are justly much esteemed.

GOLLIKOF's life of Peter the Great; a voluminous work. The former parts of this piece of biography are far superior to the latter, which are nothing more than a chaos of records, documents, anecdotes, critiques on other authors who have handled the same subject, &c. which scarcely any one will have the patience to read through. This work, however, is not without its value, as a store of archives relating to the reign of that hero, and may hereafter become a good source to some biographer of taste: the author being a wealthy merchant, retired from business, who has applied his leisure, his abilities, and fortune, solely to this performance. With great pains, and at much expence, he procured a large collection of the tzar's original letters, which, though the major part of them are perfectly insignificant, he revered as sacred relics, and has printed

printed in his work with diplomatical exactitude. Almost the whole of what concerns the great monarch is taken from other writers; and, as he is entirely unacquainted with foreign languages, he has procured whole books to be translated for this purpose. In short, the biography of Peter the Great has been the business of his whole life, and there is reason to suppose that supplemental volumes will continue to appear till grim death shall snatch the pen out of his hand.

The writings of KARAMSIN, a young man who cultivated his talents abroad, make a great noise. His first essays appeared in the Moscovian Journal, a periodical work of which he was the editor. Light poetry is his department, and he has produced several pieces in that way, that have met with deserved approbation. Some of his little sentimental stories, as Julia and Eliza, have been translated both into french and german. He seems to have formed himself chiefly on the german Anthony Wall, whom he perfectly resembles, both in genius and pursuits. Like him he has written bagatelles, and adapted Marmontel's moral tales to the manners of his country. Of late an almanack of the muses, under the title of Aonides, has been published annually by him, which serves as a repository for his own

little

little effusions, and the fanciful flights of a few moscovite youths of his acquaintance.

There are no such things as russian JOURNALS and literary periodical publications. The only attempt of this nature that has ever been made, was the Moscovian Journal by Karamsin, which was afterwards continued under the name of Aglaia. But its transient duration has shewn, that these excrescencies of superior cultivation will not yet flourish in the climate of Mosco. The political newspapers that appear twice a-week, contain accounts of the new publications, occasionally accompanied with reviews of them by the several authors and translators themselves, or encomiums by the bookseller. With the newspapers appears a periodical leaf, having for title: " Agreeable and profitable pastime," consisting mostly of translations. The editor of it is professor ZACHATSKY. The political journal of Schirach is also translated into russ.

As to the business of translating, which in Germany is not upon the best footing, it has not a very inviting appearance here. Karamsin's accommodation of Marmontel's tales excepted, the rest are for the most part executed by apprentices in the art, without having a competent knowledge of their mother-tongue, and still less of the language from which they translate.

tranflate. Add to this, that they are unacquainted with foreign literature, and confequently make a miferable felection of the performances on which they lavifh their time and trouble, while the beft works that appear abroad remain untranflated.

Three french bookfhops and one german may ferve to fhew what foreign literature is moft in requeft.

Of the profeffors of the univerfity HEYM is one of the moft induftrious as an author. Befides feveral elementary books for the univerfity and the feminary for nobles, he has publifhed a Rufs Grammar for Germans, with proper felections as exercifes. From his pen has likewife come out a Geographical and Topographical Encyclopædia of the ruffian empire; and not long fince two Lexicons have proceeded from the prefs, one german and rufs in two volumes, the other a german-rufs-french dictionary, by a fociety of learned men, at the head of whom is Heym. Of this dictionary two volumes have already appeared, containing the german alphabet; probably, when the whole is completed, it may form fix volumes.

Profeffor BAUSE not long fince publifhed an occafional difcourfe in latin, wherein he treats of the progrefs of civilization in Ruffia, which, on account of several new particulars and illustrations, seems even deserving of being known abroad.

A new edition of the poetical works of DERSCHAVIN has also recently gone through the press; several of which have made their appearance in Germany, translated by Kotzebue. The effusions of this bard are unquestionably to be classed among the most exquisite airs that were ever sung to the lyre.

CHAP. VIII.

The summer. — Short duration of the spring and autumn. — Inconveniencies of the summer. — The first of May, or the german tables. — Origin of this denomination. — Promenades. — Orlof's garden. — Paschkof's house. — Sparrow-mount. — The three mountains. — The spring-water. — Vauxhall. — Beast-baiting. — Deficiency of places of entertainment. — Imperial country-palaces. — Petroffkoy. — Tzaritzin. — Ismailova. — Kuskova. — Aftankina. — Petroffkoy of count Razumoffky. — Orangeries. — Culture of the ananas. — Blooming aloe. — The moscovite hosteffes.

Mosco has, properly speaking, like the whole of northern Russia, only two seasons, the SUMMER and the WINTER; since the spring and autumn

autumn are of such short duration, as to form no more than the imperceptible transition of the two chief seasons. We will first view the pleasures of the moscovian summer, and then proceed to the delights of the winter here, whereof those who live in warmer zones can absolutely form no conception.

The SUMMER of Mosco is, on the whole, not agreeable. The heats of the long days of June and July are oppressive, and the nights are chill. The foot-walker is either smothered in a cloud of dust, or must wade through mud and dirt.

The first grand summer holiday — for the spring is entirely blotted out — is the first of May. On this day all Mosco repairs to a district of the Falcon-wood, not far from the german slobode, in carriages, on droschkas *, on horseback, and on foot. The crowd in the streets, of people going to this place, is not to be described, and is certainly unique. The most elegant carriages, in three or four rows abreast, roll forward; for on this day luxury displays all her glories, and new liveries and coaches are usually produced for the first time.

* Light one-horse carriages, like a settee without a back, on four wheels, supplying the place of hackney-coaches.

Between the carriages and the front of the houses the light droschkas run along. The officers of police are distributed about the streets to see that no disorders arise, and that the trains of carriages and droschkas keep their due distance. The Red-gate stands a few versts from the edge of the Falcon-wood, at which the principal streets leading to it converge, and henceforward the coaches are obliged to proceed in one single train. From the lines of carriages which meet at this point only a certain number of equipages are therefore let through; and, as these come from one line behind another, collisions naturally arise, the repercussions of which, in such a prodigious confluence of carriages, are frequently felt to a considerable distance; though, to avoid this as much as possible, the rows often move in a serpentine direction. This order, which the police sees very rigorously observed, is probably the reason that, amidst such an enormous crowd of coaches, chariots, chaises, and droschkas, no accident ensues. Yet it is impossible to avoid trembling at every moment for the bold horsemen prancing among the narrow spaces between the carriages, or for the poor pedestrians twisting and writhing between them and the horses. No vehicle ever leaves its line, not only for fear of the police-officers, who make the coachmen

and

and outriders pay for the contumacy by sundry strokes with a stick of no small size across their shoulders, but also from prudence, as in that case such an one must patiently wait till all the carriages are gone by and humbly creep behind the last, as he will not be let through the Red-gate alone. It does sometimes happen that an aspiring genius of a coachman will strive to break into the line again; but in that case he is almost sure to get a broken head, and perhaps a broken carriage.

Thus, after three hours of shuddering and palpitation, but also amidst a perpetual diversity of scenes and prospects, we reach the desired spot. Here our eyes are immediately presented with a view of numberless booths and tents containing all manner of refreshments. On one hand, jugglers and rope-dancers are performing their tricks, and on another the ears are saluted with the songs and vociferous mirth of a drunken crowd from a kabak*, decorated with green twigs and leafy boughs. The whole forest is alive; motley groups in their best apparel filling every part. Under every tree a company of jovial people. Equipages and droschkas and

---

* The common tippling-houses in Russia are called kabaks.

gallant horsemen parading through the vistas. Great numbers of the coach company get out, and walk in parties through the wood. Others drive in a slow and stately pace to feast their eyes on the variegated sight. Every mortal is there, to see and to be seen; till at length the coming-on of night obliges them reluctantly to terminate the delightful holiday and quit the enchanting scene.

Diversions of this nature are called PROMENADES*. There are several of them during the course of the summer, but not one is so brilliant as the first of May.

This promenade, or rather the spot where it is held, is likewise called, the German Tables †. The origin of this denomination, if we may believe tradition, is this. At the time of Peter the Great, the Germans of the Slobodes had the custom to hail the return of the warmer season, after so long a privation of the chearing sun-beams, at this extremity of the Falcon-wood, lying at no great distance from their homes. They chose for this purpose the first of May; and Peter the Great several times condescended to take part in this humble festivity. A board nailed on two posts fixed in the ground for

---

* Gulænie.   † Nemetzki Stoli.

tables

tables at various distances, with others in like manner as benches, were the only accommodations they found; and, at these tables every party ate and drank what they brought with them. Hence the vulgar appellation: "The "German Tables." The presence of the monarch drew the great people to the place; and thus by degrees this promenade came into vogue. The fine season (sometimes), and the display of wealth and luxury at length brought it to that pitch of splendour with which it is now continued; and is certainly a curious and peculiar spectacle.

The other promenades to the Maiden-field, to the three mounts, to the donskoi monastery, &c. are of an inferior kind to that we have been describing, and appear to have arisen from religious motives, as they are all on church festivals, in honour of which these have unquestionably been pilgrimages.

Of the gardens, the most frequented, after those belonging to the palace, are the gardens of count ORLOF. They are in the district of the donskoi monastery, and are laid out in the english style; not indeed completely finished, but forming a very fine plot of ground. Art here has only followed Nature. The bank of the river Moskva makes a charming easy slope,

with

with alternate gradations of heights and falls, adorned in various parts by a number of very ancient and stately trees. Hence the reader will be enabled to form some judgment of the susceptibility of improvement in the grounds; and, on learning that they were laid out by a skilful english gardener, he may get a notion of what they are become. Elegant structures, as temples, grottos, baths, obelisks, and columns are raised with taste in their appropriate places. The beautiful view of the river Moskva and the city add greatly to the charms of this delightful spot. Here all persons of fashion assemble, especially on Sundays; and the inferior classes flock for recreation on Sundays and holidays to PASCHKOF's house and gardens.

In a populous quarter of the town, on the bank of the Mochovaia, on a considerable elevation stands this enchanting palace. The entrance on the hinder side in a cross-street. Passing through a superb portal, you come into a spacious court, gradually expanding from the gate. On one side are the stables, and on the other the riding-house; both elegant structures. The house has two entrances, ascended by grand flights of steps, which unite at the first story. Thence you may go to the upper apartments, and thence again to the spacious belvedere in the cupola,

cupola, where you have a glorious prospect of all Mosco. The house itself consists of a main edifice, and two wings, connected with the body by corridores. This has a projection in the middle, with large bow-windows, and the two principal ways into the garden. This projection forms in the first story a balcony, resting on tuscan columns. High over this balcony are placed the armorial ensigns of Paschkof, borne on corinthian pillars; which, as well as the whole structure, are models of harmony and proportion. On one side of the balcony, which is furnished between the columns with the most elegant iron lattice-work imaginable, stands the goddess Flora, and on the other Ceres. The supporters to the arms are a couple of reclining figures. The top is vaulted by a cupola, terminating in a belvedere, surrounded by double columns. The wings are ornamented with colonades; and the whole is a pattern of symmetry and eurythmy. Two other colossal statues stand in front of the house, on the most elevated scite of the garden, a Mars and a Minerva, which, together with the other figures, may be ranked among the choicest productions of the chiffel.

On

On passing through the house we come to the romantic situation on the foreside of the building to the road. Here, amidst shrubberies, and over rocky fragments, through irregular mazes and serpentine walks, we descend the mount on which the house is built. Below are two marble basons, from the centre of which spring fountains; and towards the street an iron lattice of the finest workmanship incloses the whole. The garden and the ponds swarm with curious foreign fowls. Chinese geese, various kinds of papagays or parrots, white and variegated peacocks, &c. are here seen either roving about at large, or suspended to branches of trees in magnificent cages. An innumerable concourse of people assemble here on Sundays and holidays, to enjoy the fine prospect, or survey the beauties of nature and art which it contains. The gardens, the house, the court, the stables, are full of people; and even the iron-railing to the street is thronged with the gazing crowd without. Every entrance is perpetually open, not a door is shut; and servants stationed in every part, with the most civil officiousness, fly to fetch whatever is required. The owner and builder of this charming fabric is an old podradschik, or contractor, named PASCHKOF, who for several years

past

paft can only go about in a calafh. The effect produced by this houfe when lighted up, is abfolutely not to be defcribed. This illumination, which is made on all the holidays of the imperial family, is certainly one of the grandeft in all Mofco, where they vie with one another on thefe occafions.

Other places of entertainment, that are likewife much frequented, are, the SPARROW-MOUNT, an elevated fituation on the banks of the Mofkva. The view of the town from this place is excellent, and the country round it extremely beautiful.

The THREE HILLS, a very pleafant place in the neighbourhood of Mofco, obtains its name from three hills in thofe parts. An old garden, partly overgrown, on the banks of the Mofkva, with its fhady walks, are chiefly the fcene of this promenade. Here fprings that excellent water, known by the name of the three-hill-water, and fupplies a great part of Mofco, which does not abound in good fpring-water.

Stationary amufements for the fummer are but few in this capital. The principal, and almoft the only ones, are the Vauxhall and the Beaft-baiting.

The VAUXHALL owes its origin, as well as the theatre, to the genius and enterprize of Mr. Maddox.

Maddox. A neat pretty garden at the southern extremity of Mosco, is laid out for this purpose. We first enter a set of apartments, that are fitted up as toilette-rooms for the ladies. From these a long gallery leads to a grand circular hall for dancing. Adjoining to this hall is a moderate sized theatre, where little pieces, particularly operettas, are performed. From the dancing-hall we come into a large area, surrounded by a covered gallery, having in the middle an elevated station for the orchestra. The gallery is chiefly used for walking to and fro in parties, as at other places of this nature. Beyond this is the hall allotted to refreshments of all kinds. On the sides are billiard-rooms. The other avenues of the garden cannot well be visited by elegant company. In the evening the galleries are illuminated with coloured lamps, and on particular days a firework is played off. Though the place is extremely pleasant and inviting, it is however but little frequented, partly on account of its distance, and partly because in summer few of the nobility are in town. The numerous assembly at the Vauxhall is on Peter and Paul-day.

The BEAST-BAITING is the undertaking of some people of Vienna and Italians. It is kept in a circular amphitheatre of timber in front of the tverskoi Sastava, erected by the proprietors

for

for this purpose. In the ground-floor of this building are the dens of the wild beasts, and the kennels of the bull-dogs. Over these are three tier of boxes for the spectators, and in the open area, which forms the centre, the animals are baited. That diversion, however, does not here meet with such approbation as at Vienna, and therefore this edifice is now more frequently used for the display of magnificent fireworks, than for beast-baiting.

Notwithstanding the large dimensions of Mosco, and though the numerous noblesse, and the middling ranks of merchants, have a great hankering after dissipations, yet few places of accommodation for that purpose are met with. The scenes of entertainment so frequent in other cities as coffee-gardens, tea-houses, bowling-greens, and the like, where persons may pass their hours of leisure, according to their various humours, are here either entirely wanting, or are frequented only by the populace. It is the more incomprehensible how the industry of the natives has missed of this means of profit, as the entertainments above described are so little alluring, and are attended with so many inconveniencies, that it would apparently be a very easy matter to eradicate the taste for them. The distance to the Sparrow-mount, or the three hills, is not great from several quarters of the town; for instance, not above ten or twelve versts from the Slobodes, the Bosmann, the Pokrofcoe, and others. At present, to prevent fainting at the end of the journey, it is necessary to take at least liquors of some kinds, which are rendered unpotable by the heat, and which people would certainly rather pay for on the spot. At some distance from the Slobode there is indeed a german tavern, at which parties from the Slobode frequently bespeak dinners: but it stands in a barren, uninteresting district on the road to Siberia, and, in regard to its accommodations, is chiefly adapted to the use of the german artificers and tradesmen; and, therefore, is very little frequented by the distinguished part of the public of Mosco.

For want of such places of entertainment in the capital, people of all ranks form parties to the imperial country-palaces that lie in the vicinity, and to the country seats of the nobility, whose gardens and establishments are open to the public enjoyment. This species of amusement is here called, going to the green. Among the former, the pleasure-houses Petroffkoy, Tzaritzin, and Ismailova, are the principal.

PETROFSKOY is situate about three versts from the Saftava, on the Petersburg-road. The palace

was

was built, in the gothic style, by Catharine II. Belonging to it is a pleasant park, which, in favourable weather, is seldom void of walking company.

Tzaritzin is distant twelve versts from Mosco. The buildings are likewise in the gothic taste, and partly unfinished. The english garden is spacious, and full of delightful situations. Nature has done uncommonly much for this place. Water, hills, dales, and woods, interchangeably meet the eye in pleasing combinations, affording a scenery beautiful, and highly picturesque. The orangeries are vast rooms, with walks between the trees, which yield the most fragrant odours. In the hot-houses great numbers of the ananas are reared.

Ismailova, about eight versts from Mosco, has a large park belonging to it, stocked with deer, roes, wild boars, &c. animals rarely seen in these countries. The park-keeper, a hearty old German, hospitably receives all strangers who come hither to stroll about the green.

Among the country-seats of the nobles, that are visited by the Moscovites, Kuskova, Astanknia, and Petroffkoy, are the chief.

Kuskova is an estate belonging to count Scheremetof, seven versts from Mosco. Nature has acted like a mother-in-law by this district,
and

and art has been obliged to do every thing. The buildings, the gardens, and arrangements, are all in a princely style. The mansion and the theatre, the hermitage and the dutch-house in the garden, are eminently conspicuous for their elegance and taste. Entertainments are occasionally given here by the owner, in which the public at large are invited to partake. Dramatical representations, fireworks, illuminations, and dancing, are the alternate amusements at these festivities, and refreshments of all kinds are handed round to the company.

Entertainments of a similar nature are likewise given at ASTANKNIA, which also belongs to count Scheremetof, and in magnificence and taste may vie with Kuskova. It is, indeed, far superior to it in regard to situation, which is extremely pleasant and romantic.

PETROFSKOY likewise, a country-seat of count Razumoffky, not far from the imperial Petroffky, is in a charming spot. A spacious and well-kept garden, contiguous to the park, tempts numbers of the inhabitants of Mosco hither. Here, as well as at Kuskova, are vast orangeries, in which not only the superior fruit-trees of every species, but likewise pine apples in great abundance, are reared; and as this fruit is very much cultivated in the forcing-houses about Mosco, they may
commonly

commonly be had very cheap in that capital, the finest ananas costing not more than a ruble. The head-gardeners both at Kuskova and Petrofsky are Germans. The orangeries at Kuskova, even produce a superfluity of rare exotic plants, and twice within the last ten years aloes have been in full flower.

On these expeditions into the green, it is customary for the parties to take their kitchen and cellar with them. For, as all these places of resort lie at a considerable distance from town, and we must proceed, perhaps, several versts before we get into the open country, it is usual to set out early in the morning. And as absolutely nothing is to be got at the place for love or money, it is necessary to carry eatables and drinkables from home. On these occasions the moscovite landladies, who otherwise are not wont to take much notice of their guests, appear in all their splendour, and numerous parties of this kind of course beget a desire to display the talents of a good hostess before a large company. For mankind are apt to make the greatest boast of those accomplishments and virtues, to which they have the least right to pretend.

CHAP. IX.

The stay of the nobility in the country. — Description of a Podmoskovnè. — Manner of living, and amusements in the country. — Theatre. — Hunting. — New mode of husbandry. — Its introduction into Russia. — Progress of it. — The quay. — The allée. — The great merit of the police-master, Kaverin, in the embellishment of Mosco. — Noxious and troublesome method of cleansing the streets. — The swings. — Podnabinsky.

Most of the moscovite nobility pass the summer in the country, where in truth they make their stay so pleasant, that they find no loss in their absence from town. A short description of the Podmoskovnè* will give some idea of the pleasures of the country life in Russia. As hospitality is a main feature of the national character of the Russians, a visitor has nothing to apprehend from being tiresome to the landlord. The gentry here never wish their friends to be gone, but are heartily glad to detain them as long as possible.

At Tschassovna, one of these podmoskovnès, the most unconstrained sociability prevails.

---

* Every country-seat is called a Podmoskovnè, that is situate within a hundred versts from Mosco: from *pod*, near, and the name of the capital.

No one stands in the way of another in the employment of his time. The hands and feet are entirely free from any constraint of diversion or etiquette. The only law imposed by the worthy host on his guests is, that no one shall be a restraint on another.

The estate lies about thirty versts from Mosco, not far from the great troïtskoï road, on the banks of the Skalpa, a river of confiderable magnitude, which here winding its course between shores covered with shrubs and trees, through a fine romantic landscape, adds much to the beauty of the scene. The mansion of the owner stands on a hill, inclining by a gentle slope to the Skalpa. The architecture of the house is of a peculiar taste. It consists of a regular quadrangle of two stories, with a lofty turret in the middle of the roof, which at some distance gives it the look of a church. A spacious balcony runs round the house on all the four sides, affording the most delightful prospects. Exactly opposite, on an eminence, on the other side of the Skalpa, is a village with its church, the cottages being dispersed in the most picturesque manner imaginable, on the lofty bank of the river, which, to the right of this village is covered by a thick forest: the uniformity of the forest being interrupted by various roads, twisting their courses through it, and rendering the prospect more diversified and lively. On this side of the river the eye surveys, to a vast distance, fields and meadows, interspersed with villages and detached houses. To the left the elevation gradually declines, and loses itself in cultivated plains, intersected by roads, which in almost every season of the year teem with animation and activity. The interesting scenes of mowing, reaping, ploughing, and sowing, being here represented before the sight in alternate vicissitudes.

On the other side of the house, the prospect is more confined, but not less agreeable. The foreground is formed by a pleasant wood of birch trees, and tracts of arable land, through which runs the road to Mosco, planted on each side with trees. The background is a forest which opens on the right hand to admit a spacious lake. The silent forest, with the quiet lake in which the branches of the overhanging trees are seen to play, forms a real emblem of repose, and at the same time a striking contrast to the prospect we before surveyed.

At this charming residence, the practice is, with such as choose it, to rise with the sun, and ramble about the smiling region, either for the sake of enjoying a fine morning, or with the gun slung across the shoulders, to shoot something for
dinner.

dinner. At eight o'clock tea is ready in the balcony of the house: and, certainly, that refreshing beverage never tastes so pleasant as under the azure sky, amid the balmy fragrance of the adjacent woods, the sweet carols of the birds, with a glorious prospect round, and in the open, frank, and friendly converse of liberal and enlightened men. After breakfast the company disperses, every one his own way. Some go to the library and read, others are for a walk, others order horses and take a ride, while others again go and visit the improvements of the landlord in his experiments in the new methods of agriculture, till one o'clock; when all meet again and sit down to the social and mirthful board. This likewise is prepared in the balcony under the open sky. With the blue vault of heaven for the cieling, and the grand decorations of nature all around, a rural repast tastes full as well as the costly viands of the town, eaten in a large dining-hall, full of exhalations and vapours of every kind.

The dishes being removed, for the cloth remains, the company talk and laugh till the burning heat of the midday sun is over; when away go all on horseback, or on droshkas, about the adjacent country, either to see some beautiful spot,

spot, or to the theatricals of some friendly neighbour, or to the hunt.

The theatre of a ruffian nobleman, as well as the chace with dogs, call for a brief defcription, as many of thefe theatres are met with in the country, and this mode of hunting is a favourite diverfion of the ruffian nobles, during their refidence in the country.

The actors and actreffes are vaffals; felected, however, in their infancy from a multitude, and brought up to this purpofe. They are taught mufic, dancing, declamation, and foreign languages by proper mafters, and now and then become excellent performers. The orcheftra is likewife compofed of vaffals, but is commonly under the direction of a foreign leader of a band. It is really furprifing to fee fuch good acting in the country; and the pleafure received at fuch reprefentations is greatly enhanced by this circumftance, that the expectation is ufually deceived by being exceeded. This expenfive fpecies of entertainment prefents an idea of the wealth of the ruffian nobles, and the magnificent ftyle in which they live.

The diverfion of hunting is not lefs coftly. The nobleman, with his company, on horfeback, followed by upwards of a hundred dogs, with
fifteen

fifteen or twenty huntsmen on horses, some with horns, and others with couteaux de chasse, begins the course. He leaps over every hedge, ditch, gate, or whatever else is in his way; and those of the company follow him if they can: if not, they stand gaping after him till they find some safer passage. At length he reaches the forest, the poor inhabitants whereof are destined to this day's sport. Here the company divides. The principal persons take their stations at certain intervals without the wood; keeping with them the greyhounds *; while the huntsmen, with the terriers †, rush into the wood. The horns sound, the dogs set up their barking. The scared and timid animals run out of the forest, and are pursued by the greyhounds, followed in full cry by the company that were waiting without the wood, over stock and block in a furious gallop, till they have got as many hares and foxes as were unable to effect their escape. In this manner they pursue their noisy chace over a tract of twenty or thirty versts, and in the evening return home in triumph with eight or ten hares.

Ere we quit the country, however, we must take some notice of a more dignified and profitable pursuit, in which several great land-owners

* Barsii sabaki. † Kontschii sabaki.

are at present occupied, and is prosecuted by some with enthusiasm. This is agriculture upon the principles of the modern english and german farmers, and especially the culture of clover. Mr. John Richter, a German, has the honour of being the first who sowed the first seeds of this improvement in rural œconomy, which is now making such rapid progress in Russia. At the time of his leaving Germany, about twelve years ago, Schubart's improvements in agriculture were just come into high vogue. Full of the advantages which they might produce, he praised them in an emphatical manner to major Nedderhof, in whose family at Mosco he was, and who takes great pleasure in farming. He had sense enough quickly to perceive the benefits likely to arise from these innovations, and zealously set about studying Schubart's publication. Richter now wrote to Leipsick, at his request, for a parcel of clover-seed; and he began to make experiments in miniature, according to Schubart's directions, at his estate of Yellne. These attempts succeeded, and the whole farm at Yellne was soon conducted with great advantage on Schubart's principles. An acquaintance of the family, general Blankenagel, was struck with the improvements, and introduced them with great success into his village: this excited in him the

patriotic

patriotic wish to make his countrymen in general acquainted with the progress he had made in this species of culture. He therefore, in conjunction with Richter, adopted the plan of compressing Schubart's work, and translated it with the necessary alterations for suiting it to the locality of Russia. But, just as they were beginning to put their design in execution, they were accidentally separated: the general however prosecuted and completed it alone.

Rasnodofsky, at his instance, stood forward as teacher of the improved practice, and began by publishing a book, under the title of: New Agriculture *; consisting chiefly of translations from the writings of Schubart, pointing out at the same time the progress which the improved culture had made in several parts of Russia. This was in a manner the signal for an almost general revolt against the old formal practice, and clover met with the greater number of partizans, as the price of hay had been rising for several years. The alterations likewise were more easily brought about, as here are no combinations and prescriptive rights to contend with, but the lord of a village can manage his fields and grounds as he pleases.

* Novaya Zemlætælie.

In Tschaffovna the new principles of agriculture prevail unconfined; and the culture of clover is completely introduced. The proprietor annually cuts about ten thousand pood of clover, which he stacks under a moveable roof, according to Schubart's plan, with ventilators. The russian plough has given place to the english. Sowing-machines, winnowing-machines, and other implements of husbandry of recent invention are found useful to the improvement and profit of agriculture.

It is unreasonable, however, entirely to neglect the capital for the sake of the podmoskovnies. We will therefore return, and once more — swallow dust.

Between the river Moskva and the walls of the Kreml is an extremely pleasant walk which we have not yet visited, the Quay. The first proposal of it came from knæs Proforoffky, about ten years since, while he was governor of Mosco. Allées, english walks, beds of flowers, and verdant lawns alternately intermingle, and give to the whole an animated and delightful appearance. This place was for a long time the fashionable resort of the beau monde. The parts around were covered with coaches that had brought the ladies and gentlemen to the walks

from

from all quarters of the town, and the quay swarmed with persons of all ranks to such a degree that it was with difficulty one could move about. At present it is entirely deserted, partly from the caprice of all-powerful fashion, who extends her sceptre as despotically over promenades as over shawls and head-dresses; but likewise in some measure from the place being surrounded with buildings. The margin of the river Moskva, which was formerly bordered with trees, is now provided with a granit quay, and the revolution in the buildings of the Kreml extends its effects even to this spot. It is almost entirely covered with blocks of stone and materials for building.

The walks which occupy a considerable part of the Bielgorod are far more numerously frequented. The ruins of the ramparts, which encompassed this quarter of the city, are removed, the place is levelled, and planted with a double row of trees — a beautiful plot of ground, which does honour to the activity and taste of the present maitre-de-police Kaverin.

Mosco is generally indebted for many benefits to the spirit and industry of this personage. The pavement was never kept in so good a condition as for some years past: impassable and dangerous ways are levelled, and may now be passed

with

with the greatest convenience. Swampy districts are converted into pleasant situations, and the muddy canals are cleansed. One thing, however, is greatly to be wished for, that the streets could be cleaned in a different manner from that now practised. They are indeed swept once a-week; but as they are never sprinkled, such a dust is raised by this mode of cleaning, that it is not only offensive to the senses but injurious to the health; at least the eyes and the lungs must certainly suffer by it. Considering the number of people that are kept by every family, it would be very easy to water the streets properly, then to sweep them, and carry away the dirt.

One popular diversion still remains to be mentioned, and deserves notice, as it is the principal amusement of all, during the hot season. I mean the SWINGS in the easter week. These swings are constructed in various parts of the town, having about them kabaks, booths for puppet-shows, cook-shops, and the like: Podnabinsky, however, is the capital scene of this diversion. Here, in a spacious square between Zemlenoigorod and the suburbs, about thirty of these swings, roundabouts, and ups-and-downs are erected. It is at this joyful season that here the national propensity to frolicsome pastime

is

is difplayed by the populace to its full extent. Even the fuperior claffes affemble here as fpectators, and form a fecond fpectacle extremely interefting. The numerous concourfe of perfons of all ranks, who in their elegant equipages drive flowly round the diverting fpot, the goodhumoured gaiety of the populace, the hearty fatisfaction with which they enjoy thefe amufements, the ftriking fingularity of the paftimes themfelves, give thefe popular holidays fo peculiar a character, that any obferver, who would take the pains to ftudy the nation in this giddy fcene of their entertainment, might feize very ftrong lines for its delineation. He could not fail of catching the univerfal blithfomenefs, with which old and young, childhood and hoary age are animated, and which here is not quickened by a momentary impulfe, but is only elevated and placed in its moft agreeable light by a congenial opportunity. He will remark the fpirit of courtefy and gallantry, which exhibits itfelf in a thoufand little touches, as an etching in the national character by no means indifferent. Here a couple of beggars, whofe tattered garments fcarcely afford them a covering, greet one another in the moft complaifant and refpectful manner; a long ftring of queftions concerning their mutual welfare begins the dialogue, which

likewife

likewise concludes by a polite embrace. There a young fellow offers to hand his girl, glowing with paint and brandy, into the seat in which both of them are presently mounted in the air. Even in those superior regions his tenderness does not forsake him. At every anxious agitation of his lady he throws one arm about her waist, that with the other he may shew his ease and security by expressive pantomimical gesticulations. — Only one step farther, and the eye fixes on very different scenes. The same people who were before employed in such friendly salutations, are now engaged in a dispute which exhausts the prodigious treasures of russian scurrilities. All that is degrading and exasperating to human nature finds a denomination in this energetic language; and yet the clamorous disputants never lose their temper. Using the most furious gestures, exerting their throats to the utmost pitch of vociferation, amidst a profusion of the most abusive epithets, they suddenly get so close that their beards almost touch — yet without ever coming to blows. The police, well knowing that there is no danger of life or limb in these fierce debates, cools the heated parties by a shower directed at their heads from a fire-engine, always kept in readiness on these occasions, and found by long experience to be the best instrument for quelling a riot as well as for quenching a conflagration. The whole quarrel is terminated in an instant, a general shout of hootings and laughter bursts from the by-standers; and the disputants are now running arm in arm to the nearest public house to cement their renovated friendship with a glass of brandy.

In the neighbourhood of the swings, &c. wooden booths are usually erected, in which vulgar comedies are performed. Each representation lasts about half an hour, and the price of admittance is five kopeeks. As the crowd is extremely great, and the acting goes on during the whole day, the profits are very considerable both to the proprietors and the performers, which they divide among themselves. These latter, as may easily be supposed, are not artists by profession, but mere dilettanti from the inferior classes of the people, who nevertheless, under the mask of the durak*, utter a number of shrewd and witty conceits.

Though these entertainments are calculated only for the lower orders of people, yet all the fine company of Mosco in a manner partake in them, as there is a continual rotation of elegant

* Durak is the common expression for *fool*; but here it seems synonimous likewise with buffoon, harlequin, merry Andrew, Jack Pudding, &c.

and

and genteel carriages, enjoying the fight of this amufing and diverfified fcene. The Friday in the Eafter week is, however, the grand day for the quality and people of condition. On that day there is a promenade, as it is called, to Podnabinfky, which, in regard to pomp and parade, and the number of vehicles, ranks next to that upon the firft of May.

CHAP. X.

The winter. — Livelinefs of the city in that feafon. — Common length of its duration. — Praife of the winter. — Amufements of the higher claffes. — The noble affembly. — Mafquerades. — Inconveniences of that fpecies of entertainment. — Concerts. — Tafte for mufic. — Sledge parties. — The Pokroffkaia. — Trotters. — The racing-place. — The ifvofcheiks. — The ice-hills.

THE difagreeable period of duft and dirt is at length over. The want of pavement is amply compenfated by a bountiful fupply of fnow; and the light fledges fly fwiftly through the ftreets. The atmofphere is pure, and the townfman has no longer any reafon to envy the inhabitant of the country. IT IS WINTER. What life and agility reign around! The nobility from all parts hafte to the metropolis, the abode

of

of their relations and friends, the refort of superior enjoyments, the school of refined manners, the centre of commerce and business, dear, delightful Mosco. The roads are covered with carriages and sledges. Loads of provisions are coming from the remotest provinces: then the roads are excellent; over rivers and morasses nature has thrown firm and solid bridges; nothing stands in the way of diligence and industry.

The winter usually sets in about the middle of November, often earlier, and lasts till the end of March, consequently for a period of about five months. January and February are undoubtedly the finest part of the winter. The days are then grown longer, the falls of snow are not so frequent as before, the air is pure, and the sky bright; and, from the middle of January, the frost seldom exceeds ten degrees by Reaumur's thermometer, being generally not more than four or five degrees. What a pleasure it is, properly clad against the cold, to move about and take exercise in the pure elastic atmosphere of winter! How the body is hardened against distemper, and how alert are all the animal organs! In a good continued winter epidemical diseases are extremely rare; and if colds and rheums appear on the coming on of a thaw, they are immediately difperfed by the returning froft. Even the plague, which about thirty years fince raged at Mofco, was forced to yield to its falutary influence. The appearance of the city is likewife incomparably more agreeable than in the fummer. A brilliant white is reflected from the palaces and houfes. The fight is nowhere fhocked by dirt or impurity. The houfes, the ftreets and fquares are neat and clean. The mephitic vapours with which the atmofphere of large cities is always charged, no longer offend the olfactory organs. The uncontaminated breath of nature is invigorating to the fpirits and delightful to the fenfe.

Affemblies, mafquerades, concerts, the drama, form the entertainment of the fuperior ranks at this feafon of the year. We will haftily run through them, and then mingle in the chearful throng that celebrate the maflanitza, or the butter-week.

The prime grand inftitution for diffipation frequented by the nobility is the NOBLE AS-SEMBLY*. This affembly is held once a-week, in a houfe fitted up and appropriated to that ufe. Here may be had all forts of provifions and refrefhments. In fome of the rooms are

* Blagorodnie fobranie.

card-tables. From time to time balls and concerts are given. This society has subsisted for several years; and almost the whole nobility of Mosco, of both sexes, are subscribers. It is extremely well conducted, is possessed of great funds, and is likely to continue long. The MASQUERADES are under the direction of Mr. Maddox, and are given during the carnival or butter-week. They are particularly numerous and brilliant on the last days of the maslanitza, the week immediately preceding passion-week. The last masquerade, on the sunday of the first week in Lent, lasts from the morning early till twelve at night. The grand masquerade-hall at the play-house is a beautiful production of architecture, and conveniently holds four thousand persons. Otherwise, this species of entertainment is not particularly interesting, and in many respects is very troublesome. Masks in character are but seldom seen; dominos and cloaks are the usual dresses, and many persons are totally unmasked. There is little dancing, as the hall is filled by the company walking to and fro; and it is often with great difficulty that one can move about. On account of the multitude of carriages, you must often wait upwards of an hour in the street before there is a possibility of getting out for admission. But it is still worse at endeavouring to go home. Beset by a host of clamorous servants in the antechambers, running about to look for their masters, or bawling for their carriages, is already disagreeable enough; but the turmoil and perplexity is greatly increased in endeavouring to procure your own, which is frequently stationed at the distance of a verst or more from the porch of the masquerade-house. While waiting in the cold corridores we have plenty of time to bewail the folly of masquerades, and to form good resolutions for the future.

Concerts are given during Lent. The principal performers of Europe visit Mosco at this time, and find it more profitable to them than any other city in the world, London and Petersburg perhaps excepted. The violinist Hempel, the female singer Zaporiti, the blind flute-player Delon, and, in short, the famous performer on the harpsichord Hæssler, who have frequented this town for several years, will vouch for the truth of what is here asserted. The tickets for the concerts cost from two to five rubles, and the hall is never thinly filled. Several admirers of music, in opulent circumstances, take fifty or a hundred of these tickets, for the sake of encouraging the talents of the performers; who, besides, find another source of gain, no less productive,

productive, in giving leffons in mufic during their ftay at Mofco. The pay for an hour is commonly five rubles to thefe capital artifts, but the ordinary mufic-mafters, though competent in their way, are by no means fo richly paid. They are likewife engaged for private concerts, which yield them alfo a bountiful harveft. The paffion for mufic is very general in Mofco, and the harpfichord-players, Hæfsler, Weydenhammer, Seidler, Bouleau, and others, who are employed in giving leffons, earn yearly feveral thoufand rubles.

Large and magnificent SLEDGE-PARTIES, peculiarly formed for that purpofe, are here not often feen; probably becaufe the long duration of the fledge-ways deprives this diverfion of the charm of rarity, and finks it to the level of ordinary and every-day things. In various ftreets little fledges ftand for hire, as hackney-coaches do in London, in readinefs to be taken for going from one place to another of this fpacious city, or merely for a drive. But, the whole winter through, efpecially on Sundays, there is a vaft concourfe of equipages and fledges in the Pokroffkaia, a long ftrait ftreet in the neighbourhood of the german flobode. The fineft and fleeteft horfes, as well as the moft elegant fledges, are here brought forth to captivate attention.

tention. The sledges, however, of this country are not made in those fanciful and allegorical forms, nor have that curious carved-work so much admired in the sledges of Germany; they are of a simple, light, and convenient construction, without any carvings or ornaments. Neither are the horses loaded with heavy gear, and the little bells are here not known. The sledges are made of good durable stuff, covered with fine cloth or plush, and are provided with a bearskin bag, in which those who sit in them put their feet. The horse-trappings are neat and handsome without being cumbrous. The fleetest and most admired geldings are those that constantly go in a quick trot, without ever getting into a gallop. They are called TROTTERS. If the sledge be drawn by two horses, then, according to the rules of etiquette here observed, one of them gallops while the other continually trots; and if a man does not drive by this rule, he had better not make his appearance in the Pokroffkaia, or at least not on the RACING-PLACE.

The RACING-PLACE is on the river Mosco, as at Petersburg it is on the Neva, not far from the stone bridge. Here, on the ice of the river, a course of a verst in length is set off by posts, with a line of posts down the middle to separate

those

those who go one way from such as come the other. On the sides are stands and scaffolds for the spectators. On this course every Sunday races are run, at which an extraordinary enthusiasm is observable. Wagers are seldom laid in money; the whole contest being for the superlative honour of being known to possess the fleetest nag in Mosco.

This kind of races arises frequently in the streets; when two ISVOSCHEIKS * happen to come abreast with one another, both proud of the ability of their horses, neither will let the other get before him, and immediately the sharp contest begins. Even on such occasions participating spectators are not wanting, who encourage the antagonists by acclamations, give the victor their applause, and punish the vanquished by laughing at his rashness.

The ICE-HILLS in the butter-week are a sort of break-neck diversion wherein the common people take great satisfaction, and which sets the intrepidity and dexterity of the natives in the clearest light. From a high steep scaffold covered with blocks of ice, smoothed every night by quantities of water thrown from the summit, the little sledges shoot down with the swiftness of

* The drivers of the sledges in winter and the droschkas in summer that are on the stands for hire are so called.

an arrow. On either side is a tremendous abyss formed by the height of the hill; and the slightest unskilfulness or imprudence of the person in the sledge may turn it from its direction and be attended with the most dreadful consequence. But incomparably more dangerous is this spot on skaits. Till one is used to this sight, it almost makes the hair stand on end to see the hundreds that follow one another in endless succession on skaits and in sledges down this amazing precipice. Yet accidents scarcely ever happen. Indeed, if we consider that the ice is equally glib, it is impossible that he who begins the descent after another should ever overtake him, and therefore it is not likely that any collision can ensue. The impetus acquired by this fall carries the sledges and skaiters almost half a verst on the level ice below; bringing them to the opposite ice-hill, up which they ascend by steps behind, with a sledge at their back, and this returns them to the former. The highest and most frequented ice-hills are those erected on the Moskva and the Neglinnaia. At these places are also show-booths and victuallers, much visited and admired by that part of the public for whom these amusements are calculated. The crowd around, and the various scenes, are the same with those already described in speaking of the

the diverfions of the Eafter week. Women as well as men enjoy the diverfion of the ice-hills with the fame avidity; and it is impoffible to avoid comparing the appearance they prefent to a vaft cataract of human figures.

CHAP. XI.

Moral character of the Mofcovites. — Hofpitality. — Pleafures of the table. — Play. — Political difcuffions. — Toleration. — Influence thereof on friendfhip, edu- — cation, and marriage. — Companionable toleration. — Beneficence. — Liberal way of thinking in the Mofcovites in regard to wealth and ftation.

HOSPITALITY is a leading feature in the national character of the Ruffians, which is fo much the more confpicuous, as that virtue is not nearly fo extenfive among the other nations of our quarter of the globe. It is certainly one of the moft amiable virtues that are comprized under the name of humanity. Freely to welcome the ftranger under our roof, to give him food and drink, without refpect of perfon or condition, whether he be Crœfus or Irus, Apollo or Vulcan — what an amiable people, amongft whom this pure and difinterefted hof-

pitality

pitality is a native custom! In those provinces of Russia, which lie the most remote from european refinements, that fair flower of the patriarchal ages is still indigenous; but in Mosco, Petersburg, and the other enlightened parts of Russia, hospitality, though it has lost that elevated, godlike character, yet continues to be among the engaging virtues of their inhabitants.

Every one, whether acquaintance or stranger, who neither by condition nor manners is of the vulgar class, finds a hearty welcome in the house of a generous Moscovite: and the longer he stays, the better he is liked; especially in the country, where time is apt sometimes to hang heavy on hand. It is not to be denied, that interest and covetousness, or flattery and convenience, and one cannot say what else, are now and then the porters at the gate; that here and there, wealth, rank, beauty, certain accommodations or companionable talents, such as skill in play, the powers of entertaining, especially the facility of retailing news, give greatest pretensions to a good reception: but this is likewise the case everywhere; and where is the country, at least in Europe, whose inhabitants are not liable to this observation? But, in general, a person may go into every house in Mosco, where he has once been presented, without any ceremony,

mony, uninvited, and, if he choose, appear every day at table, without the least apprehension of the master being denied to him, or of being looked upon with an evil eye. Neither has he any reason to fear that his unexpected presence may create confusion in the family; as it is the practice here to set out the table every day, as if it were for an entertainment: for even in families of moderate fortunes, the table is ordinarily furnished with ten or twelve dishes, generally well-dressed, and of exquisite quality. A pretty desert is seldom wanting; and, besides the usual table-wine, several of the finer sorts and liqueurs are served round. Hence it happens, that a man of a weak stomach seldom rises from table, without being smitten by his conscience for having transgressed his rules of diet; especially if he has indulged in the jocundity into which, in such circumstances, he may easily be surprised. A customary russian meal consists of one or more cold dishes by way of luncheon, hams, bacon, dried tongues, caviar, bread, cheese, butter, &c. which are taken at a side-board while the cloth is laying for dinner. This is composed of a strong meat-soup, and schtschi*, succeeded by three or four seasoned ragouts, roasts, pastry, and several kinds of grain prepared with milk, and in which

* A russian soup made of beef and cabbage.

no nation comes up to the Ruffians. The defert, as everywhere elfe, is made up of comfits and fruits. The ordinary table-wines are Medoc and Chateau-Margot; befides, porter and englifh ale, quas and mead *, which are always placed on the table, that the guefts may help themfelves when they pleafe, without fpeaking to a fervant. The wines that at moft tables are handed round, are Hungary, Malaga, Champagne, Burgundy, Madeira, Cyprus, Mofler, Rhenifh, called in England Old Hock, &c. The nalifki, or liqueurs, are cherries, cranberries, goofeberries, currants, &c. in brandy, noyaux, and the like.

In the forenoon a relifh is taken of pickled herring, caviar, or fmoked meats, with a glafs of aqua-vitæ, which is here called a fchelken. In the fchelken the ladies as well as gentlemen all take part. The ufual time for fitting down to dinner is at one or two o'clock at lateft, and the fupper is ferved at nine or ten; fometimes, however, later, when the company is numerous, and the rubbers of whift are not over.

In general the pleafures of the table are here in high eftimation, and the fame of the man who

* Quas and mead are two ruffian drinks, whereof the former is ufed inftead of fmall beer; and is brewed from meal, balm, mint and water. The other is compofed of honey and water. Both are extremely refrefhing.

keeps

keeps a good kitchen, flies from mouth to mouth. Acquaintances are usually not formed till this matter is properly explained; and an excellent table gives a claim to the most brilliant companies. "There is glorious eating and drinking at their house," is no small praise to any family; and the man who has a fine taste, and knows how to give savoury dishes, or is a good judge in wines, plays no inferior part in society.

Even at dinner and at the tea-table, play is generally the subject of conversation. Persons of the greatest gravity hold it not beneath their dignity to analyze the games of whist, and to make profound disquisitions on them. With a face of the utmost importance, and with a power of recollection that indeed is astonishing, they relate the most interesting events of the yesterday's party. What cards each player held, what card he led, what others were played to it, for what reasons, what were the consequences — all this is delivered with the most perfect circumstantiality, and attended to with consummate patience.

A better and more interesting topic of conversation is the politics of the day, which are here discussed with a liberality and frankness not common elsewhere. The last Hamburgh gazette is discussed

discussed and debated without fear or reserve; every one taking part in the conversation, according to his sentiments or humour. This shews the good understanding and the mutual confidence that subsist between the government and the nation, and is certainly the best evidence for the goodness of the administration and the contentedness of the people.

One of the finest features of the national character of the Russians is certainly their TOLERATION, which shines at Mósco in its most brilliant lustre. This popular virtue is the fruit of those laws that have been enacted in this respect by the wise monarchs of Russia, since the æra of Alexèy Mikhaïlovitch. Faith, in matters of religion, is here never any detriment to a man. In civil affairs, in social intercourse, in friendship, in love, religion is no obstacle to success. The Moscovite never inquires, whether thou be of Cephas, or of Apollos, or of Paul. Honour and probity are the grounds of his confidence, and amiableness of any kind the source of his attachment. Hence we see, that even bigotted parents trust the education of their children to a foreigner who is of a different persuasion, if they are but convinced of his honesty. They love and esteem him, though he never attends

their

their religious rites; and meat is served to him at their tables, while they themselves keep strict fast.

A man may safely rely on the friendship of the Russians, when once he has acquired it, in spite of any difference in religion; and marriages between Russians and foreigners are contracted without the least scruple or hesitation.

Besides this religious toleration, here is still another, namely, SOCIAL TOLERATION, which is commonly a mark of good breeding and knowledge of the world. It is in contrast with a propensity to testiness and cavil, and forms the basis of good behaviour in company, and of a chearful and easy communication of sentiments and ideas. This species of toleration is likewise universal in Mosco. Every one may deliver his particular conceptions and notions on any subject whatever, without fear of flat contradiction, or of being abashed or confounded by gross replies. No one pretends to force his opinion on others by bawling and clamour, and it seldom happens that the pleasure of society is disturbed by warm debates. Every one rides his hobby-horse under the safeguard of social toleration. In short, whatever may be the source of this virtue, its charms are inestimable, and its effects beneficial.

Another

Another beautiful characteristic of the Moscovites is entitled to equal praise — it is BENEFICENCE. No pauper is sent empty away from the door; on the contrary, they hasten to the indigent to offer their mite. At all family occurrences of consequence, especially at funerals, considerable sums are distributed in alms, and it is common to purchase the discharge of prisoners by paying their debts. The rich have an eleemosynary day, at least once a-week, when all the poor who present themselves, whatever be their country or religious profession, receive money, garments, provisions, &c. according to their several necessities, or their different deserts. Private persons at times endow useful institutions of great extent, as the commercial-school founded by M. Demidof, the alms-houses of Kurakin and of Scheremetof, and even the foundling-house, which owes its foundation in part to voluntary contributions. Very frequently too, the college of general provision receives considerable sums for the relief of the distressed, and nowhere do collections for any beneficent purpose fill more rapidly than here.

One custom more deserves our honourable notice, by which the comforts of society are greatly enhanced. Those long-tailed, troublesome, minute, and insipid titles, which are still

scrupulously

scrupulously retained in many parts of Germany, are here but seldom heard. Every one, let his rank and station be what they may, is called by his pronomen with the addition of his father's, and the termination *vitch*; as, Ivan Maksimovitch, Gavrila Petrovitch, Paphnuti Romanovitch, Pankrati Gregorievitch, &c. and the ladies by adding *evna* or *ovna*, instead of *vitch*; as, Agaphia Romanovna, Yuliana Alexandrovna, Daria Aphanasievna, Anastasia Ivanovna, &c. The knæs and the graf are indeed called *illustrious* [*], and the general, or he who holds an equal rank in the civil department, has the title *excellence* [†]; yet in common conversation often only by their names, knæs Ivan Mikhaïlovitch, graf Matphey Petrovitch, &c. This laudable custom is even generally adopted by the Germans, and is observed even in speaking their native language. In short, the pride of titles and rank, of wealth or science, is here extremely rare. Whether you are noble or not; whether you reckon your income by thousands or by hundreds, no man ever inquires. Station is honourable; but moderate circumstances are no disgrace. A man is sure of being the first person in company, if he be the most agreeable.

[*] Siatelstvo.   [†] Prevoskhodytelstvo.

CHAP. XII.

Education. — Exertions on the part of parents. — Style of moscovite education. — Regard for the french language. — Aptness of the young ladies for playing on the harpsichord. — Defects in the education of females. — Requisites for a good tutor. — French masters. — German masters. — The Dætka and the Nenka. — Visin's Nedorosl.

Of the public schools we have already had occasion to speak: we shall here say something concerning the private tuition, as it is conducted by domestic teachers, or in boarding-schools.

In Mosco, as well as throughout all Russia, education is treated with all the importance that it deserves. Persons of opulence and distinction are not sparing of expence, in order to give their children a good education; not only paying the domestic tutor a salary of a thousand rubles and upwards, but likewise having the best masters for music, dancing, drawing, &c. so that the education of the children in great houses cost several thousand rubles annually. These exertions are certainly highly praise-worthy; but, on the other hand, the mode of education in general, which is now become the fashion, is extremely reprehensible.

hensible. This seems to be the proper term; though it could hardly be expected that fashion should have anything to do in the management of an affair of so much importance as education; yet when some defective practice becomes the object of general imitation, it can only be explained from the caprices of that wanton goddess.

We shall here take the liberty to make a few remarks on the prevailing mode of education in Mosco, with that discreet frankness which ought always to characterise such as wish to do good.

The knowledge of languages, and the graces of the person, seem to be the foremost considerations in the mind of the generality of parents, if not the only points to which the labours of the tutor ought to tend. Hence it arises, that in the choice of a preceptor far less attention is paid to the science and erudition that he possesses, and his integrity, than to a brilliant exterior. The chief requisite of all is, that he speak french well: for among all classes the learning of this language is the prime concern. Accordingly, it is by no means surprising that the important business of education should be committed to ignorant and uninformed persons, and occasionally even to men of dissolute manners, if they only speak french with a proper accent, and can discourse with fluency on ordinary topics. This must needs be a great disservice

disservice to the community, to which they may perhaps return young men exceedingly well skilled in foreign languages, but totally unaccomplished in head and heart. There are surely higher and better qualities which ought to be looked for from education, such as have been reckoned of great weight in all ages, and by all nations, that are not subject to the dominion of fashion, that ever retain their value, that are recommended as the only condition on which true happiness is to be obtained, and whereon, in short, everything depends: they are, Wisdom and Virtue. Who will venture to affirm, after this, that the learning of languages and the acquiring of the graces should be the principal aim of the teacher? Who sees not, how mistakenly those parents act, who in the selection of a tutor have no regard to character and sound learning, but look solely to skill in languages, and the art of figuring in the world? It is not to be denied, that the learning of foreign tongues, and especially the french, since it is so generally spoken, particularly in all courts, should no more be neglected than the elegancies of behaviour; it is only pretended here that education ought not to be confined to them alone. By the formation of the exterior, is to be understood not only what is called a good address in company, but in

general

general whatever adds to the charms and agreeableness of person, as dancing, music, drawing, riding, fencing, &c. The three former are particularly attended to, after the french tongue, in the education of young ladies. In fact, our astonishment is often excited at the progress that is made in these arts; in many families are some juvenile performers, especially on the harpsichord, who may vie with the greatest masters; and even, while children, exhibit their talents in public concerts. How prejudicial this latter circumstance must be, especially to a young woman of fashion, is obvious to every one. Certainly all the daughters of noble families in Mosco speak french, and many of them in the greatest perfection; but about houshold affairs, about the duties of mothers and wives, they know just as little as the maid that dresses them. Yet the parents would take it much amiss if they were told that their daughters had no education. How! it would be answered, our daughter, who speaks french so well, who plays so masterly on the harpsichord, who dances like an angel, who is the delight and the soul of all companies; she has no education? — " It shall be just as you
" please, madam: but permit me to say, that
" there is a good and a bad education. The
" former principally aims at forming the head
" and

"and the heart; and those matters, of which you and the lady your daughter make so much account, hold only a secondary rank; whereas the latter does exactly the reverse, as you, madam, very well know, or in tutoring the hands and the feet, oftentimes entirely forgets the cultivation of the heart and mind."

For the education of boys, a man is usually sought out who can teach french and german, mathematics, geography, history, natural history, and natural philosophy. Parents, however, inquire more concerning those sciences, mathematics excepted, to which their children ought principally to apply, as being mostly intended for the military. If the tutor can play on the harpsichord, or can draw, particularly if he have withal a good figure and genteel deportment, he is an exquisite person; the best families engage in rivalships for him; and he is certain of having a very considerable salary and distinguished treatment. Concerning his knowledge and abilities he must have a testimonial from the univerfity, or from the director of the normal schools, certifying that he has undergone an examination; which at present is pretty severe.

The number of domestic tutors in Mosco is considerable; mostly Frenchmen and Germans. Among the former are many adventurers, who have

have formerly been perruquiers, valets de chambres, cuisiniers, and one cannot tell what, who either from indigence or ambition have turned their talents to teaching. This sort of people even renders the name of utſchitel, tutor, contemptible in Ruſſia, which is otherwiſe certainly an honorable title. The german informators, as they are called, are, generally ſpeaking, men of learning in the proper ſenſe of the term, who are not come at a venture into the country, but have been written for on the recommendation of ſome competent friend. They are likewiſe generally the moſt eſteemed as perſons of great knowledge and a decent irreproachable behaviour.

Another fault in the education here is in the cuſtom of committing children from their infancy to the care and guidance of certain male and female attendants, called the Dætka and the Nenka. Theſe are vaſſals commonly taken from the houſhold ſervants, and reſemble much the pædagogues of the ancients, being not only the nurſes and attendants of the children, but are appointed to direct and to chide them. Though the beſt and moſt truſty are picked out for theſe poſts; yet it is nearly impoſſible to find among this claſs of people any that are poſſeſſed of ſuch qualities as a man would exactly chooſe to trust with the management of his children in that period of their youth which is perhaps the most important of all: for it often happens afterwards, that all the pains an expert preceptor can bestow will not heal the perversities of the mind, or correct the deviations of the heart, which have arisen from their long habits of intercourse with the dætka and nenka; perhaps without being conscious of it; the most absurd and ridiculous prejudices being usually the first aliment with which they feed the curiosity of the opening intellect. Most of them are very strong in fairy tales, in general so extremely silly that they must palsy the best understanding. This chapter may properly be concluded by a short extract from Visin's Nedorosl, a favourite piece of the russian drama, as affording a just notion of this nenkery and utschitelship at Mosco. NEDOROSL signifies the minor, the child. It is true that, since the first appearance of this play, many alterations have taken place in this respect; yet originals may here and there be found for Visin's picture. A boy of twelve or fourteen is the hero of this piece. He never appears without his nenka, who always walks behind her Mitrophanuschka (his name in the diminutive) in great concern and anxiety to do whatever may please him and keep him quiet: now

bringing

bringing him little feathers to blow about the room with his breath, then shewing him how to make soap-bubbles, at which the looby testifies great satisfaction. But he is most of all delighted with a clapper of paper, and which he handles with great dexterity, going with it first to frighten his worthy papa, and then his no less worthy uncle, which he artfully does to the great diversion of all. The parents, who are represented as living at their country-manſion in one of the distant provinces, begin at length to think that it is just the proper period to put young Mitrophanuſchka into the hand of tutors; and the resolution is immediately adopted of taking a journey to town, as the uncle, who has a very decisive voice in the family-deliberations, assures them of its being high time for that purpose, as in town many lads have quite finished their education at fifteen. On the arrival of the family in town, therefore, the first business is to find tutors for Mitrophanuſchka. They are found. They bring good recommendations with them. They are engaged. One of them, a parish-clerk, is to torment the youth, as mamma calls it, with teaching him the ruſſian alphabet; the second, a Frenchman, is to instruct him in his language. The hours of application are begun. Mitrophanuſchka weeps
bitterly,

bitterly, and will not, by any persuasion, be brought to fix his eyes on the book. He puts his fingers in his ears, while the parish-clerk, with his drawling schoolmaster-accent, is bawling to him his As, buki, vedi, glagol, dobro, yest, jivété, &c.* At length the Nenka, who never forsakes her poor Mitrophanuschka in this hour of torment, by bringing him sugar-plumbs and cakes and the paper clapper, succeeds at least so far as to make him leave off crying. The business now seems to take a favourable turn. The schoolmaster screams his letters; Mitrophanuschka munches comfits, accompanying the melody of his teacher, at intervals, with the sound of his clapper, and even occasionally muttering out a letter; while the Nenka is incessantly coaxing the dear child with all her arts and ingenuity to mind his book. The parish-clerk having finished his hour, retires; and now the Frenchman appears. With him af-

* By the way, this will be no improper place for making the reader acquainted with the names of the letters of the russian alphabet. As, buki, védi, glagol, dobro, yest, jivété, zemlia, ijé, kako, liudi, muisliété, nachè, one, pokoï, rtsi, slowo, tverdo, u, ferte, khière, tsi, therf, scha, schtscha, yérè, yeri, yer, yati, yu, ya. Formerly among these were also the letters i, zélo, yé, ksi, psi, phita, and ijitsa; but they have of late years been disused by literary persons.

fairs

fairs are sliding into a better train; and Mitrophanuschka gets through this hour by the help of sweetmeats and his clapper. The parents are charmed with both pupil and tutor, and all goes on as it should. In the evening of this day the family receives a visit from an aunt, who has not long been come from Petersburg, where she has passed some years: the conversation chiefly turns on the clever young Mitrophanuschka: they tell the aunt that the occasion of their journey to town was solely for the sake of giving this darling boy an education suitable to his rank: they talk in high terms of the great progress he has made in only one day, at the same time doing ample justice to his tutors, who are extolled as persons of uncommon talents. But they dwell with particular emphasis on the merits of the amiable Frenchman whom they have been so happy as to engage. The aunt, a great admirer of that nation, requests to have him introduced to her. He is sent for, and presently appears. " Goodlack!" she immediately exclaims, " this is my petersburg coach-" man!" The ci-devant coachman loses nothing of his presence of mind at this discovery; but, expressing his joy at finding an old acquaintance, kisses her hand; and she, according to the russian custom, presents to him her cheek:

thus

thus all continues in the former train. The detection excites not the smallest aversion in the parents, who content themselves with saying: Well, he is however a Frenchman — on the contrary, their satisfaction is rather increased by the circumstance of his being known to the aunt, who gives him a good character. The metamorphosed coachman mixes in company with the gentlemen of the house, the petersburg aunt sits down to a party at Ombre, and all divert themselves with the recollection of former times.

The Sources whence the foregoing History is drawn are the following:

Letopis Nestorova. — Chronicle of Nestor, 1 vol. 4to. St. Petersburg, 1767. — This chronicle was published from a manuscript found at Kœnigsburg, and has been considered by the ablest critics as the most faithful of all. Neither the Poles, the Bohemians, the Serbes, the Vendes, nor any other of the slavonian nations, are able to boast of an historian of such high antiquity. He was born in 1056, and at the age of sixteen entered himself of the petscherskian monastery at Kief, where he died at a pretty advanced age. His reputation for purity of life obtained him a place among the saints. His work closes with the year 1115. With the following year commences the narrative of his continuator Sylvester, dean of the monastery of St. Michael at Kief, and afterwards bishop of Pereiaslavl. The other continuators of this chronicle, which breaks off at the year 1206, are not known.

The style of Nestor is plain and simple throughout; it being chiefly his intent to preserve the remembrance of facts without embellishment. His simplicity, however, does not entirely exclude eloquence. He says nothing of the memoirs which he followed for the times anterior to those in which he wrote: but it is easy to discover that he did not work upon merely oral tradition, and that he had before him the manuscripts which he has neglected to cite. It is proved by authentic documents, that so early as the

time

time of Oleg, in the ninth century, the Ruffians had the art of writing, fince from that period they made teftaments, contracts, and treaties. Neftor and his continuators have been careful to note down in their chronicle the appearance of comets, eclipfes, and other celeftial phænomena.

Letopis Nikonova. — Chronicle of Nikon, 2 vol. 4to. St. Peterfburg, 1767. — This chronicle is not properly the work of the patriarch Nikon, whom we have feen playing a great part under the reign of tzar Alexey. But that prelate employed fome of the leifure procured him by his difgrace, in collecting a great number of chronicles, collating them, correcting one by the other, perhaps fometimes in altering them; and, having done this, he made a copy of the whole, in which he placed fo much confidence, that he pronounces an anathema againft any who fhould dare to make any alteration in it. This work brings us down to the reign of tzar Alexey; but the two volumes that are printed conclude at the invafion of Ruffia by the Tartars.

Kniga Stepennaïa, 2 vol. 4to. St. Peterfburg, 1777. — The book of degrees — fo entitled becaufe in it the hiftory of the fovereigns of Ruffia is difpofed according to the order of their defcent: thus, when the father has for his fucceffor his fon and his grandfon, they together form only one degree; and another degree commences when the throne paffes to a collateral heir. This book is not a chronicle, but a hiftory begun in the fourteenth century by the metropolitan Kyprian, in the reign of Dmitry Donfky, and continued in the fixteenth century by the metropolitan Makhary under tzar Ivan Vaffillievitch. This work is very deservedly esteemed, and the copies of it were accordingly multiplied, till at laft it was printed by the care of the learned M. Muller, counfellor of the college of foreign affairs,

affairs, and one of the most illustrious members of the academy of sciences at St. Petersburg. The authors of it, however, are justly reprehensible, for having sometimes too lightly deviated from the text of the ancient writers of the chronicles, for supplying the place of it with false and ridiculous traditions, and often spoiling their work by accounts of prodigies for the sake of pleasing the monks of their time. They had no notion of the rules of sound criticism; and their style, though dignified, is often turgid, and fails of inspiring us with the same confidence as that of the honest Nestor and his continuators.

Tzarstvennoy Letopissets. — Tzarian chronicle, 1 vol. 4to. St. Petersburg, 1772. — It conducts us from the year 1114 to the year 1472; but there is a considerable chasm in it. Every transaction, in the original manuscript, is accompanied with a miniature representation of it. It may be conjectured, that this copy, being ornamented at so great expence, was made for tzar Alexey, who was very curious of information. Though it be not extremely ancient, it is not the less worthy of confidence, and should be considered as an extract, carefully made from the ancient chronicles written by contemporaries with the facts. The chronological order is accurately preserved in it, the very style of the authors is retained, and the various phænomena of the skies are noted.

Drevney Letopissets. — Ancient chronicle, 2 vol. 4to. St. Petersburg, 1774—75. — It is printed from a copy ornamented like the foregoing, and made for the use, it may be presumed, of the same prince. It runs on from the reign of Alexander Nesfky to the year 1424.

Tzarstvennaia Kniga. — The tzarian book, 1 vol. 4to. St. Petersburg, 1769. — This is another copy resembling the two former. It contains the history of tzar Ivan Vassilievitch, sillievitch, to the year 1553, who followed the conqueft of Kazan.

Opiſſanie Kniazia Kourbſkago. — Hiſtory of tzar Ivan Vaſſillievitch, by prince Kourbſkoy. The author was a witneſs of moſt of the facts which he relates; having ſerved at the ſiege of Kazan, and having had a command during the war of Livonia. Having fallen under the difpleaſure of tzar Ivan, and dreading his vengeance, he fled into Poland. From this place of his retreat he addreſſes his work to that prince himſelf, particularizing and reproaching him boldly with his cruelties. The tzar condeſcended to anſwer him; and, without denying the facts with which he is charged, he related, in vindication of himſelf, the cauſes of complaint he had againſt his ſubjects. The performance of Kourbſkoy and that of the tzar are two valuable monuments which are preſerved only in the manuſcript.

Letopis o Miatéyakh. — Chronicle of the troubles of Moſco, 1 vol. 8vo. St. Peterſburg, 1771. — It begins at the reign of Feodor, ſon of tzar Ivan Vaſſillievitch, and ends at the reign of Alexey. If the author has not dived into the cabinets of thoſe who were at the head of affairs in the times whereof he writes, he was at leaſt very well informed of whatever could come to the knowledge of a private attentive obſerver. The epocha which he compriſes is one of the moſt intereſting in all the hiſtory of Ruſſia.

Sinopſis, 1 vol. 8vo. St. Peterſburg. The work of a credulous monk; being a dry abridgement of a part of ruſſian hiſtory, where ſome important tranſactions are haſtily noticed, while the author dwells with ſatisfaction on a number of idle and abſurd tales, invented in the cloiſters. This little book went through ſeven editions; becauſe nothing better had then been publiſhed.

Tadre

Yadro Rossiskoy Istorii. — Abridgment of russian history, 1 vol. 8vo. Mosko, 1770. — An excellent work of prince Khilkof, ambassador from Russia in Sweden, and detained prisoner by the Swedes contrary to the laws of nations, when Peter I. in 1700 declared war against Charles XII. He died when just on the point of recovering his liberty, and it was during his captivity that he wrote this work, which he finishes at the battle of Pultava.

Kazanskai Istoriia. — History of Kazan, by M. Ritchkof, 1 vol. 8vo. St. Petersburg, 1767. — The author drew up his work from a chronicle which he found at Kazan, and he has enriched it with several curious investigations.

Voédénié k Astrakhanskoy Topographii. — Introduction to the topography of Astrakhan, 1 vol. 8vo. St. Petersburg, 1774. — A work of the same author.

Opissanie Slutchaief Kassaiustchikhsia do Azova. — Account of the events which relate to the city of Azof, 1 vol. 8vo. St. Petersburg, 1768. — The learned work of M. Baër, professor of oriental languages at the academy of sciences at St. Petersburg. The original is in german.

Izvestiya Vizantiiskikh istorikof. — Extracts from the byzantine historians. — M. Stritter has under this title collected all the passages in the historians of Byzantium that relate to the northern hives who contributed to the ruin of the roman empire.

Istoriya Skiphskaia. — History of the Scythians. — A work, in manuscript of the stolnik Lizlof, who lived under the reign of tzar Mikhaïla Pheodorovitch. It would be very useful, if it were not superseded, as to the history of the Tartars of Kazan and Astrakhan, by the writings of M. Ritchkof.

Kratkoy Letopissets Lomonosova. — Brief chronology, of Lomonosof, 1 vol. 8vo. St. Petersburg, 1760. — It is impossible

impossible to include more matter in the short space of fifty pages. This little work is followed by the genealogy of the monarchs of Russia, and their alliances.

Rovest o Samozvantsakh. — History of the impostors, by prince Schtscherbatof, 1 vol. 8vo. St. Petersburg, 1774. Under this title the author has compiled the history of the adventurers, who, under false names, have attempted to usurp the throne of Russia. This work is almost entirely taken from the chronicle of the troubles of Mosco, and the abridgment of prince Khilkof. Annexed to it is a relation of the outrages of Stenka Radzin.

Istoriya Rossiskaia Tatischtscheva. — History of Russia, by M. Tatischtschef, privy-counsellor, 3 vols. 4to. — The thor, who lived under the empress Anne, took on himself nearly the same task with Nikon. It is scarcely possible to imagine that any one has ever collected and collated such a great number of chronicles as this writer. He industriously employed himself for thirty years in correcting and completing these chronicles one from the other, in modernizing the style, and in making immense researches into the antiquities of his country, from which he has drawn bold consequences, frequently very doubtful. As he seldom cites the chronicles he has followed, and gives no reason for his preferring some to the others, what degree of confidence should be placed in his work cannot be ascertained. He had brought it down to the reign of Feodor, son of tzar Ivan Vassillievitch; but the three volumes that are printed terminate at the invasion of the Tartars, and the rest was lost in a fire.

Istoriya Rossiskaia kn. Schtscherbatova. — History of Russia, by prince Schtscherbatof, 3 vols. 4to. St. Petersburg, 1770 —71 and 74. — The author always cites his authorities, which upon reference are as often found to correspond. If the

the prime character of a historian be the love of truth, this prince deserves the highest praises.

Jitié Petra Velikago. — Life of Peter the Great, 2 vols. 4to. — printed for the first time in the slavonian language, at Venice, and reprinted in 1774 at St. Petersburg, with notes by prince Schtscherbatof. A work abounding in curious remarks. The author being only intent on the veracity of his narrative, is careless of ornament. He is said to be a prelate of a slavonian church in the turkish dominions.

Istoryia Petra Velikago. — History of Peter the Great, by Pheophane Prokopovitch, archbishop of Novgorod, 1 vol. 8vo. St. Petersburg, 1773. — The author had an intimate knowledge of his hero, who frequently condescended to ask his advice. His work finishes after the battle of Pultava. It is thought by some persons that this book is falsely attributed to the archbishop of Novgorod; it is certain, nevertheless, that the original manuscript was corrected by the hand of that prelate, and that he noted in the margin the new inquiries he intended to make.

Journal Petra Velikago. — Journal of Peter the Great, 2 vol. 4to. St. Petersburg, 1770. — If that prince did not himself write this journal, he at least caused it to be written under his own inspection, and corrected it with his own hand in a great number of places. It was given to the public by prince Schtscherbatof, who has added to it some papers of importance taken from the archives.

Opissanie Sibirskago Tzarstva. — Description of the kingdom of Siberia, 1 vol. 4to. St. Petersburg, 1750. — The learned work of M. Muller, corroborated by a great variety of original documents.

Sibirskaia Istoriya. — History of Siberia, by M. Fischer, professor of the academy of sciences at St. Petersburg, 1 vol. 4to. St. Petersburg, 1774. — The author has made considerable use of M. Muller's work, to which he has added many learned and curious remarks of his own.

Opissanie Zemli Kamtshatki. — Description of Kamtshatka, by Kracheninnikof, 2 vols. 4to. St. Petersburg, 1755. — The author, being sent to Kamtshatka by the academy of sciences, composed his work from his own observations, and those of Steller, member of that academy, and died at Tiumen, in 1745, on his return from his literary travels.

Drevniaia Rossiskaia istoriya Lomonosova. — Ancient history of Russia, by Lomonosof, 1. vol. 4to. St. Petersburg, 1766. — The author was the best poet of his country, and at the same time an excellent prose-writer: but he was destitute of that critical judgment which is the chief quality of an historian.

Téjémésiatchniya-Sotchineniyá, 20 vols. 8vo. — This is a journal published monthly by the imperial academy of sciences at St. Petersburg, from 1755 to 1765. It contains a great number of very important historical pieces, the greater part composed by the learned M. Muller, well known for his indefatigable researches into russian history.

Drevniaia Rossiskaia Vivliophika. — Ancient russian library, 10 vols. 8vo. — A collection of original authentic pieces, drawn from the cabinets and archives, and published by M. Novikof. Among them are several articles of great importance.

Razsujdénié o voiné s Shvedsiéiu. — Dissertation on the war with Sweden, by baron Shafirof, vice-chancellor of the russian empire, 1 vol. 12mo. St. Petersburg, 1722. — It is a manuscript written by order of Peter I. and under his inspection. It deserves to be consulted by all who would study the history of that prince.

Istoriya Rossiskaia Tschujestrantsom. — History of Russia, in manuscript. — The author is a foreigner who lived in the

the reign of Peter I. The frequent gallicisms that occur in his ruſs diction lead one to think that he was a Frenchman. He knew nothing of the ruſſian chronicles, and has followed the livonian, ſwediſh, and poliſh hiſtorians. He may be taxed with very frequent miſtakes, and muſt therefore be conſulted with diſtruſt, though he is not without utility, eſpecially as to the hiſtory of tzar Ivan Vaſſillievitch. That prince in the laſt years of his life ſtruck ſuch terror into his ſubjects, that the Ruſſians no longer dared to commit anything to paper. Accordingly, for a period of ſeveral years, it is only from foreigners, who were at war with them, or who travelled among them, that anything is to be learnt of their hiſtory.

Povſednevniya zapiſki vremeni tzarei Mikhaila Pheodorovitcha i Alexeiya Mikhailovitcha. — Journals of the courſe of times of the tzars Mikhaïla Pheodorovitch and Alexey Mikhaïlovitch, 2 vols. 4to. Moſco, 1769. — Theſe memoirs inform us on what days the ſovereigns dined in ſtate, what officers of the court waited at table, in what manner foreign ambaſſadors were received, what officers were ſent to meet them, &c. But they likewiſe preſent us with ſome hiſtorical facts, which are of the moſt conſummate authenticity.

Rodoſlovi imperatorſkoi familii. — Genealogy of the imperial houſe. — This manuſcript, the work of ſome literary man, ought to be conſulted as containing ſome hiſtorical facts.

Rerum Moſcovitarum commentarii Sigiſmundi liberi baronis in Herberſtain. Baſilea, 1571, 1 vol. folio. — Commentary of baron Herberſtain, on Ruſſia. — The author was twice ſent on embaſſies to Ruſſia, firſt by the emperor Maximilian, and afterwards by the emperor Ferdinand. He took much pains to acquire information, and he imparts it liberally to his readers. It may be here remarked, that

that several of the works written in latin concerning Russia, in the sixteenth century, are far superior to anything that has since appeared from foreigners touching that empire.

Moscoviæ descriptio, auctore Alexandro Guagnino Veronensi. — Description of Russia, by Alexander Guagnini, of Verona. — This author enters at large into the cruelties of tzar Ivan Vassillievitch. He appears to have been well acquainted with the chronicle of prince Kurbskoy, and that he has translated entire sections from it. Guagnini had a command at Vitepsk, a place then belonging to Poland, and bordering on Russia. Here he might have an opportunity for learning many particulars from the Russians who fled into Poland to avoid the cruelties of their sovereign, and it is not unlikely that he was in connection with prince Kurbskoy.

Joannis Basilidis, magni Moschoviæ ducis, vita, a Paulo Oderbornio, tribus libris, conscripta. — Life of Ivan Vassillievitch, by Paul Oderborn. — It is rather a violent declamation against the tzar, than a history of that prince. Great confusion prevails in this work; and that defect is not compensated by the accuracy of the transactions.

Historia belli Livonici, quod magnus Moschovitarum dux contrà Livones gessit, per Tilmannum Bredenbachium conscripta. — History of the war of the grand-duke of Moscovy against the Livonians. — A work written under the dictation of a priest. It is accurate in regard to the principal facts.

These three works, that of Herberstain and some others, are comprized in a collection, entitled, *Rerum Moschoviticarum scriptores varii, Frankofurti,* 1700. folio.

Antonii Possevini Moschovia. — Moscovy, by pere Possevin, 1 vol. folio, 1587. — This jesuit was sent on an embassy in 1581, to tzar Ivan Vassillievitch, by pope Gregory XIII. His testimony is of great weight as to the object of his negotiation, and he may be trusted in his relation of the customs and transactions to which he was witness.

Etat de l'empire de Russie et grand duché de Moscovie, par le capitaine Margaret. Paris, 1669. The author, after having served in France, where he was born, was captain of a company of guards formed by tzar Dmitry, commonly called the first false Demetrius. He was intimately acquainted with that impostor, or that prince, and deserves to be consulted.

Iter in Moschoviam, &c. — Travels into Moscovy, by baron Mayerberg. folio. — The author was ambassador from the emperor to tzar Alexey Mikhaïlovitch; and is worthy of confidence in what he relates as having seen.

Travels in Tartary, Moscovy, and Persia, by Adam Olearius: folio. 1728. — The author communicates a small number of facts, with descriptions, curious enough, of several customs.

Genealogical history of the Tartars, by the khan Abulgafi Baatur. — The antient relations between the Russians and the Tartars, render this work of importance to the history of Russia.

Diarium itineris in Moscoviam dom. de Guariens et Rall, ab imperatore Leopoldo I. ad tzarum Petrum Alexiovicium ablegati extraordinarii, descriptum a Joanne Georgio Korb, secretario ablegationis Cæsariæ. Vienna austriæ, folio. — This work is extremely rare, and sells at a high price. It was written by John George Korb, secretary to the embassy from the emperor Leopold I. to Peter I. in 1698, and contains the particulars of the punishments and tortures to which the revolted strelitses were condemned. As the tzar, on this occasion, wreaked his vengeance by the most horrid cruelties, it is said, that the court of Vienna suppressed all the copies of this book, except a few that had already got abroad.

Mémoires

Memoires pour servir à l'histoire de l'empire russien, sous Pierre le grand, par un ministre étranger, résident en cette cour. La Haye, 1725. 2 vols. 12mo. — The author of this work is not mentioned; but it is certain that he visited and followed the court of Russia from 1714 to 1719. He speaks the truth, and most of the facts he relates were still recollected by persons alive, not many years ago. Whether he were in reality a minister from some foreign power, or whether that quality was falsely attributed to him by his editor, is uncertain. The same work appeared under the following title, *Nouveaux memoires sur l'état présent de la grande Russie ou Moscovie, par un Allemand résident en cette cour.* Paris, 1725, 2 vols. 12mo. Which of the two editions is the original is not known.

Historical account of the russian empire, by baron Strahlenberg, 1 vol. 4to. — The author was one of the swedish officers taken prisoners by the Russians, and sent into Siberia. He certainly had opportunities for observation and inquiry; yet his work is inferior to his reputation, and may frequently mislead the reader.

Histoire de l'empire de Russie sous Pierre le grand, par Voltaire. — If this famous author had been better furnished with materials, by those who engaged to do so, from his lively and pleasing manner of writing there is no doubt that his work would have been a masterly performance; whereas it seems to be entirely composed from mutilated and injudicious extracts from the journal of Peter the Great. It is manifest that, from the commencement of the war with Sweden, he was even left in ignorance of the circumstances of the battle of Narva, which at once diminished the glory of the victors, and the disgrace of the vanquished. A German, employed in the affairs of the cabinet, was commissioned to supply Voltaire with the necessary documents; but,

but, either because he thought himself slighted by the historian, or because he was in the intention of writing a history of the same prince, he neglected his duty. The work of Voltaire affords but a small number of facts that rest on substantial authorities; and he was, perhaps, conscious of the defects of his book, when he said: "I would have engraved on my tomb, Here lies the man who attempted to compose the history of Peter the Great."

Histoire des révolutions de Perse, depuis le commencement de ce siecle. Paris, 1750, 3 vols. 12mo. — The author adduces all the pieces which he procured at Constantinople for the composition of his work, and highly merits the confidence of his readers.

Memoires de Catharine I. 1 vol. 12mo. La Haye, 1728. — This volume, containing very few facts, is swelled with translations of state papers.

Essai sur la bibliotheque et le cabinet d'histoire-naturelle de l'académie des sciences de S. Petersbourg, par Jean Bacmeister. S. Petersb. 1776. 1 vol. 8vo. — The author introduces some historical facts into his work.

The Antidote; or an inquiry into the merits of the abbé d'Auteroche's book, translated from the french. London, 1772. — In a bitter invective against a writer of great levity, this book contains some curious and authentic advertisements on the history, the products, the commerce, and the government of Russia. The original, here badly translated, is supposed to be the production of several authors, all well informed, and having more or less share in the administration. I have been told that it was the joint performance of the late empress Catharine II. and count Peter Schuvalof.

Historical

Historical, political, and military memoirs concerning Russia, by general Manstein. London, 4to. — The author, who was general aid-de-camp to field-marshal Munich, was witness to the facts he relates, and was even employed in circumstances of a delicate nature. He is of service in regard to the reigns of Peter II. the empress Anne, the young Ivan, and the first years of Elizabeth. The english translation is extremely inaccurate; leading the reader into numberless mistakes, particularly in regard to distances, the word *mile* being uniformly retained from the german, which denotes a measure nearly six times as large as the mere english reader would be led hence to suppose.

Essai sur le commerce de Russie. Amsterdam, (Paris,) 1777. This superior work is by M. Marbault, formerly secretary to the envoy from France to Russia. The publication was surely not executed under his inspection, as such mistakes are committed in the names of persons, tribes, and places, that they are scarcely to be known.

History of the northern governments, by Mr. Williams, 2 vols. 4to. The part devoted to the history of Russia contains some truths, no remarkable observations, a great number of errors, and above all a decided partiality against the Russians. If the Russians are beaten, the author is sure that they deserved it; if they are conquerors, he shows that they had no right to be so. But, after having copiously exaggerated the defects of their government, and their ignorance in the art of war, and in naval affairs, he pronounces, that they are able to cope with all the powers of Europe, except the English.

Journal von Russland, by J. H. Busse, 1793, &c. — A monthly publication, containing a great variety of useful materials for the history and geography of Russia.

Histoire

Histoire de Russie, tirée des chroniques originales, des pièces authentiques, et des meilleurs historiens de la nation, par M. Levesque. Paris, 5 vols. 12mo. — Unquestionably the best history that has hitherto appeared of that empire.

Geschichte des russischen Reichs, by M. Merkel. Leipzig, 1795. 3 vols. small 8vo. — A judicious abstract of the foregoing.

Schlœtzer's beylagen zum neuveraendertes Russland, Haigold. 2 vols. 8vo. 1769, 1770.

Schlœtzer's probe russischer annalen, 8vo. 1768. — The learned disquisitions and elaborate researches of professor Schlœtzer are too well known and esteemed to need any farther remark.

Iftoritschefkoye ifledovaniye o meftopolofhenii drevniago Rossiskogo Tmutarakanskago kniashneaiya, &c. — Historical examination into the situation of the antient russian principality of Tmutarakan. Published by command of her imperial majesty, 1794.

Iftoritschefkoye i topografitschefkoye opissaniye gorodof Moskofskoi guberniis ich ujesdami. — Historical and topographical description of the towns of the mofcovian government and their circles. Mosco, 1788. — This government being one of the most important in the empire, and the accounts of it hitherto published being extremely defective, the work here mentioned may be reckoned among the most interesting contributions to the topography of Russia. The description of the capital is indeed only a dry register of facts, affording little entertainment in the perusal, but the data there collected render it highly welcome to geographers by profession, as enabling them to rectify many omissions and mistakes that have slipt into the descriptions of Busching, and other writers.

Moskva.

Moskau. Eine skizze von Johann Richter. Leipzig, 1799. — This lively and entertaining little work, together with that last mentioned, has furnished the greater part of what is found under that head in this volume.

Primetschaniya na istoriyu drevniya i nuneschniya Rossii gospod. Leklerka. — Remarks on the antient and modern history of Russia by M. le Clerc, by major general Ivan Boltin. St. Petersb. 1788. — The great reputation which the author of this work has obtained by it in his own country, has even excited the curiosity of foreigners, several of whom have publicly expressed their wishes, that some, at least, of the more important chapters of it were conveyed into another language. The extracts that appear in these volumes of russian history, contain the most interesting remarks of that author, (to the regret of all true antiquaries now no more) on numerous and very different subjects of the history, the politics, the religion, the manners and usages of his country, in which all the polemical attacks upon the french historian, are either entirely omitted, or so far suppressed, as to stand in no essential connection with the passages to which they were intended to relate. The difficulties attending this selection, and the pains which it cost the translator to compress the greater part of so voluminous a work into these occasional abstracts, though an unapparent merit, is yet very hard of attainment, which can only be appreciated by such as have put their patience and their diligence to a similar trial.

Materialen zur kenntniss des Russischen reichs, von Heinrich Storch. — Materials conducive to the knowledge of the russian empire. Riga, 1796. — This work, occasionally published in volumes, is an inestimable collection of such pieces, original and others, as throw any light on the knowledge

ledge of the country, affording a source of topographical, historical, and political information concerning Russia, which nothing short of the invincible industry, and diversified abilities of this author could have furnished, and by which he has proved himself a worthy emulator of his predecessor, of undecaying fame in this department, Muller, whose Sammlung Russischer Geschichte is the corner-stone of russian antiquities.

INDEX.

N. B. *The numerals refer to the volume, the figures to the page.*

A

Abo, negotiations at, broke off, ii. page 295.
Aborigines, remote antiquity of, i. 67
Abulgaſi, his derivations futile, i. 28.
Academy, noble, at Moſco, ii. 398.
Acron, the inhabitants of, their religious opinion, i. 115.
Actions, the moſt extraordinary, expreſſed in the ſame manner by the Slaves and the Latins, i. 64.
Actors and actreſſes, at Moſco, ii. 406.
Adam of Bremen, quoted, i. 26, 27.
Adjectives very ſimilar in ſlavonian and latin, i. 61.
Adrian, the laſt patriarch of the ruſſian church, ii. 131.
Adverbs, latin, i. 55.
Ætius drives the Huns back to Pannonia, i. 4.
Agraphinia, a ruſſian ſaint, i. 94.
Agriculture, on improved principles, ii. 440.
Aix-la-Chapelle, peace of, how brought about, ii. 297.
Alberik, the chronicle of, quoted, i. 23.
Alexander Yaroſlavitch, gains a complete victory over the Danes on the banks of the Neva, i. 251. Acquires the ſurname of Neſſky, and is canonized, 253.
Alexey Mikhaïlovitch, his death and character, ii. 28.
Alexey Petrovitch, loſes his father's affection, ii. 102. Declared to have forfeited his right of ſucceſſion, ii. 107.
Alienation of boors apart from the eſtate, firſt riſe of, i. 349.
Alma, a palace on the river, i. 402.
Altranſtadt, hard conditions impoſed on Auguſtus at the treaty of, ii. 83.
Amazon, ſavages on the banks of the, i. 49.
Ambaſſador, papal, properly anſwered by tzar Ivan, i. 383.
Anarchy ſprings up in the empire, i. 287.
Anathema, denounced by the patriarch, ii. 38.
Andrey contributes much to increaſe the power of Vladimir, i. 237.

Andruſſof,

Andruſſof, an armiſtice agreed on at, ii. 25.

Anhalt-Zerbſt, Auguſta Sophia Frederica of, married to the grand-duke Peter, ii. 349.

Anna, a grecian princeſs, married to Vladimir I. i. 202.

Anna Ivanovna, ducheſs of Courland, nominated empreſs, ii. 207. Sends troops to the Rhine to act againſt France, 214. Dies at St. Peterſburg, after a reign of ten years, 233.

Anne, daughter of the duke of Mecklenburg, ii. 242. Receives the oath of allegiance as grand-ducheſs of Ruſſia, 250. Seized with her huſband and conveyed to priſon, 271. Confined in the citadel of Riga, 278. Conveyed to Dunamund, and thence to Kolmogor, where ſhe dies, 279.

Antes and Slavonians ſpoke the ſame language, i. 372.

Anthony Peter Ulric, duke of Holſtein Gottorp, converted to the orthodox greek church, ii. 294. Accedes to the crown of Ruſſia, as Peter III. 339. His imprudent conduct, 350. Openly reſiſted by the archbiſhop of Novgorod, 352. Neglects to be crowned, 353. Degrading declaration of, 360. Deprived of his life, 362.

Antichriſt, Peter the Great, ii. 134.

Apothecary-garden, at Moſco, ii. 387.

Apraxin, field-marſhal, letter from Peter I. to, ii. 90. Abandons Pruſſia, ii. 305. Impriſoned at Narva, he expires on hearing of the overthrow of Beſtuchef, 307.

Archbiſhop of Novgorod, ſhut up in a monaſtery, i. 297.

Archbiſhop, caned, ii. 163.

Archimandrites, i. 120.

Arians, account of that people, i. 9.

Ariſtotle, of Bologna, taken into ſervice by Ivan I. i. 281. 364.

Armorial enſigns of Great Ruſſia, i. 134.

Army, eſtabliſhment of a regular, i. 369. Improvements in the, ii. 124.

Articles of the treaty ſigned by Oleg and Leo, i. 154.

Artillery, the art of, introduced, ii. 124.

Artiſts and mechanics ſent for from Germany, i. 298. Brought into the empire, 363.

Arts and trades introduced by Alexey Mikhaïlovitch, ii. 112.

Aſſemblies, popular, aboliſhed, i. 282. Inſtitution of, ii. 151.

Aſſembly, general, of the princes, i. 230. Noble, at Moſco, ii. 450.

Aſſeveration,

Asseveration, the highest, i. 367.
Astrakhan, Radzin's followers executed on the high roads of, ii. 26.
Athos, mount, greek manuscripts brought from, ii. 375.
Attila, terror and devastation excited by, i. 41.
Attire, simplicity of Peter the Great's, ii. 160.
Avares, called by Nestor the great Ugres, i. 6. Account of that people, i. 8. Farther particulars concerning them, i. 23.
Augustus III. king of Poland, ii. 214.
Austria and Russia, union between, dissolved, ii. 254.
Austrian camp, contagious diseases in the, ii. 225.
Azaraents, the Tartars, i. 397.
Azof, the sea of, passed by the Huns, i. 3. Peter I. resolves to construct a fleet in, ii. 65. And its territory, stipulated to lie waste and uncultivated, ii. 227.

B

Baaty, the tartar khan, destroys Pereiaslavl, i. 206.
Bakifchifaray, the tzarian palace at, i. 401.
Balk, lieutenant-general, second husband of Anna Moëns, ii. 170.
Ballads, old, sung in the villages, i. 96.
Baltic, the russian arms make a rapid progress on the shores of the, ii. 84. Connection with, of vast consequence, 99. Dominion of the, wrested from Sweden, 144.
Barbarians make all martial excellence to consist in braving death, i. 178.
Baschkirs, mix their language with the tartarian, i. 18.
Basil, Vladimir I. takes that name, and marries the princess Anna, i. 202.
Basilius and Constantine require Vladimir to be baptized before they will give him their sister in marriage, i. 201.
Baskakes, tartarian officers, i. 352.
Baptism, ceremony at, i. 124. Produces but little change in the temper of Olga, i. 170. Administered to Vladimir I. 201.
Baptist, St. John, curious ceremony on the anniversary of, i. 122.
Bear, taught to perform a curious ceremony, ii. 163.
Bears, Ivan causes malefactors to be torn to pieces by, i. 295.

Beard, of high estimation in Russia, i. 355. Ordered to be shaved, ii. 152.
Bela-vess, Bielgorod, the white town, i. 176.
Belaya Vesha, three towns of that name, i. 410.
Belgrade, articles of peace signed at, ii. 226.
Bell, the largest in the world, ii. 375.
Bells. custom of ringing, i. 128. Used for casting cannon, ii. 76.
Bely bogue, the white god, i. 119.
Berlin taken and ravaged, ii. 328.
Bestuchef. appointed vice-chancellor, ii. 286. Entirely devoted to Austria, 306. Put under arrest, 307.
Bible translated into slavonian, ii. 134.
Bielgorod, a quarter of Mosco, ii. 382.
Bird-market, at Mosco, ii. 385.
Biren, chamberlain to Anna Ivanovna, ordered not to be brought with her into Russia, ii. 209. [Where the word *not* is by accident omitted.] Comes to court, 213. A stain upon the memory of Anna Ivanovna, 238. Is her all-powerful minion, 239. His execrable barbarities, 241. Appointed guardian of the young emperor Ivan, 244. On the pinnacle of grandeur, 247. Arrested by general Mannstein, 251.
Birds that are born blind, not eaten, i. 109.
Black-book, an antient book of arithmetic, i. 423.
Blagovest, or the agreeable sound, i. 127.
Black Russia, i. 137.
Blude, a traitorous voyevode, i. 191. His merited punishment, i. 193.
Board of commerce instituted, ii. 145.
Bogue, the antient Hypanis, i. 106.
Bohemians, or Tschechs, i. 41.
Boleslaus retakes Kief, i. 218. Many places taken by him come back to Russia, 222.
Bolgarin, a monk of the holy mountain, i. 406.
Boltin, the russian antiquarian, ii 31.
Boors, tilled the ground of the nobleman on stated conditions, i. 368.
Boris assassinated in his tent, i. 217
Boris Godunof acquires enormous wealth, i. 303. With affected reluctance suffers himself to be crowned, 306.
Borka, or Arda, empire of, i. 41.
Borysthenes, origin of that appellation, i. 39. Sviatoslaf obliged to winter near the rocks of, i. 186.
Bosphorus, over against Tamatarcha, i. 408. The tauridan straits, 429.

Boyar

Boyar, manner of his parading to court, i. 353.
Boyars, what they were, i. 329.
Boyarskoi dvor abrogated, ii. 120.
Brandt, a dutch boat-builder, sent for by Peter I. ii. 60.
Britzanians, from Britzen, i. 41.
Brown, general, ordered to quit Russia, ii. 354.
Brunswick, princess of, married to Alexey Petrovitch, ii. 105.
Buddembrock and Levenhaupt, generals, badly conduct the campaign, ii. 258.
Buka, similar to the roman Monducus or Lamia, i. 109.
Bulgarians, some account of the, i. 10. 28. Lose most of their towns along the Danube, i. 177. Their country and language, i. 180.
Byzantine historians quoted, i. 176.

C

Calabria, peopled by grecian colonies, i. 77.
Calamities, a long train of, ensue to Russia, i. 227.
Calepin, Ambrose, quoted, i. 55.
Capitulation to be proposed to Anna Ivanovna, ii. 208. Torn to pieces by her, 211.
Captives, and their offspring, the only slaves, i. 347.
Carcases of the dead embalmed, i. 110.
Caspian, whence called the Khvalinskian sea, i. 395. Connected with the Baltic, ii. 145.
Catharine I. succeeds to the crown, ii. 101.
Catullus, quotation from, i. 53.
Caverns, famous, of Kief, the beginning of, i. 429.
Cedrenus, the grecian historian, i. 400.
Celtic, thought by some writers to be the parent of the latin, i. 76.
Ceremonies, idolatrous, to the god Svetovid, i. 116.
Chancellor, Richard, commander of an english vessel, goes to the tzar at Mosco, i. 361.
Character, personal, not influenced by church forms, i. 377. Of Catharine I. ii. 192.
Charges brought against Biren, ii. 251. Against fieldmarshal Munich, 273.
Charles V. emperor, Ivan Vassillievitch sends an ambassador to, i. 298.

Charles XII. not yet sixteen, ascends the throne of Sweden, ii. 72. Entirely routs the russian army, 74. Arrogant declaration of, 75. Blameably unconcerned at the progress of the Russians, 80. Forces the Russians on all sides to retreat, 84. Killed before Frederikshal, 96.
Cherkaskoy, chancellor, ii. 286.
Chétardié, M. de la, assists in the revolution, ii. 266.
Chetvert, of land, i. 344.
China, peace between Russia and, ii. 143.
Christenings go rapidly on, i. 376.
Christianity introduced into Russia, of little effect, i. 370.
Chrysopolis, from Constantinople to, over the ice, i. 430.
Chudo Morskoe, a slavonian watery god, i. 102.
Churches and schools endowed, i. 212.
Cicero, quotation from, i. 59.
Civilization, observations on the state of, in Russia, i. 325.
Civil-wars, grounds laid for, i. 213.
Clergy, impose fetters on the human mind, i. 378. Immersed in sensuality and ignorance, 380. Interested in the choice of Mikhaïla, ii. 4. Contemned by Peter I. 101. Nothing to be expected from, 116. Attempts to reform, 348. Take umbrage at Peter III. 351. Russian, have a primate, i. 221.
Climate of Mosco, ii. 368.
Club, the noblemen's, at Mosco, ii. 384.
Coffin, model of a, sent to Russia, ii. 140.
Coin, Sophia causes her impress to be stamped on the, ii. 46.
Colberg, ineffectual siege of, ii. 315. Invested, 327.
Combat, single, between plaintiff and defendant, established by law, i. 356.
Commerce subsisted early between the Russians and the Greeks, i. 147. Flourishes, 221. Laws concerning, 357.
Common people gained over by the arts of Sophia, ii. 43.
Concerts during Lent, ii. 452.
Congregations, lutheran, in Mosco, ii. 390.
Consorts, method of chusing, practised by the tzars of Russia, ii. 30.
Constantine Porphyrogenneta, the grecian emperor, i. 169. 407. 421.
Constantinople, surprising expedition to, i. 150.
Conquerors and soldiers in barbarous ages, picture of, i. 187.
Conquests anticipated by Sweden, ii. 257.
Copenhagen, Peter I. goes to, ii. 106.
Coronation of Peter II. ii. 199.

INDEX.

Court, of Petersburg, takes a softer and politer turn, ii. 237. Magnificent, 333.
Cowl, put on by the russian princes, when dying, i. 337.
Cronstadt, description and history of, i. 493. A hostile fleet appears before, ii. 190.
Crown, refused by Mikhaïla Romanof, ii. 5.
Crucifix worn about the neck, i. 127.
Cruelties committed by Igor in Paphlagonia, Pontus and Bithynia, i. 159. Of Peter the Great, admit of no palliation, ii. 161.
Cuirassiers, first added to the army, ii. 256.
Cyril, invents the russian written character, i. 376.

D

Daibog, the slavonian Plutus, i. 102.
Dalecarlians, refuse to enlist, ii. 293. Break out into open insurrection, 293.
Damascenus, St. John, the hymns of, i. 121.
Daniel, prince of Kief, obtains from the pope the title of king, i. 381. Prince of Turof, 408.
Daniela Alexandrovitch, builds the Kreml palace, ii. 376.
Dantzik, taken by field marshal Munich, ii. 218.
Dashkof, princess, enters into a conspiracy to dethrone Peter III. ii. 355.
David Igorovitch and Volodar Rostislavitch taken prisoners, i. 409.
Daun's army, menaces Berlin, ii. 319.
Debt, Russia responsible for a, due from Sweden to Holland, ii. 229.
Deity, mankind have always made of him a malignant and cruel being, i. 91.
Democratic form of government in Novgorod, gives place to the monarchical, i. 328.
Denmark, a campaign against, projected by Peter III. ii. 353.
Denomination, similarity of, the occasion of various mistakes, i. 9.
Denominations of the most striking sensible objects, i. 51.
Derbent, captured by Peter I. ii. 100.
Desna, Russians and Swedes dispute the passage of the, ii. 86.
Devastations, horrible, committed on the swedish coast, ii. 97.
Diamonds, amazing amount in, ii. 256.

Dieti boyarſkie, boyar-children, i. 344.
Dilich, his hiſtory of Hungary, i. 22, 23.
Diminutives, a multitude of, whereof the primary ſubſtantive is loſt, i. 87.
Diſagreements, between Peter and Sophia, come to a formal rupture, ii. 56.
Diſcipline, martial, improved by count Munich, ii. 234.
Diſtempers, contagious, ſeldom prevail at Moſco, ii. 369.
Diſturbances, on the ſide of Poland, ii. 19.
Ditmar's account of Kief, i. 139.
Dmitri, grand-prince, perceives that the Tartars are no longer ſo formidable as before, i. 270. Obtains the ſurname of Donſkoy, 275.
Dmitri Ivanovitch put to death by Boris Godunof, i. 304.
Dmitri, the whole party of, diſperſed, ii. 7.
Dobryna raiſes a ſuperb ſtatue to the deity Perune, i. 196.
Dogoda, a ſlavonian zephyr, i. 98.
Dolgorukies, arreſted and put to the torture, ii. 263. Recalled from Siberia and reinſtated in their poſts, 285.
Dolgoruky, Vaſſilly Lukovitch, on an embaſſy to Anna Ivanovna, ii. 209.
Dolgoruky, the ruſſian commander, ii. 23.
Domovie dukhi, domeſtic dæmons, i. 98.
Don, Ruſſia allowed to build a fortreſs on the, ii. 227.
Dorpat, city of, deſcribed, i. 465. Hiſtory of, 470.
Dreſs, alterations in, ii. 153.
Drevlians, rendered tributary by Oleg, i. 149. Igor victorious over them, i. 163. Derivation of their name, i. 166.
Drownings, decreed by Ivan the Terrible, i. 295.
Drummer, Peter the Great begins his carreer, by being, ii. 52.
Drunkenneſs, Alexey Petrovitch addicted to, ii. 104.
Duel, generally decides on right and wrong, i. 329.
Duke, title of, unknown to the antient Ruſſians, i. 222.
Dunai, the name of the Danube, i. 106.
Durak, the common expreſſion for *fool*, ii. 447.
Duroſtole, on the Danube, i. 183.

E

Eccleſiaſtical ceremonies, great reliance on, i. 376.
Eccleſiaſtics, meritorious, i. 379.
Education, plan of, purſued with Peter II. ii. 200. At Moſco, 466.

Effigy

Effigy of Peter the Great, ii. 161.

Elicon, a swifs carpenter, went to Rome, i. 78.

Elissa, the grecian city, called Olisha by the Russians, i. 400.

Elizabeth, queen of England, highly esteemed by Ivan Vasfillievitch, i. 301. Zealously employed in promoting enterprises of discovery, 360. Among her presents to tzar Ivan, sends an english physician, i. 366.

Elizabeth, daughter of Peter the Great, remains quiet during all the reign of Anne, ii. 263. Makes a solemn vow that no blood shall be shed in her attempt on the throne, 269. Attempts made to dethrone, 279. Refuses to give back the conquests made from Sweden by her father, 289. Her death and character, 330. Her reprehensible conduct towards her successor, 342.

Elmo, St. Alexey Petrovitch, under a borrowed name, at the fortress of, ii. 106.

Engineers, a corps of, first instituted, ii. 234.

Englishmen, land at Archangel, i. 301. Invited to settle in the empire 366.

Envy, between Russians and foreigners partly done away, ii. 235.

Evdokhia, Peter the Great's first wife, ii. 207.

Eugene, prince, war happily terminated by, ii. 226.

Euxine, conjoined with the Caspian, ii. 145.

Extortioners, privileged, oppress the people, ii. 16.

F

Favourites, instability of their situation, ii. 308.

Female-sex, contempt for the, invariably a characteristic of the want of civilization, i. 367.

Feodor Ivanovitch, a weak prince, i. 302.

Feodor Borissovitch, dethroned and imprisoned, i. 314.

Feodor and Ivan, the sons of Alexey Mikhaïlovitch, ii. 33.

Feodor Alexeyvitch, prudent government of, ii. 35. abruptly answers the patriarch, ii. 39.

Ferdinand, emperor, applied to for workmen by Ivan Vassillievitch, i. 299. Ivan's letter to, 364.

Ferdinand, last prince of the house of Kettler, ii. 240.

Fermor, fieldmarshal, marches into Prussia, ii. 311.

Finland, almost all, falls to Russia, ii. 96.

Finns, antiently comprised under the denomination Varages, i. 21. Two hundred of their villages burnt by the Russians, ii. 292.

Fire-arms, brought into practice in Ruffia, i. 364.
Fire, grecian, account of, i. 161.
Flemings, great gainers by the downfall of the hanfeatic league, i. 361.
Florus and Laurus, the tutelar faints of horfes, i. 123.
Food, of the antient Slavonians, i. 387.
Fools, kept for the diverfion of the court, ii. 155.
Foreign guidance and inftruction, Ruffians muft always have, i. 363.
Foreigners, at the head of affairs under the regent Anne, ii. 261. Encouraged to come into the empire, 334. At Mofco, 391, 392.
Forefts, confecrated to the idol Perune, i. 92.
Foundling-houfe, at Mofco, ii. 399.
Franc-archers, in France, i. 344.
Frederic II. Elizabeth the perfonal enemy of, ii. 301. Writes to Peter III. to warn him of his danger, 355.
Futilities, metaphyfical, brought from Greece into Ruffia, i. 209.
Futurity, the defire to dive into, natural to man, i. 107.

G

Gabriel, metropolitan of Novgorod, i. 394.
Gallitzin, Vaffilly, a fagacious minifter, ii. 37. Character of, 43. Sent into exile, 58.
Gallitzin, fpeech of prince, ii. 208.
Gardorik, or great city, i. 134.
Gedemin, duke of Lithuania feizes on Kief, i. 277.
Genealogical tables and regifters publicly burnt, ii. 38.
Germans, often confounded with the Celts, i. 76.
Getes, called by the Romans Dacians, i. 392.
Gibbets erected in Front of Sophia's convent, ii. 72.
Gleb Vladimirovitch, ftabbed by his own cook, i. 217.
Gleb Sviatoflavitch, expelled from Tmutarakan, i. 432.
Glebof, a young boyar, cruelties exercifed upon, ii. 169.
Gluck, a lutheran clergyman, ii. 171. 187.
Gods, houfhold, among the Tfchuvafhes, i. 108.
Gœrtz, a negotiation begun by, ii. 96.
Goldap, town of, plundered and burnt, ii. 303.
Golden horde, demolition of, i. 280.
Gollikof's life of Peter the Great, ii. 414.
Gonzaga, a famous fcene-painter at Mofco, ii. 411.

INDEX.

Gorants, the same with mountaineers, i. 6. 138.
Gordon, general, numbers of Scotsmen serve under, ii. 59. Defeats the rebellious strelitzes, 71.
Gori, etruscan monuments reported by, i. 82.
Gorodetz, where situate, i. 404.
Gostomuisl, grandfather of Olga, i. 165.
Goths and Russians antiently adopted many things in common, i. 1. and Huns in the regions of the Dniepr, i. 137.
Government, beneficial changes in, ii. 120.
Gramota Ustavnaia, compiled by Ivan Vassilievitch, i. 334.
Great Britain, treaty of commerce with, ii. 236.
Great Greece, the modern Calabria, i. 77.
Grecian empire attacked by Oleg, i. 149. Peace concluded with, 153.
Greece, architects invited from, i. 208. Emperor of, presents Vladimir II. with the ensigns of imperial dignity, 229. 365.
Greek emperors had Russians in their army, and especially in their fleet, i. 170.
Greeks pretend that Theodore the martyr miraculously fought for them, i. 184.
Gregory VIII. pope, letter from, to Isiaslaf I. i. 224.
Grodno, in Lithuania, abandoned by Peter I. ii. 84.
Grosjægersdorf, battle of, ii. 304.
Ground, a great extent of, necessary to men who never cultivate the earth, i. 47.
Grunstein and Schwartz, listen to Lestocq's proposal, ii. 265.
Grusinian or Georgian slobode, at Mosco, ii. 305.
Guards, the chief actors in revolutions, ii. 178. Preobrajenskoi, harsh methods employed against, 288.
Gubnaia Gramota, not known by whom composed, i. 334.
Gubnie Starosti, a book now lost. i. 337.
Gunners and bombardeers, german, taken into the russian service, i. 364.
Gymnasium, at Mosco, ii. 398.

H

Habitations, of the antient Slaves, i. 527.
Hair, heathenish rite of cutting it off, i. 125.
Halitch and Vladimir ceded to the Poles, i. 178.
Hanseatic-league, its merchandizes confiscated, i. 284. Attempts to revive its commerce, 307. Account of, 358.
Harangue of prince Sviatopolk II. i. 447.

Harion, digs himself a cavern, i. 429.
Havellanians, from their dwelling near the Havel, i. 40.
Head money, first levy of, i. 344.
Heads cut off by hundreds, ii. 165.
Heideke, an eminent lutheran preacher at Mosco, ii. 389.
Helen, the name taken by Olga at her baptism, i. 169.
Helsingfors, the Swedes surrounded near, ii. 290.
Henry IV. emperor, applied to for aid by Isiaflaf I. i. 223.
Heretic, Peter III. ii. 353.
Highways and roads, provision for, ii. 144.
Hilarion, a hermit of great sanctity, i. 377.
Hiong-nu, the real name of the Huns, i. 2.
History, sources of russian, ii. 477.
Holovtzin, the Russians submit to the Swedes at, ii. 85.
Holstein, Gottorp, duke of, son-in-law of Catharine I. ii. 190. Anthony Peter Ulric, elect heir to the swedish crown, 294.
Honour and probity, how to know a Russian of, ii. 180.
Hortus pensilis, at Petersburg, described, i. 449.
Hostilities with Sweden, cessation of, ii. 288.
Houses, of the Russians, i. 366.
Hungary, supplies Sviatoslaf with gold and horses, i. 179.
Huns, mother-country of the, i. 2. 30.

I

Japhet, Kozar the seventh son of, i. 174.
Ice-hills, diversion of the, ii. 455.
Idlers and vagrants, not tolerated, i. 351.
Jerbzimsky, Dr. a worthy lutheran pastor, ii. 389.
Jesuits, not tolerated by Peter the Great, ii. 133.
Igor, still in his minority, accompanies Oleg on his warlike expeditions, i. 146. Succeeds to the throne, i. 157. Ravages Paphlagonia, Pontus and Bithynia, i. 159.
Igor Vladimirovitch Monomachus, builds the city of Vladimir on the Kliasma, i. 232.
Igor Vsevolodovitch, killed, with his whole family, i. 232
Igumens or abbots, i. 120.
Illyrians, inhabiting the northern coasts of the Adriatic, i. 71.
Incursions by the neighbouring nations, i. 229.
Indicts, method of computing by, i. 427.
Infancy, of Catharine I. veiled in obscurity, ii. 183.
Ingria, Peter I. makes himself master of, ii. 82.

Inhabitants

Inhabitants in Petersburg, number of, i. 453.
Innovations of Peter I. excite discontent, ii. 67.
Inquisition, political court of, ii. 338.
Inscription on a marble found among the ruins of Phanagoria, i. 427.
Intense cold, record of, i. 429.
Invalids, hospital of, at Mosco, ii. 387.
Joachim Savelof, patriarch, erects a school at Mosco, ii. 381.
Journey, Peter I. undertakes his first, ii. 69.
Isiaslaf Vladimirovitch obtains Polotsk, i. 191.
Isiaslaf Yaroslavitch forced to abandon the throne, i. 223.
Ismailofsky guards, commanded by Gregory Orlof, ii. 357.
Isvoschiks, or drivers, ii. 455.
Ivan, the kupalnistt, explained, i. 94.
Ivan I. an enterprising prince, i. 278. Unites with the grand principality, 281.
Ivan Vassilkievitch II. surnamed the terrible, i. 286. A regular attendant at church, 290. His horrid cruelties, 295. Punishes corrupt judges, 296. Revises and improves the Sudebnik, 333.
Ivan, the dethroned emperor, cruelly assassinated, ii. 283.
Judgment passed on Catharine I. by a german author, ii. 193.
Judges acting and deciding partially, i. 356. Open to bribery, ii. 15. Partial, knooted, 122.
Julian calendar still used in Russia, ii. 148.
Juliana, queen of Denmark, ii. 285.
Justice, administration of, sound maxims concerning the, ii. 114. Corrected, 121.

K

Kabaks, or common public houses, ii. 421.
Kabala, a sort of contract, i. 350.
Kabardia, added to the russian empire, i. 293. The greater and the less, to remain as a frontier, ii. 227.
Kaffa or Keffa, a maritime town in the Krimea, i. 199. Russian prisoners exposed to sale at, i. 285.
Kagans, the russian princes never so called, i. 28.
Kalka, an engagement between the Russians and Tartars, near the river, i. 241. Source of the, 399.
Kalocer, a patrician, treats with the Russians in the name of Phocas, i. 182.

Kaminietz

Kaminietz taken by the Turks, ii. 27.
Kamtschatka, the acquisition of, ii. 143.
Kaptschak, Baaty khan of, i. 243.
Kaverin, maître de police at Mosco, ii. 443.
Kayzerlinguen, count, first husband of Anna Moëns, ii. 170.
Kazan, besieged by Ivan Vaffillievitch, i. 288.
Kazanskoy church, Catharine II. takes the oath in the, ii. 357.
Kertsch, from the old Kortschef, i. 429.
Kettler, the family of become extinct, ii. 230.
Kexholm and Novgorod taken by the Swedes, i. 321. ii. 8.
Kheraskof, one of the most distinguished authors of Russia, ii. 397. 414.
Khors, the slavonian Æsculapius, i. 101.
Khortschit, signification of, i. 101.
Khotyim taken by Marshal Munich, ii. 225.
Khrebates, from khrebet, a mountain, i. 41.
Kief, a town of the Sarmates, i. 4. The original building of, i. 138. Taken by a wicked stratagem, i. 147. Oleg returns victorious to, i. 153. Besieged by the Petschenegans, i. 177. A proclamation issued at, ordering all the inhabitants to be baptized, i. 203. Feasts there, i. 212. The prince of, paramount to all the rest, 235. Suffers particularly by intestine wars, 231. Horrible slaughter committed by the Tartars at the taking of, 249. Seized on by the duke of Lithuania, 277. Origin of the famous caverns at, 429.
Kiel, Peter III. born and educated at, ii. 339. 341.
Kikimora, the slavonian Morpheus, i. 100.
Kirghises submit to Russia, ii. 237.
Kischuians from the town of Kuschan, i. 41.
Kitaigorod, at Mosco, ii. 377. 413.
Kitzliar, on the borders of the Terek, ii. 256.
Kivi, so called from their dwelling in a mountainous district, i. 5.
Knaves or serfs, i. 350.
Knighthood, an order of, instituted in honour of Catharine I. ii. 185.
Knoot, Alexey Pettrovitch supposed by some to have perished by the, ii. 108.
Kœnigsberg, submits to the Russians, ii. 311.
Kolagridova, madame, the Siddons of Mosco, ii. 409.
Koliada, the slavonian god of peace, i. 102.
Koltvó, adopted from the Greeks, i. 111.
Komunes had their name from the river Kuma, i. 12.
Kondians assist the Russians against the Tartars, i. 18.

Koprenimus,

INDEX.

Kopronimus, emperor Constantine, i. 430.
Korelians, comprehended by foreigners under the same Biarmians, i. 12. 18.
Korosten, Igor slain and buried at, i. 164.
Korses, in Courland, i. 12.
Korsun, Kherson antiently so called, i. 204.
Kossoges, dwelt eastward of the sea of Azof, i. 12. 391. Subdued by Sviatoslaf, 411.
Kostroma, the family of Philaretes in a convent at, ii. 4.
Kotiak, prince of the Polovtzes, i. 398.
Kotsupan, the assassin, stoned to death, i. 402.
Kotzebue's plays, much admired at Mosco, ii. 408. 410. 411.
Kovanskey, prince, at the head of the strelitzes, ii. 46.
Kruli khan, Thamas, an embassy from, ii. 255.
Kozaks, some account of the, ii. 19.
Kozaks, Kalmuks and Tartars, behave in Prussia like real barbarians, ii. 303.
Kozares, opinions of the learned concerning the, i. 32. Called Issidones by the old writers, i. 34. Thought to be of turkish origin, i. 174.
Krasnaya ploschtschad, the red or beautiful place at Mosco, ii. 382.
Kreml, the tzarian palace at Mosco, ii. 66. Described, 370.
Krepki bogue, the strong god, i. 113.
Kreposts, or judicial documents of vassalage, i. 342.
Krimea, antiently called Khosaria, i. 430. Russian troops march into, ii. 217. Laid waste by war, 228.
Krivitsches, a sarmatian people, i. 13.
Kromer, a polish historian, i. 126.
Krossen and Frankfort on the Oder, seized on by the Russians, ii. 317.
Kumani, from the river Kuma, i. 42.
Kunnersdorf, redoubts taken that cover the village of, ii. 320.
Kupalnitzi, explanation of, i. 93.
Kupalo, a beneficent deity, i. 92.
Kures dwelt in Courland, i. 13.
Kurilly islands, a benefit to Russia, ii. 144.
Kuskova, the seat of count Scheremetof, ii. 431.
Kustrin, the siege of, raised, ii. 312.
Kymmendgard, in Finland, given up to the Russians, ii. 296.

L

Lada, the flavonian Venus, i. 94.
Laity, their notions of being a chriftian, i. 380.
Ladoga, built by Rurik, i. 144.
Ladoga-lake, fchooners built on the, ii. 80. Canal conftructed, 145. Chiefly by Munich, 234.
Language of the Huns has no fimilarity with the fcythian, &c. i. 24. Latin, indebted to the flavonian for its firft elements, i. 44. Of the Slaves and of the Latins, muft neceffarily have had the fame origin, i 63. Manner in which it is formed, i. 67. Latin derived by Voffius from the greek, i. 76.
Lanzi, on the etrufcan language, i. 82.
Lapidation, punifhment by, i. 262.
Lapland, the crew of a fhip perifh by the extreme froft on the coaft of, i. 360.
Lapukhin, Evdokhia, efpoufed by Peter I. ii. 101.
Larceny, punifhment of, i. 356.
Lafcy, general, takes the fort of Azof, ii. 220.
Latin words, moftly of grecian origin, i. 79. Roots of many only to be found in the german, i. 86.
Laudohn, an able general, ii. 318.
Laws, code of, by Ivan Vaffillievitch, i. 293. Relating to the fucceffion, ii. 109. Early ruffian, laid great ftrefs upon oaths, i. 155. Change with manners, i. 332.
Lechie, the flavonian fatyrs, i. 104.
Lefort, general, account of, ii. 52. Admiral, 64.
Leo, the philofopher, reigns in Conftantinople, i. 152.
Leftocq, phyfician to the princefs Elizabeth, ii. 261. His device for fixing her refolution, 268. Banifhed to Siberia, 300.
Letter, curious, written by the Novgorodians to their prince, i. 235. From tzar Ivan to the emperor Ferdinand, 365. From Peter I. to his fon, ii. 105. Of Frederic II. concerning Peter the Great, ii. 168. To the queen, 321. 325.
Letters, names of the, in the ruffian alphabet, ii. 474.
Liburnians occupy the fouth-eaft coaft of modern Dalmatia, i. 77.
Lietnaya, a kind of contract, i. 350.
Lieven, the modern Livonians, i. 13. 19.

Life,

Life, hard manner of, pursued by Sviatoslaf, i. 172.
Lines of the Krimea, described, ii. 218.
Literature among the Russians, i. 380. State of, at Mosco, ii. 413.
Lithuanians, derivation of that term, i. 14.
Liubitsh, assembly of the princes at, i. 417.
Livonia, afflicted by a cruel war, i. 300.
Lœvenhaupt, the swedish general, defeated, ii. 87. An advocate for a war, 258.
Lœwenwolden, a Livonian, favourite of Catharine II. ii. 189. 243.
Lope, the same with Lapland, i. 13. 19.
Lords, followed to the wars by their slaves, i. 352.
Lubeck, sends an embassy to Russia, i. 361. Bishop of, proposed to be king of Sweden, ii. 294. Elected, 296.
Luke, the evangelist, a portrait painted by, ii. 374.
Luxury, some degree of, seems to have prevailed at the court of Russia, from the time of Oleg, i. 169.

M

Maddox, an ingenious and enterprising Englishman, proprietor and manager of the theatre at Mosco, ii. 404.
Magiares, establish the ungarian kingdom, i. 14.
Malefactors, cruelly punished, ii. 337.
Magnates, origin of their arbitrary judicial authority, i. 334.
Malucha, Olga's attendant, the mother of Vladimir, i. 191.
Mamai, khan of the donskoi Tartars, i. 271. Loses a battle to the Russians, 274.
Manichees, the devotion of them not captivating to the russian missionaries, i. 197.
Manifesto, of the empress Anne, ii. 211. Of the empress Elizabeth on taking the crown. 274. Of Catharine II. concerning the prince Ivan, 281. Accusing the Swedes as authors of the war, 291. Of Catharine II. on her acceding to the throne, 358.
Manners, causes of the alteration and diversity of, i. 331.
Mannstein, adjutant-general to count Munich, ii. 232.
Manufactures and trades encouraged, ii. 139.
Maria Feedorevna, the present empress, ii. 402.
Maria Theresa, finds a friend and ally in Elizabeth, ii. 298.
Marina consents to be married to the pretended Dmitri, i. 310. Admits a second Dmitri as her spouse, 319.

Markets-

Market-place, practice of resorting to the, i. 367.
Marseillois, spoke rather greek than celtic, i. 78.
Martens and sables esteemed in proportion to the darkness of their colour, i. 157.
Martha, the former name of Catharine I. ii. 171.
May-day, how kept at Mosco, ii. 419.
Mazeppa, hetman of the Kozaks, ii. 85. 237.
Mead, a liquor much used in Russia, ii. 460.
Meetings, public, customary with the Russians, ii. 118.
Melnik, the Miller, a famous russian comedy, ii. 407.
Memel, taken by the Russians, ii. 303.
Mengden, countess, a favourite with the regent Anne, ii. 260.
Mentchikof, prince, appointed viceroy of Ingria, ii. 82. Made preceptor to Alexey Petrovitch, 103. Fans the tzar's resentments, 104. His estates in the Ukraine confiscated, 122. Originally a pye-boy, ii. 160. Gives information of a plot, 164. Resigns Catharine to Peter the Great, 171. Guilty of much oppression and injustice, 179. Orders Catharine to be proclaimed empress, 183. Keeps in favour with the tzar till his death, 188. Anxious to execute two clauses of Catharine's will, 194. Dies in exile, 198.
Merchants, german, imprisoned at Novgorod, i. 283. Of Novgorod and Pscove, in high reputation, i. 359. Polish, fall victims to the fury of the populace at Mosco, i. 362.
Meres, dwelt in the region of Rostof, i. 15.
Meschtschores, where they dwelt, i. 15.
Mesembria, from the Krim to, over the ice, i. 430.
Metropolitan, of Novgorod, writes a submissive letter in behalf of his prince, i. 236.
Mikhaïla Feoderovitch, elected tzar, i. 323.
Mikhaïla Romanof, a descendant of the antient tzars, ii. 3. Sends ambassadors to England and other countries, ii. 10. Promotes commerce with England and Persia, 112.
Miloslafsky, the family of, ii. 33.
Mind, firmness of, Peter the Great's, ii. 128.
Minei, a hymn-book, divided into months, i. 121.
Ministers, english and prussian, frequently warn Peter III. of his danger, ii. 355.
Mint and coinage, rectified, ii. 145.
Mirovitch, lieutenant, forms a plan for delivering the captive Ivan, ii. 283. Pays for it with his head, 285.
Mitrophanuschka, a character in the play of Nedoross, ii. 472.

INDEX.

Mittau, an embassy dispatched to, ii. 209.
Moëns, Anna, beloved by Peter the Great, ii. 170.
Moëns, de la Croix, ii. 172. Beheaded, 175.
Mokos, a slavonian deity, i. 97.
Moldavia, hospodar of, ii. 92. Conquered by the Russians, ii. 222. Restored to the Turks, 227.
Monasteries, not to purchase villages without the consent of the tzars, i. 336. Reformed, ii. 132.
Mongoles quit their antient seats, i. 238.
Monks, greek and russian, i. 120.
Monosyllables, slavonian and latin, i. 48.
Monuments, etruscan, reported by Dempster, i. 82.
Mordvines, formerly called Meren, i. 19.
Morosof, entrusted with the education of Alexey Mikhaïlovitch, ii. 14.
Mosco, origin of, i. 268. Horrid massacres and conflagrations at, 276. The great bell conveyed to, 282. Ravaged and burnt by the Poles, 322, ii. 9. Tranquillity restored in, ii. 17. Tremendous procession at, 47. Triumphal entry of Peter I. into, 64. A second, 81. On the victory at Pultava, 89. A mathematical school at, 135. A gigantic city, ii. 365.
Mstislaf Vladimirovitch, obtains the honourable surname of the Great, i. 229. Builds a church to the mother of God, i. 396. Vladimirovitch, prince of Tmutarakan, 419.
Munich, count, ordered against the Turks, ii. 217. Complained of by the court of Vienna, 223. Ambitious and vain, 249. Obtains the post of minister, 252. The punishment he had brought on Biren, retaliated on, 272.
Murom, prince of, subdued by Oleg Sviatoslavitch, i. 414.
Muromes, inhabited the district of Murom, i. 15.
Murder, common among the antient Slavonians, i. 327. Might be retaliated by the relations, 354. Statutes concerning, ii. 113.
Music and dancing encouraged at court, ii. 237.
Mythology, slavonian, no probability of obtaining a complete system of, i. 90.

N.

Names, proper, terminations of, ii. 465.
Narishkin, Alexey's second consort of the family of, ii. 33.
Narva, city of, described, i. 457. Curious discovery made near, 464.

Natalia, the tzaritza, two brothers of, murdered, ii. 45.
Nations, all alike at particular periods of their history, i. 178.
Navy, Peter I. desirous of obtaining a, ii. 61. Created by him, 127. Augmented, 189.
Nedorosl, the Spoiled Child, a favourite russian comedy, ii. 410. 472.
Nessky. St. Alexander, order of knighthood of, i. 253.
Neglinnaiya, a river at Mosco, ii. 366.
Nestor, enumerates the nations tributary to Russia, i. 21. Quoted, i. 35. Treaty of peace between Oleg and the Greeks, preserved in his antient chronicle, i. 153. Speech of Igor's counsellors reported by, i. 163. Makes the Russians always victorious, i. 184. His merit in writing a history, 380. Tatischtschef's remarks on, i. 403. Wrote the life of St. Nikon, i. 405.
Nicholas, St. the wonder-worker, a singular favourite of God, i. 121.
Niemtzi, the Germans, why so called, i. 325.
Nikon, St. and the monk Bolgarin, travel together, i. 407. Returns to Tchernigof, 428. Nikon, the metropolitan, acquires great merit, ii. 17. Receives all petitions addressed to the tzar, 129.
Niya, the slavonian Pluto, i. 102.
Nœtburg, at the origin of the Neva, captured by Peter I. 81.
Nobility, pedigrees of, destroyed, ii. 38.
Noblemen, without exception, to serve in the wars, i. 353.
Nobles, universally soldiers, i. 368.
Novgorod Severski, account of, i. 140. The Varages become masters of, i. 142. Its republican spirit breaks out afresh, i. 145. And Kief, the sovereign of, first assumes the style of grand-prince, 215. The antient love of liberty revives at, i. 234. The chief mart of the russian commerce, 235. Relieved by Alexander Nessky, 255. Pressed hard upon by Ivan I. 281. Shocking cruelties inflicted at, 297. Municipal laws of, i. 354. A scarcity at, ii. 129.
Nouns of number, french and english, derived from the latin, i. 50.
Numbers, of late invention among all nations, i. 49.
Nuns, obliged to keep schools, ii. 133.
Nyenschantz, taken from the Swedes, ii. 81.
Nystadt, treaty of, ii. 229. Sweden requires to be annulled, 288. Adopted as the basis of a new one, 296.

Oath,

INDEX.

O

Oath, of allegiance, new, ii. 212.
Oaths, methods of taking, i. 371.
Obdores, incorporated in the imperial title, i. 19.
Obeses, now the Georgians, i. 395.
Observatory, erected, at St. Petersburg, ii. 137.
Odnodvortzi, why they gave themselves that appellation, i. 345.
OEsel and *Mohn*, islands of, i. 485.
Officers, swedish, disseminate arts, ii. 142.
Oktoich, a book of canticles, i. 121.
Oleg, a kinsman of Rurik, obtains the sovereign power, and unites the slavonian territory to that of Novgorod, i. 145. Fixes the seat of his dominion at Kief, 149. Commits horrid depredations in the territory of Constantinople, 152.
Oleg Sviatoslavitch, obtains the country of the Drevlians, i, 180. Slightly mentioned in history, 188. Taken prisoner by the Kozares, 408.
Olga, Igor's widow, revenges the murder of her husband, i. 165. Baptised at Constantinople, 168. Dies at an advanced age, and canonised, 179. No female sovereign after her, till Catharine I. ii. 183.
Opritschniki, a body of informers, i. 295.
Oranienbaum, the palace of, ii. 357.
Oranienburg, the dethroned Ivan confined in the monastery at, ii. 279.
Orlofs, the brothers, conspire to dethrone Peter III. ii. 355. Count, his gardens, at Mosco, 423.
Orphan and foundling houses established, ii. 149.
Oskold and Dir, sovereigns of Kief, basely murdered, i. 148.
Ostad, the slavonian Comus, i. 102.
Ostermann, plenipotentiary at Nystadt, ii. 98. Count, some particulars of, 196. Contributes to annul the capitulation, 212. Heads a party, 253. Warns the regent Anne of her danger, 267.
Otchakof, submits to count Munich, ii. 222.
Otrepief, a monk, gives out that he is prince Dmitri, i. 309.

P

Palatine, mount, the part of Rome first inhabited, i. 60.
Panin, count, conspires to dethrone Peter III. ii. 355.

Parents, reverence of children to, ii. 117.
Paschkof's house and gardens, ii. 424.
Passport put into the hand of the dead, a fiction, i. 112.
Patericon, written by Nestor, i. 394.
Patkul, Johann Reinhold, a livonian nobleman, ii. 77. Complains of the russian soldiery, 125.
Patriarchs, great power of the, ii. 128.
Patriarchate, resigned by Nikon, ii. 129. Abolished, ii. 132.
Patriarch's horse led by the tzar, ii. 130.
Patronymics in several languages, i. 88.
Patzinakians, or Petschenegans, i. 421.
Paulus Jovius, extract from, ii. 31.
Peasantry, systematic vassalage of the, i. 370.
Pedigrees, books of, kept with great care, ii. 36.
Pelim, in Siberia, Biren exiled to, ii. 251.
Pereiaslavetz, dreadful slaughter committed at, i. 183.
Pereislavl, Vladimir Sviatoslavitch, dies at, i. 431.
Perekop, the only passage through the lines of the Krim, ii. 218.
Permiaks, converted by Stephen to the christian faith, i. 19.
Perry, captain, attends Peter the Great from London, ii. 140.
Persia, disturbances in, ii. 100. A treaty of commerce with, 113. Negotiation with, 215.
Perune, the chief of the slavonian deities, i. 90. Thrown into the Borysthenes, i. 202.
Petchenegans attack the Russians, i. 158. Commit horrid barbarities in Bulgaria, 163. Besiege Kief, 177. Humbled by Yaroslaf, 220.
Peter the Great, the tzars prior to him desirous that the empire should have little connection with other countries, ii. 31.
Peter II. greatly beloved by the nation, ii. 200. Letter from to his sister, 202.
Peter III. accedes to the crown of Russia, ii. 339.
Peterhof, the empress at the palace of, ii. 357.
Petersburg, tzar Peter lays the foundation of ii. 81. City of, described, i. 454.
Petschores, the present Samoyedes, i. 15.
Phænomena of nature, names of some, i. 56.
Phanagoria, in the isle of Taman, i. 388. 407. 426.
Phocas, the patrician, encounters the Russians, i. 162. Nicephorus, implores aid of Sviatoslaf, i. 176.

Philaretes,

Philaretes, metropolitan of Roftof, ii. 3. Appointed patriarch, ii. 10.

Phyficians and apothecaries, encouraged to come from Germany, i. 366.

Phyficians, at Mofco, ii. 393.

Plato, metropolitan, preaching encouraged by, ii. 381.

Plautus, quotation from, i. 62.

Plays, fpiritual, at Kief and Mofco, ii. 153.

Plot to murder Peter I. detected, ii. 68.

Podmoſkovnè, defcription of, ii. 434.

Podnabinſky, diverfions at, ii. 444.

Polabes, from the Laba or Elbe, i. 40.

Poland, Kief devolves to, i. 277. Livonia ceded to, 300. and Sweden, fruftrated in their defigns on the ruffian throne, ii. 6. Peace concluded with, 48. Spirit of party in, occafions great misfortunes, 76. Election of a king of, 213.

Polelia, the flavonian Hymenæus, i. 94.

Poles, little reliance to be placed on the, ii. 1. Lay Mofco in afhes, 9. Extremely corrupt, 78. Limited in their free choice of a king, 213.

Politics had at leaft an equal influence with devotion in the early converfions to chriftianity, i. 200.

Polnotatzko, a wife lawgiver, i. 330.

Polotſk, the prince of, defeated and killed, with his two fons, by Vladimir, i. 191.

Polotzani, fuch as dwelt on the Polota, i. 41.

Police, inftitution of, i. 440.

Polkan, the giant, ridiculous ftories of, i. 103.

Pomeranians, thofe that lived near the fea, i. 40.

Pope, fends deputies to perfuade Vladimir I. to embrace the ritual of Rome, i. 196. Receives an abrupt anfwer from prince Alexander, 382. The abomination of the Ruffians, ii. 67.

Popof, Mikhaila, his dictionary, i. 89.

Popeus, a god of the antient Scythians, i. 91.

Population of Mofco, ii. 368.

Poſt-office, early attempts at erecting, ii. 146.

Potchnaya, a thoufand Ruffians in a day often baptized in that rivulet, i. 375.

Poteſchniye, companions of Peter the Great, ii. 51.

Potzvid, the flavonian Boreas, i. 98.

Praſkovia Feodorevna, i. 437.

Pravda, or law, preface to the, i. 330.

Precedence, table of, ii. 149.

L L 3

Prekraſna,

Prekrasna, Olga surnamed, from her beauty, i. 165.
Preobrajenskoi guards, guilty of great excesses, ii. 287. 335.
Preposition, negative, i. 84.
Princes, russian, offer their assistance to Alexander Nessky, i. 272.
Principalities, separate, gradually formed, i. 226.
Printing-offices, at Mosco, ii. 413.
Printing-press set up in Mosco, i. 381.
Printz, ambassador from Prussia, ii. 167.
Prititch, general, attempts to succour Kief, i. 177.
Procopius, the first who mentions the Slavenians, i. 90. Quotation from, i. 371.
Professors of the university of Mosco, ii. 417.
Promenades, public, at Mosco, ii. 422.
Prona, the ruins of a town near that river, i. 389.
Pronouns, not the parts of speech first formed, i. 51. Relative, invented after the verb, 69.
Prussians, originally Sarmates, i. 15.
Pruth, peace of the, ii. 94. 216.
Pscove, the native place of Olga, i. 164. The rival of Novgorod in commerce, 285. A false Dmitri at, finishes his career at the gallows, ii. 8.
Ptolemy, mentions the Chuni, i. 26.
Pultava, decisive battle of, ii. 88.
Punishments, dreadful, inflicted on the ringleaders of a revolt, ii. 71.
Pustoschkin, Paul Vassillievitch, i. 425.
Putkammer, general, killed in action, ii. 324.
Pysbiki, a future generation of pygmies, i. 103.

Q

Quarrel, decided by single combat, i. 204.
Quas, a russian liquor, ii. 460.
Quay, at Mosco, originated with prince Prosorofsky, ii. 443.
Quays, visited by Peter I. ii. 144.
Question, penal, i. 341.

R

Radimitches, rendered tributary by Oleg, i. 149.
Raezan, or Riazan, a famous old city, i. 386.

Rava, Peter I. has a conference with the king of Poland at, ii. 72.
Razumoffky, count, hetman of the Kozaks, ii. 355.
Rededa, prince of the Kossoges, killed by Mstislaf, i. 391.
Relics, holy bones and other, imported from Constantinople, i. 375.
Religion, what Peter the Great did for, ii. 127.
Religions, different, missionaries dispatched by Vladimir I. to inquire into, i. 197.
Religious societies increase by vexations, but not by contempt, i. 170.
Repnin, prince Nicholas, governor of Livonia, ii. 173.
Reval, description and history of, i. 474. Ivan I. provoked by the populace of, i. 284.
Revelation, divine, in favour of Mikhaila Romanof, ii. 5.
Revenues, great deficiencies in the, ii. 122.
Revolutions in Russia easily brought about, ii. 178. Elizabeth's effected without bloodshed, 260.
Riga, description and history of, i. 479.
Rogvolode, the daughter of, confers her hand on Yaropolk, i. 191.
Romanof, the family of, becomes extinct, ii. 202.
Romans, imagined by the antient Russians to be of larger stature than the rest of mankind, i. 103.
Romanus, emperor, offers tribute to Igor, i. 162. Treaty with, 412.
Romodanoffky, prince, titular tzar of Mosco, ii. 162.
Rostislaf, of Volhynia, i. 419.
Rostof, bishop of, deposed by the metropolitan, i. 379.
Rugen, the Slavonians of, had their peculiar deities, i. 114.
Rurik, a chieftain of the Varages, i. 142.
Russalki, nymphs of the forests and waters, i. 103.
Russia, how called by the antient northern writers, i. 25. Antient, its extent, 133. Governed by Oleg, thirty-three years, 156. Attacked by the Petchenegans, 158. A long series of calamities befal, 227. Invaded by the Mongoles, 240. Dependent on the Tartars, 256. Foundation of that power which enabled it by degrees to shake off the yoke of the Tartars, 269. The kazan-tartarian empire annexed to, 290. Christianity becomes the national worship in, 384. Tmutarakan re-united to, 387. Her consequence increases in Europe, ii. 11. Makes some progress in civilization under Alexey Mikhaïlovitch, 30. More closely connected with the rest of Europe, 82. Extension and aggrandisement of, 99. Opens a considerable trade with China, 115. Arts and

Speech of Sviatoslaf to his army on going to battle, i. 175.

St. Petersburg, some account of, i. 435.

Stanislaus Leschinsky, elected king of Poland, ii. 79. 240.

Statue of Peter the Great, described, i. 449.

Stavutshan, the Turks completely routed by Marshal Munich, near, ii. 225.

Stenka Radzin, a revolt headed by, ii. 24. His robberies about Astrakhan, 113.

Stepennaiya kniga, or book of degrees, i. 388.

Stockholm, french influence great at, ii. 214. Greater still, 228.

Stoglaf, or book of a hundred chapters, i. 337.

Stone, for the pedestal of the famous statue of Peter the Great, transport of, i. 450.

Strelitzes, when first formed, i. 289. What the janissaries are at Constantinople, ii. 42. Excesses committed by them, 45.

Strikofsky, the polish historian, i. 390.

Stroganof, curious to gain a knowledge of Siberia, i. 291.

Substantives, slavonian and latin, i. 58. 88.

Succession, hereditary, abolished by Peter the Great, ii. 110.

Sudebnik, a double collection of statutes, i. 331. Consists of ninety-seven clauses, i. 336.

Svenald continues his attachment to Yaropolk, i. 189.

Sviatoi Vit, means both Sviatovid and St. Vitus, i. 118.

Sviatoslaf Igorievitch, i. 165. 431. Prohibits none from submitting to baptism, 168. has no turn for the grave concerns of government, 171. Partitions his states among his children, 179. Hardly escapes captivity, 184. Defeated and killed, 186. His character, 187.

Sviatoslof Yaroslavitch, i. 406.

Sviatovid, worshipped in the isle of Rugen, i. 114. Exchanged by the Bohemians for St. Vitus, i. 118.

Sventeld assists Olga by his counsel, i. 165.

Sviatopolk I. succeeds Vladimir, i. 216. Takes to flight and dies on the road, 220.

Sukanin, chief of a conspiracy against Peter I. ii. 69.

Sumarokof, the russian historian, his encomium on Feodor Alexeyvitch, ii. 40.

Summer-season, at Mosco, ii. 419.

Superstition tinges the hands of its pontifs in blood, i. 91. Absurd and sanguinary, 119.

Superstitions practised by the ignorant vulgar of all nations, i. 111.

Supremacy of the church recovered to the sovereigns, ii. 132.

Sweden, an unsuccessful war with, i. 300. Jealousy of, ii. 1. And Poland, frustrated in their views on the russian throne, ii. 6. Cessions made to Russia by, at the treaty of Nystadt, 97. 229. King of, only the shadow of a monarch, 229.

Swedes, defeat the Poles and deliver Mosco, ii. 8. Lose part of their possessions on the Baltic, 79. Generally victorious over the Russians in a pitched battle, 83.

Sword, brethren of the, order of, i. 484.

Synod, the holy directing, constituted, ii. 132.

Syranes, baptized by Stephen Permskoi, and become Russians, i. 18.

T

Taganrok, demolition of the fortifications at, ii. 216.

Taman, an inscription found in the island of, i. 387. Professor Pallas goes to, 425.

Tamatarcha on the same site with Phanagoria, i. 407.

Tartarian slobode, at Mosco, ii. 395.

Tartars, first invasion of Russia by the, i. 240. Terrible as enemies, 244. The power of, considerably divided, 279. The second false Dmitri killed by, 320. Give a check to Alexey's conquests, ii. 22.

Taupins, under Charles VII. of France, i. 345.

Taurida, Vladimir I. marches through, i. 412.

Tcherny bogue, the black god, i. 119.

Temudschin, since called Tschinghiskhan, i. 239.

Territory, new distributions of, i. 230.

Terror, general, inspired by Biren, ii. 252.

Teutonic order, in Livonia, i. 486.

Theatre, at Mosco, ii. 404. Private, of a russian nobleman, 438.

Theodosia, besieged by Vladimir I. i. 199.

Theophanes, the patrician, attacks the Russians by surprise, i. 160. Bishop, ii. 110.

Thrace, John Zimisces makes an incursion into, i. 182.

Tmutarakan, Mstislaf, prince of, takes possession of the country of the Kossoges, i. 12. Inquiry into the situation of, 385. Captured by Sviatoslaf I. 415. What its name implies, 425. Directly opposite Kertsch, 429.

Toleration, excites the fury of the clergy, ii. 133. A distinguished feature of the russian character, 462.

Tolstoi

INDEX.

Tolstoi, Peter Andreyevitch, ii. 167. Manages the affairs of the russian cabinet, 183. Exiled to Siberia, 198.
Torjok, set on fire, i. 422.
Torkes, mistaken for the Turks, i. 15.
Torture, use of the, i. 340.
Town, taken by storm, an uncommonly dreadful spectacle, i. 290.
Towns, several, built by Rurik, i. 357.
Trade, between the English and Russians, commencement of, i. 360.
Trade and commerce, school of, at Mosco, ii. 402.
Translations made from foreign languages, ii. 136.
Trigliva, the slavonian Hecate, i. 99.
Triodion, a book of anthems, i. 121.
Trizna, or funeral repast, i. 110.
Tschalmates, mingled with the Tartars, i. 17.
Tschassovna, described, ii. 434.
Tscheremisses, so called from their situation to the eastward, i. 20.
Tschervonnaia Rossia, or Red Russia, i. 136.
Tschislenie liudi, or numbered people, i. 352.
Tschudes, signifies acquaintances or neighbours, i. 17.
Tschuvasches, the antient Bilirians, i. 20.
Tver, built by Vsevolod III. i. 422.
Turkestan, on the banks of the Taras, i. 41.
Turkey, hostilities with, ii. 49.
Turks, of like origin with the Tartars, i. 31. Compelled to acknowledge the sovereignty of the tzars over the Kozaks, ii. 34. Drawn into a war against Persia, 216.
Twelve select men, judicial decisions referred to, i. 355.
Tzar, when first used, i. 286.
Tzargrad, Constantinople so called, i. 151. 421.
Tzaritzin, english garden at, ii. 431.
Tzar Morski, the slavonian Neptune, i. 102.
Tzars, method practised by them in chusing a bride, ii. 32. Antient, shewed themselves but seldom to the people, ii. 66. Title of, exchanged for that of emperor, 98.

V

Vadim, the valiant, a famous Novgorodian, i. 143.
Vagabonds, and other useless members of society, i. 351.

Valdemar,

INDEX.

Valdemar II. king of Denmark, lays the foundation of Narva, i. 458.
Varages, swedish, norman, english and russian, i. 142.
Varagians, who they were, i. 10.
Varro, etymology of, i. 54.
Vassilly Ivanovitch, enabled to keep the Tartars in awe, i. 285.
Vassilly Dmitrievitch, causes himself to be crowned, i. 277.
Vassilly-ostrof, whence so called, i. 436.
Vatitches, i. 11. a slavonian nation, i. 176.
Vauxhall, established by Mr. Maddox, at Mosco, ii. 427.
Veliki knez, improperly translated grand duke, i. 222.
Veneta, built by the slaves, i. 38.
Vengeance, personal, strictly forbidden, i. 368.
Verb, the first that would have been imagined in any language, i. 62. Had at the beginning, perhaps, only the infinitive. i. 69.
Vesses, dwelt on the White-sea, i. 11.
Victims, human, thrown into the waters, i. 107.
Victory, a dear, to the Russians, i. 274.
Vienna, Alexey Petrovitch, goes to Charles VI. at, ii. 106.
Vier, count de, a portuguese adventurer, ii. 197. Knooted and sent to Siberia, 198.
Virgil, quotation from, i. 54.
Vishnei-Volotshok, canal with sluices at, ii. 145.
Vizir, deposed and banished, ii. 95.
Vladimir, a natural son of Sviatoslaf, obtains Novgorod, i. 180. Ambitious and obdurate, 188. Retires to the Varagians, 190.
Vladimir I. obstinately bigoted to idolatry, i. 196. Extorts baptism by force of arms, i. 199. Saves his life by hiding himself under a bridge, i. 207. Dies of grief, i. 208. Is styled the Great, i. 210. Canonized, 215. Order of knighthood established in his honour, 216. His friendship courted by the Greeks and Bulgarians, 373.
Vladimir, the antient city of, i. 231. Calamities brought on it by the Tartars, 246.
Vladislaf, of Poland, elected tzar of Russia, ii. 4.
Vogulitsches, inhabit mount Ural, i. 18.
Voivode, a leader in war, i. 326.
Volga, piratical parties on the, i. 422.
Volos, the god of cattle, i. 371.
Voloti, whether the Slavonians worshipped giants under the name of, i. 103.

Vorontzof,

526   INDEX.

Vorontzof, count, succeeds Bestuchef, ii. 307. Countess Elizabeth, 349.
Voskresenskoi nunnery, when built, i. 438.
Vossius derives the latin language from the Greek, i. 76.
Votes, a tribe dwelling between the Volkhof and the Neva, i. 11. 18.
Vreech, a swedish captain, founds a school at Tobolsk, ii. 139.
Vyborg-side, at St. Petersburg, i. 437.

U

Udores inhabited the province of Tomsk, i. 20. Farther particulars concerning them, i. 22.
Uglitsches, contend for their liberty, i. 157.
Ugres, account of them, i. 16.
Ukraine, the Tartars there chastised, ii. 218. Count Lascy winters in the, 222.
Ulric, Anthony, duke of Brunswic, ii. 243. Dies in prison, 279.
Ultramontanes, who went from the north-west into Italy, i. 78.
Uloshenies, published, i. 333. ii. 113.
Umbria, antient inhabitants of, i. 85.
Ungrians invade the roman territory, i. 176.
Union, of the russian and latin churches, attempted by the roman pontiffs, i. 381.
University of Mosco, ii. 396.
Uschakof, general, ii. 174.
Uspenskoy cathedral, at Mosco, the russian monarchs crowned there, ii. 374.
Ustavnaia Gramota, i. 338.

W

Wachter, of opinion that the latin language originated in the teutonic, i. 76.
War, always declared just and necessary by politicians antient and modern, i. 159. Uniform consequences of, i. 195. The principal occupation of the Slaves, 326.

Wars,

Wars, bloody, frequently bring nothing about, ii. 13. That are attended with no alteration in the state of nations should occupy but a short space in history, ii. 222.

Warsaw, archives brought thence to Petersburg, ii. 13.

Waters held in great veneration by the Slavonians, i. 106. Day of the consecration of, ii. 267.

Wedel, general, joined by the king of Prussia, ii. 318.

Weights and measures, regulated, ii. 144.

Weymar, account of the russian army in Prussia, by a person of, ii. 309.

Wife, dependent on the husband, i. 368.

Will, one of the first sentiments declared by men, i. 65.

Winter-season, at Mosco, ii. 448.

Words, in what manner inverted or changed, i. 79. Orthography of russian, i. 129.

Workmen, none but foreign, employed in ship-building, ii. 65.

Workshops, Peter I. leaves his throne to gain knowledge in, ii. 144.

Y

Yagujinsky, lieutenant-general, reveals a secret, ii. 172. 210.

Yamboly, made the seat of empire by Sviatoslaf, i. 177.

Yamburg, an antient structure discovered near, i. 464.

Yaropolk Sviatoslavitch has Kief for his portion of the empire, i. 179. Is informed by Svenald of the death of his father, i. 186. His character, 188. Takes up arms against his brother Oleg, i. 189. Murdered by some Varagians, i. 192.

Yaroslaf, prince of Novgorod, drives Sviatopolk from Kief, i. 218. Laws in being before his time, 330. Vladimirovitch dies at Kief, i. 432.

Yaroslaf Vladimirovitch, the founder of Dorpat, i. 466.

Yaroslavian statutes, i. 340.

Yasses, the sea of Azof probably denominated from them, i. 17. 391. Subdued by Sviatoslaf, 411.

Yassy, the capital of Moldavia, Peter marches to, ii. 93. Taken by marshal Munich, 225.

Yatveges, dwelt in Poland, i. 17. 195.

Yausa, a river at Mosco, ii. 366.

Yegorof, major, his account of a discovery, i. 425.
Yemians, the same with Biarmians, i. 11.
Yermak, Timofeyef, conquers Siberia, i. 292.
Youths, sent to travel, ii. 137.
Yugdores, a great and powerful nation on the river Yuga, i. 17.
Yurievetch Livonskoi, Dorpat so called by the Russians, i. 465.
Yurin Tsiul, general of the Kozares, i. 401.
Yury, prince, shorn of his hair, i. 126.
Yury II. transfers the residence to Suzdal, i. 135.
Yury, or George, his marriage feast, i. 245. His unfeeling behaviour towards his unhappy father, i. 266.
Yutland, Horsens in, the family of prince Ivan permitted to retire to, ii. 285.

Z

Zaikonospasky monastery, in Mosco, ii. 380.
Zakoffky, Lazarus, general, i. 423.
Zaporogian Kozaks return under the russian sceptre, ii. 237.
Zaruski, an accomplice of Marina, ii. 7.
Zemlenoigorod, a quarter at Mosco, ii. 367. 386.
Zenovia, the slavonian Diana, i. 99.
Ziethen and Seidlitz, generals, perform miracles of prowess, ii. 313.
Zimisces, John, assassinates and succeeds Nicephorus, i. 181.
Zimtserla, the slavonian Flora, i. 103.
Znitch, a slavonian deity, i. 101.
Zolotaiya baba, the golden matron, i. 113.
Zorndorf, cause of the misfortune at, ii. 317.
Zubof, Plato Alexandrovitch, governor of Taurida, i. 426.

THE END.

Printed by A. Strahan, Printers Street, London.

CPSIA information can be obtained at www.ICGtesting.com
Printed in the USA
LVOW090047241112

308567LV00015B/865/P

9 781141 875689